The Church's Worship
The 1979 American Book of Common Prayer in a Historical Perspective

Thaddaeus A. Schnitker

The Church's Worship

The 1979 American Book of Common Prayer in a Historical Perspective

Eugene, Oregon

Wipf and Stock Publishers
199 W 8th Ave, Suite 3
Eugene, OR 97401

The Church's Worship
The 1979 American Book of Common Prayer in a Historical Perspective
By Schnitker, Thaddaeus A.
Copyright©1989 by Schnitker, Thaddaeus A.
ISBN 13: 978-1-60899-114-3
Publication date 9/15/2009
Previously published by Peter Lang, 1989

*To all Episcopal lay persons
who carry out the mission of the Church
of restoring all people to unity
with God and each other in Christ*

Table of Contents

Table of Contents		vii - viii
Prologue		ix - xii
Acknowledgments		xiii
Text		1 - 218

1.	The Prayer Books of 1549, 1552, 1559, 1604, 1637, and 1662	1 - 47
1.1	The Henrician Reformation	1 - 14
1.2	The Book of Common Prayer 1549	15 - 25
1.3	The Book of Common Prayer 1552	25 - 29
1.4	Queen Mary and the Reaction	29 - 30
1.5	The Book of Common Prayer 1559	31 - 37
1.6	The Book of Common Prayer 1604	37 - 40
1.7	The Book of Common Prayer 1637	40 - 42
1.8	Civil War and Interregnum	42 - 43
1.9	The Book of Common Prayer 1662	43 - 47
2.	The American Prayer Books of 1789, 1892, and 1928	49 - 104
2.1	The Colonies in the Seventeenth Century	49 - 53
2.2	The Colonies in the Eighteenth Century	53 - 58
2.3	The United States of America	58 - 60
2.4	The Book of Common Prayer 1789	60 - 68
2.5	Social and Ecclesiastical Life in the First Half of the Nineteenth Century	68 - 73
2.6	The Oxford Movement and the Episcopal Church	74 - 81
2.7	William Augustus Muhlenberg and the Muhlenberg Memorial	81 - 83
2.8	Social and Ecclesiastical Life in the Second Half of the Nineteenth Century	83 - 86
2.9	The Book of Common Prayer 1892	86 - 88
2.10	Social and Ecclesiastical Life at the Turn of the Century	88 - 96
2.11	Social and Ecclesiastical Life from the Turn of the Century to 1928	96 - 97
2.12	The Book of Common Prayer 1928	98 - 104
3.	The Prayer Book of 1979	105 - 150
3.1	Social and Ecclesiastical Life between 1928 and 1950	105 - 108
3.2	The Liturgical Movement within the Episcopal Church	108 - 116
3.3	Currents of Life between 1950 and 1979	116 - 119
3.4	Preliminaries to the Revision Process, a Lambeth Conference, and the Second Vatican Council	119 - 127
3.5	The Revision Process of the Book of Common Prayer	127 - 149
3.6	Conclusions	149 - 150
4.	The Church's Liturgy according to the 1979 Book of Common Prayer	151 - 179
4.1	Special Features of the 1979 Prayer Book	151 - 162
4.1.1	The Book for the Liturgy	151 - 154
4.1.2	The Role of the Laity in the Celebration of the Liturgy	155 - 156
4.1.3	Comprehensiveness and Adaptation	156 - 158
4.1.4	Reverence for Tradition	158 - 159

4.1.5	Social Concern and the Adoption of Contemporary Ideas	160
4.1.6	The Eucharist as the Central Liturgy	161
4.1.7	Variety and Flexibility	161 - 162
4.2	Holy Baptism	162 - 169
4.3	"Confirmation"	169 - 171
4.4	The Holy Eucharist	171 - 179
5.	The Mystery of Initiation: The Newness of Life	181 - 212
5.1	The Setting: Paschal, Doxological, and Eucharistic	181 - 186
5.2	The Celebration: The Covenant, the Water, and the Spirit	186 - 196
5.3	The Interpretation: The Dignity of a Faithful	197 - 202
5.4	The Fulfillment: The Eucharist	202 - 212
6.	Epilogue	215 - 218
7.	Select Bibliography	221 - 234
7.1	Sources	221 - 227
7.1.1	The Bible, Patristic Texts, and Ancient Liturgical Material	221
7.1.2	Reformation to 1662	222 - 223
7.1.3	American Period to 1928	223 - 224
7.1.4	1928 to 1979, including the Liturgical Movement	224 - 226
7.1.5	Overlapping Periods	226 - 227
7.2	Studies	227 - 234
8.	Index	235 - 246
8.1	Index of Names	235 - 240
8.2	Index of Biblical References, Patristic Texts, and Ancient Liturgical Material	241 - 242
8.3	Index of Subjects	243 - 246

Prologue

This study is about a dream: a dream of the Episcopal Church about its own life before God. It is a great dream because it is about one of the most important duties, if not the most important task, of the Church: to worship and glorify the Living God. The Episcopal Church has set out its own attempts of living up to the significance of this great dream in a book of which the first version will see its bicentennial in 1989: the *Book of Common Prayer according to the use of the Episcopal Church*. This book manifests the deepest roots of the Church's existence in God's life-giving mercy and goodness which are recorded in joyful celebration.

The present version of this book which has been used in the Episcopal Church since 1979 is the material with which this study is concerned. This *Book of Common Prayer* has been hailed as "perhaps the most splendid achievement of the modern liturgical movement in any Protestant church,"[1] although the Episcopal Church would have some reservations about its inclusion among the Protestant denominations.[2] This prayer book deserves the close attention of liturgists from the various churches and denominations because of the many new features to be found in it, be it in the expression of texts and rubrics, or in the underlying theological ideas and suppositions, all of which try to give form to the vision of the Church in its worship of the Living God. It is with this book that this study concerns itself.

Nobody will deny that there is always a dichotomy between the textual contents and rubrical directions of a liturgical book and all the provisions in it, and the actual performance and celebration of the liturgy in the parishes and congregations. Liturgical life in practice cannot be learned from the study of books. But this latter issue is not within the scope of the present research; it is, again, concerned with the official prayer book and its history.

This study is not intended as a commentary on the 1979 prayer book, nor as a history of the *Book of Common Prayer* in general, or of the American prayer book in particular; all this has been done elsewhere in a very scholarly manner; the reliance on these publications is gratefully acknowledged.[3] Even less is it the purpose to write a history of the Anglican Communion or of the Episcopal Church, either for the past 450 years, or for a particular period; this, too, has been done before.[4]

---

[1] Geoffrey Wainwright, "'E pluribus unum:' Questions of Unity and Diversity on the Ecumenical and Liturgical Scene in the USA," in *Communio Sanctorum: Mélanges offerts à Jean-Jacques von Allmen* (Genève: Labor et Fides, 1982), p. 294.

[2] See the preamble to the constitution of the Episcopal Church.

[3] The standard commentary on the 1979 *Book of Common Prayer* is Marion Josiah Hatchett, *Commentary on the American Prayer Book* (New York: Seabury, 1981). The standard work on the history of the Anglican liturgy in general is Geoffrey John Cuming, *A History of Anglican Liturgy*, 2nd ed. (London: Macmillan, 1982); on the American prayer book, exclusive of the present one, reference has to be made to John Wallace Suter and George Julius Cleaveland, *The American Book of Common Prayer: Its Origins and Development* (New York: Oxford University Press, 1949); the standard commentary on the 1928 prayer book is Massey Hamilton Shepherd, *The Oxford American Prayer Book Commentary* (New York: Oxford University Press, 1950).

[4] For the history of the Church of England in general, see John Richard Humpidge Moorman, *A History of the Church in England*, 3rd ed. rpt. with corrections (London: Black, 1980); for the reformation period, Arthur Geoffrey Dickens, *The English Reformation*, 7th ed. (New York: Schocken Books, 1980), and Geoffrey Rudolph Elton, *Reform and Reformation: England, 1509-1558*, The New History of England (Cambridge, MA: Harvard University Press, 1977), are to be consulted. For the history of the Episcopal Church, mention is to be made of James Thayer Addison, *The Episcopal Church in the United States 1789-1931* (1951; rpt. Hamden, CT: Archon Books, 1969), Raymond Wolf Albright, *A History of The Protestant Episcopal Church* (New York: Macmillan; London: Collier-Macmillan, 1964), and David E. Sumner, *The Episcopal Church's History 1945-1985* (Wilton, CT: Morehouse-Barlow, 1987). In the broader context of all churches in the United States, Sydney Eckman Ahlstrom, *A Religious History of the American People*, complete and unabridged in 2 vols. (Garden City, NY: Image Books, 1975) is the standard reference.

In the course of the history of the Anglican liturgy, certain ideas recur with a constancy which makes them so obvious as to demand attention; these are underlying themes upon which the texts of the prayer books are based, rather than expressions in the books themselves. To the author of this study, the three ideas most manifest throughout the English and American prayer books are those of uniformity of worship, the search for apostolic liturgy, and the possibility of adaptation. It will be intelligible that, due to the political circumstances in England with the ecclesiastical situation so closely interwoven, the first of these themes flourished in the prayer books of the sixteenth and seventeenth centuries, based on the respective parliamentary legislation. The quest for adaptation to the local situation dimly emerged from the preface of the 1662 prayer book and is transparent in the American prayer books, to such a degree that the more recent the books become, the easier it is to detect this possibility. The search for the closest possible approach to whatever is regarded as the letter or the spirit of a true liturgy of the primitive Church runs through the entire history of the Anglican liturgy, from the English Reformation through the most recent revision of the American prayer book.

It is above all in the liturgical texts and rites in the prayer books that notions and ideas current at the time of the production of a prayer book come to the fore. These ideas will be mentioned in this study, too. Very often they are closely linked to the political or economic situation of the day, and the ties of this social environment with the liturgical life of the Church deserves attention, possibly more so than has hitherto happened. The author does not deny that his own unemployment during the longest part of the research on this book has sharpened his focus above all for the economic circumstances of the life for the vast majority of the people for whom the prayer books had been made.

As it would have been totally out of the scope of this present study to present all parts of the liturgical life of the Church of England and the Episcopal Church, this book is concerned with the sacraments of Christian initiation as examples of the incarnation of those historical ideas in the Church's liturgy. The rites or parts of the Christian initiation were chosen because baptism and the eucharist were always regarded as owning a special dominical institution and were held, therefore, in highest esteem in the Anglican Communion. The confirmation, on the contrary, has received so different interpretations in the course of Anglicanism[5] that it might rightly be called the crux for any revision process of the liturgy. The relation of confirmation to baptism, and the integrity of the baptismal rite, were the most dominant subjects of discussion during the most recent revision of the prayer book in the United States. It is, therefore, only natural that attention is focused on these parts of the Church's liturgy.[6]

Chapter One of the present study shows the influence of the English Reformation upon the different editions of the prayer book. A prominent place is thereby given to Henry VIII and his mind on ecclesiastical affairs. This chapter leads up to the 1662 *Book of Common Prayer*, still the sole legal prayer book in the Church of England.[7]

---

[5] For an account of the different interpretations, see John Douglas Close Fisher, *Confirmation Then and Now*, Alcuin Club Collections, 60 (London: SPCK, 1978), especially pp. 142-52; Ronald Cloud Dudley Jasper, "Christian Initiation: The Anglican Position," *Studia Liturgica*, 12 (1977), 118; Leonel Lake Mitchell, "Revision of the Rites of Christian Initiation in the American Episcopal Church," *Studia Liturgica*, 10 (1974), 27-28; and Louis Weil, "Christian Initiation in the Anglican Communion: A Response," *Studia Liturgica*, 12 (1977), 126-28.

[6] As far as the eucharist is concerned, this book is not a study of the eucharistic liturgy in itself but only insofar as it is connected with baptism (and confirmation) as a part of the initiatory process. Therefore, the revision of the eucharistic liturgy in the 1960s and 1970s has not been traced in different stages; only the final results are shown.

[7] In 1980 the Church of England published *The Alternative Service Book 1980* which contains "Services authorized for use in the Church of England in conjunction with The Book of Common Prayer;" but the authorization runs out on December 31, 1990, with the future prospects as yet undecided. As the 1662 *Book of Common Prayer* has been established by Act of parliament and still is on the statutory books, only parliament

Chapter Two gives an account of the situation of the *Book of Common Prayer* in America, from the time of the colonies to the publication of the 1928 prayer book, the predecessor to the present one.

Chapter Three outlines the revision process of the liturgy of the Episcopal Church, beginning with the publication of the series Prayer Book Studies in 1950 and seriously worked on since 1967. It is the story of an adventure in introducing, or reintroducing, patterns or material to the liturgy which were not known to the Episcopal Church and the Anglican Communion in general. It culminates in the ratification and authorization of the 1979 *Book of Common Prayer*.

Chapter Four surveys some characteristic lines of the new prayer book and gives a profile of the rite of baptism as it is restored with the reintegration of the bestowal of the gift of the Holy Spirit; the rite of a new concept of confirmation, as the reaffirmation of baptismal vows; and the rites of the eucharist which can be celebrated according to different patterns.

Chapter Five is devoted to a theological-spiritual interpretation of baptism according to the new book, and its close links, within the pattern of Christian initiation, with the eucharist, a theme which deserves a closer link than it has been given in the past.

The epilogue can be rather short: it sums up how much the Church lives up to its great dream of worshipping the Living God. Life before God is not a set of restrictions molded as a strict liturgical uniformity but the total of being in touch with the Church's own historical roots, in this instance in the attempt of an approach to liturgical forms dating back to periods close to the apostolic era, which enable this body to be flexible and to respond to present-day situations in the adaptation to contemporary needs and challenges. The lessening of the restraint of uniformity, after it had been the guiding principle in the English prayer books, in favor of more flexibility and ways of adaptation, and the vastly greater resources and use of the apostolic liturgy (especially in the 1979 *Book of Common Prayer*) are very evident. The ambivalent understanding of confirmation is mentioned again as the one focal point for the future work of education for liturgy. It is suggested that the issue is not so much one of a necessity for a public affirmation of faith but the interpretation of the pastoral office of the bishops which will have to be changed.

A personal statement might be allowed to the author before giving some technical explanations concerning the study. This book has been written with a profound sense of affection and admiration for the liturgy of the Episcopal Church, and for this church in general. Since the first participation in a eucharist on Thanksgiving Day 1978 at Grace Cathedral, San Francisco, the (then proposed and now definitive) prayer book has been a constant source of spiritual nourishment and inspiration for the present writer. If at times the judgment of a given feature or of an underlying theme in the prayer book might seem harsh or unfair, it is written with the intention of revealing those items in order that they might be corrected, if possible. Love of the prayer book of the Episcopal Church determines the relation of the author to the subject.

An attempt has been made in this study to let the documents, which have been relevant to the course of the history scrutinized here, speak for themselves. The contents of those texts give a clearer indication of their purpose and position than the present writer could achieve; moreover, as a number of them might not easily be available to the reader, preference is given to verbal quotations over against paraphrasing the texts. The contents of those texts, of

---

could legally abolish it--which it is most unlikely to do as the calamities in 1927/28 have shown and have been echoed in the discussion of the Worship and Doctrine Measure in parliament in 1974. See Gavin White, "'No-one is free from Parliament:' The Worship and Doctrine Measure in Parliament, 1974," in *Religion and National Identity: Papers Read at the Nineteenth Summer Meeting and the Twentieth Winter Meeting of the Eccclesiastical History Society*, ed. Stuart Mews, Studies in Church History, 18 (Oxford: Blackwell, 1982), pp. 557-65.

course, are not subject to the present writer's authority; for the selection of them, however, he takes full responsibility.

All texts are given in modernized spelling. Preference is given throughout this entire study to the use of the name "(The) Episcopal Church" instead of the earlier one "Protestant Episcopal Church in the United States of America;" the shorter title is also used as the only one throughout the 1979 *Book of Common Prayer*.

American English is employed throughout the writer's text. A special effort has been made in the fourth and fifth chapters to use so-called inclusive or non-sexist language by choosing words or grammatical constructions which do not require the personal pronoun "he." This is done firstly out of respect for the employment of this language pattern in the 1979 prayer book, and secondly out of conviction that the use of a particular language pattern is more revealing than often intended; the present writer agrees with the intentions that govern the application of this speech pattern.

Scriptural texts are mostly quoted from the Revised Standard Version of the Bible which is also used, if necessary, in the 1979 *Book of Common Prayer*.

Acknowledgments

This book has its origin in the *thèse d'agrégation* of the author submitted in 1986 to the Theological Faculty of the University of Fribourg (Switzerland) under the title "The Quest for Uniformity, Apostolic Liturgy, and Adaptation: The 1979 *Book of Common Prayer* according to the Use of the Episcopal Church in a Perspective of Historical Ideas." Gratitude is due to this body for accepting the study and according the *venia legendi* in the field of liturgiology.

The original thesis was written under the supervision of the Rev. Dr. Jakob Baumgartner, S.M.B., professor of liturgiology at that university. He was the best teacher the author could possibly have wished for.

Dr. John H. Erickson, sometime professor and chairman of the Department of English at Erie Community College, New York, read the drafts in regard to a proper use of American English.

The late Rev. Dr. Geoffrey Cuming, Oxford, read the first chapter on the period from Henry VIII to 1662. The Rev. Dr. Marion J. Hatchett, professor of liturgics and music at the University of the South, Sewanee, Tennessee, read the second through fourth chapters about the American prayer books. He also made available a copy of his unpublished master's thesis on Thomas Cranmer and the rites of Christian initiation, as well as his--at that time also still unpublished--doctoral dissertation on the making of the first American prayer book. The Rev. Dr. Massey H. Shepherd, Jr., Sacramento, California, read the third chapter on the revision process leading to the 1979 prayer book. All three experts have endorsed the manuscript and given much encouragement.

The Archives of the Episcopal Church at Austin, Texas, the library at Nashotah House, Wisconsin, the Bodleian Library, Oxford, and the library of the Institute of Historical Research at the University of London opened their material and resources for this study.

The Rev. Dr. Louis Weil, formerly professor of liturgics at Nashotah House, Wisconsin, was very helpful in mailing sources not available in West Germany.

The Liturgical Institute at Trier, West Germany, has been so kind as to grant a subsidy to the printing of this book, a contribution that is gratefully acknowledged.

To all the persons named here as well as to countless others who have in some way or other given assistance, help, and encouragement, the author is very thankful and appreciates what they have done for him.

The Prayer Books of 1549, 1552, 1559, 1604, 1637, and 1662

The *Book of Common Prayer* as used in the Church of England which is the parent body of the Episcopal Church is one of the effects of the ecclesiastical, political, and social changes summarized under the name "Reformation."

The Henrician Reformation

The Reformation in England was, as far as its driving force and its constitutional implications are concerned, a reformation from above; neither a single theologian nor the désire of the masses but the necessities of the king caused it to happen, resulting in a body politic, both secular and ecclesiastical, which is unique among the effects of the Reformation. With all means legally possible (and sometimes quite beyond the legality), the country was turned from a nation that had lived with a sovereign as temporal head and the pope in Rome as spiritual head in a balance which had sometimes been so weak as to invoke serious clashes, into a state that acknowledged one common head only, a nation which was to become uniform in its sole direction to the king; a prince whose head was two heads, yet if one were attacked the other would retaliate all the more violently.

Henry VIII (born on June 28, 1491, proclaimed king on April 23, 1509, died on January 28, 1547) had his mind set on his hold over the Church from the beginning of his reign. A preserved autograph shows that he intended the coronation oath he had to swear during his coronation on June 24, 1509 to be changed from an expression of the rights and freedom of the Church to be kept, into a text that made these rights and liberties subject to his interpretation of law, his jurisdiction, and his royal dignity.[1] Only insofar as these would not be touched upon could the normal life of the Church continue. Early absolutism has rarely found a clearer phrasing.[2]

The world had to wait, however, for more than two additional decades to see the meaning of his royal prerogatives.[3]

---

[1] British Museum, Cotton, Tiberius E VVV, fol. 89. A photographic reproduction can be found in Leopold Wickham Legg, ed., *English Coronation Records* (Westminster: Constable, 1901), no. 21, pp. 240-41. The text is reprinted in Thaddäus A. Schnitker, "Kirche, Staat und Liturgie: Zwei bedeutsame Jahre im Leben der Kirche von England, 1533 und 1833," *Liturgisches Jahrbuch*, 33 (1983), 109:

[The proposed text:]
The king shall swere at ye coronacion that he shall kepe and mayntene the right and the libertees of holie church of old tyme graunted by the rightuous Cristen kinges of Englond.

[The text as *changed* by Henry:]
The king shall *then* swere at ye coronacion that he shall kepe and mayntene the *lawfull* right and the libertees of holie church of old tyme graunted by the rightuous Cristen kinges of Englond *to the holy chirche of inglond nott preiudyciall to his Jurysdiccion and dignite ryall.*

However, the rephrased text was not used.

[2] Percy Ernst Schramm, *A History of the English Coronation*, trans. Leopold George Wickham Legg (Oxford: Clarendon, 1937), pp. 216-17.

[3] John Jay Scarisbrick, *Henry VIII*, English Monarchs (London: Eyre Methuen, 1981), p. 384, disputes the early date of the autograph: he would have the alterations made after the Act in Restraint of Appeals (24 Hen. 8, c. 12) 1533 or after the Act of Supremacy (26 Hen. 8, c. 1) 1534. Neither act, however, provided for

In the meantime, on October 11, 1521, Pope Leo X, after more than ten years' pressure from English delegations, had to bestow on Henry the title of "Defender of the Faith," a royal style that put the English sovereign *on par* with his archrival, the King of France, and with his parents-in-law.[4] He had "earned" this honor by writing a defense of the seven sacraments against Martin Luther's *De captivitate babylonica*, presented with great humility to the pope. In his dedicatory letter Henry saw great advantages in a strong uniform religion for a well-functioning state; and at the moment Roman doctrine held the sway.[5]

Eight years later, on August 9, 1529, the "Reformation Parliament" was summoned, linked in timing to Henry's divorce case from Queen Catherine of Aragón but, as far as intentions were concerned, more or less independent from it; it was to sit in several sessions from November 3, 1529 until April 14, 1536[6] and to produce the most revolutionary legislation in the constitutional history of England. Seven bills were passed from 1532 through 1534 which marked the end of the two provinces of the Church in England in communion with the See of Rome and established the Church of England, divided into two provinces, with the See of Canterbury holding the metropolitan dignity. Step by step, the first five bills (and the last one) gave to the prince those unlimited powers which were in the sixth and most famous one designated as the supreme headship of the king over the Church. It was the sucessful attempt by Henry to concentrate as much power and rule in his hands as possible; there was to be one king, one country, and one Church, the latter two entirely dominated by the former.

The first bill, the Conditional Restraint of Annates (23 Hen. 8, c. 20),[7] passed in the third session, January through March 1532, restricted the payment of money to Rome after the appointment to a bishopric or archbishopric. Persons lacking the documents from Rome due to the non-payment were nonetheless to be duly consecrated. The right to nominate such a person rested with the king.[8] Should the pope retaliate by putting the country under excommunication or interdict, all the sacraments and divine services were ordered by the parliament to be ministered nonetheless. Still,

---

this change which, given the predilection of the Tudor legislation for listing even miniscule details, could easily have been done, nor were there any notes on a change in the phrasing of the oath around that time. Above all, there are no allusions to the designation of England as an empire, to the king as emperor, or to the royal supremacy all of which could have easily been worked into the text. It is therefore improbable that the change should have been made at so late a date.

[4] For the history of the fight for a royal style and the politicking behind the scenes, see John William McKenna, "How God became an Englishman," in *Tudor Rule and Revolution: Essays for G. R. Elton from His American Friends*, ed. Delloyd J. Guth and John William McKenna (Cambridge: Cambridge University Press, 1982), pp. 34-43.

[5] *Assertio septem sacramentorum aduersus Mart[inum] Lutherum* (Parisiis: Desboys, 1562), p. 2: "Postquam enim in administratranda republica maximam semper vim, maximumque momentum, religionem habere multo vsu aduertimus, vt primum maturiores annos attigimus, coepimus eius contemplari nonnihil studii impendere."

[6] The sessions: first: November 4 to December 17, 1529; second: January 16 to March 31, 1531; third: January 15 to March 28, 1532; fourth: April 10 to May 14, 1532; fifth: February 5 to April 7, 1533; sixth: January 15 to March 30, 1534; seventh: November 3 to December 18, 1536: Frederick Maurice Powicke and Edmund Boleslaw Fryde, eds., *Handbook of British Chronology*, Royal Historical Society: Guides and Handbooks, 2, 2nd ed. (London: Royal Historical Society, 1961), p. 535.

[7] For a summary of how English pieces of legislation are quoted, see Schnitker, "Kirche, Staat und Liturgie," 105-06, note 1; for the regnal years of the English monarchs, see *Guide to Law Reports*, 4th ed. (London: Sweet & Maxwell; Edinburgh: Green, 1962), pp. 27-31. The text of this bill: Henry Gee and William John Hardy, eds., *Documents Illustrative of English Church History* (London: Macmillan, 1896), no. 49, pp. 178-86.

[8] This had effectively been the case since the Norman conquest, with all the inevitable clashes ensuing.

our said sovereign the king, and all his natural subjects, as well spiritual as temporal, [are] as obedient, devout, catholic, and humble childen of God and Holy Church, as any people [are] within any realm christened.9

The second bill, the Act in Restraint of Appeals (24 Hen. 8, c. 12),10 passed in the fifth session on February 4, 1533, has been called "the foundation stone of the new order."11 It can hardly be overestimated in its implications both for the proper selfunderstanding of the state and for the results it showed in the life of the Church. Eight surviving drafts and four fragments show the energy bestowed on this act.12 It is quite probable that at the moment of voting on it only a small minority, if any, was aware of the impact of this act: it was the severance of England from Rome that was affected by it, and the classification of England as a nation independent of any foreign power. The preamble13 designated "this realm of England" as "an empire ... governed by one supreme head and king, having the dignity and royal estate of the imperial crown of the same" to whom every person in the country owed "a natural and humble obedience." This supreme head had been given by God "plenary, whole, and entire power, preeminence, authority, prerogative and jurisdiction" to do justice to everybody and to ultimately determine all matters that could possibly happen to his subjects, a power exercized on the one hand without any interference of any foreign prince or potentate, which included the See of Rome, and on the other hand both in temporal and spiritual respect. As the Roman curia had encroached upon the indepedence of England and had attracted many legal proceedings that were not only lengthy and tedious but also expensive due to the fees, this act attempted to restore the ancient order by forbidding any redress or appeal to any court or instance outside the country, and by establishing the exclusive responsibility of the English courts, both in temporal and spiritual matters. Any appeal to Rome would be liable to the provisions of the Statute of *Praemunire*;14 the stages of appeal were outlined. All clergy of the realm were bound to disobey any possible interdict or excommunication issued by Rome and to administer the sacraments as usual. Two major premises are obvious in this act: that the country is an empire, a nation totally independent from any other power in all respects, and that the sovereign has "the imperial crown ... by the goodness and sufferance of Almighty God," which means nothing less than a God-given absolute and unlimited authority over both State and Church not subject to any human restriction.15 The king in the center of his empire: the king *is* the center of his empire in its totality.

The five remaining acts were "merely" explications of this basic principle of the English Reformation as far as the shape of the Church of England was concerned. The next three statutes were passed in the sixth session of the parliament, January through March 1534.

---

9 Gee and Hardy, *Documents*, no. 49, p. 180.

10 Gee and Hardy, *Documents*, no. 50, pp. 187-95.

11 Scarisbrick, *Henry VIII*, p. 272.

12 Stanford Eugene Lehmberg, *The Reformation Parliament 1529-1536* (Cambridge: Cambridge University Press, 1970), p. 164.

13 "Es handelt sich [in der Gesetzgebung der Tudorzeit] nicht mehr um relativ kurzgefaßte Verordnungen, sondern um wortreiche Ausführungen, die in ihren Präambeln zum Teil den Charakter politischer Willenserklärungen tragen.": Werner Teubner, *Kodifikation und Rechtsreform in England: Ein Beitrag zur Untersuchung des Einfluses von Naturrecht und Utilitarimus auf die Idee einer Kodifikation des englischen Rechts* (Berlin: Duncker & Humblot, 1974), p. 42.

14 "The three *Praemunire* statutes (1353, 1365, 1393) were designated to check papal encroachments against the rights of the Crown; they were ... the outcome of temporary situations and speedily disregarded. ... So loosely, however, had its text [of 1393] been drafted that in subsequent times lay lawyers began to envisage its use as a multi-purpose weapon against ecclesiastical jurisdiction.": Arthur Geoffrey Dickens, *The English Reformation*, 7th ed. (New York: Schocken Books, 1980), p. 87.

15 Walter Ullmann, "'This Realm of England is an Empire,'" *Journal of Ecclesiastical History*, 30 (1979), 185.

The Submission of the Clergy and the Restraint of Appeals (25 Hen. 8, c. 19)[16] meant that the Convocations of Canterbury and York could be summoned by the king only. The church legislation needed the royal assent to become effective, no canons were to be passed contrary to the royal prerogative or the statues of the realm, and appeal to Rome was liable to the penalties of the Statutes of *Praemunire*. Appeals of exempt monasteries that formerly went to "the Bishop of Rome, otherwise called pope," were to go to the Court of Chancery of the king.

The following Act about Ecclesiastical Appointments (25 Hen. 8, c. 20)[17] repeated that all nominations to archbishoprics and bishoprics were to be made by the Crown, which would send letters missive to the election body (convent or chapter) containing the name of the person to be elected; after the election, the bishop-elect was to do homage to the king, who would then confirm the election and order the consecration. Disobedience to these directions attracted the penalties of the Statutes of *Praemunire*. The king was hereby given the power to man the bishops' bench, who were at the same time spiritual lords of the realm, with persons of his persuasion, an opportunity he readily seized whenever possible.[18]

The next long Act Forbidding Papal Dispensations and the Payment of Peter's Pence (25 Hen. 8, c. 21)[19] gave most of the dispensing power formerly held by Rome to the Archbishop of Canterbury, dependent of course on the approbation of the supreme lord of the country, as "this your grace's realm recognis[es] no superior under God, but only your grace." However, this power was said to be vested in king and parliament as well as king and council. No payment to Rome was to be made, no visitation from that see was to be allowed, and no oath of allegiance to the Bishop of Rome was permitted. Buried in between all the technical provisions of this act was the intention that

> this Act, nor any thing or things therein contained, shall be hereafter interpreted or expounded, that your grace, your nobles and subjects, intend, by the same, to decline or vary from the congregation of Christ's Church in any things concerning the very articles of the Catholic faith of Christendom or in any other things declared, by Holy Scripture and the word of God, necessary for your and their salvations, but only to make an ordinance by policies necessary and convenient to repress vice.[20]

One day after the sixth session of the Reformation Parliament ended, on March 31, 1534, the Canterbury Convocation which had been meeting parallel to the parliament was voting in the present assembly (January 16 to December 19, 1534) on the question "whether the Roman Pontiff has any greater jurisdiction bestowed on him in the Holy Scripture in this realm of England than any other foreign bishop?" The result: thirty-four negative, four positive, and one doubtful vote. The York Convocation, sitting from May 5, 1534 to February 3, 1535,[21] concurred "unanimously, with no dissentient" on May 5 of that year.[22]

All this prepared and cleared the way for what has usually been regarded as the climax of the breach with the Apostolic See, the Act of Supremacy, passed probably on November 16, 1534.[23]

---

[16] Gee and Hardy, *Documents*, no. 51, pp. 195-200.

[17] Gee and Hardy, *Documents*, no. 52, pp. 201-09.

[18] Taken together with the Act of Conditional Restraint of Annates (23 Hen. 8, c. 20), the first of the seven reformation statutes that acknowledged this power of the king, it is interesting to note that of the twenty-one English and Welsh bishops given for 1540 by Philip Hughes, *Religio depopulata*, Vol. II of *The Reformation in England* (London: Hollis & Carter, 1954), pp. 5-8, fifteen were appointed after 1532, the date of 23 Hen. 8, c. 20; only six were named to their sees before.

[19] Gee and Hardy, *Documents*, no. 53, pp. 209-32.

[20] Gee and Hardy, *Documents*, no. 53, p. 225.

[21] The dates of the Convocations: Powicke and Fryde, *Handbook of British Chronology*, pp. 564-65.

[22] Gee and Hardy, *Documents*, no. 58, pp. 251-52 for both Convocations.

[23] The ambassador of Charles V to the English court, Eustace Chapuys, reported on November 17, 1534 to the emperor that he had heard that morning that the king had been declared by act of parliament supreme head of

From as early as 1531 on, Henry had a position like the Hebrew priest-king in mind, and he had let his desire be known to his Lord Chancellor, Sir Thomas More, and the Convocation[24] which at that time had been able to resist.[25] In exchange for not being put under the provisions of the Statutes of *Praemunire* by cooperation with the then Archbishop of York and *legatus a latere* of the Holy See, Cardinal Wolsey, both Convocations had bribed the king with an immense sum and had granted him the title of "protector and supreme head of the English church and clergy so far as the law of Christ allows."[26] From June 20, 1534 on, declarations of chapters, universities, and other institutions were recorded acknowledging the king as the head of the Church of England.[27] Little is known about the circumstances of the parliamentary debate and passage; apparently there were no obstacles or unexpected delays,[28] and the contents of the act were by that time evident to all. The remarkable shortness of the act (26 Hen. 8, c. 1)[29] is directly contradictory to its intended meaning and the consequences deriving from it. The parliament simply confirmed that the king was and had been recognized as being by the Convocations, namely "the only supreme head in earth of the Church of England, called *Anglicana Ecclesia*" with all the privileges, authorities, and profits belonging to it. Part of this title was the power "to visit, repress, redress, reform, order, correct, restrain, and amend all such errors, heresies, abuses, offenses, contempts, and enormities, whatever they be."

This fullness of royal prerogatives falls just short of ministerial functions and is otherwise the English version of a pope's office; this is exactly what Henry wanted. He was eager to exercize this authority, be it even in matters of faith. The combinations of his amateur theological knowledge and his utter self-glorification and self-righteousness would have posed a serious obstacle to the theological integrity of the emerging Church of England if he had bestowed the majority of his time on the execution of his new title; nobody could have legally prevented him from carrying out a *caesaro-papism* of the worst kind.[30]

---

the English Church. "They have also ratified all that was ordained at the last parliament against the Holy See.": James Gairdner, ed., *Letters and Papers, Foreign and Domestic, of the Reign of Henry VIII: Preserved in the Public Record Office, The British Museum and Elsewhere in England*, Vol. VII (London: Longmans, Trübner, 1883), no. 1437. The date of November 3 which is sometimes given refers to the opening of the parliamentary session on that day. The roll of the parliament gives this act under no. 8 of this session: Gairdner, *Letters and Papers*, VII, no. 1377. However, on November 4, 1534 already Thomas Cranmer, Archbishop of Canterbury, announced to the Convocation that from now on he was to be called metropolitan of England, no longer *legatus natus* of the Apostolic See: Lehmberg, *Reformation Parliament*, p. 214. This change of style, indicating the break with Rome, could mean the passage of the supremacy act on the first working day of the parliamentary session. On the other side, this could also mean a measure of "foresighted disobedience:" of all the lords spiritual, the Archbishop of Canterbury had the best record of attendance at the parliamentary debates; in total he was forty-one days present in 1534: Lehmberg, *Reformation Parliament*, appendix A, p. 257. Another clue might be that it was counted as the first chapter of the statutes passed in the twenty-sixth regnal year of Henry (April 22, 1534 to April 21, 1535).

[24] Steven W. Haas, "Martin Luther's 'Divine Right' Kingship and the Royal Supremacy: Two Tracts from the 1531 Parliament and the Convocation of Clergy," *Journal of Ecclesiastical History*, 31 (1980), 324-25.

[25] Geoffrey Rudolph Elton, *Reform and Reformation: England, 1509-1558* (Cambridge, MA: Harvard University Press, 1977), pp. 144-45.

[26] The story of this shady bargaining is told by Scarisbrick, *Henry VIII*, pp. 273-81, and Dickens, *English Reformation*, pp. 103-04.

[27] Gairdner,*Letters and Papers*, VII, nos. 865, 891, 921, 1024-25, 1121, 1216, 1377, 1594.

[28] Lehmberg, *Reformation Parliament*, p. 202.

[29] Gee and Hardy, *Documents*, no. 55, pp. 243-44.

[30] As is known, Emperor Maximilian I (1493-1519) in 1511 was seriously contemplating to unite the emperorship and the papacy in his hands in order to reform the Church and of course have some financial resources available for his political and military plans. He signed letters with "Maximilian, future pope." Henry VIII was not the only monarch to be plagued by the apparently irresistable temptation to be supreme head of his

So far, parliament had granted him his "heart's desires" culminating in this supremacy act. He as well as the country was free from any temporal or spiritual bond with anybody or anything abroad, and he was the center of the realm. Yet, due to the phrasing of this as well as the other statutes, there arose the unresolved problem of who it in fact was that had been given the supreme headship, and by whom it had been given. Some of the texts suggest that it was the king's person that had been granted an untransferable style; some others, however, indicate that it was the king-in-parliament, the sovereign together with the Lords and Commons, that held this title of supremacy as, after all, the legislative body had apportioned this power in his hand.[31] And even if it were the king's person only who had been vested with this authority, the confirmation as consistent with theology by the Convocations, and the preamble of the Act in Restraint of Appeals (24 Hen. 8, c. 12) implied that it was a God-given prerogative. Can any body bestow anything on somebody who has no superior to himself but God? These questions have never in theory been answered. Fortunately the successors to Henry, his minor son Edward and his daughters Mary and Elizabeth, were either afraid or not unscrupulous enough to exercize the supreme headship in a way envisaged by their father. The Church of England might otherwise have been subject to a disaster.

After this high point of the royal Reformation, the last statute, the Suffragan Bishops Act (26 Hen. 8, c. 14).[32] came as something of sheer necessity for a good working of the everyday life of the Church and as an anticlimax. It provided for the establishment by the parliament of additional titular sees in England and Wales so that the king could present persons to the archbishops to be consecrated bishops suffragan.

With the passage of this act the parliamentary reformation of the Church found its conclusion during Henry's lifetime. Whatever else was voted on by the two Houses or decided by the king was not in the context of this constitutional change. The Church of England had been established, a church that in its outward life revolved around the king. After the liturgical changes resulting in and effected by the *Book of Common Prayer* 1549, this church found itself equipped with a double center which demanded uniformity by the whole nation: the Supreme Head[33] and the *Book of Common Prayer*.

The genius of the king and his legislators in their ability to sell a personal ambition of Henry, a radical breach with what was undisputedly seen as the (personal and institutional) center of the Church, a theological revolution, to the English people with questionable historical arguments;[34] to show the continuity of the present institution with the former one; and to leave intact the medieval shape of the Church that now was the Church of England, is certainly to be marveled at.[35] But it was a very fragile settlement, as it was tailored to Henry's designs and lust for power, prestige, and money.[36]

---

people in all respects; he just was the only one to succeed in his plans. See Aloys Schulte, *Kaiser Maximilian I als Kandidat für den päpstlichen Stuhl, 1511* (Leipzig: Dunckler & Hublot, 1906).

[31] See the excellent treatment of this question by Scarisbrick, *Henry VIII*, pp. 383-423 ("The Royal Supremacy and Theology"), esp. pp. 392-98.

[32] Gee and Hardy, *Documents*, no. 59, pp. 253-56.

[33] The Treasons Act of November 1534 (26 Hen. 8, c. 13) (Gee and Hardy, *Documents*, no. 57, pp. 247-51) made it a high treason "to deprive them [the king, the queen who at that time was Anne Boleyn, or the heir presumptive who at that time were Princesses Mary and Elizabeth] or any of them of their dignity, title, or name of their royal estate, or . . . publish and pronounce . . . that the king our sovereign lord should be heretic, schismatic, tyrant, infidel or usurper of the crown." Penalty for such high treason was death. See James Walter Weingart, "The Concept of Treason in Tudor England," Dissertation Northwestern University 1976.

[34] For example, in the preamble to the Act in Restraint of Appeals (24 Hen. 8, c. 12).

[35] William Holdsworth, *A History of English Law*, Vol. I, ed. Arthur Lehman Goodhart and Harold Greville Hanbury, 7th ed. rev. (London: Methuen; Sweet & Maxwell, 1966), pp. 590-91.

[36] The imperial ambassador Chapuys wrote on November 28, 1534 to Charles V: "The king, who, as head of the church in his kingdom, was intending to take back into his hands all church property, and distribute only a frugal sustenance to ministers of the church, is for the present satisfied to leave the churchmen in possession of

Other factors, mainly in the realm of ideas philosophical and theological, of persons appearing on the stage, and of economic problems, contributed to the Reformation in England. They are at least worthy of mention.

The first half of the sixteenth century was an age that saw deep-rooted feelings of anticlericalism come to the surface. Resentment against the negligence of pastoral duties to the detriment of the cure of souls[37] as well as against the pluralism of priests[38] and the accumulation of lands and money by the prelates of the Church ran high. The epitome of all this was Cardinal Thomas Wolsey, *parvenu* at the king's court and at one time the most pwerful man in England after Henry. The "well-merited unpopularity"[39] of the *legatus a latere* of the Apostolic See before his fall in November 1530 certainly helped the growth of hatred by the laypeople (and some of the lower clergy) of all prelacy and everything Roman. These feelings were voiced in an official petition by the House of Commons to the king[40] to look into the conduct of bishops, their financial dealings, and their unjust accusations of heresy. The clergy was even said to sometimes deny the ministration of the sacraments if the sum of money were deemed insufficient. The answer of the bishops[41] was an unsuccessful attempt to destroy the fears of the Commons and to purge themselves of the charges. As Henry wanted the upper hand over the Church, as yet against the resistance of the bishops' bench, the strong feelings of the House of Commons were very welcome, and it was not for nothing that during his reign the Lower Chamber of the parliament rose to an equal status with the House of Lords in which the prelates could voice their views.

Another reason for the rise of anticlericalism was the gradual growth of a literate laity. The potentials of book-printing with its rapid increase of production and foundation or refoundation of institutions of higher learning were important not only for the upper classes; lower classes, too, were affected by these changes. The first appointment ever of a non-cleric to the lord chancellorship of the realm was one of the signs of this shift.[42]

Humanism on the philosophical side and the *devotio moderna* on the theological side were two more contributing factors. The age of the "New Learning" brought about a surgence of literary, historical, and philosophical ideas,[43] together with a new critique of the medieval view of life as upheld by the Church's authorities. As theology, and even the text of the

---

their property, provided they will contribute to him a yearly rent of 30,000 l st. [= pound sterling], and grant him the first fruits of all benefices. It is true he has always taken by apostolic privilege the revenue of vacant bishoprics but now he claims the whole revenue, not only of the bishoprics but of all other benefices, which amounts to an inestimable sum. Since the king is determined to bleed the churchmen, he has done much better to do it thus than to take all their goods, to avoid the murmur and hatred, not only of the clergy but of the people, especially of those who have endowed churches, or of their successors; moreover, it would have been necessary to stop the mouths of many people, to give the greater part of those goods to gentlemen and others.": Gairdner, *Letters and Papers*, VII, no. 1482. Although biased, it was nonetheless a very accurate account of Henry's utter greediness.

[37] Arthur Geoffrey Dickens, *Reformation and Society in Sixteenth-Century Europe* (London: Thames & Hudson, 1966), pp. 36-39.

[38] See Joel Arthur Lipkin, "Pluralism in Pre-Reformation England: A Quantitative Analysis of Ecclesiastical Incumbency, ca. 1490-1539," Dissertation The Catholic University of America 1979.

[39] Philip Hughes, *"The King's Proceedings,"* Vol. I of *The Reformation in England*, 3rd ed. (London: Hollis & Carter, 1954), p. 111.

[40] Gee and Hardy, *Documents*, no. 46, pp. 145-53.

[41] Gee and Hardy, *Documents*, no. 47, pp. 154-76.

[42] Sir Thomas More, one of the greatest European humanists, October 26, 1529 to May 16, 1532: Powicke and Fryde, *Handbook of British Chronology*, p. 86.

[43] See William Paul Haugaard, "Renaissance Patristic Scholarship and Theology in Sixteenth-Century England," *Sixteenth Century Journal*, 10,3 (1979), 37-60.

Bible,[44] were not spared a profound questioning by the representatives of humanism, the results were bound to help bring the fall of the *ancien régime*. The *devotio moderna* limited its criticism to overblown cults of saints and relics which had replaced the primacy of Christ in Christian devotion, and to utterances of late medieval piety of questionable value, in favor of personal religion and a simplified piety suitable for laypersons.[45]

Erastianism was flourishing during Henry's reign. Marsiglio of Padua's *Defensor Pacis* had been published two centuries earlier (1324); the ideas expressed were common knowledge and more or less accepted. More than a century before Henry had acceded to the throne, in 1408, King Henry IV had exercized what Henry VIII had in mind as the royal prerogative to determine church affairs by ensuring one loyalty of the whole nation in the Great Schism of the Church. The king and not the archbishops or any other church authority had become the supreme power in ecclesiastical matters.[46] It was not a new field whereupon Henry sowed; he did it more intensely than others and reaped the fruits.

Facts, rather than ideas, that helped to create a climate in which the Reformation could grow included economic problems that arose in the first half of the sixteenth century.

Some time between 1470 and 1520 an accelerating rise in population began. Between 1525 and 1545 the total population increased by more than twenty percent, from about 2.3 to about 2.8 million people, with all the subsequent food, employment, and sanitation problems. Due to internal migration, the capital of the country rose to a prominent place among the European cities: around 1500 it had about 33,000 inhabitants; by 1650 it counted around 400,000 people; and by the end of the seventeenth century over half a million people lived in London.[47] Hand in hand with the increase in population went a period of a colder climate, together with poor harvests, from about the mid-sixteenth century on. In the sixteenth century, the economy was still one at a predominant subsistence level, and the by far greater part of society had hardly any income available for purchases beyond the basic needs. Roughly half the population of England lived under the poverty line.[48] People whose only comfort in their struggle for survival is an existence which is tied into the complex life of the Church, and the promise of a reward in the next world, are bound to react to any changes which might threaten their way of life and cut the ground under their feet; reforms in church

---

[44] See James Barrett Miller, "Scripture and the English Reformation, 1526-1533," Dissertation Fuller Theological Seminary, School of Theology 1982.

[45] Reinhold Mokrosch, "Devotio moderna: II. Verhältnis zu Humanismus und Reformation," *Theologische Realenzyklopädie* 8, p. 616.

[46] Margaret Harvey, "Ecclesia Anglicana, cui Ecclesiastes noster Christus vos prefecit: The Power of the Crown in the English Church during the Great Schism," in *Religion and National Identity: Papers Read at the Nineteenth Summer Meeting and the Twentieth Winter Meeting of the Ecclesiastical History Society*, ed. Stuart Mews, Studies in Church History, 18 (Oxford: Blackwell: 1982), pp. 230-32. See John Joseph Martin, "Doctrinal Authority in the Church on the Eve of the Reformation," Dissertation University of California Los Angeles 1978; *Reform and Authority in the Medieval and Reformation Church*, ed. G. Fitch-Lytle (Washington: The Catholic University of America Press, 1981).

[47] D. C. Coleman, *The Economy in England 1450-1750* (London: Oxford University Press, 1977), pp. 12, 19-20. Roger Mols, "Population in Europe 1500-1700," in *Sixteenth and Seventeenth Centuries*, ed. Carlo Maria Cipolla, The Fontana Economic History of Europe, 2 (Glasgow: Collins, 1974), pp. 28-29, 42-43, gives slightly different numbers: early sixteenth century: 40,000-60,000; early seventeenth century: 150,000-200,000; end of seventeenth century: more than 400,000 people in London. Although an ordinance by Thomas Cromwell in 1538 imposed the registrations of baptisms, marriages, and deaths in the parishes, and despite the fact that in 1600 about half of the English parishes had such registers, it is still difficult to come to agreement upon numbers of the population.

[48] Walter Minchinton, "Patterns and Structure of Demand 1500-1750," in *Sixteenth and Seventeenth Centuries*, ed. Carlo Maria Cipolla, The Fontana Economic History of Europe, 2 (Glasgow: Collins, 1974), pp. 88-89; Domenico Sella, "European Industries 1500-1700," in *Sixteenth and Seventeenth Centuries*, ed. Carlo Maria Cipolla, The Fontana Economic History of Europe, 2 (Glasgow: Collins, 1974), p. 357.

life receive a response by the populace, as will be seen in the following decades.[49] Besides, the first half of the sixteenth century was an era of high inflation in which above all food and fuel prices rose sharply, whereas the real wages declined to the same degree. It came to a "savage depression of the living standards of the lower half of the population."[50]

During the 1530s several attempts were made for political reasons to come to an alliance with the German Lutheran princes, but these were utterly to no avail as the princes always insisted on an adoption of the Lutheran principles of faith in England as a precondition for any political relations. Lutheran books were known and discussed in Cambridge and elsewhere by 1520, and Martin Luther's ideas were spread throughout the realm, albeit vaguely in the beginning,[51] but concrete tendencies are difficult to assess in the following decade and even harder to point out.

In 1532, however, some of these lines convened in a person who was to become one of the most important figures in the English Reformation for two decades and, as far as the liturgical provisions emanating from this period are concerned, one of the most outstanding creative personalities of all times.

The octogenarian Archbishop of Canterbury, William Warham, died on August 22, 1532. Henry's choice for a successor fell on the person who had had the brilliant idea to propose to the king that the opinions of European universities should be sought regarding the divorce case, in order to lend support to Henry's position. Thomas Cranmer, the Archdeacon of Taunton, had been made ambassador to the court of Charles V in January 1532. Although having been ordained to the presbyterate some time between 1516 and 1520, he had, after having come into contact with the Lutherans in Lent 1532 in Nuremberg, secretly married a niece of the Nuremberg reformer Andreas Osiander in the summer of 1532. This was "a gesture by which Cranmer secretly but unequivocally committed himself to Lutheranism. The priest who had been married by Osiander could not easily return to the ranks of orthodoxy."[52] For the first time after almost two centuries not a bishop was transferred to the See of Canterbury but a presbyter chosen.[53] Pope Clement VII authorized Cranmer's consecration with the issue of eleven bulls on March 3, 1533; at the same time he bestowed the pall on him. The new archbishop was consecrated on March 30 of that year by the Bishops of Lincoln (John Longland), Exeter (John Voysey), and St. Asaph (Henry Standish). Before his consecration, however, in the presence of five witnesses, during the consecration

---

[49] The observation by Minchinton, "Patterns and Structure of Demand 1500-1750," p. 169, comprises only half the truth: "For the mass of the population, whose major endeavours were to keep body and soul together, to feed themselves, to clothe themselves and to obtain some degree of protection from the elements for themselves and their families, the degree of change may well have been less perceptible." At least in the period discussed here, alterations in religion obtained a much higher degree of fierce response than economic changes.

[50] Christopher Hill, *Reformation to Industrial Revolution: A Social and Economic History of Britain 1530-1780* (London: Weidenfels & Nicolsen, 1967), p. 64.

[51] See James Edward McGoldrick, *Luther's English Connection: The Reformation Thought of Robert Barnes and William Tyndale* (Milwaukee: Northwestern Publishing House, 1979). As no other European country was as dependent upon especially the textile trade in the fifteenth, sixteenth, and early seventeenth centuries as was England (Kristof Glamann, "European Trade 1500-1750," in *Sixteenth and Seventeenth Centuries*, ed. Carlo Maria Cipolla, The Fontana Economic History of Europe, 2 [Glasgow: Collins, 1974], p. 501), it is understandable that religious ideas from abroad were first known in the harbor towns in Southeast England and in London and were spread mainly through the Merchant Adventurers who had connections with Bruges, Antwerp, and other important trade and fare centers in Europe.

[52] Jasper Ridley, *Thomas Cranmer* (Oxford: Clarendon, 1962), p. 47. It is worth pondering the suggestion by Marion Josiah Hatchett, "Thomas Cranmer and the Rites of Christian Initiation," M.A. Thesis General Theological Seminary 1967, p. 219: "It is interesting to consider how different Cranmer's rites might have been if it had been in Rome or in Geneva rather than in Nuremberg that he had found the woman he loved."

[53] The last Archbishop of Canterbury to be consecrated bishop after his nomination was Simon Islif, elected September 20, 1349, consecrated December 20, 1349, died April 26, 1366: Powicke and Fryde, *Handbook of British Chronology*, p. 211.

itself, and while being given the pall, he read aloud a solemn protestation that no oath to the pope which he would be taking at the consecration would be binding if it was against the law of God, against the king or the commonwealth, or the laws or prerogatives of England; he would feel free to reform the Christian religion and the government of the Church in a direction furthering the prerogatives of the Crown.[54] The king could not have asked for a more subservient primate. His belief in the divine rights of the monarch, in royal absolutism, and in unlimited supremacy of the sovereign stands out as a very extreme type of erastianism.[55] In Cranmer Henry found a very helpful and reliable archbishop who by virtue of his office made the reformation of the Church easier than might have been the case with a more resistant man.

The ideas dominant in the first half of the sixteenth century were prone to give to the people affected a hitherto unknown measure of liberty (with the exception of the erastianism). Establishing the irreplaceable value of the individual whose horizon is opened and whose life needs no longer be dominated totally by the Church's absolute power and authority is a force clearly running in a centrifugal direction. The grip of the king upon the English people by virtue of his not only being the sovereign but also the Supreme Head of the Church is all the more remarkable and astonishing. Uniformity remained the catchword of the day despite all these currents.

The king had been given the power in the Supremacy Act (26 Hen. 8, c. 1) to visit ecclesiastical institutions and to order all matters "for the conservation of the peace, unity, and tranquillity of this realm." Through his viceregent for ecclesiastical affairs, Thomas Cromwell,[56] Henry took the obligation seriously. Two royal injunctions were issued, the first in the summer of 1536,[57] the second in September 1538.[58] The first was mainly concerned with the uprooting of

> the Bishop of Rome's pretended and usurped power and jurisdiction within this realm, and for the establishment and confirmation of the king's authority and jurisdiction within the same, as of the supreme head of the Church of England[59]

as well as with the conduct of the clergy who were to take their duty of the cure of souls seriously; besides, "Sacrament [sic] and sacramentals be duly and reverently ministered in the parishes." The second set of injunctions envisaged the same problems: instructions in the faith were to be given to people, superstitions were to be extirpated, the clergy were to live in an orderly manner. Nobody was allowed to "alter or change . . . any prayer or divine service otherwise than is specified in the said Injunctions, until such time as the same be so ordered and transposed by the king's highness's authority."[60] Two changes were immediately provided for: the feastday of St. Thomas Becket was abolished--it was politically inappropriate and not to the advancement of the king's supreme authority--and the invocation of saints in the litany would be better omitted in favor of the following Christ-centered

---

[54] Ridley, *Cranmer*, pp. 55-58.

[55] Dickens, *English Reformation*, p. 168; Gregory Dix, *The Shape of the Liturgy*, 2nd ed. (1945; rpt. London: Dacre, 1975), p. 640; Ridley, *Cranmer*, pp. 65-66; Scarisbrick, *Henry VIII*, p. 386. Attempts to whitewash Cranmer (Geoffrey Rudolph Elton, "Cranmer, Thomas," *Theologische Realenzyklopädie* 8, p. 229) are doomed given the letters and words of the archbishop himself and his actions, which were determined only by the wishes of the prince and none else.

[56] See Joseph Simon Block, "Church and Commonwealth: Ecclesiastical Patronage during Thomas Cromwell's Ministry, 1535-1540," Dissertation University of California Los Angeles 1973; Alan Lauffer Hayes, "The Viceregency in Spirituals in England, 1535-1540," Dissertation McGill University 1975.

[57] Gee and Hardy, *Documents*, no. 62, pp. 269-74.

[58] Gee and Hardy, *Documents*, no. 63, pp. 275-81.

[59] Gee and Hardy, *Documents*, no. 62, p. 270.

[60] Gee and Hardy, *Documents*, no. 63, p. 280.

suffrages. These second act of injunctions also brought the breakthrough of the translation of the Bible into English, as they foresaw that a copy of "the whole Bible of the largest volume, in English" be set up in the church for the parishioners; the reading was to be encouraged. The English version thus licensed was that of the "Great Bible," so called because of the size, a revision in 1537 by John Rogers of the former translations by William Tyndale (1526) and Miles Coverdale (1535), which in turn had been heavily influenced by the Luther and Zurich translations of the Bible.[61]

Henry's concern in church affairs, however, was not limited, to visitations. He wanted uniformity not only in outward matters but in the essentials of the faith, too. Although lacking any special theological education,[62] the Supreme Head was empowered to "order all errors and heresies," a duty he discharged in a most astonishing manner.[63]

In 1536 the king had the Canterbury Convocation ratify what were officially called *Articles about Religion*[64] but what came to be known as the Ten Articles. As they were of course published "by the King's authority" and provided with a preface by Henry, they showed his "most chief, most ponderous," and most weighty concern "that [God's] holy word and commandments may sincerely, without let or hindrance, be of our subjects truly believed, and reverently kept and observed." "To the honour of God and ours, the profit, tranquillity, and quietness of all you our most loving subjects,"[65] the three sacraments of baptism, penance, and the altar, the justification, and some provisions about the liturgical order (images, saints, rites and ceremonies) were dealt with. The sacrament of baptism was described in a quite traditional manner, without any extravagancies, as "instituted and ordained in the New Testament by our Saviour Jesus Christ . . . for the remission of sins, and the grace and favour of God." Children dying in their infancy were said to be "undoubtedly saved thereby, and else not."[66] The few sentences on the eucharist expressed a belief in the transsubstantiation without using the word.[67] All the "laudable customs, rites, and ceremonies" which were a few years later abolished were upheld and were "to be used and continued as things good and laudable, to put us in remembrance of those spiritual things that they do signify," including "the hallowing of the font, and other like exorcisms and benedictions by the ministers of Christ's church."[68] Although these Ten Articles have been said to be a rapproachment with the German Lutherans,[69] they were rather orthodox in what they said, even in the question of justification.[70]

The omission of four of the seven traditional sacraments was corrected a year later in what came to be known as The Bishops' Book. The *Institution of a Christian Man*,

---

[61] Basil Hall, "Bibelübersetzungen: III/2. Übersetzungen in andere germanische Sprachen, Übersetzungen ins Englische," *Theologische Realenzyklopädie* 6, pp. 248-50.

[62] Scarisbrick, *Henry VIII*, pp. 4, 15, discards with good reasons the notion first expressed in 1672 that Henry had been destined by his father for the See of Canterbury; but in 1502, when Henry was nine years old, his older brother died, thereby leaving the throne of England in the future to Henry. Theology was one of his pastimes, not a prime occupation.

[63] Scarisbrick, *Henry VIII*, p. 405, quotes from the sources that Henry himself corrected the first commandment in The Bishops' Book as reading: "Thou shalt not have, nor repute any other God, or gods, but me Jesu Christ;" and the Lord's Prayer was to end: "and suffer us not to be led into temptations."

[64] [Charles Lloyd, ed.,] *Formularies of Faith Put Forth by Authority during the Reign of Henry VIII: viz. Articles about Religion, 1536, The Institution of a Christian Man, 1537, A Necessary Doctrine and Erudition for any Christian Man, 1543* (Oxford: Clarendon, 1825), pp. 1-20.

[65] Lloyd, *Formularies of Faith*, pp. 3-5.

[66] Lloyd, *Formularies of Faith*, pp. 6, 7.

[67] Lloyd, *Formularies of Faith*, pp. 11-12.

[68] Of Rites and Ceremonies: Lloyd, *Formularies of Faith*, p. 16.

[69] Dickens, *English Reformation*, pp. 175-76.

[70] "This word Justification signifieth remission of our sins, and our acceptation or reconciliation into the grace and favours of God, that is to say, our perfect renovation in Christ. . . . Sinners attain this justification by contrition and faith joined with charity.": Lloyd, *Formularies of Faith*, p. 12.

containing the exposition or interpretation of the common creed, of the seven sacraments, of the ten commandments, and of the Pater noster and the Ave Maria, justification, and purgatory[71] was completed in July 1537 by a committee of bishops and theologians and submitted to the king. The dedicatory letter to the king explained that

> albeit, most dread and benign sovereign lord, we do affirm by our learnings with one assent, that the said treatise is in all points so concordant and agreeable to holy scripture, as we trust your majesty shall receive the same as a thing most sincerely and purely handled, to the glory of God, your grace's honour, the unity of your people, the which things your highness, we may well see and perceive, doth chiefly in the same desire: yet we do most humbly submit it to the most excellent wisdom and exact judgment of your majesty, to be recognised, overseen, and corrected, if your grace shall find any word or sentence in it meet to be changed, qualified, or further expoinded, for the plain setting forth of your highness' most virtuous desire and purpose in that behalf. Whereunto we shall in that case conform ourselves, as to our most bounden duties to God and to your highness appertaineth.[72]

Indeed, this is the predominance of the Supreme Head over the truth of Holy Scripture![73] Of special interest in the first part of the book on the creed is the treatise on the ninth article, "And I believe that there is one holy catholic and universal church,"[74] the longest of all expositions. The holy Church, so it was stated, is catholic, "that is to say, that it cannot be coarcted or restrained within the limits or bonds of any town, city, province, region, or country; but that it is dispersed and spread universally throughout all the whole world." Yet this Church consists in particular churches that are "the very parts, portions, or members of this catholic and universal church." No church has any superiority or dominion over the others, which holds true for the Church of Rome, too.

> The unity of this one catholic church is a mere spiritual unity, consisting in . . . the unity of Christ's faith, hope, and charity, and in the unity of the right doctrine of Christ, and in the unity and uniform using of the sacraments consonant unto the same doctrine.[75]

These "outward rites, ceremonies, traditions, and ordinances" could be instituted by the churches' governors. All churches were "called" apostolic churches because all were founded on the faith and doctrine of the apostles. The Church of England, therefore, claimed to be a true member of the catholic Church, to the same degree as the Church of Rome and other churches stated. The explanation of the sacrament of baptism was identical with that of the Ten Articles.[76] The confirmation was seen in the traditional theological context prevalent at that time and was strongly upheld as a sacrament.[77] The eucharist was interpreted along the lines of the Ten Articles, without any deviation from catholic belief.[78]

A statute was passed by the parliament in June 1539 that came to be known as The Six Articles Act (31 Hen. 8, c. 14).[79] The Supreme Head, "intending the conservation of the same Church and congregation [of England] in a true, sincere, and uniform doctrine of Christ's

---

[71] Lloyd, *Formularies of Faith*, pp. 21-211.

[72] Lloyd, *Formularies of Faith*, pp. 26-27.

[73] For some revealing and almost embarrassing passages in The Bishops' Book not relevant to the topic of this chapter, and for an attempt by Henry himself to revise the statements of the book, see Ridley, *Cranmer*, pp. 121-25.

[74] Lloyd, *Formularies of Faith*, pp. 52-57.

[75] Lloyd, *Formularies of Faith*, p. 56.

[76] John Douglas Close Fisher, ed., *Christian Initiation: The Reformation Period, Some Early Reformed Rites of Baptism and Confirmation and Other Contemporary Documents*, Alcuin Club Collections, 51 (London: SPCK, 1970), pp. 73-75; Lloyd, *Formularies of Faith*, pp. 92-94.

[77] Fisher, *Christian Initiation*, pp. 221-22; Lloyd, *Formularies of Faith*, pp. 94-96. See Hatchett, "Cranmer," pp. 33-34.

[78] Lloyd, *Formularies of Faith*, pp. 100-01.

[79] Gee and Hardy, *Documents*, no. 65, pp. 303-19.

religion," had six questions proposed to parliament and Convocation. Henry himself partook in the deliberations of parliament, so as to make sure that his private convictions and predilections would be expressed in the answers. Transsubstantiation was upheld; communion under both kinds was not necessary *ad salutem* to all persons; the marriage of priests was forbidden by the law of God; private masses were to be continued and were "agreeable to God's law;" and auricular confession was expedient and necessary. Together with the heavy penalties which ranked the offenders among the heretics, with consequent burning, this act was a crushing defeat for the reforming party.

A revision and slight correction of The Bishops' Book appeared in 1543 which, though written chiefly by a few bishops, was prefaced by a declaration of the king and so inevitably came to be known as The King's Book. Officially titled *A Necessary Doctrine and Erudition for any Christian Man*,[80] this book has been described as "the handsomest monument of Henry's experiment in Anglo-Catholicism."[81] Here, too, the doctrine of the Church was upheld as being the Church which exists in several places under several heads in several churches so that the unity among them

> is conserved and kept by the help and assistance of the Holy Spirit of God, in retaining and maintaining of such doctrine and profession of Christian faith, and true observance of the same, as is taught by the scripture and the doctrine apostolic.[82]

Diversity of traditions and ceremonies were said to be no obstacle to this unity. All this signified that the authority and jurisdiction of the Church and Bishop of Rome was a usurpation and not to be acknowledged in any other church, and that the Church of England was a member of the whole catholic Church. The section on the sacrament of baptism was almost identical with its predecessor, The Bishops' Book, with regard to contents, though expanded by an exposition on original sin and concupiscence.[83] The last paragraph introduced the idea of a covenant, which was to become a common-place argument in the sacramental theology of the Church of England and the Anglican Communion:

> This sacrament of baptism may well be called a covenant between God and us, whereby God testifieth, that he for his Son Christ's sake justifieth us, that is to say, forgiveth our sins, and endueth us with his Holy Spirit, and giveth us such graces, that thereby we be made able to walk in the ways of justice ordained by God to be exercised of us in this present life, to the glory and praise of God: and so persevering, to enjoy the fruit of the life everlasting. And we again, upon our part, ought most diligently to remember and keep the promise that we in baptism have made to Almighty God, that is, to believe in him, only to serve and obey him, to forsake all sin, and the works of Satan, to mortify our affections of the flesh, and to live after the Spirit in the new life.[84]

The scriptural warrant for this was said to be Romans 6:3-4. The section on the eucharist was greatly expanded.[85] The doctrine of transsubstantiation was confirmed in the strongest possible terms. The aspects of this sacrament as "a permanent memorial of his mercy and the wonderful work of our redemption" and as the "Eucharistia, that is to say, the sacrament of thanks and blessing"[86] were not forgotten. Communion under one kind only was defended, the necessity of preparation before the reception was stressed, and the notion of the communion and unity of the receiver of this sacrament with the whole Church was sustained.

---

[80] Lloyd, *Formularies of Faith*, pp. 213-377.
[81] Dickens, *English Reformation*, p. 185.
[82] The Ninth Article: Lloyd, *Formularies of Faith*, p. 246.
[83] Fisher, *Christian Initiation*, pp. 76-79; Lloyd, *Formularies of Faith*, pp. 253-57. See Hatchett, "Cranmer," pp. 39-40.
[84] Fisher, *Christian Initiation*, p. 79; Lloyd, *Formularies of Faith*, p. 256.
[85] Lloyd, *Formularies of Faith*, pp. 262-69.
[86] Lloyd, *Formularies of Faith*, pp. 264-65.

As to the sacrament of confirmation,[87] the matter was said to be "their [the bishops'] prayers and imposition of their hands upon them [the confirmands], and consigning them with holy chrism," and the effect would be "so corroborated and established in the gifts and graces before received in baptism, that they should not lightly fall from the same;" the statements of The Bishops' Book were repeated. As far as matters of liturgy and of liturgical theology were concerned, this book can be valued as affirming sound doctrine which was nonetheless open to further developments.

The last years of Henry's life saw the attempt to bring uniformity not only to the structure of the Church (royal supremacy) and the faith of the Church of England (The King's Book) but also to the liturgy. Archbishop Cranmer proposed to the Canterbury Convocation on February 14, 1542 an amendment and correction of all service books; one year later the king's will was made known that all liturgical books be reformed in a way that points to an exclusively biblical basis for the texts used in the liturgy.[88] The proceedings did not meet with much success, however, and, except for minor changes mainly in the direction of omitting the name of the pope, the books were reissued as before. The only part of the liturgy which was actually changed and continued to be used, with minor alterations, in the several editions of the *Book of Common Prayer* is the litany, composed by Thomas Cranmer in response to a royal mandate in August 1543 and issued on June 11, 1544. The litany was abbreviated by the omission of the invocation of the saints, in accordance with the second royal injunctions of September 1538. But the remarkable feature about the text is the arrangement of the petitions in sets of two, three, or four. Cranmer hereby achieved a flow in the phrasing very consonant with the rhythm of petition and answer. A word-by-word comparison[89] reveals the superior handling of the material by Cranmer:

> bold handling of traditional forms, notably by abbreviation and conflation; borrowing from different portions of the Sarum rite; insertion of Reformed elements into the traditional framework; and occasional recourse to a totally unexpected source.[90]

The first and oldest part of the liturgy, according to the *Book of Common Prayer*, reveals two aspects of the life of the (Henrician) Church of England. Liturgical uniformity is officially[91] dependent upon the king's will. As all matters in the Convocations and everything pertaining to the liturgy needed the royal assent to be executed, it was secured that the texts reflected the official theological policy of the sovereign, including, if necessary, polemics.[92] Except for the newly composed parts that can be judged on their own merits, the eclecticism exercized in the revision of the liturgy (and later of other parts) renders it difficult to come to a commonly agreed-upon interpretation of the material by both its users and the churchmen building their argumentation upon it.

---

[87] Fisher, *Christian Initiation*, pp. 228-29; Lloyd, *Formularies of Faith*, pp. 289-90.

[88] Geoffrey John Cuming, *A History of Anglican Liturgy*, 2nd ed. (London: Macmillan, 1982), p. 32; Walter Howard Frere, *A New History of The Book of Common Prayer: With a Rationale of Its Office*, rev. and rewritten on the basis of the former work by Francis Procter, 3rd impr., with corrections and alterations (London: Macmillan, 1910), pp. 30-31; Hatchett, "Cranmer," p. 48.

[89] Frank Edward Brightman, ed., *The English Rite: Being a Synopsis of the Sources and Revisions of The Book of Common Prayer*, 2 vols, 2nd ed. rev. (1921; rpt. Farnborough: Gregg, 1970), I, lviii-lxviii, 174-85.

[90] Cuming, *History*, pp. 35-36; p. 37 an example for a collation of all sources used for one petition.

[91] Susan Elizabeth Bridgen, "The Early Reformation in London, 1520-1547: The Conflict in the Parishes," Dissertation Cambridge [1979], pp. 207-09, indicates that in the 1530s and 1540s the attitude in London towards worship was changing. Not obeying the still strict church rules was now often tantamount to sympathy with officially heretical ideas; as the liturgical forms in the city churches depended on the incumbent, certain parishes followed reformist ideas, others conservative practices.

[92] To be delivered by the Good Lord "from the tyrannye of the bischoppe of Rome and all his detestable enormities" (Brightman, *English Rite*, I, 176) was certainly nothing short of propaganda.

The Book of Common Prayer 1549

The Reformation in England came to a turn when Henry VIII died on January 28, 1547 while holding Archbishop Cranmer's hand. He had left the education of his son Edward to persons of radical Protestant persuasion; and "the Earl of Hartford, Sir Edward Seymor, [was] to be Lord Protector and Governor of the King's Majesty and this realm of England." The imperial crown now belonged to "Edward the Sixth, King of this realm of England, France, and Ireland, Defender of the Faith, &c., and of the churches of England and also of Ireland the Supreme Head, immediately under God, on earth."[93] Edward was nine years old when he ascended to the throne; but the real power belonged to his uncle, the Lord Protector, whom he soon created Duke of Somerset.

The royal prerogatives were used to ensure the progress of the Reformation. Injunctions were given in 1547 for

> the advancement of the true honour of Almighty God, the suppression of idolatry and superstition throughout all his realms and dominions, and to plant true religion, to the extirpation of all hypocrisy, enormity and abuses.[94]

Most of the popular piety people had been used to was to be abolished; the supreme headship of the king was to be expounded, and the conduct of the clergy was to be regulated. Liturgical alterations were foreshadowed: nobody was to alter or change the order and manner "of common prayer or divine service, otherwise than is specified in these injunctions, until such time as the same shall be otherwise ordered and transposed by the king's authority."[95] The epistle and gospel of the High Mass were to be said in English rather than in Latin; English lessons were introduced as additional readings in Morning and Evening Prayer.[96]

On November 4, 1547, the *Gloria, Credo, Sanctus/Benedictus, and Agnus Dei* of the opening mass of the new parliament were sung in English.[97] An Act of this parliament for Receiving the Sacrament of the Altar under Both Kinds (1 Edw. 6, c. 1)[98] revealed for the first time not only the intent to take care of a uniform belief of all subjects but also that "the common use and practice both of the Apostles and of the primitive Church, by the space of 500 years and more after Christ's ascension"[99] was responsible, next to Christ's own command, to administer the sacrament under both kinds and to the people present who had to prepare themselves for the reception. Uniformity of belief, as we see here, was directed towards uniformity in practice, both being rooted in a claim of apostolic origin.

The uniformity in practice was advanced by a proclamation by the Duke of Somerset in the king's name on February 6, 1548.[100] Nothing was declared so much "to tend to the disquieting of his realm as diversity of opinions and variety of rites and ceremonies concerning religion and worshipping of almighty God." Nobody, therefore, was allowed to "omit, have done, change, alter or innovate any order, rite or ceremony commonly used and

---

[93] Charles Wriothesley, *A Chronicle of England during the Reigns of the Tudors, from A.D. 1485 to 1559*, ed. William Douglas Hamilton, 2 vols. (Westminster, 1870, 1875; rpt. New York: Johnson, 1965), I, 179, 178.

[94] Edward Cardwell, ed., *Documentary Annals of the Reformed Church of England: Being a Collection of Injunctions, Declarations, Orders, Articles of Inquiry, &c. from the Year 1546 to the Year 1716*, new ed. in 2 vols. (Oxford, 1844; rpt. Ridgewood, NJ: Gregg, 1966), I, no. 2, pp. 4-31.

[95] Cardwell, *Documentary Annals*, I, no. 2, p. 13.

[96] Cardwell, *Documentary Annals*, I, no. 2, pp. 13-14.

[97] Wriothesley, *Chronicle*, I, 187.

[98] Gee and Hardy, *Documents*, no. 67, pp. 322-28.

[99] Gee and Hardy, *Documents*, no. 67, p. 327.

[100] Cardwell, *Documentary Annals*, I, no. 7, pp. 42-45.

frequented in the church of England" unless abolished by royal writ. Rites for Candlemas, Ash Wednesday, Palm Sunday, and Good Friday, however, were prohibited.

The next month saw the definitive entry to a proper liturgy for the Church of England by the publication of the Order of Communion.[101] It was prepared during a "long conference;" but either the conference must have been rather shortlived, or else the Order must have been prepared beforehand;[102] it was intended to bring a liturgical framework to the Act of Receiving in Both Kinds (1 Edw. 6, c. 1) that had been passed on December 17, 1547; the publication date of the Order is March 8, 1548. The royal proclamation preceding the Order demanded of every person

> with such obedience and conformity to receive this our ordinance and most godly direction, that we may be encouraged from time to time further to travail for the reformation and setting forth of such godly order, as may be most to God's glory, the edifying of our subjects, and for the advancement of true religion.[103]

The actual version of the Order is mainly derived from Martin Bucer's work in Cologne resulting in the *Einfaltiges Bedencken*, a church order published by authority of Hermann Wied, Archbishop of Cologne, in 1543 and translated in 1545 into Latin as *Simplex ac pia deliberatio*.[104] The Order itself consisted of addresses to the congregation, a general confession and absolution, scriptural sentences as "Comfortable Words," the "Prayer of Humble Access," the administration, and a final blessing, all of which (except for the first exhortation to the congregation) was to be said after the communion of the priest, and everything of course said in English.

In May of that year the services, Morning Prayer, Mass, and Evening Prayer, were entirely in English in St. Paul's and other churches in London. The anniversary mass for Henry VII on May 12, 1548 also was entirely in English, including the Words of Institution in the Canon.[105]

The execution of all the liturgical innovations envisioned in the injunctions and the Order of the Communion was inquired during a visitation held in the diocese of Canterbury in 1548.[106] The metropolitan seems to have made up a first (and, as the events of the years to come would show, preliminary) balance of the reformation of both the liturgical life of the Church of England and the life style of the clergy; uniformity was at least ensured in his own diocese.

Thomas Cranmer it is, too, who was the principal actor in the next step of the Reformation, the production of the *Book of Common Prayer*.

A committee was appointed consisting of the Archbishop of Canterbury and some other bishops and theologians who, "having as well eye and respect to the most sincere and pure Christian religion taught by the Scriptures, as to the usages in the primitive Church," were to draw up "a uniform quiet and godly order" for the whole realm.[107] This committee met from September 9, 1548 on; the discussions seem to have lasted for no longer than three weeks; therefore, a draft must have been prepared beforehand.[108] Given Cranmer's expertise in

---

[101] Colin Buchanan, ed., "The Lord's Supper according to the Book of Common Prayer," in *Coena Domini: Die Abendmahlsliturgie der Reformationskirchen im 16./17. Jahrhundert*, hrsg. Irmgard Pahl, Spicilegium Friburgense, 29 (Freiburg [Schweiz]: Universitätsverlag, 1983), nos. 530-40, pp. 388-94.

[102] Henry Albert Wilson, Introd., *The Order of the Communion, 1548: A Facsimile of the British Museum Copy C. 25, f. 15*, Henry Bradshaw Society, 34 (London: Harrison, 1908), pp. xxiv-xxv.

[103] Wilson, *Order of Communion*, n.p. [plate 3].

[104] Geoffrey John Cuming, *The Godly Order: Texts and Studies Relating to the Book of Common Prayer*, Alcuin Club Collections, 65 (London: SPCK, 1983), pp. 68-90.

[105] Wriothesley, *Chronicle*, II, 2.

[106] Cardwell, *Documentary Annals*, I, no. 10, pp. 49-59.

[107] Act of Uniformity 1549 (2&3 Edw. 6, c. 1): Gee and Hardy, *Documents*, no. 69, pp. 358-66.

[108] Cuming, *History*, p. 45.

arranging liturgical forms[109] and his intentions to carry out his duties as metropolitan for the further reformation of the Church, there can be no doubt that this first draft must have been his. Six more bishops and six other members participated in the discussions.[110] The final results of the committee work as well as the bill for the introduction of the *Book of Common Prayer* were subject to parliamentary debate in mid-December. When on January 15, 1549 the bill was voted upon, three of the six bishops who had been members of the preparatory committee voted against it.[111] The bill had been passed through both Houses of parliament by January 21; it received the royal assent on March 14 and became effective on Pentecost Sunday of that year, June 9, 1549. That day became the watershed, for the ordinary man and woman in the pew[112] as well as for the liturgy in England in general.[113]

The Act of Uniformity (2&3 Edw. 6, c. 1)[114] carried parliamentary authority, despite the royal supremacy to which neither a direct reference nor an allusion was made in the text. The uniformity in liturgical matters was, therefore, based on the same triad as the uniformity in the church structure by claiming the royal supremacy. Lords, Commons, and king cooperated in establishing this form. The act itself began with a lament over the formerly accepted divergencies in the different variations of the Roman rite, the so-called Use of Sarum, the by far most widespread one, of York, of Bangor, and of Lincoln. The diversification had enjoyed a long tradition, and a ritual according to the Use of Sarum had been republished as recently as 1543.[115] The difference in the celebration of the mass cannot in honesty have attracted much attention of the laity, and probably of the lesser clergy, either, as they were minor ones.[116] Nonetheless, for the sake of uniformity, the legal and acknowledged existence of different rites in the one realm had to be mentioned as undesirable. Another cause of offense, and one home-made, was the "now of late much more divers and sundry forms and fashions" in all churches, owing to the different stages of the Reformation as well as the predilection of the incumbents for the various persuasions. All this diversity was to be suppressed in favor of the one uniform order, rite, and fashion of common and open prayer and administration of the sacraments. The ensuing book was called *The Book of the Common Prayer and Administration of the Sacraments, and other Rites and Ceremonies of the Church, after the use of the Church of England*. The longest part of the act, however, was given to the provisions for offenders who would not use the book and its rites and texts. The penalties

---

[109] John Wickham Legg, ed., *Cranmer's Liturgical Projects : Edited from British Museum ms. royal, 7, B. IV*, Henry Bradshaw Society, 50 (London: Harrison, 1915), pp. 3-22 (first version of Morning and Evening Prayer), 115-53 (second version of Morning and Evening Prayer). See Cuming, *Godly Order*, pp. 56-67; Cuming, *History*, p. 46.

[110] Cuming, *History*, pp. 45-46; John Wallace Suter and George Julius Cleaveland, *The American Book of Common Prayer: Its Origins and Development* (New York: Oxford University Press, 1949), pp. 41-42, give the names and their positions in church politics.

[111] Together with five other bishops; the three other bishops on the committee voted in favor of it, together with the two archbishops and five other bishops: Philip Hughes, *Religio depopulata*, Vol. II of *The Reformation in England* (London: Hollis & Carter, 1954), p. 106 note 2.

[112] "To the common man the use of the English language must have seemed by far the strongest element of novelty.": Dickens, *English Reformation*, p. 219.

[113] Biting in his attack Gregory Dix: "With an inexcusable suddenness, between a Saturday night and a Monday morning at Pentecost 1549, the English liturgical tradition of nearly a thousand years was altogether overturned. Churchgoing never really recovered from that shock.": *Shape of the Liturgy*, p. 686.

[114] Gee and Hardy, *Documents*, no. 69, pp. 358-66.

[115] Arthur Jefferies Collins, ed., *Manuale ad vsum percelebris ecclesie Sarisburiensis: From the Editions Printed at Rouen in 1543 Compared with Those of 1506 (London), 1516 (Rouen), 1523 (Antwerp), 1526 (Paris)*, Henry Bradshaw Society, 91 (Chichester: Moore & Tillyer, 1960).

[116] William Maskell, ed., *The Ancient Liturgy of the Church of England according to the Uses of Sarum, York, Hereford, and Bangor and the Roman Liturgy Arranged in Parallel Columns*, 3rd ed. (Oxford, 1882); rpt. New York: AMS Press, 1973). Differences in the textual and ritual shape of the uses were more or less limited to prayers not audible to the congregation, and gestures not visible to them.

ranged up to life imprisonment. Disagreement, therefore, with the book itself and with its features was clearly foreseen. Some exceptions to the general rule of a vernacular liturgy were permitted for persons learned in languages and for the two universities (Cambridge and Oxford). Additions to the texts by psalms or prayers taken out the Bible to be used in public were allowed.

The act supposed in its underlying ideas that every person in the realm was a member of the Church of England and, therefore, legally bound to use its liturgy; to be subject to the king was to be a member of the king's Church; and this was enforceable by law.[117] The one uniformity, acknowledging the king's title of supreme headship, was here necessarily followed by the other uniformity in matters of faith and worship.

Copies of the *Book of Common Prayer* were on sale on Ash Wednesday, March 7. St. Paul's and other churches in London began to use it in the beginning of Lent, at the same time abolishing private masses.[118] On March 25 of that year Francis Dryander, a Spaniard who, together with other reformers, had come to England recently, wrote a letter to Heinrich Bullinger in Zurich in which he told that

> a praiseworthy reformation has taken place in matters of religion.... It is generally reported that the mass is abolished.... [It] is entirely directed to the right institution of public worship in churches.[119]

Those things which he called "puerilities" that still remained he expected to be amended shortly. On June 5, after having seen the book, Dryander wrote anew to Bullinger, this time commending the book:

> You will see that the summary of doctrine cannot be found fault with, although certain ceremonies are retained in that book which may appear useless, and perhaps hurtful, unless a candid interpretation be put upon them.... This reformation must not be counted lightly of; in this kingdom especially, where there existed heretofore in the public formularies of doctrine true popery without the name.[120]

Four days later, on June 9, the book became the sole legal liturgical agenda in the realm of England and Wales.

The title of the book indicated that it was a collection of the books formerly necessary for celebrating the liturgy: breviary, missal, lectionary, pontifical, ritual are united in one volume. Two features of the title are remarkable: distinction was made between "rites" and "ceremonies," and the liturgy was considered to be the liturgy of the Church as it was celebrated in the Church of England. The meaning of the word "ceremonies" was indicated in the visitation articles for the diocese of Canterbury 1548, where the clergy was to be asked to "open and declare" to the visitors "the true use of ceremonies (that is to say) that they be no workers nor works of salvation, but only outward signs and tokens, to put us in remembrance of things of higher perfection."[121]

The preface of the book is a curiosity in that it did not deal with anything but the common prayer, now mattins and evensong, and did not explain any of the further features.[122] At the end of the book appeared a section "Of Ceremonies, why some be abolished and some

---

[117] Stefan Schlosshauer-Selbach, *Staat und Kirche in England*, Europäische Hochschulschriften: Reihe 2, 153, Dissertation München 1976 (Frankfurt: Lang, 1976), pp. 3-4.

[118] Wriothesley, *Chronicle*, II, 9.

[119] Hastings Robinson, trans. and ed., *Original Letters Relative to the English Reformation: Written during the Reigns of King Henry VIII., King Edward VI., and Queen Mary, Chiefly from the Archives of Zurich*, Parker Society, 28, 2nd portion (Cambridge: Cambridge University Press, 1847), pp. 349-50.

[120] Robinson, *Original Letters*, II, 351.

[121] Cardwell, *Documentary Annals*, I, no. 10, p. 54.

[122] Brightman, *English Rite*, I, 34-38; Edgar Charles Summer Gibson, ed., *The First and Second Prayer Books of Edward VI*, Everyman's Library, 448 (1910; rpt. London: Dent; New York: Dutton, 1964), pp. 3-5.

retained" which was more revealing as to the purpose of the publication.[123] A distinction was made between superstitious and uncorrupt ceremonies; the first were to be rejected, the second might be retained. It would be each country's privilege and duty to use such ceremonies "as they shall think best to the setting forth of God's honour and glory."

Additional notes clarified the questions of appropriate vestments which were surplice (and a hood equivalent to the academic degrees).[124] The only strictly episcopal insignia left was the pastoral staff. The people's gestures during the celebrations were left to their discretion.

The contents of the book can be divided into six categories:
the common prayer, mattins and evensong, with tables and calendars for the distribution of the psalms and lessons;
the proper texts of Sundays and feastdays for the celebration of the Lord's Supper;
the ordinary texts of the Lord's Supper;
the other sacraments and sacramental celebrations: baptism, confirmation, including a catechism,[125] matrimony, visitation of the sick and communion;
other rites: burial, and purification of women;
the commination, a penitential service for Ash Wednesday.

The two most controversial features in the book are the "Supper of the Lord and the holy Communion, commonly called the Mass," and the "Administration of public Baptism to be used in the Church."

The order of the Lord's Supper followed rather closely the use of Sarum.[126] Two collects for the king were provided for use after the collect of the day, one of which was to be said each time. The first was not free of allusions to the royal supremacy.[127] After the creed followed the first of the exhortations from the 1548 Order of Communion, admonishing the congregation about the danger of an unworthy reception of the sacrament. Provision was made for a second incitement to come to communion if the parishioners were negligent. This text, too, was taken from the Order of Communion of the previous year. Those who wished to communicate came to a place in the choir or other convenient place near the altar to follow the progress of the celebration.

The Canon deserves special attention.[128] It was introduced after the *Sanctus* with the exclamation "Let us pray for the whole state of Christ's church." What followed were basically intercessions on behalf of the king and state authorities, the clergy, and for all people, especially the present congregation. After a commemoration of the saints and a prayer for the departed, the Canon was continued with a christological part emphasizing Christ's redemptive death, and an epiclesis over the gifts. After the institution narrative the anamnesis flowed into an offering of our sacrifice of praise and thanksgiving and our whole life. An epiclesis for a worthy reception of the sacrament ended this Canon, of which it has

---

[123] Brightman, *English Rite*, I, 38-44; Gibson, *Prayer Books*, pp. 286-88.

[124] Brightman, *English Rite*, II, 926; Gibson, *Prayer Books*, pp. 288-89.

[125] See Lynn Diane Durbin, "Education by Catechism: Development of the Sixteenth Century English Catechism," Dissertation Northwestern University 1987.

[126] Brightman, *English Rite*, II, 638-720; Colin Buchanan, ed., *Eucharistic Liturgies of Edward VI: A Text for Students*, Grove Liturgical Study, 34 (Bramcote, Notts.: Grove Books, 1983), pp. 7-20; Gibson, *Prayer Books*, pp. 212-30.

[127] "that we his subiectes (duely consydering whose auctoritie he hath) maye faithfully serue, honour, and humbly obeye him, in thee, and for thee:" Brightman, *English Rite*, II, 646; Buchanan, *Eucharistic Liturgies*, p. 8; Gibson, *Prayer Books*, p. 213. See John Wickham Legg, "The Regalism of the Prayer-book," in *Some Principles and Services of the Prayer-Book Historically Considered*, ed. John Wickham Legg (London: Rivington, 1899), pp. 168-71.

[128] Brightman, *English Rite*, II, 684-94; Buchanan, *Eucharistic Liturgies*, pp. 13-15; Buchanan, "Lord's Supper," nos. 544-58, pp. 396-401; Gibson, *Prayer Books*, pp. 221-23.

been said that "its most remarkable feature is its mere existence. . . . The abolition of the Canon was an article of faith with all the Continental Reformers."[129]

After the Lord's Prayer and the Peace the other parts of the 1548 Order of Communion followed: an invitation to a general confession, the general confession spoken by one person as the representative of the congregation, the absolution, the "Comfortable Words" with sentences from Scripture, and a prayer said by the priest asking for humble access to "these holy mysteries." After the administration of the sacrament a sentence from Scripture was proposed. The final prayer asked for a life worthy of a life in Christ's mystical body. The blessing concluded the celebration.

Provisions were made for some omissions at weekday communions. Rubrics concerning the communion material, about the frequency of reception, and the manner of reception brought the section on holy communion to an end. Except for the vernacular the most striking feature of this communion order for the ordinary people might well have been the requirment to come forward to the chancel at the offertory if they were to receive communion, and to stay there through the rest of the celebration.[130]

The two principal sources in this order of the Lord's Supper were the Sarum Use and, for the parts originating in the 1548 Order of Communion, the *Einfaltiges Bedencken* of the Cologne Reformation. The same sources will be encountered in the order of public baptism; this also holds true for the confirmation rite.

The order of public baptism[131] immediately began with a rubric reminding the congregation that in antiquity baptism had been administered only at Easter and Pentecost; as this custom could not be retained, the sacrament was to be administered on Sundays and other holy days in the presence of the greatest number of people which, as the next rubric directed, was at Morning and Evening Prayer. The public administration of baptism was to serve the congregation as a reminder of their own baptism.

After an inquiry upon a possible earlier baptism of the child, the priest explained the nature of baptism, which is regeneration and a new birth in water and the Holy Spirit. Children are "baptized with the Holy Ghost, and received into Christ's holy church." Luther's well-known "Flood Prayer" followed, invoking God's mercy upon the children "to sanctify them with thy Holy Ghost, that by this wholesome laver of regeneration, whatsoever sin is in them, may be washed away." The child whose name had been asked was signed on the forehead and breast with the sign of the cross. The prayer from the Sarum rite was said asking that the children might enjoy the everlasting benediction of God's heavenly washing and might come to the eternal kingdom. One exorcism only followed, a combination of several texts in the Sarum Use,[132] imploring the "unclean spirit" to depart and to remember that his judgment was at hand; afterwards he was not again to exercize any tyranny over the child. Mark 10:13-16 was read. A long introduction to the creed, preceded by the Lord's Prayer, once again outlining God's mercy towards the child, was addressed to the congregation. After those two texts God was asked to increase and confirm the faith. The children were received into the Church. Whereas all this was done at the church door, the priest and the godparents now moved to the font. The central act of baptism, the renunciation, the questions of belief, the question after the willingness to be baptized--all addressed to the child--, the baptism by a threefold immersion, the giving of the white vesture signifying the innocence which was to be kept blamelessly, and the anointing on the head "with the unction

---

[129] Cuming, *History*, p. 54.

[130] Brightman, *English Rite*, II, 662; Buchanan, *Eucharistic Liturgies*, p. 12; Gibson, *Prayer Books*, p. 219. See George William Outram Addleshaw and Frederick Etchells, *The Architectural Setting of Anglican Worship: An Inquiry into the Arrangements for Public Worship in the Church of England from the Reformation to the Present Day* (London: Faber & Faber, 1948), p. 28.

[131] Brightman, *English Rite*, II, 724-46; Fisher, *Christian Initiation*, pp. 89-95; Gibson, *Prayer Books*, pp. 236-42. See Hatchett, "Cranmer," pp. 101-25.

[132] "Exorcizo te, immunde spiritus;" "Nec te latet sathana;" "Ergo, maledicte diabole:" Collins, *Manuale Sarisburiense*, pp. 28-29.

of [God's] holy Spirit" were done with every child individually. The conclusion of the administration of baptism was another exhortation to the godparents to care for a Christian upbringing and education of the child baptized. Morning or Evening Prayer was then continued.

As soon as the child knew the creed, the Lord's Prayer, and the Ten Commandments, and was instructed in the catechism, he was to be brought to the bishop to be confirmed by him.

A provision was made for a prayer of sanctification over the water which should be changed once a month.[133] An epiclesis of the Spirit was here invoked over the water so that all who would be baptized in the water might be spiritually regenerated and made the children of everlasting adoption. Eight petitions were added asking for the virtue of a life worthy of the baptism for all who were to be baptized in that font. The third part of the text, after alluding to John 19:34 and Matthew 28:19, desired the fullness of grace for those baptized.

It has been noted that the order in the 1549 *Book of Common Prayer* kept the structure of its immediate precedent, the Sarum Use, while most of the texts were taken from the *Einfaltiges Bedencken* of the Cologne Reformation.[134] The whole rite was simplified, yet in general liturgically conservative.[135] It has acquired a strong un-exorcizing note, to the advantage of an emphasis for this sacrament "as the sacrament of the Holy Spirit, as the entrance into a convenant relationship, as effective for regeneration or new birth, as a dying and rising again with Christ."[136]

Provisions for baptism of adults were not made; the necessity was not seen.

As the godparents had been charged with the supervision of the Christian education of the baptized, so it was the bishop's duty to make sure that the persons had learned what they ought to know, as well as been able to answer the questions of the catechism. The confirmation was the "reward" for this knowledge. The administration of this rite was therefore inevitably linked with the years of discretion, and not with baptism.

The structure of the rite[137] was that of the use of Sarum,[138] but the meaning was drastically altered.

The sevenfold gifts of the Spirit were invoked upon the confirmands in the first prayer. Thereafter the bishop asked Christ to sign those persons and to mark them to be his for ever by virtue of his cross and passion, and to confirm and strengthen them "with the inward unction of thy Holy Ghost." The bishop made the sign of the cross on the forehead and laid his hands upon them, accompanied by an explanatory formula. After the Peace the children were prayed for, "unto whom (after the examples of thy holy apostles) we have laid our hands, to certify them (by this sign) of thy favour and gracious goodness toward them," that they would be guided by God's hand and by his Holy Spirit. A blessing of the children concluded the service. The anointing was abolished, despite the fact that The King's Book still regarded the unction as one of the matters of the sacrament.[139] It was to those who could confess "by their own mouth" that the confirmation was administered.

> For Cranmer [as the author of the rite] Confirmation is not the infusion of the Holy Ghost, nor is it the completion of Baptism, but an examination in the profession which was made for the

---

[133] Brightman, *English Rite*, II, 738-40; Gibson, *Prayer Books*, pp. 245-46.

[134] Cuming, *History*, p. 60; Hatchett, "Cranmer," pp. 76, 101-02, 129, 211; Max Keller-Hüschenmenger, *Die Lehre der Kirche im frühreformatorischen Anglikanismus: Struktur und Funktion* (Gütersloh: Mohn, 1965), p. 165.

[135] John Mark Meredith Dalby, "Christian Initiation: The Background and Formation of the Prayer Book Pattern," Dissertation Nottingham 1977, p. 129.

[136] Hatchett, "Cranmer," p. 129.

[137] Brightman, *English Rite*, II, 792-98; Fisher, *Christian Initiation*, pp. 241-43; Gibson, *Prayer Books*, pp. 250-51. See Hatchett, "Cranmer," pp. 131-46, esp. pp. 141-46.

[138] Collins, *Manuale Sarisburiense*, pp. 166-67.

[139] Lloyd, *Formularies of Faith*, p. 290.

child at Baptism, with prayer that the Holy Ghost might give 'strength and constancy' to those who come to 'the yeres of discrecion' and have learned their Catechism.[140]

Confirmation was a prerequisite for admission to holy communion, as the last rubric demanded. The last rubric before the catechism gave a theological statement which was to become a stumbling block to many generations of non-conformists:

> And that no man shall think that any detriment shall come to children by deferring of their confirmation: he shall know for truth, that it is certain by God's word, that children being baptised (if they depart out of this life in their infancy) are undoubtedly saved,[141]

an echo of the same statement in The King's Book.[142]

The reactions today to the 1549 *Book of Common Prayer* are totally different from those of the contemporaries.

As to the literary qualities of the book, although "there is no evidence that contemporaries were overawed by the literary excellence" of that publication,[143] yet it was especially the sixty-nine translations from Latin originals which revealed Cranmer's craftsmanship, since in those he succeeded in an unrivaled succinctness without being verbose.[144]

Two factions are discernable in the recent discussion of this most important self-produced book of the Church of England. The first recognizes the book as one that succeeded in reforming the ancient liturgy of the Church; Cranmer's conservatism is made responsible for a not stronger reformed book but for a liturgy whose "dignity, sobriety, compactness, and practicality make it a peculiarly English vehicle of devotion."[145] The influence of Reformation theology is readily acknowledged, and the Lutheran church orders and other Continental material is discerned, but the basic catholicity of this book is defended and outlined.[146] The opposing party stresses the irrevocable break with the past, the doctrinal revolution apparent in the prayer book, the imposition "upon an unwilling church and people by a theological and political minority,"[147] the abolition of most of what was sacred to the English people, and in general an innovation rather than a reformation underlying the purpose of the book.[148] Representatives of both sides agree, however, that there are discernable underlying principles; whether Cranmer has succeeded in working along these lines again is a matter of dispute.

---

[140] Hatchett, "Cranmer," p. 146.

[141] Brightman, *English Rite*, II, 778; Gibson, *Prayer Books*, p. 247.

[142] Lloyd, *Formularies of Faith*, p. 290.

[143] Dickens, *English Reformation*, p. 220.

[144] James Ashton Devereux, "The Collects of the First Book of Common Prayer as Works of Translations," Dissertation University of North Carolina 1964, pp. 50-114, 139, 144, 177-81.

[145] Horton Davies, *From Cranmer to Hooker, 1534-1603*, Vol. I of *Worship and Theology in England* (Princeton: Princeton University Press, 1970), p. 165.

[146] Roger Thomas Beckwith, "Thomas Cranmer and the Prayer Book," in *The Study of Liturgy*, ed. Cheslyn Jones, Geoffrey Wainwright, and Edward Yarnold (London: SPCK, 1978), pp. 73-74; Brightman, *English Rite*, I, pp. lxxix-lxxxi; Davies, *From Cranmer to Hooker*, pp. 165-66; Frere, *History*, p. 54; William Paul Haugaard, *Elizabeth and the English Reformation: The Struggle for a Stable Settlement of Religion* (Cambridge: Cambridge University Press, 1968), p. 13; Edward Craddock Ratcliff, "The Liturgical Work of Archbishop Cranmer," *Journal of Ecclesiastical History*, 7 (1956), 195-96; Luther Dotterer Reed, *The Lutheran Liturgy: A Study of the Common Liturgy of the Lutheran Church in America*, 2nd ed. rev. (Philadelphia: Muhlenberg, 1959), p. 132.

[147] William Jardine Grisbrooke, "The 1662 Book of Common Prayer: Its History and Character," *Studia Liturgica*, 1 (1962), 146.

[148] Dix, *Shape of the Liturgy*, pp. 647-82; Grisbrooke, "1662 Book of Common Prayer," 146, 152-53, 158; Hughes, *Religio depopulata*, pp. 142-43-149.

These rules are "scripturalness, catholicity, purity, simplicity, intelligibility, commonness, orderliness."[149]

The reactions of the contemporaries were much more militant. Immediately after the *Book of Common Prayer* had come into effect, the country saw several uprisings, notably in Devonshire, Cornwall, Norfolk, and Oxfordshire, in which religious, social, and economic problems all had a share. The Devonshire rebellion had the strongest anti-Protestant and anti-innovative motives, demanding nothing short of a withdrawal of the *Book of Common Prayer* and a reintroduction of the liturgy prior to 1548.[150] Only two months later, on August 5, could this rebellion be overcome.[151]

Some priests who had to comply with the regulations of the Act of Uniformity (2&3 Edw. 6, c. 1) and of the *Book of Common Prayer* apparently resorted to a minimalist observance only. Articles drawn up after Pentecost 1549 to ensure the obedience of the provisions showed a revealing picture:

> 2. Item, For an [sic] uniformity, that no minister do counterfeit the popish mass, as to kiss the Lord's table; washing his fingers at every time in the communion; blessing his eyes with the paten, or sudary; or crossing his head with the paten; shifting of the book from one place to another; laying down and licking the chalice of the communion; holding up his fingers, hands, or thumbs, joined toward his temples; breathing upon the bread or chalice; shewing the sacrament openly before the distribution of the communion; ringing of sacrying bells; or setting any light upon the Lord's board at any time; and finally to use no other ceremonies than are appointed in the king's book of common prayers [sic], or kneeling, otherwise than is in the said book.[152]

Uniformity clearly was not (yet) achieved by the act and the book. The Bishop of London, Edmund Bonner, received a royal rebuke for his resenting the book and his perseverance in what was now "much idolatry, vain superstition, and great and slanderous abuses."[153] In order to advance the use of the prayer book which was said to be "grounded upon holy scripture, agreeable to the order of the primitive church, and much to the reedifying of our subjects," therefore superior to anything the realm had seen before, all books heretofore used in the Latin liturgies after the Use of Sarum, Lincoln, York "or any other private use" were to be collected and destroyed according to a royal command of December 25, 1549.[154] One of the more radical Protestants in the country, John Hooper,[155] who would be appointed bishop in July 1550, wrote to Bullinger on December 27, 1549 about the state of acceptance of the order of the Lord's Supper:

> The public celebration of the Lord's supper is very far from the order and institution of the Lord. Although it is administered in both kinds, yet in some places the supper is celebrated three times a day. Where they used heretofore to celebrate in the morning the *mass* of the apostles, they now have the *communion* of the apostles; where they had the *mass* of the blessed virgin, they now have the *communion* which they call the communion of the virgin; where they had the principal, or high mass, they now have, as they call it, the high

---

[149] Hughes, *Religio depopulata*, p. 149. See Beckwith, "Cranmer," pp. 73-74.
[150] Dickens, *English Reformation*, pp. 220-22.
[151] Wriothesley, *Chronicle*, II, 20.
[152] Cardwell, *Documentary Annals*, I, no. 15, p. 75.
[153] Cardwell, *Documentary Annals*, I, no. 17, pp. 78-80. Cf. no. 18, pp. 80-82, and no. 19, pp. 83-84.
[154] Cardwell, *Documentary Annals*, I, no. 20, pp. 85-88.
[155] In a letter of Bullinger March 27, 1550, he wrote: "I am so much offended with that book, and that not without reason, that if it not be corrected, I neither can nor will communicate with the church in the administration of the supper.": Hastings Robinson, trans. and ed., *Original Letters Relative to the English Reformation: Written during the Reigns of King Henry VIII., King Edward VI., and Queen Mary, Chiefly from the Archives of Zurich*, Parker Society, 23, 1st portion (Cambridge: Cambridge University Press, 1846), no. 38, p. 79.

communion. They still retain their vestments and the candles before the altar; in the churches they always chant the *hours* and other hymns relating to the Lord's supper, but in their own language. And that popery may not be lost, the mass-priests, although they are compelled to discontinue the use of the Latin language, yet most carefully observe the same tone and manner of chanting to which they were heretofore accustomed in the papacy. God knows to what perils and anxieties we are exposed by reason of men of this kind.[156]

The following year, 1550, saw the rearrangement of the bishops' bench with men of strong persuasions.[157] In March the book appeared which was to enable the Church of England to secure its own reformed clergy: *The form and manner of making and consecrating of Archbishops, Bishops, Priests, and Deacons*,[158] commonly called the Ordinal.[159] The Protestant party gradually won the upper hand;[160] iconoclasms occurred;[161] and a revision of the *Book of Common Prayer* was on its way.[162]

In the beginning of 1551, on January 5, a publication appreared whose influence on the *Book of Common Prayer*, as it was to be reedited the next year, is "extremely difficult to assess"[163] yet which carried great clout, as it was written by Martin Bucer, the principal person behind the *Einfaltiges Bedencken* of Cologne; he had come to Cambridge in 1549 and had been asked by Thomas Cranmer to give his views on the rites and ceremonies of the prayer book. In his *Censura or Critical Examination* Bucer "found nothing in them which was not taken from the word of God, or at least upon a reasonable interpretation was not opposed to it."[164] For each of the rites of the books (the Ordinal was included in his examination) he gave his assessment, commended what ought to be retained, proposed amendments, and urged what ought to be abolished. He supported his arguments with quotations from the Church Fathers and writings of the first centuries.[165] As regards the eucharistic Canon, he prefered that the epiclesis over the gifts be changed to an invocation over the persons "that with true faith we may receive in these mysteries the body and blood of thy Son to be the food and drink of eternal life," as an epiclesis over the gifts would be

---

156 Robinson, *Original Letters*, I, no. 36, p. 72.
157 See Stephen Michael Lyons, "Conflict and Controversy: English Bishops and the Reformation, 1547-1558," Dissertation Brown University 1980.
158 Brightman, *English Rite*, II, 928-1017; Gibson, *Prayer Books*, pp. 291-317.
159 For a detailed study, see Alan F. Detscher, *The Evolution of the Rite for the Ordination of Priests in the Protestant Episcopal Church in the United States of America from Its Pre-Reformation English Origins to the Book of Common Prayer, 1979: An Historical Study*, Diss. Rome 1981 (Romae: Pontificium Institutum Liturgicum, 1981), pp. 67-127.
160 Letter of Peter Martyr to Bullinger, January 27, 1550: Robinson, *Original Letters*, II, no. 227, pp. 477-80; Visitation articles for the diocese of London, about the beginning of June: Cardwell, *Documentary Annals*, I, no. 21, pp. 89-93; Injunctions for the diocese of London, before November 24: Cardwell, *Documentary Annals*, I, no. 21, pp. 93-96.
161 For example, during the Pentecost week in London, following the visitation: Wriothesley, *Chronicle*, II, 41; the Privy's Council order to take down altars: Cardwell, *Documentary Annals*, I, no. 24, pp. 100-02.
162 Cuming, *History*, p. 75; Gerrit Jan van de Pol, *Martin Bucer's Liturgical Ideas*, Dissertation Groningen 1954 (Assen: Van Gorcum, [1954]), pp. 142-69.
163 Cuming, History, p. 73; Robert Stupperich, "Bucer, Martin," *Theologische Realenzyklopädie* 7, p. 264, sees "einen großen Einfluß auf die endgültige Gestalt dieses Buches."
164 Edward Charles Whitaker, ed., *Martin Bucer and The Book of Common Prayer*, Alcuin Club Collections, 55 (Great Wakering: Mayhew-McCrimmon, 1974), p. 12.
165 "Wie Erasmus schätzte Bucer die alte Kirche, sie galt ihm als Vorbild. Daher wollte er sich auch nach den Kirchenvätern richten, um den früheren Zustand festzustellen, der bei der Restitution wieder erreicht werden sollte.": Stupperich, "Bucer," p. 265. See Donald W. Taylor Carr, "The Influence of Patristic Writings on the Ecclesiology of Martin Bucer," Dissertation The Southern Baptist Theological Seminary 1981; Hughes Oliphant Old, *The Patristic Roots of Reformed Worship* (Zürich: Theologischer Verlag, 1975).

tantamount to "the infinitely wicked and blasphemous dogma of the transsubstantiation."[166] Other parts of the order of the Lord's Supper were "of perfect purity and consistent with the words of the Holy Spirit,"[167] especially those that were introduced by way of the 1548 Order of Communion. As far as baptism and confirmation are concerned, he was eager to have the godparents answer the questions in their own name, promising assurances for the children, because the baptizands themselves "cannot yet understand or say anything."[168] In general Bucer opined about the "ceremonies and rites which in themselves are not opposed to the work of God" that

> care will need to be taken that these rites and instruments of religious practice are provided and used in the manner required by the rule of the Holy Spirit which is admirably set out in this book: that is to say, to ensure that no place is abandoned to any ancient wickedness, to provide nothing obscure which the people cannot understand, nothing which is not weighty and suitable to the work of building up faith in Christ and to the dignity of the cross of Christ.[169]

The Book of Common Prayer 1552

The year 1552 witnessed the republication of the *Book of Common Prayer*.

An ensuing Act of Uniformity, replacing the former one (2&3 Edw. 6, c. 1), was introduced by March 9, 1552, the final vote was taken on April 6, the royal assent was given on April 14, and it became effective November 1, All Saints' Day, 1552. Of the twelve bishops voting on this bill, the two archbishops and eight bishops were in favor of it; two opposed.[170]

The second Act of Uniformity (5&6 Edw. 6, c. 1)[171] had a twofold purpose: the first part commended the first *Book of Common Prayer* as "a very godly order . . . agreeable to the word of God and the primitive Church, very comfortable to all good people desiring to live in Christian conversation, and most profitable to the estate of this realm." Yet some people had wilfully excused themselves from church attendance. For the sake of uniformity in the entire realm, all persons without exception were to resort to their parish church or chapel to follow the services. Church authorities were charged with punishing people for neglect. This section of the act is a classical expression of the Church as "the State in prayer" without any provision for non-conformists or scruples of conscience.[172] The second part tried to explain the changes made in the new prayer book with "the more plain and manifest explanation [and] the more perfection of the said order . . . to make the same prayers and fashion of service more earnest and fit to stir Christian people to the true worshipping of Almighty God." The Ordinal was now an integral part of the *Book of Common Prayer*. The penalties for non-compliance with the intent of this act were the same as in the first Act of Uniformity (2&3 Edw. 6, c. 1) and ranged up to life imprisonment.

---

166 Whitaker, *Bucer*, pp. 52-54.
167 Whitaker, *Bucer*, p. 64.
168 Whitaker, *Bucer*, pp. 96-114.
169 Whitaker, *Bucer*, pp. 142-44.
170 Hughes, *Religio depopulata*, p. 123.
171 Gee and Hardy, *Documents*, no. 71, pp. 369-72.
172 John Richard Humpidge Moorman, *A History of the Church in England*, 3rd ed. rpt. with corrections (London: Black, 1980), p. 186.

As regards the new *Book of Common Prayer* there is general agreement among historians[173] and liturgists[174] that this book is more a "really revolutionary departure from the first"[175] than a natural evolution leading gently from the 1549 book to the present one.[176] Although Thomas Cranmer, due to political circumstances, could not have his entire way in the production of the 1552 book,[177] he still had a decisive hand in the making of it.

The book itself had undergone an important change of title. It was no longer a book used for the liturgy "of the Church after the use of the Church of England" but a book for "common prayer, and administration of the Sacraments and other rites and Ceremonies 'in' the Church of England."[178] The contents of the book made no claim to represent the (purified) liturgy of the Church but were for the exclusive use of the Church of England.

The preface and the section on ceremonies were more or less literally retained.[179]

The most controversial of all contents of the book certainly is the "Order for the administration of the Lord's supper or holy Communion."[180] It had been thoroughly remodeled so as to make certain theological doctrines clearer and to remove any possibility of mistaking the communion service for a popish mass. The altar had become the Lord's table; the priest stood not "afore the middle of the table" as in 1549 but "at the north side of the table;" the two short sides of the table, therefore, pointed to an east-west direction. As a note before Morning Prayer indicated, the appropriate vestment of all liturgies, including the communion service, was "neither alb, vestment, nor cope," but for a bishop a rochet sufficed, for a priest and deacon a surplice.[181]

After the preparatory collect the Ten Commandments were read, after which followed the collect of the day and one of the two collects for the king. The normal pattern was then used as before. After the money offering the prayer "for the whole state of Christ's church militant here in earth" was inserted, which in 1549 had formed the first part of the Canon after the Preface and *Sanctus*, but this time without any mentioning of the saints and departed. An exhortation was proposed for reminding the persons to receive the sacrament more frequently. A second exhortation was added admonishing the people to receive the communion worthily prepared by a good Christian life. And yet a third lengthy exhortation[182] was given, taken from the 1548 Order of Communion and in 1549 inserted after the creed, warning the congregation against an unworthy reception of the sacrament. The general confession with absolution by the priest for those intending to receive communion followed, after which the Comfortable Words from Scripture were pronounced. The Preface was said, succeeded after

---

[173] Dickens, *English Reformation*, pp. 247-49; Elton, *Reform and Reformation*, p. 365; Moorman, *History*, pp. 189-91.

[174] Dix, *Shape of the Liturgy*, p. 672; Grisbrooke, "1662 Book of Common Prayer," 159; Frere, *History*, p. 85; Ratcliff, "Liturgical Work," 200-02.

[175] Elton, *Reform and Reformation*, p. 365.

[176] Beckwith, "Cranmer," pp. 71-72.

[177] Clifford William Dugmore, "The First Ten Years, 1549-59," in *The English Prayer Book 1549-1662* (London: SPCK, 1963), pp. 10-11, 15, 26.

[178] Brightman, *English Rite*, I, 3; Gibson, *Prayer Books*, p. 319.

[179] Brightman, *English Rite*, , 35-45; Gibson, *Prayer Books*, pp. 321-26.

[180] Brightman, *English Rite*, II, 639-721; Buchanan, *Eucharistic Liturgies*, pp. 21-33; Buchanan, "Lord's Supper," nos. 577-81, pp. 406-08 (slightly confusing arrangement); Gibson, *Prayer Books*, pp. 377-93.

[181] Brightman, *English Rite*, I, 127; Gibson, *Prayer Books*, p. 347.

[182] One wonders whether in the light of so prolonged, and verbose (of course, after the creed was to follow an sermon or homily which ordinarily was not marked by shortness), and tenacious a part like the section between the creed and the following general confession, the *Book of Common Prayer* even after its almost *verbatim* restitution in 1559 was ever obeyed to the extend envisioned and made obligatory by the Act of Uniformity. People might have shown a reaction different from being "stirred up" to devotion, in particular as they were bound on Sundays and holy days to attend Morning Prayer, which of course could be the setting of public baptism with all the exhortations again, the litany, and the communion service, which were joined together in the morning; attendance at Evening Prayer was to follow.

the *Sanctus* not immediately by the Canon but by the prayer asking for humble access to the Lord's table, thereby giving the Canon which was then said an instantanous reference to the distribution of the communion which happened immediately after the institution narrative. The epiclesis before the narrative, which no longer asked for an action of the Holy Spirit, was no longer over the gifts but, as Bucer had proposed, over the recipients, and the narrative itself was pronounced without any gestures. The communion was given to the people in their hands, not, as had been provided for in 1549, in the mouth. The ensuing formula at the distribution asked the person to remember Christ's death and be "thankful." After the communion the Lord's Prayer was said, followed by an abridged version of what had in 1549 been the anamnesis which now was dropped, the offer of ourselves as "a reasonable, holy, and lively sacrifice," and the petition that "this our bounden duty and service" might be accepted. This prayer could be substituted by the one proposed in 1549 as a postcommunion prayer, giving thanks for the communion and for the retention of ourselves in Christ's mystical body and asking for a life worthy of God's providence. The *Gloria in excelsis* and the final blessing concluded this service.

Should there be no communion, six collects were provided to be said after the offertory. Rubrics governed the number of communicants (at least three), the matter of the bread (ordinary one; the remaining bread and wine was at the curate's own disposal), the frequency of the communion for every parishioner (at least three times a year whereof Easter was one day), and the (in)famous black rubric inserted after the book had been commissioned to the printer, declaring that kneeling at the reception of the communion was not intended as adoration as bread and wine would remain what they were, but as a humble and grateful acknowledgment of the benefits given by Christ.

Whatever can be said about the rearrangement of the texts, the majority of the scholars agree that this order comes close to an essentially Zwinglian idea of the eucharist as a mere commemoration of Christ's redemptive sacrifice.[183] The breaks with the past are evident, and one might consider the change in the title of the book not unreasonable in view of the alterations.

The same heavy remodeling held true for the "Ministration of Baptism to be used in the Church."[184]

The preface was virtually unaltered and required the baptism in public when the most number of people would be together; the setting remained at Morning or Evening Prayer.

The changes were done more by virtue of omission and rearrangement than of tampering with the texts. The one remaining exorcism in the 1549 book was left out; the signing with the cross was shifted to a position right after the dipping in the water. As the whole rite took place at the font without any movements of the parties concerned, the procession from the church door to the font became unnecessary. The rubric governed that the renunciations were asked of the godparents, no more of the children, though still addressed in the second person singular, answered once by them; this procedure was repeated for the questions concerning the belief. It was not in their own name that the godparents answered but "a promise of the child's future faith."[185] The text serving as the blessing of the water once a month in the 1549 book was now incorporated in a shortened version into the setting of every baptism, being remodelled to petitions for the children without any traces of a sanctification of material. The immersion into the water with the Trinitarian formula followed, the execution of the dipping being left to the discretion of the priest. The ensuing signing with the cross was made a gesture of the child's reception into "the congregation of Christ's flock." The giving of the white vesture and the anointing were abolished without any substitution. As a thanksgiving for the regeneration and grafting of the baptized children into the body of Christ's

---

[183] For a good survey, see Cuming, *History*, p. 81.

[184] Brightman, *English Rite*, II, 725-47; Gibson, *Prayer Books*, pp. 394-99; Peter John Jagger, ed., *Christian Initiation 1552-1969: Rites of Baptism and Confirmation since the Reformation Period*, Alcuin Club Collections, 52 (London: SPCK, 1970), pp. 12-18. See Hatchett, "Cranmer," pp. 176-95.

[185] Cuming, *History*, p. 82.

congregation, the Lord's Prayer was said, followed by a petition for a life worthy of being partakers of Christ's death and, as was asked, also of his resurrection, so that they might inherit the everlasting kingdom. The last exhortation to the godparents concluded the rite. The rubric at the end mandated that the children be brought to the bishop for confirmation as soon as thy would know the creed, the Lord's Prayer, the Ten Commandments, and the catechism.

The similarities between the last part of the order of baptism and the order of communion have been observed and noted.[186] In baptism as well as in communion, the elements were set apart, the worthy reception of the elements and of the grace was prayed for, the dominical words were recited with the application of the elements to the persons intended, and the Lord's Prayer was said. A thanksgiving for the sacrament was recited, for the "incorporation in the mystical body" (communion), the "incorporation into thy holy congregation" (baptism), so that they were "also heirs, through hope, of thy everlasting kingdom, by the merits of the most precious death and Passion of thy dear son" (communion), "as he [the infant] is made partakers of the death of thy son, so he may be partaker of his resurrection; so that finally with the residue of thy holy congregation, he may be inheritour of thine everlasting kingdom" (baptism). These parallels were not accidental, as for Thomas Cranmer the manner of Christ's presence in baptism and in the eucharist was the same; it was a presence "by faith, and spiritually," as the archbishop himself acknowledged. "For no more is truly he corporally or really present in the due ministration of the Lord's Supper, than he is in the due ministration of Baptism; that is to say, in both spiritually by grace." The power of both sacraments was "in the action and ministration," and God worked not in the elements "but in them that duly receive the same."[187]

The one omission that was more than "a reduction of ceremonies"[188] was the abolition of the unction after the immersion, as the ritual dimension of the giving of the Spirit in baptism; life in Christ is not possible except in the Holy Spirit.[189]

The confirmation service had undergone one change only, but at the very heart of the rite.[190] The petition after the invocation of the sevenfold gifts of the Spirit, that the children were to be confirmed and strengthened "with the inward unction of the Holy Spirit," was entirely dropped without a substitution. The text accompanying the laying on of hands, which was not preceded by a crossing on the forehead, asked for the defense "with thy heavenly grace, that he [this child] may continue more and more, until he come unto thy everlasting

---

[186] Cuming, *History*, pp. 82-83; Hatchett, "Cranmer," pp. 203-04.

[187] Henry Jenkyns, ed., *The Remains of Thomas Cranmer, D.D. Archbishop of Canterbury* (Oxford 1833), II, 412-13; III, 30, 229, 350; quoted in Hatchett, "Cranmer," pp. 97-98. Cf. Cranmer's Answers to the Devonshire rebels, 1549: "The water of baptism, and the holy bread and wine of the holy communion, none other person did ordain, but Christ himself.... And Christ ordained his bread, and his wine, and his water, to our great comfort, to instruct us and teach us what things we have only by him.... Our Saviour Christ ordained the water of baptism to signify unto us, that as water washes the bodies outwardly, so be we spiritually within washed by Christ from all our sins. And as the water is called water of regeneration, or new birth, so it declareth unto us, that through Christ we be born anew, and begin a new life towards God; and that Christ is the beginning of this new life.": John Edmund Cox, ed., *Miscellaneous Writings and Letters of Thomas Cranmer* (Cambridge: Cambridge University Press, 1846), p. 176.

[188] Dalby, "Christian Initiation," p. 298. Cf. p. 295.

[189] It is true that Cranmer's intentions for the 1552 rites were "that it is the act of Baptism in water in the name of the Trinity rather than any other means which effects regeneration, incorporation into the church, the giving of the name, the conferring of the seal, the anointing of the Spirit, and the giving of arms to fight." (Hatchett, "Cranmer," p. 195) But how is "any additional ceremonial action ... explanatory of what happens in this action" (Hatchett, "Cranmer," p. 205) when there was hardly any ceremonial left, especially no unction symbolizing the gift of the Holy Spirit?

[190] Brightman, *English Rite*, II, 793-99; Gibson, *Prayer Books*, pp. 408-09; Jagger, *Christian Initiation*, pp. 20-21. See Hatchett, "Cranmer," pp. 195-200, esp. 198-200.

kingdom." Without the sign of the Peace the service was concluded with the prayer provided in 1549, and a blessing.

This order was a ritual rendering of the second rubric preceding the catechism and confirmation rite, that "by imposition of hands and prayer they [the baptized] may receive strength and defense against all temptations to sin, and the assaults of the world and the devil."[191] As this rubric had preceded the 1549 rite too, the change in the wording and gesture made "explicit the rationale which is spelled out in unequivocal terms in Cranmer's writings[192] and in the introductory rubrics of the 1549 rite."[193]

The 1552 *Book of Common Prayer*, more than its predecessor, was a radical break with the past, carefully removing every trace of the liturgical order that was followed in the realm until a few years ago. There was no doubt that England was a Protestant country.

The services according to this book were begun on November 1. On that day "all copes and vestments were put down through all England, . . . and the Bishops [left] their crosses, so that all priests and clerks should have none other vestments, at service nor communion, but surplices only."[194]

The book's fate was a short-lived one, but even so was accompanied by church robberies on such a grand scale in April and May 1553 that all inventories of the churches in the realm, except for a cup and tablecloths for the communion board, were to be brought to the Tower to be handed over to the king's use; immeasurable treasures were taken away.[195]

Queen Mary and the Reaction

After King Edward's death on July 6, 1553 and some turmoil due to the rivalry between Lady Jane Grey's pretensions to the throne and the aspirations of Princess Mary, daughter of Henry VIII and Catherine of Aragón, Mary was proclaimed new queen on July 19, which was "so joyful news . . . that the inestimable joys and rejoicing of the people cannot be reported.[196] The austere reign of the boy king[197] and the church terror of the Duke of Somerset and later of the Duke of Northumberland had come to an end. As it had been known everywhere that Mary had steadfastly kept to the old religion, everybody knew what her accession meant. The dichotomy became obvious when on August 10 "the Queen's highness had a solemn mass of Requiem sung within the chapel in the Tower for the King," whereas a public service of communion and burial according to the 1552 *Book of Common Prayer* was held at Westminster Abbey.[198] Although her conscience of course could not allow her to adopt the royal title of "Supreme Head of the Church of England," she had nevertheless to act as such in order to pursue her ways. In her first proclamation about religion, dated August 18, 1553, she wished that the religion she had "ever professed from her infancy hitherto . . . were of all her subjects quietly and charitably embraced," although she would refrain from compelling

---

[191] Brightman, *English Rite*, II, 777; Gibson, *Prayer Books*, p. 404; Jagger, *Christian Initiation*, p. 19, no. 5.

[192] "Confirmation . . . is prayer by the bishop 'in the name of the church' that the Holy Ghost might give 'strength and constancy, with other spiritual gifts' to those confirmed.": Hatchett, "Cranmer," p. 94.

[193] Hatchett, "Cranmer," p. 200. See Dalby, "Christian Initiation," p. 298.

[194] Wriothesley, *Chronicle*, II, 78-79.

[195] Wriothesley, *Chronicle*, II, 83-84.

[196] Wriothesley, *Chronicle*, II, 88-89.

[197] See Edward Louis Coyle, "The English Josiah: A Psychological Portrait of King Edward VI," Dissertation Northwestern University 1976.

[198] Wriothesley, *Chronicle*, II, 96-97.

anybody to this step until "further order, by common assent, may be taken therein,"[199] The reestablishment of the old religion was to determine all her activities as far as the Church and liturgy were concerned. A week later, on August 24, the Latin services were resumed in some of the churches in London, "not by commandment but of the people's devotion."[200]

The queen's first Act of Repeal (1 Mar., stat. 2, c. 2), passed in the autumn of 1553, repealed nine acts passed under her predecessor, thereby restoring the status quo of 1547.[201] This affected the liturgical innovations of the reception of the sacrament under both kinds (1 Edw. 6, c. 1), the first Act of Uniformity (2&3 Edw. 6, c. 1), the act establishing the Ordinal (3&4 Edw. 6, c. 12), and the second Act of Uniformity (5&6 Edw. 6, c. 1). After December 20, 1553, the liturgical order was that of 1547, which in effect meant the Latin mass and all the other celebrations according to the several Uses, "throughout the whole realm of England and all other the queen's majesty's dominions," a regulation that was duly observed everywhere.[202] Most of the other ecclesiastical legislation affecting the church structure (royal supremacy), the clergy discipline, and the formerly customary ceremonies were dealt with in Mary's injunctions of March 4, 1554.[203] Whereas the liturgical reaction against the Reformation was carried out from Palm Sunday 1554 on so that the Roman ritual was completely restored,[204] the following months and years saw the repeal of all anti-Roman legislation from 1529 on,[205] including of course the Act of Royal Supremacy (26 Hen. 8, c. 1). The "conversion of this realm to the catholic faith and church" on January 25, 1555 concluded the process of un-reforming the country.[206] On February 24, 1556 a writ for burning Thomas Cranmer, who had been deprived of his see on December 11, 1555 and of his episcopal and presbyteral orders on February 14, 1556, was issued by Philip and Mary.[207] March 21 of that year saw both the burning of Cranmer and the ordination of his successor, Cardinal Pole, himself of the royal family, who as *legatus a latere* had reconciled England to Rome, to the presbyterate; the next day he was ordained bishop.[208] As in their lives, so in their deaths Mary and her Archbishop of Canterbury were not divided: Mary died on November 17, 1558, Cardinal Pole one day later.[209]

Mary's reign had fallen from an enthusiastic reception by the people in the beginning to an unforeseeable and intensely low regard, to be attributed both to the nearly three hundred burnings of persons convicted of heresy, a number too great to bear, and to the queen's marriage treaty and wedding with the widower king of Spain, Philip II, which proved to be an utterly unpopular step.[210] These events served to alienate the sovereign from the people, and to both her subjects and successor the deaths of the two most important persons of the realm within two days must have looked providential.

---

[199] Cardwell, *Documentary Annals*, I, no. 28, pp. 114-17; Gee and Hardy, *Documents*, no. 72, pp. 373-76.
[200] Wriothesley, *Chronicle*, II, 101.
[201] Gee and Hardy, *Documents*, no. 73, pp. 377-80.
[202] Wriothesley, *Chronicle*, II, 105.
[203] Cardwell, *Documentary Annals*, I, no. 30, pp. 120-25; Gee and Hardy, *Documents*, no. 74, pp. 380-83.
[204] Wriothesley, *Chronicle*, II, 113.
[205] The second Act of Repeal (1&2 Phil. & Mar., c. 8): Gee and Hardy, *Documents*, no. 76, pp. 385-415.
[206] Wriothesley, *Chronicle*, II 126. It is worth to be noted that this reconciliation of the country with the See of Rome was arranged for being done on the feastday of the Conversion of St. Paul, the former persecutor of the true Church.
[207] Cardwell, *Documentary Annals*, I, no. 40, pp. 201-03.
[208] Wriothesley, *Chronicle*, II, 134.
[209] Wriothesley, *Chronicle*, II, 141-42.
[210] Moorman, *History*, pp. 193-97.

The Book of Common Prayer 1559

Elizabeth, daughter of Henry VIII and Anne Boleyn, was proclaimed queen the same day as Mary died. Her leanings had always been known to be toward a position close to Henry's ideas of a national Church.

In her first proclamation to forbid preaching she immediately allowed the epistle and gospel, the creed, and the Lord's Prayer to be said in English as well as the use of the English litany as was at that time recited in her own chapel. Other measures would be taken by the parliament.[211] On January 15, 1559 Elizabeth was crowned at Westminster Abbey according to the Latin liturgy, but the mass, with minor changes, was celebrated by the dean of her chapel, as no bishop wanted to have a hand in altered liturgical rites.[212] On January 25 parliament began its sessions. On February 9 the Lower House began with the reading of a bill "to restore the supremacy of the Church of England &c. to the Crown of this realm," introduced by the government. After some heavy politicking behind the scenes, the bill was extended to include a Protestant service which would have made it a measure of both supremacy and uniformity. A committee of the House of Lords redrafted it to its original form. The supremacy bill, agreed to by both Houses, was ready for royal assent by March 22. As Easter that year fell on a particularly early date (March 26), a royal proclamation was issued declaring that from Easter onwards the communion was to be given under both kinds. Instead of giving the assent and ending parliament, the queen adjourned parliament on Good Friday, March 24, to April 3. After the reassembly both Houses passed the supremacy bill. A uniformity bill, without any book annexed, was introduced into the Commons on April 18. This measure, too, was rapidly passed by both Chambers. At the closing session of parliament on May 8 both bills received the royal assent.[213] Elizabeth saw herself vested with almost the same powers as her father.

The Act of Supremacy (1 Eliz. 1, c. 1)[214] repealed the second Act of Repeal 1554 (1&2 Phil. & Mar., c. 8) and revived ecclesiastical legislation of Henry VIII and Edward VI. "All usurped and foreign power and authority, spiritual and temporal" was forever excluded from the country, and the highest ecclesiastical jurisdiction was "united and annexed to the imperial crown of the realm." An oath of supremacy was to be taken, under heavy penalties. Despite the length, this act curiously never spoke about the queen's "supremacy over the Church of England." The only time this prerogative was mentioned was the phrasing of the oath which declared the queen's highness to be "the only supreme governor of this realm, and of all other her highness's dominions and countries, as well in all spiritual or ecclesiastical things or causes, as temporal." From the beginning on Roman Catholics,[215] and radical Protestants[216]

---

211 Cardwell, *Documentary Annals*, I, no. 42, pp. 208-10; Gee and Hardy, *Documents*, no. 77, pp. 416-17.

212 William Paul Haugaard, "The Coronation of Elizabeth I," *Journal of Ecclesiastical History*, 19 (1968), 170. See Angelo Joseph Louisa, "The Marian Bishops: A Study of the Backgrounds and Ecclesiastical Activities of the Marian Episcopate," Dissertation Univsity of Minnesota 1985.

213 John Earnest Neale, *Elizabeth I and Her Parliaments 1559-1581* (London: Cape, 1953), pp. 41-81.

214 Gee and Hardy, *Documents*, no. 79, pp. 442-58.

215 For the difficult position of the remaining Roman Catholics in England, and the influence of Roman Catholics from abroad, see Thomas Marshall Caughron, "Elizabethan Catholicism: The Dilemma of Split Allegiance," Dissertation Claremont Graduate School 1981; John Joseph Larocca, "English Catholics and the Recusancy Laws 1558-1625: A Study in Religion and Politics," Dissertation Rutgers University, The State University of New Jersey (New Brunswick) 1977; William Thomas Walker, "Tridentine Reforms and Recusancy in England during the Sixteenth and Seventeenth Centuries," Dissertation University of South Carlonia 1983; Garnett Lee White, "Anglican Reactions to the Council of Trent in the Reign of Queen Elizabeth I," Dissertation Vanderbilt University 1975.

216 The most prominent Continental reformer influencing the Church of England in the sixteenth and seventeenth centuries, and the one who became the most influential contemporary theologian, was John Calvin

who had begun to reappear in the country immediately after Elizabeth's accession after a period of exile on the Continent during Mary's reign, united in opposing any lay headship over the Church. Elizabeth was, for her own conscience's sake as well as for the sake of preventing any strife, content to stand as it were outside the church authorities, even if she mostly got her way when she interfered in ecclesiastical affairs in the years to come.[217]

The Act of Uniformity (1 Eliz. 1, c. 2)[218] was marked by a short revival of the second *Book of Common Prayer* according to the Act of Uniformity 1552 (5&6 Edw. 6, c. 1), effective from June 24, 1559 on, with the four alterations specified, and long provisions for penalties if a person would offend against this reestablishment, ranging up to life imprisonment. Two more clarifications and orders in liturgical matters were foressen in the act. First,

> that such ornaments of the church, and of the ministers thereof, shall be retained and be in use, as was in the Church of England, by authority of Parliament, in the second year of the reign of King Edward VI, until other order shall be therein taken by the authority of the queen's majesty . . . or of the metropolitan of this realm;[219]

second,

> that, if there shall happen any contempt or irreverence to be used in the ceremonies or rites of the Church, by the misusing of the orders appointed in this book, the queen's majesty may . . . ordain and publish such further ceremonies or rites, as may be most for the advancement of God's glory, the edifying of His Church, and the due reverence of Christ's holy mysteries and sacraments.[220]

The *Book of Common Prayer* 1559 altered the 1552 book in only four instances.[221] The litany no longer petitioned deliverance "from the tyranny of the Bishop of Rome, and all his detestable enormities."[222] Whereas in the 1549 book the words of administration of the Body of Christ had been "The body of our Lord Jesus Christ which was given for thee, preserve thy

---

whom the so-called puritans looked to as their foreign guide. See Robert Tillman Kendall, *Calvin and English Calvinism to 1649*, Oxford Theological Monographs (Oxford: Oxford University Press, 1979). As to Calvin's ideas on baptism, see John Wheelan Biggs, "The Development of Calvin's Baptismal Theology 1536-1560," Dissertation University of Notre Dame 1988. During the later Tudor and early Stuart periods, 126 editions of his works appeared in English. See David Harry Stam, "England's Calvin: A Study of the Publication of John Calvin's Works in Tudor England," Dissertation Northwestern University 1978.

[217] Claire Cross, *The Royal Supremacy in the Elizabethan Church*, Historical Problems, Studies and Documents, 8 (London: Unwin; New York: Barnes & Noble, 1969), pp. 19-23. However, the claim by Cross that whereas Henry exercized his supremacy as "the King alone" Elizabeth fulfilled her function of supreme governor as "Queen-in-Parliament" (pp. 23-24) has to be corrected to a certain degree in the light of what Cross herself states, that "Elizabeth repeatedly, on her own initiative interfered in questions of faith and doctrine, albeit mainly in a negative way.": p. 68.

[218] Gee and Hardy, *Documents*, no. 80, pp. 458-67.

[219] The second regnal year of Edward VI was January 28, 1548 to January 27, 1549 (*Guide to Law Reports*, p. 28). The first Act of Uniformity (2&3 Edw. 6, c. 1) was passed on January 21, 1549 "with the assent of the Lords and Commons in this present Parliament assembled, and by the authority of the same" (the royal assent on March 14, 1549 made it an act of the second and third regnal years). There can be no doubt that reference in the Elizabethan Act of Uniformity (1 Eliz. 1, c. 2) was to this first Act of Uniformity (2&3 Edw. 6, c. 1) and, thereby, to the provisions for vestments as were outlined in the *Book of Common Prayer* 1549.

[220] William Keatinge Clay, ed., *Liturgical Services: Liturgies and Occasional Forms of Prayer Set Forth in the Reign of Queen Elizabeth*, Parker Society, 27 (Cambridge: Cambridge University Press, 1842) contains forty-nine such additional prayers in excess of the editions of the *Book of Common Prayer*.

[221] John E. Booty, ed., *The Book of Common Prayer 1559: The Elizabethan Prayer Book*, Folger Documents of Tudor and Stuart Civilization, 22 (Washington: Folger Shakespeare Library: London: Associated Universities Press, 1976).

[222] Brightman, *English Rite*, I, 177.

body and soul unto everlasting life," the words of administration of the Blood reading accordingly, they had been changed in the 1552 book to "Take and eat this, in remembrance that Christ died for thee, and feed on him in thy heart by faith, with thanksgiving;" the delivery of the cup had been accompanied by saying: "Drink this in remembrance that Christ's blood was shed for thee, and be thankful." The two sentences for the administration of bread and wine were now, in the 1559 book, linked together[223]--a curious method to make the theological implications purposely ambiguous. The so-called black rubric on kneeling at the reception was suppressed.[224] And the ornaments' rubric before Morning and Evening Prayer essentially repeated the provisions of the Uniformity Act, without the saving clause of a further possible amendment.[225]

These four alterations have mostly been taken to represent a swing in a more Catholic direction: as the queen could not have the 1549 book restored, she would try to amend the 1552 book in a way more conforming to her own taste.[226] The pressure in the parliament for a uniform order representing the theological and liturgical ideas of the returned exiles that had been heavily influenced by John Calvin was extreme, and it would continue throughout Elizabeth's reign.

The next year saw the publication of a Latin version of the prayer book, *Liber Precum Publicarum*,[227] a rather conservative, not entirely accurate translation of the 1559 book, done by Walter Haddon in a renaissance Latin style,[228] to facilitate the improvement of the students' command of that language in the universities and colleges.[229]

The most important part of the "Elizabethan Settlement" regarding the liturgy of the Church of England, besides the Act of Uniformity and the prayer book, was the "Advertisements," articles drawn up by Elizabeth's Archbishop of Canterbury, Matthew Parker, who in 1565 had tried in vain to obtain the queen's assent to them and then published them under his own authority in the spring of 1566.[230] With all clarity possibly wished for, the aim of uniformity in doctrine and ritual was proclaimed in the preface, setting the tone not only for this document but for the whole *régime* of Elizabeth's church governance:

> The queen's majesty, of her godly zeal, calling to remembrance how necessary it is to the advancement of God's glory, and to the establishment of Christ's pure religion for all her loving subjects, especially the state ecclesiastical, to be knit together in one perfect unity of doctrine, and to be conjoined in one uniformity of rites and manners in the ministration of God's holy word, in open prayer and ministration of sacraments, . . . hath by her letters directed unto the Archbishop of Canterbury and metropolitan, required, enjoined, and straightly charged, that . . . some orders might be taken, whereby all diversities and varieties among them of the clergy and the people might be reformed and repressed, and brought to one manner of uniformity throughout the whole realm.[231]

---

[223] Brightman, *English Rite*, II, 700-01.

[224] Brightman, *English Rite*, I, clxx, 721; Booty, *Book of Common Prayer 1559*, p. 268. See Cuming, *History*, p. 91.

[225] Brightman, *English Rite*, I, 127.

[226] Patrick Collinson, *The Elizabethan Puritan Movement* (London: Cape, 1967), p. 34; Cross, *Royal Supremacy*, p. 75; Haugaard, *Elizabeth and the English Reformation*, pp. 109-10.

[227] Clay, *Liturgical Services*, pp. 299-430.

[228] Cuming, *History*, pp. 92-93; Haugaard, *Elizabeth and the English Reformation*, p. 113; Frank Streatfield, *Latin Versions of the Book of Common Prayer*, Alcuin Club Pamphlet, 19 (London: Mowbray, 1964), pp. 2-7.

[229] Literae patentes reginae de forma precum publicarum Latine vertenda, dated April 6, 1560: Cardwell, *Documentary Annals*, I, no. 50, pp. 280-82.

[230] Cardwell, *Documentary Annals*, I, no. 65, pp. 321-31; Gee and Hardy, *Documents*, no. 81, pp. 467-75.

[231] Cardwell, *Documentary Annals*, I, no. 65, pp. 321-23; Gee and Hardy, *Documents*, no. 81, pp. 467-68.

Among other things, observance of the orders in the *Book of Common Prayer* was to be enforced and frequent communion was to be desired. A solution to the controversy around the vestments of the clergy in cathedral and collegiate churches as well as in parishes was attempted by prescribing the appropriate apparel (surplice, and a cope for the communion service in cathedral and collegiate churches). Kneeling was enjoined for the reception of the communion; moving the baptismal font was forbidden, as was the baptism over a basin.[232]

The advertisements, expedient as they were intended, did not stop either the more external quarreling over vestments or the more profound questions about church policy in general, discipline, governance, and liturgy that had come to the focus in the meantime. A proclamation by the queen reminding the church and state authorities of the Act of Uniformity (1 Eliz. 1, c. 2) and the penalties for trespassing it, issued on October 20, 1573,[233] and even a special act against puritans passed in 1593[234] came too late to save the intention of the Elizabethan settlement: within the one church in the realm, which is the Church of England, both to comprehend all subjects of the Crown and to hold to a uniformity of belief and liturgy. Comprehension and uniformity were incompatible with each other in Elizabeth's era.[235]

The church party that more than others was to determine the fate of Elizabeth's church was the puritans, a movement within the Church of England, which is at the same time so multiform and so difficult to define[236] that besides generalizations only certain common features concerning the liturgy can be pointed at. The common religious denominator of this group was the desire to advance the reform of the Church beyond what had been achieved in the Church of England, to abolish popish abuses, to take away things not ordained by God's pure Word, so that what had been tolerated as things indifferent, which in many cases had been retained and under Elizabeth even enforced, should not be used. Some circles of the puritans did not confine these questions of authority in the Church to patterns and details of worship but extended them to questioning of the appropriateness of a female supreme governor or of a visible Supreme "Head" over the Church at all. As the years went by, the puritans changed their own outlook; therefore, the early movement is not necessarily identical with later groups.[237]

As to the differences between the two parties which later came to be known as "Anglicans" and "Puritans," there was a constancy in refusing certain ceremonies and provisions of the prayer book as not in accordance with the Word of God or as having been

---

[232] Some of the more radical clergy had taken to baptize in front of the congregation so as to facilitate the participation of the people, but with the help of a temporary resource of a basin containing the baptismal water.

[233] A proclamation against the despisers or breakers of the orders prescribed in the book of common prayer: Cardwell, *Documentary Annals*, I, no. 79, pp. 383-87.

[234] Gee and Hardy, *Documents*, no. 86, pp. 492-98.

[235] This assessment of course does not take away the many positive results of the settlement; and without so stubborn a supreme governor as Elizabeth much would have been defeated or lost during the latter part of her long reign. For a positive evaluation of the settlement, see Sydney Eckman Ahlstrom, *A Religious History of the American People*, complete and unabridged in 2 vols. (Garden City, NY: Image Books, 1975), I, 130-31; Collinson, *Elizabethan Puritan Movement*, pp. 32, 35; Cross, *Royal Supremacy*, p. 75; Geoffrey Rudolph Elton, "Elisabeth I.," *Theologische Realenzyklopädie* 9, pp. 512-13.

[236] The expert on the puritan movement, Patrick Collinson, gives a sarcastic comment on the attempts to come to grasp with the phenomenon: "Much of this literature [on puritanism], perhaps too much, is hung up on the elementary difficulty of defining the object of investigation: a debate conducted among a group of blind-folded scholars in a darkened room about the shape and other attributes of the elephant sharing the room with them.": "A Comment: Concerning the Name Puritan," *Journal of Ecclesiastical History*, 31 (1980), 483-84.

[237] For an appraisal of the puritans in the sixteenth century, see Geoffrey William Bromiley, *Baptism and the Anglican Reformers* (London: Lutterworth, 1953), pp. 158-59; Collinson, *Elizabethan Puritan Movement*, pp. 25, 28, 59-60, 463; Davies, *From Cranmer to Hooker*, p. 255; Elton, "Elisabeth I.," pp. 511-12; Willem Nijenhuis, "Calvin, Johannes," *Theologische Realenzyklopädie* 7, p. 589.

usurped by the papists on the side of the puritans; therefore, they ought to be refused. The surplice and the outdoor dress for the clergy was the greatest stumbling block. Then,

> the puritans would object with monotonous consistency to signing with the cross and addressing interrogatories to the infant in baptism, baptism by midwives [in emergency cases], the rite of confirmation, kneeling at the communion and the use of wafer-bread [as enjoined by royal injunctions of 1559], the giving of the ring in marriage, the purification of women after child-birth, the retention of such terms as "priest" and "absolution," the observation of saints' days, bowing at the name of Jesus and "exquisitie singing in parts" and organs.[238]

The other side of the coin was the willingness of this party to conform to a liturgy they considered better reformed and more in accordance with the ancient and apostolic Church;[239] and, above all, preaching was to take precedence over liturgical forms: the pure Word of God over man-made ceremonies.[240]

The puritans voiced strong objections against some regulations and underlying theological doctrines about baptism. The sign of the cross was regarded as constituting a new sacrament, "as if regeneration were by baptism, and incorporation by crossing,"[241] therefore not to be done. Private baptism was to be entirely abolished as God's promises would be given and sealed in the church; baptism by women was to be forbidden as women ought to be silent; besides, as the puritan movement was a heavily clerical faction, lay people were not listened to by the pastors and were not given any voice in determining church affairs--how much less women who should dare administer one of the two sacraments ordained by God; the interrogatories were to be asked to the congregation, as these were the elected, gifted with God's grace and ready to answer it; and godparents should not be allowed to substitute for the real parents of the child.[242]

The puritans were confined during Elizabeth's reign to voicing their opposition and to attracting the utter dislike and even enmity of the queen. They were silenced for the moment, but the further history of the *Book of Common Prayer* is incomprehensible without their steady attempts to move the liturgy, and thereby the Church, in their own direction.

More important perhaps than any other theologian or divine was Richard Hooker (1553-1603), whose *Laws of Ecclesiastical Polity*[243] was the major victory point for the Church of England in its defense against the puritans. He took their arguments to task and answered

---

[238] Collinson, *Elizabethan Puritan Movement*, p. 36. See Davies, *From Cranmer to Hooker*, pp. 69-70; William Sydnor, *The Real Prayer Book: 1549 to the Present* (Wilton, CT: Morehouse-Barlow, 1978), pp. 25-26.

[239] Collinson, *Elizabethan Puritan Movement*, pp. 356-57, 364-65; Davies, *From Cranmer to Hooker*, p. 70.

[240] Collinson, *Elizabethan Puritan Movement*, p. 358; Samuel H. Garrett, "Prayer Book Presence in Colonial America," in *Worship Points The Way: A Celebration of the Life and Work of Massey H. Shepherd, Jr.*, ed. Malcolm C. Burson (New York: Seabury, 1981), p. 65.

[241] Quest 95 of "A Survey of the Booke of Common Prayer;" quoted in: Horton Davies, *The Worship of the English Puritans* (Westminster: Dacre, 1948), p. 63.

[242] Collinson, *Elizabethan Puritan Movement*, pp. 369-70; Davies, *Worship of Puritans*, pp. 69-70; Haugaard, *Elizabeth and the English Reformation*, pp. 121-22.

[243] John Keble, ed., *The Works of That Learned and Judicious Divine Mr. Richard Hooker: With an Account of His Life and Death by Isaac Walton*, 7th ed., rev. by Richard William Church and Francis Paget, 3 vols., Burt Franklin Research and Source Works Series, 546: Philosophy Monograph Series, 34 (Oxford, 1888; rpt. New York: Franklin, 1970).

them in a way that made him one of the pillars of Anglican theology.[244] He defended royal supremacy in rather mild terms, as more a matter of convenience than of absolute necessity:

> Visible government is a thing necessary for the Church; and it doth not appear how the exercise of visible government over such multitudes every where dispersed throughout the world should consist without sundry visible governors; whose power being the greatest in that kind so far as it reacheth, they are in consideration thereof termed so far heads.[245]

The entire fourth book of the Laws was devoted to questions of ritual, ceremony, and uniformity, which was defended as safeguarding the principle that "the due and decent form of administering those holy sacraments [of baptism and communion] doth require a great more" than saying the Lord's words over the elements.[246] Most of the fifth book was given to vindicating the right of the Church of England to set up a form of common prayer and of the administration of the sacraments. Baptism and eucharist were taken not

> for bare resemblances or memorials of things absent, neither for naked signs and testimonies assuring us of grace received before, but (as they are indeed and in verity) for means effectual whereby God when we take the sacraments delivereth into our hands that grace available unto eternal life, which grace the sacaments represent or signify.[247]

He defended both the sign of the cross in baptism,[248] the interrogatories to the infants and the answers on their behalf by the godparents,[249] and lay baptism, even by women, in case of necessity.[250]

In all these positions Hooker may well be regarded as representing what came to be classical Anglican theology; the church would benefit from it in the next century.

Elizabeth I died on March 24, 1603, after more than forty-four years on the throne. Her last years were characterized by two conflicting ideas. The church that through her settlement had become an established one had taken hold of the majority of the population. But comprehension, the one church for the one people of the empire, was never achieved. On the surface of the church, and of society at large, it was rather calm, and internally the church matured. But other elements were active which would be determining factors in the two following reigns.

The year before her death saw another heavy outbreak of the "plague," with a death toll of at least 33,000 people, more than a quarter of the population in London alone, caused by a steady migration to the capital, a series of bad harvests in the previous twenty years, and the complete lack of any sanitary regulations.[251] The past two generations had seen a great redistribution of landed property and a large-scale sale of crown lands, partly to finance the

---

[244] See Günther Gaßmann, "Hooker, Richard," *Theologische Realenzyklopädie* 15, pp. 581-83; Olivier Loyer, *L'Anglicanisme de Richard Hooker*, 2 vols. (Paris: Champion, 1979); John Kenneth Reynold Luoma, "The Primitive Church As a Normative Principle in the Theology of the Sixteenth Century: The Anglican-Puritan Debate over Church Polity As Represented by Richard Hooker and Thomas Cartwright," Dissertation The Hartford Seminary Foundation 1974.

[245] VIII, iv,7: Keble, *Hooker*, III, 381. Cf. VIII, ii,5: Keble, *Hooker*, III, 343-45; VIII, iv,1,6: Keble, *Hooker*, III, 368, 374-80.

[246] IV, i,2: Keble, *Hooker*, I, 418. Cf. the entire fourth book: Keble, *Hooker*, I, 416-88.

[247] V, lvii,5: Keble, *Hooker*, II, 258. "Underlying the passage is the concept of the Covenant which is fundamental for an understanding of the classical Anglican teaching on the sacraments.": Louis Weil, "Worship and Sacrament in the Teaching of Samuel Johnson of Connecticut: A Study of the Sources and Development of the High Church Tradition in America, 1772-1789," Dissertation Institut Catholique 1972, p. 128.

[248] V, lxv,1-5: Keble, *Hooker*, II, 317-20.

[249] V, lxiv,1-6: Keble, *Hooker*, II, 307-17.

[250] V, lxii,1-22: Keble, *Hooker*, II, 280-304.

[251] Mols, "Population," p. 75; Coleman, *Economy of England*, p. 93 (calling the death toll an "underestimate" and the real figures "appreciably higher").

costly wars England had to fight in the sixteenth century. This change of property resulted in two phenomena. The "middle class" especially (merchants, richer artisans, peasantry, well-to-do farmers) became more distinguished and more important in politics, due to their rising wealth.[252] As the former monastic and chantry land had belonged to the now outlawed Roman Church, Henry, Edward, and Elizabeth had created a vast interest in Protestantism: only the reformed church could guarantee the preservation of the tenure.[253] It was this "middle class" and the lower gentry that could afford to engage in education, to buy and read the Bible, and to voice their sentiments in church affairs. These people became "the backbones of Puritanism,"[254] eager to advance the religion into an even more reformed direction, if possible after the church at Geneva. They were stimulated by what was later called "the Protestant work-ethic;" and as wealth was God-given, and poverty was a sign of idleness and wickedness, they did everything to increase their property and to prevent any overthrow of their tenure. This resulted in keeping the poor in their poverty, heavily restricting improvement of the lot of these people, and emphasizing the importance of self-help. Indeed, "Puritanism was in large part a social as well as a religious phenomenon. . . . For many of the middle class, Puritanism was a knife and fork question."[255] After the near-famine conditions of the 1590s due to bad harvests and ever-rising food prices, England saw some efforts of private charity with apprenticeships and almshouses for the poor. In 1601 a Poor Law was passed in an attempt to regulate the worst effects of the hand-to-mouth existence by forcing the parishes to support the deserving people. Others saw a solution which they thought would be more effective: they advocated the emigration to America with the promise of free land.[256] However, the first attempts of settlement foundered, and it took another twenty to thirty years before the emigration to the colonies ran on a significant scale.

On the other side, the last years of "the faery queen" were not without splendid climaxes, either. William Byrd, John Dowland, Christopher Marlowe and William Shakespeare made that period one of grandeur for the English culture.

The Book of Common Prayer 1604

Elizabeth was succeeded by James I, the first Stuart on the English throne who as James VI had reigned over Scotland since 1567. He was a direct descendant from Henry VII and could, therefore, lay claim to the English throne. With him the personal union between England and Scotland began which in 1707 became a real union of the two countries.

On his way to London James was presented what afterwards came to be known as the Millenary Petition due to the alleged number of subscribers.[257] By it the authors, puritans from England, hoped to draw the king on their side as they trusted that his acquaintance with a thoroughly reformed church government, which in 1560 had been established by the Scottish parliament along presbyterial lines according to the Geneva model, would make a further reform of the Church of England more feasible. The subscribers, "all groaning as

---

[252] Hill, *Reformation to Industrial Revolution*, pp. 39-40; Minchinton, "Patterns and Structure of Demand 1500-1750," p. 161.
[253] The reconciliation of England with the Church of Rome was passed by the parliament only under the condition that the confiscated and sold monastic and chantry land needed not be given back to the Church; the Lords and Commons would not vote against their own personal stake in this great redistribution of the country's estate: The second Act of Repeal, 1554 (1&2 Phil. & Mar., c. 8): Gee and Hardy, *Documents*, no. 76, pp. 394, 401, 403-09.
[254] Hill, *Reformation to Industrial Revolution*, p. 39.
[255] Hill, *Reformation to Industrial Revolution*, p. 89.
[256] Hill, *Reformation to Industrial Revolution*, pp. 73-78.
[257] Gee and Hardy, *Documents*, no. 89, pp. 508-11.

under a common burden of human rites and ceremonies," asked for a relief from the "abuses" which they had long voiced in the past. It was the same list as before, concerning baptism, the communion, some other rites, and the conduct of clergy, as well as church discipline. In order to pacify the parties concerned, the king convoked a conference to be held January 12-18, 1604 at Hampton Court. Nine bishops, seven deans, and two divines met with four representatives of the puritan side. One of the three main topics of the conference, according to James' will, was to be liturgical grievances, in particular confirmation, absolution, and private baptism. At the end of the conference, several points of rephrasing were agreed upon, among other things that

> to confirmation shall be added the word of catechizing, or examination of the children's faith.
> ... The private baptism shall be called by the ministers and curates only; and all these questions that insinuate women or private persons, to be altered accordingly.... The cross in baptism was never counted any part in baptism, nor sign effective, but only significative.[258]

On February 9 of that year, 1604, the king issued a letter to the Archbishop of Canterbury and others in which he, invested with "all such jurisdictions, rights, privileges, superiorities, and preeminences, spiritual and ecclesiastical" that were "by authority of parliament of this our realm united and annexed to the imperial crown of the same," authorized certain changes in the *Book of Common Prayer*.[259] Private baptism at home was to be administered by "the minister of the parish, or any other lawful minister that can be procured." The confirmation was to be titled such: "The order of confirmation, or laying on of hands upon children baptised, and able to render an account of their faith, according to the Catechism following." The rubric before the actual confirmation was to read "Confirmation, or laying on of hands."

A royal proclamation for the use of the *Book of Common Prayer* was issued on March 5, 1604.[260] Discharging himself of "of the chiefest of all kingly duties, that is, to settle the affairs of religion, and the service of God before their own," he authorized the *Book of Common Prayer* as outlined in his letter to the Archbishop of Canterbury. Although he thought the arguments of the puritan party at the Hampton Court conference "weak and slender," he agreed "that some small things might rather be explained than changed." Any further alteration of the *Book of Common Prayer* was not to be expected or attempted. In the printed editions, the rubrics preceding the private baptism were altered in the direction that excluded the baptism by anybody but the clergy.[261] The title of the confirmation was enlarged as had been agreed upon.[262]

All these results can hardly be said to have been a success for the puritans; their dissatisfaction and disappointment[263] must have certainly been all the harder as not only were the issues they had fought not taken away, but they were explained and enjoined with new authority.[264]

Even worse times were upon them, as indeed on every person who did not conform to the strict rule of the king and the Archbishop of Canterbury, after Charles I had succeeded his

---

[258] Edward Cardwell, *A History of Conferences and Other Proceedings: Connected with the Revision of The Book of Common Prayer from the Year 1558 to the Year 1690*, 3rd ed. (Oxford, 1849; rpt. Ridgewood, NJ: Gregg, 1966), pp. 214-15; an account of the Hampton Court Conference by William Barlow, Dean of Chester and one of the participants: pp. 167-212.

[259] Cardwell, *History of Conferences*, pp. 217-25.

[260] Cardwell, *History of Conferences*, pp. 225-28; Gee and Hardy, *Documents*, no. 89, pp. 512-14.

[261] Brightman, *English Rite*, II, 749.

[262] Brightman, *English Rite*, II, 793.

[263] On a regional level, see Ogbu Uke Kalu, "The Jacobean Church and Essex Puritans: A Regional Study on the Enforcement of Church Discipline and on the Survival of Puritan Nonconformity, 1603-1628," Dissertation University of Toronto 1973.

[264] Frederick Shriver, "Hampton Court Revisited: James I and the Puritans," *Journal of Ecclesiastical History*, 33 (1982), 62-69.

father to the throne on March 27, 1625. For him the will of the king superseded everybody and everything,[265] and for eleven years, 1629-1640, no parliament was summoned.

In November 1628 Charles declared that as he was "by God's ordinance, according to our just title, Defender of the Faith, and Supreme Governor of the Church, within these our dominions" it was "most agreeable to this our kingly office, and our own religious zeal, to conserve and maintain the Church committed to our charge." This was done by "requiring all our loving subjects to continue in the uniform profession [of the true doctrine of the Church of England], and prohibiting the least difference from the said Articles." He made it perfectly clear who held the ultimate authority in the Church:

> We are Supreme Governor of the Church of England; and . . . if any difference arise about the external policy, concerning injunctions, canons or other constitutions whatsoever thereto belonging, the clergy in their convocation is to order and settle them, having first obtained leave under our broad seal so to do, and we approving their said ordinances and constitutions, providing that none be made contrary to the laws and customs of this land.

Even matters of doctrine depended on him:

> Out of our princely care . . . the churchmen may do the work which is proper unto them, the bishops and clergy, from time to time in convocation, upon their humble desire, shall have license under our broad seal to deliberate of, and to do all such things as, being made plain by them, and assented unto by us, shall concern the settled continuance of the doctrine and discipline of the Church of England now established; from which we will not endure any varying or departing in the least degree.[266]

Although the House of Commons presented a resolution to the king on February 24, 1629 in which they complained about the growth of popery in the realm and requested remedies to undo the influence of this development,[267] the king did not heed the warning and by his dismissal of parliament on March 10, 1629 showed his own determination to proceed with his ideas on "his" church.

He increasingly relied on a man who had rapidly risen through the hierarchy: William Laud.[268] As Bishop of London and later Archbishop of Canterbury he exercized an autocratic rule over the Church of England with a zeal that was only rivaled by his absolute loyalty to the king, and he tried to extend his influence even beyond the borders to the presbyterian Kirk of Scotland. His seemingly authoritarian policies, however, were nourished by an admirable fountain of inspiration: a clear look upon the conditions of the people of his time. As he saw Church and state as a unit and the society as a living organism, he took great interest in the conditions of the poor. Individualism, the password for any good puritan, did not find any mercy in his eyes as it was detrimental to Church and state. Wealth and property carried a responsibility for the community and were not given for the exclusive enjoyment by the owners only.

> The tragedy of Laud lies in the fact that he offended, through his policies, the pride of the nouveaux-rich in their wealth. He made it seem wrong to possess or to get wealth, as indeed it was, in Laud's view, unless there was a concurrent responsibility. . . . Puritanism had taught the English middle class their virtues and had sanctified their vices. The power of money was

---

[265] See Robert Malcolm Smuts, "The Culture of Absolutism at the Court of Charles I," Dissertation Princeton University 1976.

[266] His Majesty's Declaration: Cardwell, *Documentary Annals*, II, no. 136, pp. 221-25; Gee and Hardy, *Documents*, no. 91, pp. 518-20.

[267] Resolutions on religion presented by a committee of the House of Commons: Gee and Hardy, *Documents*, no. 92, pp. 521-27. See Allen Ward Croesmann, "Critics of the Crown: Leadership in the House of Commons during the Early Parliaments of Charles I, 1625-1629," Dissertation Harvard University 1976.

[268] Bishop of St. David's 1621, transferred to Bath and Wells 1626, transferred to London 1628, transferred to Canterbury 1633: Powicke and Fryde, *Handbook of British Chronology*, pp. 206, 241, 212.

so strong and so closely connected with God's will that no authority could stand in its way... . The puritan was convinced of his sure election to salvation, and he could neither see nor feel that the poverty of the poor was not always the result of stupidity or of sin but rather of the economic practices which enriched one group while it impoverished another.... On the other hand, Laud was fighting for the unity of all groups in both Church and State.[269]

It is, therefore, very understandable that he very much disliked puritanism, and that these feelings were answered with hatred by the puritans. His beheading on January 10, 1645, during the civil war, was at least as much a revenge by the puritan part of society for his social policies and his constant reminder of their shortcomings, as it was the execution of a man who had tried to increase the influence of the Church of England on all parts of society. His insistence on the use of the texts, rites, and symbols which were customarily denounced by the puritans were added to the list of his "crimes" but were certainly not the real cause for his fate.

In liturgical matters he was much given to an outward expression of the inward reality of liturgy, the adoration of God. Within the context of the regualtion of the prayer book it was his aim that everybody "worship the Lord in the beauty of holiness" and that "the whole earth stand in awe of him."[270] Concerning liturgical material his name is linked, although rightly to a certain degree only, to *The Book of Common Prayer and Administration of the Sacraments and other parts of divine service for the use of the Church of Scotland* 1637.[271]

The Book of Common Prayer 1637

From 1619 on attempts had been made to issue a liturgy in Scotland, substituting the English prayer book. On May 13, 1634 royal instructions were issued to proceed with a compilation of a Scottish liturgy "as near that of England as might be." A copy of the English prayer book with a few alterations was signed by the king on September 28, 1634. The royal instructions "reflect the views of a somewhat small-minded and sacerdotally inclined layman, rather than of a churchman interested in doctrine and other larger issue."[272]

While this book was being printed, James Wedderburn, the then dean of the chapel royal, sent notes to Archbishop Laud concerning some further revision; these were submitted to the king who referred them back to a committee consisting of Laud, William Juxon of London,[273] and Matthew Wren of Norwich. The results of the deliberations were again submitted to the king. He finally signed a copy of the book that was to be published, on December 20, 1636. The books did not come from the press until April or May 1637.[274] On July 23, 1637 when

---

[269] J. Hallock Morgan, "The Economic Policies of Archbishop Laud," *Anglican Theological Review*, 47 (1965), 224-26. See Richard Henry Tawney, *Religion and the Rise of Capitalism: A Historical Study* (1926; rpt. Harmondsworth, Middlesex: Penguin Books, 1984), pp. 174-75, 177, 235-36.

[270] Ps 96:9 (prayer book version).

[271] Gordon Donaldson, *The Making of the Scottish Prayer Book of 1637*, Edinburgh University Publications: History, Philosophy and Economics, 3 (Edinburgh: Edinburgh University Press, 1954), pp. 95-247.

[272] Donaldson, *Scottish Prayer Book*, p. 47.

[273] See Thomas Alexander Mason, "The Political and Episcopal Career of William Juxon, 1582-1663, Bishop of London, Lord High Treasurer and Archbishop of Canterbury," Dissertation University of Virigina 1975.

[274] Brightman, *English Rite*, I, clxxxvi-clxxxvii; Cuming, *History*, pp. 107-08; Donaldson, *Scottish Prayer Book*, pp. 41-59; William Jardine Grisbrooke, *Anglican Liturgies of the Seventeenth and Eighteenth Centuries*, Alcuin Club Collections, 40 (London: SPCK, 1958), pp. 1-18; Sydnor, *Real Prayer Book*, pp. 33-34.

the book was introduced in the cathedral church of St. Giles in Edinburgh, a riot broke out which immediately silenced the book; it was not used again afterwards.[275]

Both the merits of the book and the disastrous reception must be credited more to Bishop Wedderburn and the king than to Archbishop Laud; but nonetheless his name was linked to the "Romanizing" book in public. The communion office especially, however, is of utter importance as it was the immediate predecessor of what the Episcopal Church in America adopted for its own first prayer book.

The preface of the book made an immediate appeal to antiquity and uniformity:

> The Church of Christ hath in all ages had a prescript Form of Common Prayer, or Divine Service, as appeareth by the ancient Liturgies of the Greek and Latin Churches. This was done, as for other great causes, so likewise for retaining an [sic] uniformity in God's worship: a thing most beseeming them that are of one and the same profession.[276]

The links with the liturgical of the Church of England were stressed, even for those rites "not as yet received nor observed in our Church."

The section "Of Ceremonies why some be abolished, and some retained"[277] was almost literally taken over from the *Book of Common Prayer* 1604,[278] which in turn had the same phrasing as those of 1552 and 1549.

As to the order of baptism[279] and to the order of confirmation or laying on of hands,[280] they were almost *verbatim* adopted from the 1604 English prayer book, except for small editorial changes.[281] However, the prayer after the first address to the godparents and people in the order of baptism, which had been molded after Luther's Flood Prayer, received an express epiclesis over the water:

> Almighty and everlasting God, which . . . by the baptism of thy well-beloved son Jesus Christ, didst sanctify the flood Jordan, and all other water, to the mystical washing away of sin:
> (Sanctify this fountain of baptism, thou which art the sanctifier of all things.)[282]

The insertion of this invocation of God's blessing of the element, and not of the persons only, was a deliberate parallel to the remodeling of the eucharistic prayer which was given an explicit epiclesis, too.

The prayer book is mostly remembered and quoted for its "Prayer of Consecration" in "The Order of the Administration of the Lord's Supper, or holy Communion."[283] The Prayer of Humble Access, following in the 1604 prayer book immediately after the Preface, was shifted to a position immediately before the reception of communion. The section of the eucharistic prayer preceding the institution narrative was given an express epiclesis:

---

[275] Donaldson, *Scottish Prayer Book*, p. 83; Edward Patrick Echlin, "Was Laud's Liturgy Wholly Laud's?" *Historical Magazine of the Protestant Episcopal Church*, 37 (1968), 114.

[276] Donaldson, *Scottish Prayer Book*, p. 101.

[277] Donaldson, *Scottish Prayer Book*, pp. 104-05.

[278] It is noteworthy that the title of the book omitted any reference to "ceremonies" altogether, a bow towards the objections of the Scots and the puritans: Donaldson, *Scottish Prayer Book*, p. 65.

[279] Donaldson, *Scottish Prayer Book*, pp. 205-11; Jagger, *Christian Initiation*, pp. 12-18.

[280] Donaldson, *Scottish Prayer Book*, pp. 221-22; Jagger, *Christian Initiation*, pp. 20-21.

[281] The major change was the substitution throughout the whole book of the word "presbyter" for the word "priest" as had been employed in the English prayer books (Donaldson, *Scottish Prayer Book*, p. 63), certainly without any intentional exclusion of the bishops. On the other side, whereas the 1604 *Book of Common Prayer* had sometimes used the word "minister" for the confirmation service, the 1637 *Book of Common Prayer* made clear that it was the bishop who conducted the service.

[282] Donaldson, *Scottish Prayer Book*, p. 206; Jagger, *Christian Initiation*, p. 14 n. 1.

[283] Buchanan, "Lord's Supper," nos. 591-98, pp. 410-12; Donaldson, *Scottish Prayer Book*, pp. 183-204; the prayer of consecration (officially beginning after the Preface): pp. 198-200.

Hear us, O merciful Father, we most humbly beseech thee, and of thy Almighty goodness vouchsafe so to bless and sanctify with thy word and Holy Spirit these thy gifts and creatures of bread and wine, that they may be unto us the body and blood of thy most dearly beloved Son.[284]

The institution narrative was provided with rubrics governing the gestures of taking the presbyter's paten in the hand and of laying the presbyter's hand "upon so much [of the wine] as he intends to consecrate." The following part of the prayer was titled "Memorial or Prayer of Oblation," so that the entire eucharistic prayer was said before the Lord's Prayer, the Prayer of Humble Access, and the distribution of communion. The "memorial which thy Son hath willed us to make" was done "with these thy holy gifts."[285] The prayer was continued with a petition for acceptance of "this our sacrifice of praise and thanksgiving," for the benefits of Christ's passion, and for a worthy reception of the communion. This prayer book, therefore, succeeded in restoring the ancient pattern of a eucharistic prayer.

The formula for the distribution of the communion was the old one of the 1549 prayer book without any addition: "The body (blood) of our Lord Jesus Christ, which was given (shed) for thee, preserve thy body and soul unto everlasting life," to which the communicant answered, "Amen."[286]

For the first time in the history of the *Book of Common Prayer* a large-scale return to expressions of the first prayer book took place; the communion service has been hailed as "the first genuinely Anglican liturgy" and "as a vehicle of traditional faith and practice."[287] This order of communion played an important role in the securing of the episcopate for the Episcopal Church in the United States and in the making of the first American prayer book.

Civil War and Interregnum

As the 1637 prayer book was seen by most as yet another sign of increasing popery in the Church of England, and since some bishops went out of their way to ensure the enforcement of elaborate ceremonial and a rearrangement of church interiors so as to fit their ideas,[288] it is no wonder that the nobility and gentry, whose majority were puritans themselves or sympathetic to their cause, became all the more disenchanted with the discipline and liturgy of the Church of England. The episcopate especially was the subject of much debate and ridicule, and its abandonment was demanded.[289] The House of Commons, increasingly influenced by Scottish members[290] whose religious background was the Kirk which had taken Geneva as its great example to follow, on September 1, 1641 issued on its own behalf resolutions on ecclesiastical innovations.[291] In the following years, liturgical rites were the cause of much strife in the realm. It climaxed in the solemn league and covenant of

---

[284] Buchanan, "Lord's Supper," no. 594, pp. 410-11; Donaldson, *Scottish Prayer Book*, pp. 198-99.
[285] Buchanan, "Lord's Supper," no. 596, p. 411; Donaldson, *Scottish Prayer Book*, p. 199.
[286] Buchanan, "Lord's Supper," no. 601, pp. 412-13; Donaldson, *Scottish Prayer Book*, pp. 200-01.
[287] Grisbrooke, *Anglican Liturgies*, p. 18.
[288] For example, the "Particular orders, directions, and remembrances given in the diocese of Norwich upon the primary visitation of the reverend father in God, Matthew [Wren] lord bishop of that see": Cardwell, *Documentary Annals*, II, no. 143, pp. 537-45.
[289] The root and branch petition of December 11, 1640: Gee and Hardy, *Documents*, no. 97, pp. 537-45.
[290] Peter King, "The Reasons for the Abolition of the Book of Common Prayer in 1645," *Journal of Ecclesiastical History*, 21 (1970), 335.
[291] Gee and Hardy, *Documents*, no. 100, pp. 551-52.

September/October 1643 which was imposed on every Englishman over eighteen years of age.[292] Every person taking this league swore to advance the reformation of the Church of England "in doctrine, worship, discipline, and government, according to the word of God and the example of the best reformed Churches" so as to move the Church of England as close to the Kirk as possible. The episcopate was to be utterly abolished. In August 1642 the civil war had begun. The *Book of Common Prayer* was declared illegal in 1644; the episcopacy was abolished at the same time. Liturgy had become not an expression of unity and uniformity but of war, disunity, and hatred. On January 10, 1645 William Laud was beheaded; on January 30, 1649 Charles I underwent the same fate.[293]

The Book of Common Prayer 1662

The life of the Church of England and that of the *Book of Common Prayer* began anew with what was later called the "Restoration." Whatever had been abolished came to be valued as an object of worth, affection, and reverence; the monarchy, episcopacy, and prayer book fell into this category.

Charles II who had been in Breda, The Netherlands, was invited by parliament in 1660 to come back to England. On May 14, 1660 he issued the "Declaration of Breda."[294] In it he promised a pardon to all who had had a part in the turbulence of the years past. For the first time not a strict *régime* in church matters would be enforced but the different opinions concerning religion were acknowledged and protected:

> ... and because the passion and uncharitableness of the times have produced several opinions in religion, by which men are engaged in parties and animosities against each other (which, when they shall hereafter unite in a freedom of conversation, will be composed or better understood), we do declare a liberty to tender consciences, and that no man shall be disquieted or called in question for differences of opinion in matter of religion, which do not disturb the peace of the kingdom.[295]

On May 29 of that year Charles returned to England; the monarchy was restored.[296]

Although the surviving eleven English and Welsh bishops showed in the beginning of the Restoration a remarkable lack of concern and interest in the securing of episcopal succession,[297] nonetheless five new bishops were consecrated on October 28, 1660, seven on December 2 of that year, and four on January 6, 1661, so that the bishops' bench was complete again and the episcopacy restored.[298]

---

[292] Gee and Hardy, *Documents*, no. 107, pp. 569-74.

[293] See Peter Hammond Schwartz, "Kings on Horseback: On the Meaning of the Trial and Execution of Charles I," Dissertation University of California, Berkeley 1984.

[294] Gee and Hardy, *Documents*, no. 114, pp. 585-88.

[295] Gee and Hardy, *Documents*, no. 114, p. 587.

[296] Charles II counted his regnal years from the execution of his father; he therefore returned to England and became sovereign in his twelfth regnal year (January 30, 1660 to January 29, 1661). All parliamentary acts are officially cited accordingly: *Guide to Law Reports*, pp. 29-30.

[297] Anne Whiteman, "The Restoration of the Church of England," in *From Uniformity to Unity, 1662-1962*, ed. Geoffrey Fillingham Nuttall and Owen Chadwick (London: SPCK, 1962), pp. 48-49.

[298] Ian M. Green, *The Re-establishment of the Church of England 1660-1663*, Oxford Historical Monographs (Oxford: Oxford University Press, 1978), pp. 81-98, 255-56; Whiteman, "Restoration," p. 65. It was reported that during their first visitations the bishops carried out large-scale confirmations; these celebrations often lasted the whole day, and numbers were given between two hundred and "nera a 1000 of all sorts." It must have been a delight for all, especially the bishops. (Green, *Re-establishment*, pp. 141-42).

On October 25, 1660 Charles issued another declaration concerning ecclesiastical affairs.[299] It was an irenic document trying to see the good will of all sides who would have a part in the affairs of the church, the presbyerians who had stated their usual grievances again in June 1660,[300] as well as the "Laudians" who wanted to preserve the "Catholic elements in the Anglican heritage" as the "clear mark of distinction for all the varieties of Protestantism to be found in the anarchical English Church."[301] The church discipline was regulated by limiting the excessive powers of the bishops. Regarding the liturgy the king wrote:

> We are very glad to find, that all with whom we have conferred, do in their judgements approve a liturgy, or set form of public worship to be lawful; which in our judgement for the preservation of unity and uniformity we conceive to be very necessary: and though we do esteem the liturgy of the church of England, contained in the book of Common Prayer, and by law established, to be the best we have seen; and we believe that we have seen all that are extent and used in this part of the world, and well know what reverence most of the reformed churches, or at least the most learned men in those churches have for it; yet we find some exceptions made against several things therein, we will appoint an equal number of learned divines of both persuasions, to review the same, and to make such alterations as shall be thought most necessary, and some additional forms (in the scripture phrase as near as may be) suited unto the nature of the several parts of worship, and that it be left to the minister's choice to use one or other at his discretion.[302]

As to ceremonies, the king had become disenchanted with those churches that had abolished them, but for the time being those who object to them might dispense with them until further measure. The signing with the cross in baptism, the bowing at the name of Jesus, and the wearing of the surplice also fell into this category. Finally, the concession of liberty to tender consciences, first issued from Breda, was renewed.

On March 25, 1661 the conference announced in the declaration was summoned by the king with the purpose

> to advise upon and to review the said Book of Common Prayer, comparing the same with the most ancient liturgies which have been used in the Church in the primitive and purest times; and to that end to assemble and meet together.

Alterations were allowed to be made; but "all unneccessary abbreviations of the forms and liturgy, wherewith the people are already acquainted and have so long received in the Church of England," were to be avoided.[303]

This conference in the Savoy took place April 15 to July 24, 1661.[304] The puritan party went to great lengths to outline every grievance they had against the *Book of Common Prayer* in general as well as in matters of detail; these were submitted to the bishops and participants of the other side.[305] The bishops' answer to the exceptions of the ministers was just as bulky and showed an almost wilfull neglect of concern for the request by the puritans; none of the by now characteristic demands was acknowledged as just, let alone conceded; only seventeen miniscule concessions were made.[306]

For the puritan side this was to be the last chance and attempt to alter the *Book of Common Prayer*; the outcome of the conference and the ensuing prayer book excluded them from any further active role in the liturgical life of the Church of England. Partly overlapping

---

[299] Cardwell, *Documentary Annals*, II, no. 149, pp. 285-301; Cardwell, *History of Conferences*, pp. 286-98.
[300] Cardwell, *History of Conferences*, pp. 277-86.
[301] Whiteman, "Restoration," p. 39.
[302] Cardwell, *Documentary Annals*, II, no. 149, pp. 296-97.
[303] Order for the Savoy Conference: Cardwell, *History of Conferences*, pp. 298-302; Gee and Hardy, *Documents*, no. 115, pp. 588-94; contained therein the king's writ: pp. 588-93.
[304] Cuming, *Godly Order*, pp. 142-53.
[305] Cardwell, *History of Conferences*, pp. 303-35.
[306] Cardwell, *History of Conferences*, pp. 335-63.

the conference, the Canterbury Convocation had taken place in May and November/December of 1661. When it was closed on December 20, the revision of the prayer book had been approved and subscribed by members of both Houses of both Convocations.[307] The fair copy of the revised prayer book came before the Lords on February 25, 1662; on April 15 and 16, the Commons debated on it; on May 8 the Act of Uniformity was passed by the Lords; on May 19, 1662 this act received the royal assent; and it became effective on August 24 of that year.[308]

This Uniformity Act (14 Car. 2, c. 4)[309] finally reinstalled the third element of the restoration process, the *Book of Common Prayer*. To this book open and public consent was to be given by the minister; those refusing were to be deprived and without any benefice. Incumbents who were not episcopally ordained on or after August 24, 1662 were to be deprived and without any benefice. Other provisions concerning church discipline in connection with the liturgy were made, each accompanied, in case they were disobeyed, by heavy penalties.

St. Bartholomew's Day 1662 became the watershed in the history of the Church of England. Although there were (re-)ordinations of presbyterian ministers, about a thousand incumbents refused the oath and lost their benefice and living.[310] Neither side was content with the result of the deliberations because, despite the nearly six hundred changes, mostly miniscule ones, in the texts and rubrics of the prayer book, it was substantially the 1552 book, which for both sides was unsatisfactory.[311] Not even the "Laudian" party which had a good deal to propose in what later became known as the Durham Book, a 1619 edition of the prayer book in which Bishops Cosin and Wren, who had made good use of the 1549 prayer book and the Scottish one of 1637, had entered their corrections, really won.[312] The conservative mood of the parliament was against any substantial change of what had become dear to them.

The book itself received a title that clarified its contents: *The Book of Common Prayer and Administration of the Sacraments And Other Rites and Ceremonies of the Church According to the Use of the Church of England Together with the Psalter or Psalms of David as they are to be sung or said in Churches And The Form or Manner of making, ordaining, and consecrating Bishops, Priests, and Deacons*.[313]

Curiously the book opened with a printing of the Act of Uniformity not of Charles II (14 Car. 2, c. 4) but of Elizabeth I (1 Eliz. 1, c. 2).

A preface had been written for this book by Robert Sanderson in which the right of the Church to change rites and ceremonies if necessary was defended.[314] Adaptation, therefore,

---

[307] Proxies of the Lower House of the York Convocation and Bishop John Cosin of Durham, whose diocese belongs to the York province, were present during the discussions and signed the documents. It has been enthusiastically said that "[t]he Restoration Prayer Book, unlike its predecessors, possessed the authority of a National Synod of the Church of England.": Edward Craddock Ratcliff, "The Savoy Conference and the Revision of the Book of Common Prayer," in *From Uniformity to Unity, 1662-1962*, ed. Geoffrey Fillingham Nuttall and Owen Chadwick (London: SPCK, 1962), p. 130.

[308] Ratcliff, "Savoy Conference," pp. 141-44.

[309] Gee and Hardy, *Documents*, no. 117, pp. 600-19.

[310] Moorman, *History*, p. 252.

[311] Nonetheless, of the *Book of Common Prayer* 1549 it was said in the beginning of the Uniformity Act (14 Car. 2, c. 4) that it was "agreeable to the word of God and usage of the primitive church," a claim both sides would have denied: Gee and Hardy, *Documents*, no. 117, p. 600.

[312] For a thorough discussion of the Durham Book and an edition of all the entries, see Geoffrey John Cuming, ed., *The Durham Book: Being the First Draft of the Revision of the Book of Common Prayer in 1661* (London: Oxford University Press, 1961).

[313] Brightman, *English Rite*, I, 3. The phrase ". . . of the Church According to the Use of the Church of England" suggests a return to the title of the *Book of Common Prayer* 1549 clarifying that it is the liturgy of the Church which is celebrated in a particular manner.

[314] Brightman, *English Rite*, I, 27-33.

"according to the various exigency of times and occasions" was acknowledged as legitimate. The attempts to abolish the prayer book either during the Interregnum or by some of those opposed to it were deemed useless; in the course of the prayer book restoration, propositions that had been rejected were thought of as "either of dangerous consequence . . . or else of no consequence at all, but utterly frivolous and vain." The general aim of the revision was said "not to gratify this or that party in any their unreasonable demands: but to do that which to our best understandings we conceived might most tend to the preservation of peace and unity in the Church." Some of the new features were outlined, among other things an office of baptism of such as are of riper years,

> which although not so necessary when the former Book was compiled, yet by the growth of Anabaptism, through the licentiousness of the later times crept in among us, is now become necessary and may be always useful for the baptizing of Natives in our Plantations, and others converted to the Faith.[315]

The former preface was added, although now renamed "Concerning the service of the Church."[316] The text "Of Ceremonies, why some be abolished and some retained" had also been kept.[317]

The actual changes in the "Order for the Administration of the Lord's Supper, Or holy Communion" were many, but only a few were important in substance.[318] The prayer for the whole state of Christ's Church militant here in earth, after the giving of alms and oblations, was at the end said also for the departed, asking for grace to follow their example and to be with them partakers of God's heavenly kingdom.[319] Rubrics governed the ritual at the institution narrative with taking the elements into the hands, breaking the bread, and laying the hands on bread and the vessels.[320] Immediately after the administration of the communion, rubrical provisions were given for a re-recitation of the institution narrative in case either one of the elements was spent before the end of the communion; and the remains were to be placed on the altar and covered with a cloth.

As to "The Ministration of Public Baptism of Infants to be used in the Church," four alterations of more than editorial value could be noted.[321] In strong reactions to the demands of the more zealous puritans, the question about the renunciation was asked of the godparents as "dost thou, in the name of this child, renounce . . .,"[322] whereas the former prayer books had had a phrasing insinuating an address to the child. An additional question was asked after the inquiry to be baptized in this faith: "Wilt thou then obediently keep God's holy will, and commandments, and walk in the same all the days of thy life? Answer: I will,"[323] a characteristic addition to be found in this form or expanded in all subsequent American prayer books. The prayer containing the allusions to Christ's open side and to Matthew 28 had received a petition to "sanctify this water to the mystical washing away of sin," a blessing of the element of the water.[324] The crucial signing with the cross was even strengthened with a rubric that the priest should make a cross upon the child's forehead.[325]

The newly created "Ministration of Baptism to such as are of riper years, and able to answer for themselves"[326] had been prepared in May 1661 mainly by George Lloyd, Bishop

---

[315] Brightman, *English Rite*, I, 33.
[316] Brightman, *English Rite*, I, 35-39.
[317] Brightman, *English Rite*, I, 39-45.
[318] Brightman, *English Rite*, II, 639-721; in excerpts: Buchanan, "Lord's Supper," nos. 606-35,pp. 414-26.
[319] Brightman, *English Rite*, II, 663-65.
[320] Brightman, *English Rite*, II, 693; Buchanan, "Lord's Supper," no. 625, p. 421.
[321] Brightman, *English Rite*, II, 725-47; Jagger, *Christian Initiation*, pp. 22-29.
[322] Brightman, *English Rite*, II, 735; Jagger, *Christian Initiation*, p. 26, no. 11.
[323] Brightman, *English Rite*, II, 737; Jagger, *Christian Initiation*, p. 26, no. 11.
[324] Brightman, *English Rite*, II, 741; Jagger, *Christian Initiation*, p. 27, no. 13.
[325] Brightman, *English Rite*, II, 741; Jagger, *Christian Initiation*, pp. 27-28, no. 16.
[326] Brightman, *English Rite*, II, 761-77.

of St. Asaph.[327] All the questions and addresses otherwise directed to the godparents were said to the baptizand here, taking into account that he/she was responsible for him/herself. Instead of Mark 10:13-16, the reading from the gospel was John 3:1-8.

The confirmation order was no longer interrrupted by the catechism.[328] It began with a question by the bishop:

> Do ye here in the presence of God, and of this congregation, renew the solemn promise and vow that was made in your Name at your Baptism; ratifying and confirming the same in your own persons, and acknowledging yourselves bound to believe and to do all those things which your Godfathers and Godmothers then undertook for you? And everyone shall audibly answer: I do,[329]

a felicitous insertion of a link with baptism. After the imposition of hands the Lord's Prayer was said by the bishop. After the next prayer for grace for the confirmed person and before the final blessing, a prayer was added asking for a life after the commandments of God and for the preservation of body and soul. The last rubric after the order extended the admission to communion not only to those who were confirmed but also to those who were "ready and desirous to be confirmed,"[330] no doubt in view of what the preface to the book had meant with "our plantations," the colonies, to which the attention now turns.

---

[327] Cuming, *History*, p. 126.
[328] Brightman, *English Rite*, II, 793-99; Jagger, *Christian Initiation*, pp. 30-33.
[329] Brightman, *English Rite*, II, 793; Jagger, *Christian Initiation*, p. 30, no. 3.
[330] Brightman, *English Rite*, II, 799; Jagger, *Christian Initiation*, p. 33, no. 13.

The American Prayer Books of 1789, 1892, and 1928

The Colonies in the Seventeenth Century

At the time of the Restoration, in 1660, "the plantations" in North America had a total population of about 75,000 souls, one-fifth the size of London; thirty years later, after the Glorious Revolution in which James II, who had succeeded his father in 1685, was declared deposed and King William III and Queen Mary II were called to the throne as joint monarchs in 1689,[1] the number of inhabitants had about trebled, to 210,000; still a decade later, in 1700, the colonies had 250,000 residents.[2]

The typical colonist in the seventeenth century was a small farmer; the economy was nine-tenths based on agriculture and the production of raw materials.[3] This orientation was of great advantage to the motherland as it provided England with desperately needed material and at the same time created an additional market for English goods.[4] The economic concept of mercantilism, introduced in England by Henry VIII,[5] was working well: England was self-sufficient in the satisfaction of its demands, and the balance of trade was positive. There was another advantage of possessing colonies: Whereas in England there was an oversupply of labor and a scarcity of land, the situation in the colonies was the reverse, a vast country with insufficient numbers of settlers. The promise of owning landed property in North America figured as an incentive for those eager to improve their conditions, albeit under extreme hardship, especially on the frontier, and served as a relief for the English job market.

A momentous and far-reaching event occurred when in 1619 the first slaves from the West Indies and Africa were introduced to work in the colonies. Virginia, which had been founded by Sir Walter Raleigh in 1584 (although there was no permanent settlement until 1607), had in 1620 a population of 2,200 which included 26 Blacks. In 1660, 2,920 out of the total colonial population of 75,000 were Blacks; in 1700, more than ten percent (27,817 out of 250,888) were Blacks. Except for the colony of New Amsterdam, which in 1664 became New York, the slaves were for more than eighty percent concentrated in the southern colonies.[6] They worked on cotton fields and tobacco plantations which settlers, who could afford to do so, had implanted. As those agricultural enterprises were labor-intensive and slaves had to be bought, the vast majority of those workers were treated as expensive property: loyally and well, so that their capacity for work and energy was kept, but denied the rights and possibilities of the white population.

Everyday life in the colonies for the "average" colonist was a monotonous routine of hard work in order to get the best results out of the farmland[7] and to support a large family. Little,

---

[1] Ensuing Bill of Rights: 1 Will. & Mar., sess. 2, c. 2: Gee and Hardy, *Documents*, no. 122, pp. 645-54; Toleration Act: 1 Will. & Mar., c. 18: Gee and Hardy, *Documents*, no. 123, pp. 654-64.

[2] Ben J. Wattenberg, ed., *The Statistical History of the United States from Colonial Times to the Present: Historical Statistics of the United States, Colonial Times to 1970*, prep. by the United States Bureau of the Census (New York: Basic Books, 1976), Z 1-19, p. 1168.

[3] Harold Underwood Faulkner, *American Political and Social History*, Educational Manual, 270 (New York: Crofts, 1943), pp. 49-51.

[4] In the seventy-nine years from 1697 to 1776, the value of the imports from England to the colonies exceeded the value of the exports from the colonies to England, measured in pounds sterling, in forty-nine years, among which in the uninterrupted period from 1745 to 1774: Wattenberg, *Statistical History*, Z 213-14, pp. 1176-77.

[5] See Michael W. Watts, "Tudor Economic Thought after the Reformation: A 'Genre' of Early English Mercantilism," Dissertation The Louisiana State University and Agricultural and Mechanical College 1978.

[6] Wattenberg, *Statistical History*, Z 1-9, p. 1168.

[7] Faulkner, *History*, p. 50, speaks of "unscientific agriculture" and unbelievably bad treatment of livestock.

if any, time was left for amusement. Illiteracy was widespread in the colonies, and only in New England was a rudimentary general public education present since the mid-seventeenth century. Intellectual life was very much the exception, and among the professionals only the ministry could develop reasonably.[8]

The tiny minority that could afford to spend some energy on following and discussing philosophical and intellectual currents was, at the end of the seventeenth century, attentive to England's most influential philosopher of that time, John Locke (1632-1704). As an empiricist and rationalist, Locke saw as the end of society and as the duty of the government "the preservation of their [men's] property:"[9] their lives, liberties, and estates.[10] If the government did not fulfill this charge, neglected it or exercized it by unlawful means,

> the people are at liberty to provide for themselves by erecting a new legislative differing from the other by the change of persons, or form, or both, as they shall find it most for their safety and good.[11]

Concerning strictly philosophical and religious questioons, Locke saw the foundations of reason and knowledge in the experience and in the "perception of the operations of our own minds."[12] This human knowledge would be superior even to divine revelation, as the latter would be subject to the assent of our intuitive knowledge. Only those that would be

> beyond the discovery of our natural facilities and above reason, are, when revealed, the proper matter of faith. . . . If the provinces of faith and reason are not kept distant by these boundaries, there will, in matters of religion, be no room for reason at all, and those extravagant opinions and ceremonies that are to be found in the several religions of the world will not deserve to be blamed. . . . For, to this crying up of faith in opposition to reason, we may, I think, in good measure ascribe those absurdities that fill almost all the religions which possess and divide mankind. . . . For men, having been principled with an opinion that they must not consult reason in the things of religion, however apparently contradictory to common sense and the very principles of all their knowledge, have let loose their fancies and natural superstition, and have been by them led into so strange opinions and extravagant practices in religion that a considerate man cannot but stand amazed at their follies and judge them so far from being acceptable to the great and wise God, that he cannot avoid thinking them ridiculous and offensive to a sober, good man.[13]

Eighty years later, the constitutional consequences of Locke's view of governmental duties became manifest in the struggle for independence from Great Britain. The opinions held on the relationship between faith and reason found a reaction in the religious developments of the mid-eighteenth century.

Almost from the beginning of the settlement on, all the way through the colonial period, and down to present-day politics, one of the most prominent and significant aspects of American civilization and culture has been what is commonly called American

---

[8] In 1636 John Harvard left a legacy for a college in Cambridge, Massachusetts, which was later named after him; this was the first school of higher education in North America. The first college to be affiliated with the Church of England was that of William and Mary, founded in 1693. The major purpose of all colleges was the training of ministers: Faulkner, *History*, pp. 58, 60, 62-63.

[9] See Johannes Hahn, *Der Begriff des Property bei John Locke: Zu den Grundlagen seiner politischen Philosophie*, Europäische Hochschulschriften: Reihe 20, 134 (Frankfurt/M.: Lang, 1983).

[10] John Locke, *A Treatise of Civil Government*, 1690, II, ix,123-24; quoted in: Pierre Vitoux, *Histoire des idées en Grande Bretagne*, 3e éd. (Paris: Colin, 1969), p. 255.

[11] *A Treatise of Civil Government*, 1690, II, xix,220; quoted in: Vitoux, *Histoire des idées*, p. 257.

[12] *An Essay Concerning Human Understanding*, 1690, II, i,4; quoted in: Vitoux, *Histoire des idées*, p. 249.

[13] *An Essay Concerning Human Understanding*, 1690, IV, xviii, "Of Faith and Reason," 7, 11; quoted in: Vitoux, *Histoire des idées*, pp. 252-53. See Serge Hutin, *La philosophie anglaise et américaine*, "Que sais-je?", 796 (Paris: Presses Universitaires de France, 1958), pp. 25-27.

Millenialism.[14] It is the conviction that the New World, at that time especially New England, is the earthly paradise, the place where God's purpose with humanity will finally come to be fulfilled. The new colonies were the location "where the Lord will create a new Heaven and a new Earth."[15] This paradise is God's gift for His chosen people, and just as the natural resources as well as the chance to start an entirely new life in the American colonies show that these people are God's own and favored by Him, so, too, does He bestow special blessings upon these people. God is (almost) an American. From this awareness of being the real chosen race, the holy nation, and God's own people, flows the necessity to fight against all that is un-godly. What that is, was and is determined by the concrete circumstances of those who struggle in this battle. In the seventeenth and eighteenth century New England colonies, everything Anglican and popish was un-godly and to be rooted out. In the eighteenth century fight for independence, the king was seen as the personification of a rule unjust and contrary to God's laws. Fear of Catholicism in the nineteenth century, because it was the source of oppression under man-made un-godly religious rule and, at the same time, the religion of millions of immigrants pouring into the United States, has its roots here, just as the ideological (and armed) warfare against Communism in the twentieth century. Whenever the colonies, or later the United States, underwent a profound revitalization in awakenings, this divine purpose laid at the heart of the process of rejuvenation. Hand in hand with this easily recognizable religious interpretation of the nature and destiny of the American people went a secular strain: the emphasis on everything that is new and young. The New World and New England as well as many place names testify to this. And the young and strong were not only those who were needed for cultivating the land and building the country so that everybody could enjoy its fruits, they were also the incarnation of the best in life.

Without acknowledging the presence of these messianic ideas, especially in New England, and the (later) secular derivatives from it, it is difficult to realize the inner dynamics of the American history, the shaping of the American mind, and the historical ideas influential for the religious situation from the beginning.

The majority of those people who emigrated to the colonies in the seventeenth century were either nonconformists and dissenters from England who were dissatisfied with the situation at home and, therefore, tried to establish what they regarded as "pure religion" in New England,[16] or Protestants from Continental Europe.[17] Of the thirteen colonies which declared their independence from Great Britain in 1776, the eight northern colonies (Massachusetts, New Hampshire, Rhode Island, Connecticut, New York, New Jersey, Pennsylvania, and Delaware) at best tolerated the worship according to the *Book of Common Prayer* among the life of other churches and denominations. The church life in these colonies was heavily molded by Calvinistic theology, imported by the settlers who had tried to escape the alleged impurities of the established church in England. Massachusetts and Pennsylvania were at the ends of the ecclesiastical specter. Until 1691, when a royal governor was

---

[14] See Christopher Merriman Beam, "Millenialism in American Thought, 1740 to 1840," Dissertation University of Illinois at Urbana-Champaign 1976; John Richard Hales, "Time's Last Offspring: Millennialism in America from John Cotton to James Fenimore Cooper," Dissertation State University of New York at Binghamton 1985; Ray Hodgson Macsorley, "Millennialism in Eighteenth Century America," Dissertation University of Maryland College Park 1983.

[15] Edward Johnson, in the middle of the seventeenth century; quoted in: Mircea Eliade, *The Quest: History and Meaning in Religion* (Chicago: University of Chicago Press, 1969), p. 94.

[16] Hugh Gerard Gibson Herklots, *The Church of England and the American Episcopal Church: From the First Voyages of Discovery to the First Lambeth Conference* (London: Mowbray; New York: Morehouse-Barlow, 1966), p. 28. The history of the religious conditions in the colonies from the beginnings of their settlement cannot possibly be summarized here; it would exceed the scope of this treatise. See Ahlstrom, *Religious History*, I, 169-323 for the seventeenth century. Ahlstrom's account and interpretation are followed throughout this book, unless otherwise stated.

[17] Ahlstrom, *Religious History*, I, 290-323.

appointed for Massachusetts and a certain degree of toleration of other religions took hold, this colony had a history of gross intolerance of other than the Congregational churches, of persecution and ejection of other believers, and of utter intransigence towards any deviation from the most closely watched everyday life, patterned after puritanical ideas.[18] Pennsylvania, on the other side, was to become "a model state where people of divers ethnic and religious backgrounds could live together under equitable laws in a single commonwealth."[19] Although the Quakers dominated the colony due to William Penn's own allegiance to that society, their tolerance provided for an otherwise unheard-of degree of acceptance of other religions. It was, therefore, not without significance that most of the early decisive events in the constitutional and religious history of the colonies that declared their independence in 1776 took place in Philadelphia, the capital of that colony, that was founded in 1682 by William Penn himself. The remaining six northern colonies were dominated by puritans, and only insofar as they were royal colonies with a charter spelling out the degree of religious tolerance that had to be followed could there be any measure of benevolence towards churches other than the ones formerly established in those parts of the country.

In the five southern of the thirteen colonies (Virginia, Maryland, South Carolina, North Carolina, Georgia) was the Church of England officially and legally the established church. From the first charter for Virginia in 1606 through the charter for Georgia in 1732, the Church of England was given the full support of the English and colonial agencies that were responsible for the governance of the colonies. Other Protestant churches, however, were not excluded, and members could exercize the religion according to their own rules.

It is no surprise to learn that outside the southern colonies "the Church of England during most of the seventeenth century was only a flickering and uncertain reality in the American colonies. In hardly a dozen localities was there a self-sufficient parish or a sustained ministry before 1700."[20] A group persecuted in one country and being the domineering party in another will indeed hardly welcome members of the class they suffered from. At the end of the seventeenth century a distinction must therefore still be made between the underdog position which the Church of England held in the northern colonies, and the rather fully grown parish life which could be found in the southern colonies.[21] For example, the Virginia charter establishing the colony in 1606 for the Virginia company declared,

> that the true Word of God and Christian faith be preached, planted and used ... according to the doctrine, rite and religion now professed and established within our [the sovereign's] realm of England.[22]

However, the biggest obstacle to a full religious life for the members of the Church of England, including the liturgy, was the lack of bishops. To the extent that the prayer book provided for episcopal services and demanded the presence of bishops, these parts of the worship life of the Church could not be conducted in the colonies. Although Archbishop William Laud (1573-1645) had foreseen this urgency and had completed the preparations for sending a bishop to the American colonies by 1638, the settlers never saw an active bishop on their soil before independence.[23] Confirmations and ordinations, therefore, never took place

---

[18] Ahlstrom, *Religious History*, I, 182-211. Even after the independence from Great Britain and the ratification of the federal Constitution, Massachusetts provided in its state constitution for the establishment of the Congregational Church as state church until 1833: Samuel Eliot Morison and Henry Steele Commager, *The Growth of the American Republic*, 5th ed. rev. and enlarged (New York: Oxford University Press, 1962), I, 243.

[19] Ahlstrom, *Religious History*, I, 156. Cf. pp. 264-71.

[20] Ahlstrom, *Religious History*, I, 272.

[21] See Garrett, "Prayer Book Presence," p. 62, for the quotation from a vestry meeting of Christ Church Parish, Middlesex County, Virginia, on June 2, 1684 which shows that the church life had settled to a fully normal and regular pattern in that state.

[22] Quoted in: Garrett, "Prayer Book Presence," p. 60.

[23] Raymond Wolf Albright, *A History of The Protestant Episcopal Church* (New York: Macmillan; London: Collier-Macmillan, 1964), p. 22.

in the colonies, and everybody who wanted to receive these two rites had to undergo all the labors and expenses of going to England. The absence of bishops was due not only to a lack of interest in the affairs of the church life in America on the part of the English bishops as well as state authorities, but also to a resentment of their presence on the part of the settlers and authorities in the colonies where the Church of England was not officially established. They could not see a bishop not living in grandeur and almost princely stature,[24] and were not willing to have them serve also as state functionaries as they were and are in England by virtue of their office.

> To put it in a sentence, the story of the Church of England in the thirteen colonies before 1776 is a story of what happens to an episcopal Church when it tries to live and thrive without bishops. The record on the whole is not a happy one.[25]

The Colonies in the Eighteenth Century

The colonial life underwent a change of fundamental importance: Second and third generation colonists began to feel like, and to consider themselves as, "Americans," no longer English(wo)men or Scots. As the colonies had been granted a certain degree of autonomy and representation of the people in representative Houses, the shape and influence of which differed from one colony to the other, and although they still lacked the full rights of a parliament, the dependence on the Crown became less visible than in the motherland. The structure of everyday life consolidated. Not only were increasingly more specialized professions carried out, but an intellectual elite could little by little grow and influence the social and political outlook with its philosophy. Above all in the South, an aristocracy of big landowners could develop, giving work to a sizable number of dependent White and Black families on their cotton and tobacco farms. In the seventeenth century England and Scotland had been the most important emigration countries; this distinction turned in the eighteenth century to the northern and central European countries. Above all Germans flocked into the American colonies, and by the time of the independence more than one-fifth of the population had non-English-speaking ancestors. The three most "un-English" colonies were New York, New Jersey, and Pennsylvania.[26] During the seventy years from the turn of the century until 1770, the total population grew more than eightfold; the number of the Black slaves, however, increased at even twice this rate, sixteenfold.[27] In 1700 more than eighty percent of the Black population lived in the southern colonies, in 1770 almost ninety percent.[28] The demographic developments and the totally different living conditions in the eighteenth century colonies made it almost unavoidable that the legal and political character of the country would at some day be changed from a colony to an independent state.

The traditions that had brought the settlers to the colonies went on with steadiness and almost unbroken zeal. The New England colonies continued to be strongholds of puritanism which took on the form of Congregational churches, and the political and ecclesiastical powers were interwoven with each other. Due to their settlement with several independent

---

[24] Minchinton, "Patterns and Structure of Demand 1500-1750," p. 97, gives a table with the income distribution in late seventeenth-century England. The bishops belonged to the first category of people (peers, baronets, greater office holders) having an annual income in excess of £200.

[25] James Thayer Addison, *The Episcopal Church in the United States 1789-1931* (1951; rpt. Hamden, CT: Archon Books, 1969), p. 55. Cf. pp. 27, 50.

[26] Wattenberg, *Statistical History*, Z 20-23, p. 1168.

[27] Total population 1700: 250,888; 1770: 2,148,076. Black population 1700: 27,817; 1770: 459,822: Wattenberg, *Statistical History*, Z 1-19, p. 1168.

[28] 1700: 22,611 out of the total of 27,817 Blacks; 1770: 411,362 out of the total of 459,822: Wattenberg, *Statistical History*, Z 1-19, p. 1168.

strains of immigrations and the variable forms of political proprietorship, the middle colonies came the closest to any semblance of religious tolerance, although Jews and Roman Catholics were excluded from conducting their own worship almost everywhere.[29] The southern colonies saw the Church of England established but provided for the right of the other Protestant churches to exist and exercize their own affairs.

The greatest obstacle for an efficient ministry and a normal church life among the members of the Church of England was the scarcity or absence of priests who would exercize their vocations in the colonies. As life was not attractive on the frontier and the church was denied the advantages of a state church except in the southern colonies, only those whose vocation to adventure was as great as that to the ministry would sail to the New World. Those who had studied for the ministry in the colonies themselves had to cross the ocean to receive the ordination in England, with all the ensuing labor and expenses. Such a candidate for ordination from the colonies had to present to the Bishop of London, who had the albeit somewhat spurious and not entirely undisputed title to oversee all the missionary activities of the Church of England and to be the ecclesiastical superior for all congregations in the colonies, a set of documents from the home parish and those who had cared for his education, before he could be ordained; this included the promise of a "title," the guarantee of a congregation to make up for his living.[30]

The situation improved somewhat, although not to the extent necessary, when, due to the initiative of Thomas Bray (1656-1730),[31] the "Society for the Propagation of the Gospel in Foreign Parts" was founded in June 1701.[32] The purpose of this society was the assistance of the parishes and the clergy in mission countries and the colonies, the center of activity being the North American colonies, until the Declaration of Independence in 1776. Material and personal help began to flow. Between 1748, the beginning of the records of ordination papers in the register of the Bishop of London, and 1775, 409 clergymen were ordained, or, if they had served as priests in England before, licensed, for working in the American colonies.[33] This clergy, recruited both from American members of the church and from Englishmen, had to serve about 400 congregations by 1775, with a total membership of less than 20,000.[34] The society, moreover, repeatedly received requests for more copies of prayer books.[35]

---

[29] Ahlstrom, *Religious History*, I, 403-17. See James Hennesey, *American Catholics: A History of the Roman Catholic Community in the United States* (New York: Oxford University Press, 1981), pp. 36-54.

[30] The editor of the Fulham Papers has added a note if any additional information in excess of this set of documents was supplied. It appears that, although being technically possible and legally prescribed, the candidates did not receive the confirmation before the ordination, as the rubric or the instruction at the end of baptism and of confirmation provided (Brightman, *English Rite*, II, 747, 799). It might, however, be presupposed for candidates who received their education in England or Scotland. Three cases were recorded in the eighteenth century where young men from the American colonies who were going to school in England were recommended by a letter to the Bishop of London for confirmation: William Wilson Manross, ed., *The Fulham Papers in the Lambeth Palace Library: American Colonial Section, Calendar and Indexes* (Oxford: Clarendon, 1965), pp. 297-311; III 43-44, V 277-78, VII 265.

[31] See Henry P. Thompson, *Thomas Bray* (London: SPCK, 1954).

[32] See Anne Elizabeth Polk Diffendal, "The Society for the Propagation of the Gospel in Foreign Parts and the Assimilation of Foreign Protestants in British North America," Dissertation The University of Nebraska-Lincoln 1974; Henry P. Thompson, *Into All Lands: The History of the Society for the Propagation of the Gospel in Foreign Parts, 1701-1950* (London: SPCK, 1951).

[33] Frederick Vandever Mills, *Bishops by Ballot: An Eighteenth-Century Ecclesiastical Revolution* (New York: Oxford University Press, 1978), p. 7.

[34] Addison, *Episcopal Church*, p. 74; Garrett, "Prayer Book Presence," p. 86; Arthur Carl Piepkorn, "Episcopal Churches," in *Protestant Denominations*, Vol. II of *Profiles in Belief: The Religious Bodies of the United States and Canada*, ed. Arthur Carl Piepkorn (San Francisco: Harper & Row, 1978), p. 215.

[35] William Wilson Manross, ed., *SPG Papers in the Lambeth Palace Library: Calendar and Indexes* (Oxford: Clarendon, 1974), nos. XIII 126-27, 132-33, 161-63.

Due to these developments the still excessively long Sunday services were conducted with a regular pattern that presupposes an established ministry, permanent church structures, and as much "normalcy" as possible.[36] The prayer book that was used was, of course, that of 1662.

Slowly but steadily, Anglicanism gained ground even in puritan New England, and in those colonies it became a High Church affair in a conscious counter to the Congregational churches. It profited from a theological dispute among the theologians of those churches. In 1722 a great defection took place within the Congregational ministry when the entire faculty of Yale College (two teachers) and two ministers from Connecticut went to England to seek episcopal ordination. Outstanding among those apostates was Samuel Johnson (1696-1772), who had become acquainted with English literature and writings by Anglican theologians with a high view on church structure and an esteem for the liturgy of the Church of England.[37] He had been given a copy of the *Book of Common Prayer* and began to appreciate the orderliness and agreement with Scripture of the prayers and liturgical formulas. The liturgy of the Church of England had become an asset rather than a liability for a convincing church life. For more than twenty years Samuel Johnson "became the dominant influence for Prayer Book worship and practice in the northern American colonies."[38] His theology centered upon the *Book of Common Prayer*.[39] His influence was to be felt for decades.[40]

The eighteenth century has been called "The Century of Awakening and Revolution,"[41] marking the two climaxes of the intellectual and political order in North America. The revival period in the 1730s and 1740s, the Great Awakening, did not bear directly on the liturgy according to the *Book of Common Prayer*, unless in New England by an inflow of those disenchanted with the underlying theology or the manifestations of undisciplined and embarrassing behavior of groups or individuals into the orderliness of the Church of England. In the southern colonies, the denominations which originated in the Awakening or made the most of it, the Baptists and Methodists, drained members of the Church of England from their former allegiance. But as undoubtedly the experience and ideology of the Awakening were major factors in the molding of the American ecclesiastical, intellectual, and political life, this phenomenon cannot be neglected here.

Awakenings are "periods of fundamental ideological transformation necessary to the dynamic growth of the nation in adapting to basic social, ecological, psychological, and economic changes."[42] The periods and developments that can be described as awakenings are revitalizations of the cultural and intellectual system so that disjunctions and disparities between old beliefs and new realities, and chasms between traditional norms and fresh experi-

---

[36] Marion Josiah Hatchett, "A Sunday Service in 1776 or Thereabouts," *Historical Magazine of the Protestant Episcopal Church*, 45 (1976), 373-84, describes the normal pattern for a regular service on Sunday morning: Morning Prayer, possibly baptism, possibly churching of women after childbirth, litany, antecommunion or eucharist. Around 2 o'clock in the afternoon: Evening Prayer and possibly a burial; all services enlarged with metrical psalms or other hymns.

[37] See Donald Francis Marc Gerardi, "The American Doctor Johnson: Anglican Piety and the Eighteenth-Century Mind," Dissertation Columbia University 1973; Sean Collins Murray, "The Reverend Samuel Johnson, 1696-1772: Anglican Protagonist in Colonial America," Dissertation State University of New York at Buffalo 1975.

[38] Garrett, "Prayer Book Presence," p. 77.

[39] See Weil, "Worship and Sacraments."

[40] William Anthony Clebsch, *American Religious Thought: A History*, Chicago History of American Religion (Chicago: University of Chicago Press, 1973), pp. 59-60.

[41] Ahlstrom, *Religious History*, I, 325.

[42] William Gerald McLoughlin, *Revivals, Awakenings, and Reform: An Essay on Religion and Social Change in America, 1607-1977*, Chicago History of American Religion (Chicago: University of Chicago Press, 1978), p. 8. This present section leans heavily on McLoughlin's theoretical interpretation of the nature and significance of awakenings: *Revivals*, pp. 1-23.

ence, can be overcome. The awakendings are brought about by the perception that in its intellectual understanding and experience of daily life, society aberrs too much from the moral and religious legitimization of church and state authorities.

Any such awakening or revivalist period can be divided in four patterns. First, a period of individual stress, marking the dichotomy between the experience of the individual and the traditions of society at large; second, a period of cultural distortions, in which the defenders of the old values are in battle with the exponents of a vision of a possible or necessary new order; third, a period of profound emotional and intellectual turmoil, confusion, and excitement which affects every member of society, being the throes of the new order to come; and fourth, a period of clarification, of working on the new model according to which experience, culture, and authority are interpreted, and of restructuring the old institutions.

All this takes on a religious significance in the American awakenings as these developments are seen as a furthering of God's light upon His revelations. Revivals and awakenings are not secular movements but a profound religious experience:

> There is no conservative tradition in America because God is not conservative. God is an innovation. American culture is thus always in the making but never complete. . . . America, the New World, has easily become a metaphor for the New Eden; it is "the new Garden in the West," where, unspoiled by old and corrupt institutions (monarchy, an established church, a nobility), man might create a perfect moral order with perfect moral freedom. From its first settlements, not only in Pilgrim Plymouth but in almost every colony, America has been an utopian experiment in achieving the Kingdom of God on earth. Our Revolution was justified on these terms in 1776. Our history has been essentially the history of one long millenarian movement. Americans, in their cultural mythology, are God's chosen, leading the world to perfection. Every awakening has revived, revitalized, and redefined that cultural core.[43]

Phenomenologically revivals and revitalization movements superabound with symbols and experiences of death and rebirth: death to the old ways and patterns, and rebirth into spiritual renewal. Within society this renewal takes shape in considerably restructured institutions. In the American colonies, this social revision after the First Great Awakening was possible and was carried out in the War of Independence and the building of the Republic, which can easily be seen as a result of the process of renewal and of the struggle against the evil of the old political structure.

The First Great Awakening 1730-1760 was "a broad intercolonial phenomenon--indeed, the first such,"[44] and was a contributing factor in the molding of the coloners' awareness of themselves as Americans rather than English subjects. The four stages mentioned above were present in this revival, too. From about 1700, and more intensely from about 1720, strain was felt between the economic ambitions of the people who had grown moderately rich and, on the other side, the ideas of the clerymen who still clung to a settler's or frontier mentality. Itinerant preachers traveling from one place to the other were beginning to tell people about the religious significance of their new condition, and to preach that they were not lost and abandoned by Providence. Revival meetings, often for days in a row, were marked by heavy attendance and the arousal of much emotion. These revivals attempted to convince individuals that they could repent of their wrong ways and be saved, even in their present economic situation. It was the "joy of salvation" that they were to incur. During these meetings scenes charged with the utmost emotional upheaval took place; while these emotional scenes were viewed as signs of genuine conversion by some, they were clearly repellent to others.

All the churches were affected by the experience of revitalized Christianity, but mostly in negative ways: The spiritual needs of the parishioners had been taken better care of by those traveling preachers and, sometimes self-appointed, evangelists, than by the official clergy; and the individual person realized that he or she did not need a clergyman, a church, or a

---

[43] McLoughlin, *Revivals*, pp. 18-19.
[44] Ahlstrom, *Religious History*, I, 354.

liturgy to get into a personal relationship with God. On the other hand, two churches gained from the Awakening. The Methodist churches and the Baptist churches became firmly rooted especially in the South, due to their ability to respond in very flexible ways to the exigencies and the spiritual hunger of those eager to be affected by the Awakening. The Calvinist theology was revitalized in New England, especially through the efforts of Jonathan Edwards (1703-1758), the "most significant preacher and theologian of the American colonial time."[45] He once summed up the ultimate mission of puritan America as revitalized and given new vigor:

> It is not unlikely that this work of God's Spirit, so extraordinary and wonderful, is the dawning, or at least a prelude, of that glorious work of God, so often foretold in Scripture, which, in the progress and issue of it, shall renew the world of mankind.... And there are many things that make it possible that this work will begin in America.[46]

In the northern colonies, many of those who were appalled by the sometimes extreme and almost hysterical manner in which the conversion process was expressed on the preacher's as well as the individual's side found the worship according to the *Book of Common Prayer* all the more attractive and changed their allegiance to the Church of England, which was not an established church in these colonies and, therefore, could not be a socially dominant body.[47] Together with the convincing eloquence of Samuel Johnson, the First Great Awakening was the reason why the Anglican Church could get a foothold in the North and become a community with a rather High Church outlook there.

On the contrary, the Church of England in the southern colonies lost members, due to the preaching results of those itinerant evangelists. As they professed religion as an immediate affair between the individual and God, everything else was of secondary importance or even an impediment to achieving the soul's salvation.

Seen in its totality, the experience of the First Great Awakening, felt throughout every community (family, place, church, and colony), helped to loosen the links with the past, cut through church and colonial lines, and prepare the way for ideological and political consequences which followed almost inevitably in the next generation.

This Awakening, with its view of the old beliefs as incompatible or irrelevant to the needs of the American society as it had emerged in the first half of the eighteenth century, went hand in hand with the great philosophical current of that era, the Enlightenment; and prominent advocates of a new interpretation of the faith suiting the American experience were influenced by both streams, like Jonathan Edwards,[48] however mutually exclusive these currents may sometimes look. Persons like Benjamin Franklin (1706-1790) and particularly Thomas Jefferson (1743-1826), eminent among the Founding Fathers, were strong voices for the theological dimension of the Enlightenment, deism, albeit in a somewhat moderate form.

The emphasis was on simplicity of faith, against all the intricacies of medieval scholasticism and post-Reformation rigidity, on the proper role and cooperation of humanity in its relation with deity, and on ethics and morality for a virtuous life without any casuistry. Differences in the creeds of the churches were regarded as almost irrelevant as long as there was agreement on the acknowledgment of the one God; church policies, forms of worship, and doctrinal teachings were of only secondary importance.[49] "Reason" and "progress" were words frequently recurring as being the means for building up a better world which, according

---

[45] "der bedeutendste Prediger und Theologe der amerikanischen Kolonialzeit:" Hugh Lawrence Bond, "Edwards, Jonathan," *Theologische Realenzyklopädie* 9, p. 300.

[46] Quoted in: McLoughlin, *Revivals*, p. 77. See Eliade, *Quest*, pp. 94-95.

[47] Alan Heimert, *Religion and the America Mind: From the Great Awakening to the Revolution* (Cambridge, MA: Harvard University Press, 1966), pp. 118-19.

[48] Ahlstrom, *Religious History*, I, 427.

[49] Christof Gestrich, "Deismus," *Theologische Realenzyklopädie* 8, p. 394.

to the American disciples of the protagonists of Enlightenment and deism, would naturally begin in, and radiate from, America.

This awareness of the mission of the American people was the common denominator for the dream of the Pilgrim Fathers and most of the other colonists of the seventeenth century, the revitalization movement in the First Great Awakening, and the philosophical and religious ideas of the Enlightenment.

The United States of America

Equipped with renewed vigor and faith in themselves and their destiny, more than two million colonists[50] from the middle of the eighteenth century on saw themselves faced with measures from the motherland which hindered the expansion of their political rights as inhabitants of a British colony and their trade with other countries. A clash was inevitable.[51] A Continental Congress was convoked, seating representatives of all thirteen colonies. After a resolution of independence had finally been introduced (on June 7, 1776) and voted upon (on July 2, 1776), "The unanimous Declaration of the thirteen united States of America" was accepted and issued by the Continental Congress on July 4, 1776.[52] Its central ideas originated in Thomas Jefferson's Enlightenment philosophy; the document itself was drafted by a committee of which Jefferson was a member:

> We hold these truths to be self-evident, that all men are created equal, that they are endowed by their Creator with certain unalienable Rights, that among these are Life, Liberty and the pursuit of Happiness.[53]

Governments which have no power but by the consent of those governed would be instituted to secure those rights; if they did not live up to their duties they might, under special circumstances, be altered or abolished. A long list of *gravamina* against the British Crown, the parliament,[54] and King George III personally justified exactly this extreme measure:

> We, therefore, the Representatives of the united States of America, in General Congress, Assembled, appealing to the Supreme Judge of the world for the rectitude of our intentions, do, in the Name, and by Authority of the good People of these Colonies, solemnly publish and declare, That these United Colonies are, and of Right ought to be Free and Independent States, that they are Absolved from all Allegiance to the British Crown. . . . And for the support of this Declaration, with a firm reliance on the Protection of Divine Providence, we mutually pledge to each other our Lives, our Fortunes and our sacred Honor.[55]

The heavy influence of the philosophy of John Locke, especially in the section on the duties and the abolishment of the government, is evident throughout the document; his ideas offered the rationale for severing the ties with the Crown and government. Another trait that is highly visible is the use of vocabulary and notions borrowed from the concept of the deists: Nature's God, the Creator, the Supreme Judge, and the Divine Providence are titles which did not commit to any specific creed, let alone to any of those churches that were by law

---

[50] 1760: 1,593,625; 1770: 2,148,076: Wattenberg, *Statistical History*, Z 1-19, p. 1168.

[51] The political and economic history of the fight for independence is not the subject of this section and can be read in every history book.

[52] The text: Henry Steele Commager, ed., *Documents of American History*, Crofts American History Series, 5th ed. (New York: Appleton Century Crofts, 1949), no. 66, pp. 100-03.

[53] Commager, *Documents of American History*, no. 66, p. 100.

[54] See Mary Barbara Allen, "The Question of Right: Parliamentary Sovereignty and the American Colonies, 1763-1774," Dissertation University of Kentucky 1981.

[55] Commager, *Documents of American History*, no. 66, p. 102.

established in several of the colonies.⁵⁶ A third very characteristic thread through this document was the reliance on the concept and the representation of the people. The declaration was not written on behalf of any imagined or real political body but the most basic one, the people living in the territory. No institution could substitute for this entity. Throughout the history of the United States, and of the Episcopal Church, the precedence of the constituency, the people or the members of the church, over the government has been closely watched and safeguarded.

The consequence of this Declaration of Independence was a division within the people between those favoring the step, and the royalists who wanted to remain loyal to the Crown. About 100,000 of the latter group emigrated to the West Indies, Canada, or Great Britain during or after the War of Independence.

Great Britain did not recognize the independence according to the international laws until the Treaty of Paris September 3, 1783.

One effect of the Declaration of Independence, and of its acknowledgment by Great Britain, was especially grave for the Church of England in the former colonies: its ties with the Church of England were cut, and the king could no longer be supreme governor.⁵⁷ The material help and the licensing of persons for work in America came to an end. Since the Church had been particularly linked with the state in Great Britain, the Church, too, was viewed with suspicion. Church historians agree that the American Revolution was an almost devastating blow to the integrity of the Church of England in America.⁵⁸

It was the people of the United States again that issued the most fundamental document of the nation, the Constitution.⁵⁹ It was voted upon by a convention of representatives from the thirteen states on September 17, 1787:

> We the People of the United States, in order to form a more perfect Union, establish Justice, insure domestic Tranquillity, provide for the common defence, promote the general Welfare, and secure the Blessings of Liberty to ourselves and our Posterity, do ordain and establish this Constitution for the United States of America.⁶⁰

---

⁵⁶ See John F. Berens, "Divine Providence and the American Enlightenment, 1740-1815," Dissertation Marquette University 1975.

⁵⁷ In the light of the importance of the royal supremacy for the life of the Church of England, at least at the time of the American Revolution, it is more than surprising to find little evidence of any qualms of conscience, realizing that, with the severance from the king as having the supreme authority in temporal matters, the supreme governorship was abolished, too. Herklots, *Church of England*, pp. 103-04, quotes from a letter of the Rev. Philip Reading, SPG missionary in Delaware and an Oxford graduate, written on August 25, 1776, as given by Clara Olds Loveland, *The Critical Years: The Reconstitution of the Anglican Church in the United States of America, 1780-1789* (Greenwich, CT: Seabury, 1956), p. 3: "The Church of England has no longer an existence in the United Colonies of America.... My reason for speaking in this manner is as follows: I look upon the King's supremacy and the constitution of the Church of England to be so intimately blended together that whenever the supremacy is either suspended or abrogated the fences of the Church are then broken down and its visibility is destroyed." Marion Josiah Hatchett, *The Making of the First American Book of Common Prayer: 1776-1789* (New York: Seabury, 1982), p. 38, gives examples of local decisions by the vestries to omit the prayers for the king from the liturgy.

⁵⁸ Addison, *Episcopal Church*, p. 51; Ahlstrom, *Religious History*, I, 446; Ahlbright, *History*, p. 123; Garrett, "Prayer Book Presence," pp. 87-89.

⁵⁹ Commager, *Documents of American History*, no. 87, pp. 139-45. Between 1776 and 1784, the former colonies had, through their respective state legislative procedures, issued state constitutions which remained in force for the state territory even after the ratification of the federal Constitution. See Daniel Lee Hailman, "Abolishing the Forms to Which They Are Accustomed: Constitutional Changes as the Colonies Became States, 1776-1784," Dissertation Auburn University 1983.

⁶⁰ Commager, *Documents of American History*, no. 87, p. 139.

The Constitution in its original form contained nothing about religious affairs. The first ten Amendments which were added to the Constitution in 1791, the so-called "Bill of Rights," which had been demanded by some states, provided for the guarantee of human rights. The first article deals with religion: "Congress shall make no law respecting an establishment of religion, or prohibiting the free exercize thereof."[61]

The former Church of England in the United States therefore could not hope for any help from any civil authority in its struggle for realignment and reconstitution, not even in the former colonies where the church had been established. It was solely its own task, with all the attendant opportunities and dangers. On the other hand, it would be free of interference from anybody outside, in the process of finding its own identity.

The Book of Common Prayer 1789

Since it was clear that the English hierarchy no longer had any authority over church matters in America, but that an organizational structure had to be established to conduct the temporal and spiritual aspects of church life, conventions in several states were held, comprising both clergymen and laymen, to deal with those matters. A rather low-keyed and secret gathering by ten clergymen in the state of Connecticut on March 25, 1783 elected Samuel Seabury, who had been a chaplain to the British troops in America and a High Churchman, to go to England in order to seek consecration as a bishop.[62] Since this was not legally possible in England--the oath of allegiance to the king was still a precondition for being consecrated--Seabury turned to the Scottish bishops and was consecrated on November 14, 1784 by the Bishop of Aberdeen and Primus of Scotland (Robert Kilgour), his coadjutor (John Skinner), and the Bishop of Ross and Murray (Arthur Petri). The Church in America had gotten its first bishop--the first Anglican bishop outside the British Isles--and most of the episcopal functions could now be carried out.[63]

On the day after the consecration, a concordat between Seabury and the Scottish bishops was signed. Articles IV and V dealt with liturgical matters. Article IV stated that the signatories

---

[61] Commager, *Documents of American History*, no. 87, p. 146. See Thomas John Curry, "The First Freedoms: The Development of the Concept of Freedom of Religion and Establishment of Religion in America from the Early Settlements to the Passage of the First Amendment to the Constitution," Dissertation Claremont Graduate School 1983. This section of the First Amendment was patterned after the statute for religious freedom that was adopted by the Virginia parliament on January 16, 1786; this text again had been drafted by Thomas Jefferson.

[62] The Anglican Church in Connecticut still was under the strong influence of the High Church teachings of Samuel Johnson. Bishop Seabury's father, Samuel Seabury, had been a Congregational minister before going to England to become, after his ordination, an SPG missionary in Connecticut; this conversion too had been the result of Johnson's efforts: Ahlstrom, *Religious History*, I, 285.

[63] The 1979 *Book of Common Prayer* makes in its calendar provisions to commemorate the day of Seabury's consecration liturgically. The validity of his consecration, however, was not undisputed, and the debate about it and the rivalry between Seabury and William White and Samuel Provoost, the two other bishops who, after the passing of a law on June 26, 1786 allowing the consecration of Americans by English bishops without the administration of the oath of allegiance to the king, had been consecrated by English bishops on February 4, 1787, marred the General Convention of 1789 a great deal.

agree in desiring that there may be as near a conformity in worship and discipline established between the two Churches, as is consistent with the different circumstances and customs of nations.⁶⁴

Article V dealt with the eucharist:

> As the celebration of the Holy Eucharist, or the administration of the Sacrament of the body and blood of Christ, is the principal bond of union among Christians, as well as the most solemn act of worship in the Christian Church, the Bishops aforesaid agree in desiring that there may be as little variance here as possible; and though the Scottish Bishops are very far from prescribing to their brethren in this matter, they cannot help ardently wishing that Bishop Seabury would endeavor all he can, consistently with peace and prudence, to make the celebration of this venerable mystery conformable to the most primitive doctrine and practice in that respect, which is the pattern the Church of Scotland has copied after in her Communion Office, and which it has been the wish of some of the most eminent divines of the Church of England, that she also had more closely followed than she seems to have done since she gave up her first reformed Liturgy, used in the reign of King Edward VI, between which, and the form used in the Church of Scotland, there is no difference in any point, which the Primitive Church reckoned essential to the right administration of the Holy Eucharist. In this capital article, therefore, the Eucharistick [sic] service, in which the Scottish Bishops so earnestly wish for as much unity as possible, Bishop Seabury also agrees to take a serious view of the Communion Office recommended by them, and if found agreeable to the genuine standards of antiquity, to give his sanctions to it, and by gentle methods of argument and persuasion, to endeavor, as they have done, to introduce it by degrees into practice, without the compulsion of authority on the one side, or the prejudice of former custom on the other.⁶⁵

In terms mild and yet convincing, the principle of the preeminence of a liturgy consistent with what at that time was thought to be genuine apostolic pattern was established, be it even at the cost of abandoning the former allegiance to the 1662 *Book of Common Prayer*. The eucharistic prayer to which the text refered had however been in use in parishes which had their origins in Scottish rather than English immigrants, especially in the southern colonies; it was therefore not an unknown entity to either Bishop Seabury or other churchmen.

An allusion was made in this article to a series of revisions of the *Book of Common Prayer* by "some of the most eminent divines of the Church of England," by which were meant the so-called non-jurors. After the deposition of James II on December 11, 1688 and the accession of King William III and Queen Mary II, with an equal right to the throne, on February 13, 1689, some of the English clergy refused to abandon their oath of loyalty to James II, even as he had become a Roman Catholic, in favor of the new sovereigns. In time these clergy were deposed and the vacancies filled with new, loyal appointments. Gradually this group of non-jurors, to whom in 1689 even Archbishop William Sancroft of Canterbury belonged, became not only a reservoir for the politically dissatisfied but also for those who had become disenchanted with the liturgy and theology of the Church of England. They quickly took the 1549 book as their example, but they also published their own forms of service. The members of this Anglican group invested a great amount of time in patristic and liturgical studies in order to establish a liturgy as much genuinely in accord with the primitive liturgies as possible. Since, politically speaking, all Scottish bishops were non-jurors, the efforts by the divines and scholars showed their first fruits in Scotland where, following the revisions of the communion service of 1637 in 1722, 1723, 1735, and 1755, the eucharistic li-

---

⁶⁴ Marion Josiah Hatchett, "The Making of the First American Prayer Book," Dissertation General Theological Seminary 1972, p. 99.

⁶⁵ Hatchett, "First American Prayer Book," pp. 99-100. See Herklots, *Church of England*, pp. 96-99, esp. p. 98.

turgy that Bishop Seabury was to consider and, if possible, to introduce was that of 1764.[66] A characteristic feature, common to all revisions and proposals, was a constant appeal to the primitive Church;[67] the recovery of the apostolic liturgy was a primary concern.

A year after Seabury's consecration, a convention of the "Southern States" met in Philadelphia on September 27, 1785.[68] The next day a committee was appointed,

> consisting of one Clerical and one Lay Deputy from the Church in each state, to consider of and report such alterations in the Liturgy, as shall render it consistent with the American revolution and the constitutions of the respective states: And such further alterations in the Liturgy, as it may be adviseable for the Convention to recommend to the consideration of the Church here represented.[69]

The committee began its work immediately. On October 5 a resolution was passed appointing a committee whose task it was to publish the prayer book with the changes necessary due to the American Revolution, as well as those recommended by the revising committee. The book ordered by this resolution came out in 1786 as *The Book of Common Prayer, and Administration of the Sacraments, And Other Rites and Ceremonies, As Revised and Proposed to the Use of the Protestant Episcopal Church*.[70]

In comparison with the numerous other attempts of revision in the seventeenth and eighteenth centuries,[71] this proposed book of 1786 was not overly dependent on the theological currents of its day, although they had left their traces.

The preface of the book was an exercise in outlining the various influences, desires, and principles of the reform.[72] The right of the Church to alter its liturgy was confirmed and upheld, as the discipline of the Church had to conform to "the various exigencies of times and

---

[66] For the sometimes slightly confusing history of the interdependence between the non-jurors' and the Scottish liturgies, see Cuming, *History*, pp. 135-45; Grisbrooke, *Anglican Liturgies*, pp. i-xv, 71-159; Hatchett, *First American Book of Common Prayer*, pp. 22-28.

[67] Grisbrooke, *Anglican Liturgies*, p. xiv.

[68] The history of the first American prayer book has been masterly told by Hatchett in his doctoral dissertation "First American Prayer Book," 1972, and in a revised publication of it *First American Book of Common Prayer*, 1982. What follows in the text is an outline of the events of the years 1785-1789. In this case it has been deemed impeding rather than helpful to refer constantly to those two standard works on this subject. Only additions to the matter from other sources as well as verbal quotations are indicated.

[69] Hatchett, "First American Prayer Book," p. 123; Hatchett, *First American Book of Common Prayer*, p. 52.

[70] The rather curious name "Protestant Episcopal Church," in the 1789 constitution of the Church officially adopted as "Protestant Episcopal Church in the United States of America," seems to have been a blend of the habit of the church in Maryland which distinguished between the "Catholic," that is, the Roman Catholic Church, and the "Protestant," that is, the Church of England which in that state seems to have held a monopoly on the designation "Protestant," on the one side; and the speech habit of the church members in Pennsylvania which adopted the name "Episcopalians" that had become a synonym for the Anglicans in England around 1650, on the other side. The terminology was then simply fused so that the "Anglican episcopalians" could be distinguished from "Roman episcopalians.": Robert W. Shoemaker, *The Origin and Meaning of the Name "Protestant Episcopal"* (New York: American Church Publication, 1959), pp. 51, 120-21. Owing to the growing dissatisfaction with the name, the General Convention of 1967 confirmed a change of the constitution made at the previous Convention in 1964, thereby giving it legal status in the church, to adopt as an equally fitting name the self-designation "The Episcopal Church." Since the 1979 *Book of Common Prayer* itself and all liturgical material in which reference to this church is made give as the only name "The Episcopal Church," this use is adopted entirely throughout the text of this study.

[71] Hatchett, *First American Book of Common Prayer*, pp. 6-36.

[72] William McGarvey, *Liturgiae Americanae or The Book of Common Prayer as Used in the United States of America: Compared with the Proposed Book of 1786 and with the Prayer Books of The Church of England and an Historical Account and Documents* (Philadelphia: [Sunshine], 1895), pp. 9-33.

occasions," a repetition of a statement in the preface of the 1662 English prayer book which was in its entirety quoted in this 1786 preface. Even the example of the Roman Catholic Church was cited:

> This is not only the doctrine of the Church of England, and other Protestant Churches, but likewise of the Church of Rome; which hath declared, by the Council of Trent--"That the Church always had a power of making such constitutions and alterations in the dispensation of the Sacraments, provided their substance be preserved entire, as, with regard to the variety of circumstances and places, she should judge to be most expedient for the salvation of the receivers, or the veneration of the Sacraments themselves.[73]

The example of the Church of England with regard to alterations was furthermore outlined, giving 1549, the publication of the first prayer book, as the date of the Reformation in England, after which year several revisions or attempts thereof had been carried out, in particular the abandoned effort to revise the 1662 book in 1689.[74] The preface continued:

> When, in the course of divine providence, these American States became independent with respect to civil government, their ecclesiastical independence was necessarily included: and the different religious denominations of Christians in these states were left at full and equal liberty to model and organize their respective Churches and forms of worship and discipline, in such manner as they might judge most convenient for their future prosperity, consistently with the constitution and laws of their country.[75]

The occasion not only to change the texts referring to the civil authorities but also to incorporate further alterations if deemed necessary or useful was welcomed; an outline of the amendments compared with the 1662 book was given for each office. At the end the essential unity with the Church of England was once again stressed.

In the "Order for the Administration of the Lord's Supper, or, Holy Communion," the following changes are noteworthy.[76] The two collects for the king were omitted, with no substitution. The Nicene Creed was omitted here as throughout the entire book. The general confession between the exhortations and the Comfortable Words was to be said by all instead of one person as the representative of those intending to receive communion. All other texts and rubrics of the celebration were taken over from the 1662 book, including the eucharistic prayer. At the end the rubrics about kneeling and adoration of the consecrated elements were eliminated. Here as well as in other parts of the book, the term "minister" was substituted for "priest."

The "Ministration of Public Baptism of Infants, To be Used in the Church" had undergone a few but significant changes.[77] The rationale for the presence of the congregation at baptism, that it would serve as a reminder of one's own baptism, was omitted in the first rubric. The parents could be admitted as additional sponsors, if desired--a halfway meeting of the puritan objections against the use of godparents. Of the two opening prayers, only one

---

[73] McGarvey, *Liturgiae Americanae*, pp. 9-11. Concilium Tridentinum, sessio 2 (July 16, 1562), Doctrina de communione sub utraque specie et parvulorum, cap. 2: "Declarat [synodus], hanc potestatem perpetuo in ecclesia fuisse, ut in sacramentorum dispensatione, salva illorum substantia, ea statueret vel mutaret, quae suscipientium utilitati seu ipsorum sacramentorum venerationi, pro rerum, temporum et locorum varietate, magis expedire iudicaret.": Josephus Alberigo, et al., eds., *Concilium Oecumenicorum Decreta*, ed. tertia (Bologna: Istituto per le scienze religiose, 1973), p. 726.

[74] See Timothy John Fawcett, *The Liturgy of Comprehension 1689: An Abortive Attempt to Revise The Book of Common Prayer*, Alcuin Club Collections, 54 (Southend-on-Sea: Mayhew McCrimmon, 1973).

[75] McGarvey, *Liturgiae Americanae*, p. 25.

[76] McGarvey, *Liturgiae Americanae*, pp. 213-57.

[77] McGarvey, *Liturgiae Americanae*, pp. 259-73.

needed by said. The renunciations were dropped entirely.[78] The Apostles' Creed was no longer asked but was replaced by the question:

> Dost thou believe all the Articles of the Christian Faith, as contained in the Apostles' Creed; and wilt thou endeavour to have this Child instructed accordingly?
> Answ. I do believe them; and by God's help will endeavour so to do.
> Minister. Wilt thou endeavour to have him brought up in the fear of God, and to obey his holy Will and Commandments?
> Answ. I will, by God's assistance.[79]

It was left to the discretion of the sponsors whether the sign of the cross on the forehead would be made or not. If not, reference to this gesture in the formula of accepting the baptized into the congregation was to be omitted--after more than two hundred years a fulfilling of one of the wishes of the puritans. References to regeneration as one of the effects of baptism were left out of the text. The rubric stating that baptized children, dying before they commit actual sin, would be undoubtedly saved, was also excluded.

The "Ministration of Baptism of such as are of Riper Years and able to answer for themselves" was an adaptation of the same order in the 1662 book along the lines of the revision of the infant baptism; the same textual changes and rubrical alterations applied.[80]

The proposed revision of "The Order of Confirmation, or laying on of hands upon those who are baptized and come to years of discretion" was a rather heavy one.[81] The rational aspect of confirmation was highlighted. In an additional second question before the prayers, the willingness to promise to live in the faith in which the candidates were instructed, and the obedience to God's will and commandments, was asked; an affirmative response was to be given. The direction of the first prayer and the invocation of the Holy Spirit and his gifts upon the candidates, said by the bishop, had been altered. Whereas in the 1662 prayer book God had, in this prayer, been seen as the one who had regenerated the candidates by water and the Holy Spirit, forgiving them all their sins, He was now regarded as the one who had received the candidates into the Church by baptism,[82] and had given them the grace to confess now in their own persons the faith wherein they had been instructed according to the promise made for them by the godparents at baptism. It was knowledge which was to be strengthened by the confirmation, not the sacramental reality of baptism.

The impression left by this proposed revision is one of non-resistance to some pressure of then current theologies and philosophical ideas, most obvious in the deletion and substitution of the interrogatories in baptism.[83]

In the meantime Bishop Seabury had returned from Scotland. As alterations of the liturgy were thought of by him as being the business of bishops, he was against the proposed book. At the same time he presented the Scottish communion office to the Connecticut

---

[78] That this ancient part of the baptismal liturgy should be dropped, is not altogether surprising. Deism had its heyday and certainly influenced the deliberations about the book, albeit in sometimes subconscious ways. As renunciations by essence tell about a previously inferior or incomplete state of the person to be baptized, it was only natural that those allusions should give way to an emphasis on the equal value of all believers and to moral teachings. At the time of the publication of the book, a justification for dropping the renunciations was hardly necessary. The same holds true for the omission of all references to regeneration: There needs not come a better or more godly quality inside the baptized as all human beings are equal before their Creator.

[79] McGarvey, *Liturgiae Americanae*, p. 267.

[80] McGarvey, *Liturgiae Americanae*, pp. 283-97.

[81] McGarvey, *Liturgiae Americanae*, pp. 307-13.

[82] The reference to regeneration had been dropped.

[83] Rather than wondering why there had been an inroad of deism into the liturgy of the Episcopal Church, it could reasonably be asked why there had not been a greater part of surrender to the theory of deism, and subsequently be marveled at the lack of it. It would have been easy, for example, to drop allusions to, or expressions of, the sinful state, or the Episcopal Church in contrast to other churches. In this respect, the proposed book was still a "conservative" revision of the 1662 book.

convention on September 22, 1786 which, however, seems to have been rejected by the clergy of that state.

The delegates from the "Southern States" met anew in Philadelphia July 28 to August 8, 1789 in order to ratify the proposed book, but voted to postpone any action to allow the delegates from the New England states to participate. The convention reassembled at the same place September 29 to October 16 of that year, with Seabury and others present. A seperate House of Bishops was set up so that the Convention became a two-chamber system, one of the bishops, and one of clerical and lay deputies from each state, both having the right to originate actions. At this Convention, the proposed book was scrutinized again in the two Houses. Amendments were passed about the definite shape of the new prayer book, and the Scottish communion prayer was adopted for use in the church, substituting the 1662 book.

> Many have considered the inclusion of the revised form of the Eucharistic Prayer from the Scottish Communion Office as the greatest improvement in the 1789 book. Seabury has often been given the credit for this, but it seems highly doubtful that this prayer would have made its way into the book on his recommendations. Several other individuals probably deserve as much credit as he.... Seabury met staunch resistance when he tried to promote its use in Connecticut, but the state conventions of Maryland and Pennsylvania proposed a revision of the Eucharistic Prayer based on the Scottish prayer. Though Seabury may have influenced the form which the final revision took, he could not single-handedly have carried the day for it, and should not be given undue credit.[84]

This Convention certainly was the most important ever held by the Episcopal Church. For the first time, delegates from all state conventions came together to act on behalf of the whole church. Bishops, clergy delegates, and lay delegates had a say in all matters brought before the Convention; the church clearly was not a purely clerical institution. A constitution and a set of canons were adopted, and the *Book of Common Prayer* ratified. The Church of England in America had become the Episcopal Church. Due to the strict separation of church and state in America, the Episcopal Church was able and, for that matter, forced to break with almost one and a half millenia of interference of the state in church matters. This church establishment was "an ecclesiastical revolution."[85] Besides, the bishops could be and were elected by clergy and laity alike: the recovery of a system lost since centuries.

"In the founding of the Protestant Episcopal Church in the United States of America ecclesiastical union and a uniform liturgy came hand in hand. Neither might have been possible without the other."[86]

The first American prayer book bore a title in which only the Church's name differed from the 1662 prayer book: *The Book of Common Prayer, and Administration of the Sacraments and other Rites and Ceremonies of the Church, According to the Use of the Protestant Episcopal Church in the United States of America, Together with the Psalter, or Psalms of David.*

A ratification of the official character of the book was printed after the table of contents.[87]

---

[84] Hatchett, *First American Book of Common Prayer*, p. 112. See Marion Josiah Hatchett, *Commentary on the American Prayer Book* (New York: Seabury, 1981), pp. 359-60.

[85] Frederick Vandever Mills, "Mitre without Sceptre: An Eighteenth Century Ecclesiastical Revolution," *Church History*, 39 (1970), 365. See Addison, *Episcopal Church*, p. 65; Ahlstrom, *Religious History*, I, 449; Ahlbright, *History*, p. 140.

[86] Hatchett, "First American Prayer Book," p. 6.

[87] McGarvey, *Liturgiae Americanae*, p. 6. The ratification of the 1789 book has been printed *verbatim* in all editions of the prayer book, even after the revisions in 1892, 1928, and 1979.

The following preface was a condensation of that of the proposed book, leaving out the summary and arguments for the changes.[88]

The "Order for the Administration of the Lord's Supper, or, Holy Communion" was a revision of the communion service of the 1786 proposed book.[89] After the decalogue at the beginning of the service, the Summary of the Law according to Matthew 22:37 40 might be added, after which a collect for purity was to be said, asking God to direct us in the ways of His laws so that we might be preserved in body and soul. After this collect the collect of the day was said. The epistle and gospel were followed by either the Apostles' or the Nicene Creed, unless it had been read immediately before at Morning Prayer. After the prayer for the whole state of Christ's church militant, the three exhortations were to be given about the nature and frequency of communion. Except for the epiclesis, the eucharistic prayer was adopted from the 1764 Scottish communion office. Whereas the 1764 book read:

> And we most humbly beseech thee, O merciful Father, to hear us, and of thy almighty goodness to bless and sanctify, with thy word and Holy Spirit, these thy gifts and creatures of bread and wine, that they may become the Body and Blood of thy most dearly beloved Son,[90]

the 1789 American book read after "these thy gifts and creatures of bread and wine:"

> that we, receiving them according to thy Son our Saviour Jesus Christ's holy institution, in remembrance of his Death and Passion, may be partakers of his most blessed Body and Blood.[91]

After the eucharistic prayer a hymn might be sung. The rubric governing the consecration of additional material directed that both bread and wine would have to be consecrated, not either one alone. To this purpose almost the entire eucharistic prayer was to be repeated from the post-*Sanctus* up to the just-quoted epiclesis, therefore saying the central parts--praise, institution narrative, anamnesis, epiclesis--again. The only rubric that was kept at the end stipulated that the remaining consecrated species were to be reverently eaten and drunk by the ministers and communicants after the service.

In the "Ministration of Public Baptism of Infants, To be used in the Church," some of the theological ideas of the 1662 book had been reinstated while other features of the proposed book of 1786 had been retained.[92] Directions that the baptism was to be administered at the font were given. Of the first two prayers, again only one needed be said. If there were more than one baptism per month, the gospel reading, the explanatory exhortation ensuing, the prayer for the giving of the Holy Spirit to the child, the address to the godparents about their duties, and--after the interrogatories which were asked of the sponsors in the name of the child--the prayer for a fruitful reception of the sacrament might be omitted.[93] The

---

[88] McGarvey, *Liturgiae Americanae*, pp. 8-32. This text too has been retained in all prayer books, also those of 1892, 1928, and 1979.

[89] McGarvey, *Liturgiae Americanae*, pp. 212-56.

[90] Bernard Wigan, ed., *The Liturgy in English* (London: Oxford University Press, 1962), p. 44, with the 1764 corrections, p. 45.

[91] McGarvey, *Liturgiae Americanae*, p. 240. This change had originated in the 1786 state conventions of Maryland and Pennsylvania. It passed the committee of the 1789 General Convention responsible for the eucharistic rite probably because of the known bias of the three clergymen serving on it in favor of an Evangelical outlook and with sympathies to the Methodists; the two laymen came from the Northeast: Hatchett, *First American Book of Common Prayer*, pp. 122-24. Nonetheless, this text too derived from the 1637 Scottish prayer book: "these thy gifts and creatures of bread and wine, that they may be unto us the body and blood of thy most dearly beloved Son; so that we, receiving them according to thy Son our Saviour Jesus Christ's holy institution of his death and passion, may be partakers of the same his most precious body and blood.": Buchanan, "Lord's Supper," no. 594, pp. 410-11; Donaldson, *Scottish Prayer Book*, pp. 198-99.

[92] McGarvey, *Liturgiae Americanae*, pp. 258-72.

[93] One ought not to forget that the proper setting for baptism was still the excessively long Sunday morning service which, celebrated with due reverence, intermingled with the singing of hymns, and interspersed

renunciation was reinstated in the same phrasing as the 1662 book provided, to which the godparents had to answer. The question for the faith remained in the simple form: "Dost thou believe all the Articles of the Christian Faith, as contained in the Apostles' Creed?" The questions for the willingness to be baptized and to live according to God's will were then asked. If the sponsors rejected the signation with the cross, nothing was to be done or said, according to their wishes, although the rubric stated that "the Church knows no worthy cause or scruple concerning the same." The invitation to give thanks for the regeneration of the infant, as well as this respective phrase in the ensuing prayer, were reinstated.

The "Ministration of Baptism to such as are of Riper Years, and able to answer for themselves" was a revision of the same order as in the proposed book of 1786; there was hardly a difference from the 1662 English book.[94] It is, however, surprising to have had the questions of renunciation and belief asked of the sponsors even in the case where the baptizands could answer for themselves; the 1662 book and the 1786 proposed book had had them addressed to the persons to be baptized. The signing with the cross might be omitted, too. A rubric at the end allowed the baptism of adults in private houses in consideration of extreme sickness, although even here in the presence of "a convenient number of persons." Two more rubrics respectively governed the order of a baptism of an adult person and of an infant at the same time, and the rule that for persons not baptized as infants, yet brought to baptism before the years of discretion, the office for public baptism of infants was to be used.

The "Order of Confirmation, or laying on of Hands upon those who are baptized and come to Years of Discretion" is a picture book example of a conservative mood prevalent in a prayer book revision: every change proposed in 1786 was disapproved, and the order of the 1662 prayer book reinstated in its entirety.[95] The emphasis on knowledge had disappeared, and the reference to regeneration and forgiveness of sins had been reinserted. It was a *verbatim* adoption of the order that had been legally obligatory, but had not been able to be used, in the colonies.

As was the case with the first English prayer book of 1549, the first American book also lacked what was known as the Ordinal. The next General Convention in 1792 added this part to the *Book of Common Prayer*.

After 1793 a "Standard Book," authorized by Convention, was kept to secure the accuracy of the several printings, which could be done by any recommended printer.

At the 1808 Convention an addition was proposed to the constitution, which was adopted in 1811, stating that for any future alteration of, or addition to, the prayer book the changes were to be proposed to one General Convention, thereafter to be made known to the convention of every diocese or state, and only then adopted at the subsequent General Convention. Any revision process, therefore, had to last at least three years from the first proposal to the adoption.[96]

The first American prayer book was the result of a revision necessitated by the political situation, but it quickly turned into an occasion for adapting the book to facilitate liturgical life under the special circumstances of life in the United States. It must be attributed to the strong conservative mood of persons like Bishops White and Seabury, and others, that rationalism, deism, and unitarianism did not gain much influence. As can be seen in the correspondence between the outstanding members of the Convention of 1786, the editorial committee resulting, and the members of the first General Convention 1789, as well as from

---

with exhortations and longer sermons on their proper places, wa a matter of hours rather than of quaters of an hour. The permission to leave out the prayers for the giving of the Holy Spirit and for a fruitful reception of the sacrament may be, in our eyes, unfortunate and to be regretted. But human nature does take its toll even in divine services.

[94] McGarvey, *Liturgiae Americanae*, pp. 282-96.
[95] McGarvey, *Liturgiae Americanae*, pp. 306-12.
[96] Hatchett, *First American Book of Common Prayer*, pp. 134-36.

the minutes of the several state conventions, an appeal to the primitive Church and to the liturgy of the first centuries was the reason for retaining or regaining features in the book that otherwise might have been sacrificed to the contemporary ideologies. This can be seen through a comparison to other attempts at prayer book revision at the time.[97] For this, as well as for the other revisions of the American prayer book, it holds true that "Anglican worship in this country has reflected both a strong attachment to tradition and a readiness to adapt to current circumstances."[98]

Social and Ecclesiastical Life in the First Half of the Nineteenth Century

The years preceding the beginning of the century were marked by both excitement, apathy, and hope in, and a vision of, the political future--as well as exhaustion from the upheavals that went along with the birth and early years of the Republic. In 1792, a certain Dr. Samuel Currie could write eulogies on life in the United States almost as if it were heaven on earth:

> North America is the only portion of this spacious globe where man can live securely, and enjoy all the privileges to which he has a native right. In this enviable and favoured region there is no proud usurping aristocracy, no ecclesiastical orders with exclusive privileges, no kings with arbitrary power or corrupting influence, no venal parliaments composed of different ranks and opposing interests. ... None of the enervating refinements of luxury or dissatisfaction are to be found here; but here all the necessities and convenience of life abound, and a pleasing equality and decent competence are everywhere displayed. Here the dignity of the human species is restored, and man enjoys all the freedom to which he is entitled; for he is a member of the government he obeys, and a framer of the laws by which he is governed.[99]

These people, numbering more than four million in that year,[100] had the city of New York as their capital; in 1800, a then still muddy place named after the first President, George Washington, took over that dignity. It was laid out in the intersection between the northern and southern states and built on such a magnificent scale that the buildings and streets seemed to be out of all proportions. The republic wanted to represent.

Regular and everyday life was not as much affected by the results of the War of Independence and the structuring of the republic as it could have been. It was still dominated by the rural style. Only five towns had more than 20,000 inhabitants,[101] and the impact of the Industrial Revolution that was going on with increasing rapidity in Great Britain was not yet felt in the United States.

After the process of making necessary changes due to the new political circumstances, the formerly established churches saw themselves in a spiritual slump, with no signs of vigor

---

[97] Hatchett, *First American Book of Common Prayer*, pp. 28-36, 144-48.

[98] Harry Boone Porter, "Toward an Unofficial History of Episcopal Worship," in *Worship Points The Way: A Celebration of the Life and Work of Massey H. Shepherd, Jr.*, ed. Malcolm C. Burson (New York: Seabury, 1981), p. 99.

[99] Samuel Currie, *Historical Account of the Climate and Diseases of the United States of America ... Collected principally from Personal Observation and the Communications of Physicians of Talents and Experience* (Philadelphia, 1792), pp. 408-09; quoted in: Henry Steele Commager, *The Empire of Reason: How Europe Imagined and America Realized the Enlightenment* (Garden City, NY: Anchor Press Doubleday, 1978), pp. 109-10.

[100] 4,194,000: Wattenberg, *Statistical History*, A 6-8, p. 8.

[101] Philadelphia (with 70,000 people the largest city), New York, Baltimore, Boston, and Charleston: Faulkner, *History*, p. 206-08.

or health. For the Episcopal Church the two decades after the ratification of the 1789 prayer book have been described as "the lowest low-water mark of the lowest ebb-tide of spiritual life in the history of the American Church," in which it "showed few symptoms of vitality and made little progress" because it "seemed hardly aware of the mission and the purpose of a Church."[102] Rationalism, indifference, desolation, and simple carelessness, especially on the side of the bishops and priests, are given as reasons for this lack of life.

Commencing with the last decade of the eighteenth century, personal as well as institutional stress began to build up again.[103] Is human nature *per se* sinful or good, is it to be trusted or not, does it have a free will or not? These questions represented a mounting conflict between the ministers and theologians upholding Calvinistic traditions, and the representatives of the Enlightenment and deism. A new awakening of the Christian spirit was called for. Whereas in the southern states Baptists and Methodists had somehow managed to keep their vigor of the First Great Awakening alive and to carry it over to the scattered outposts of the frontier territories of the West, the northern states felt the necessity to clarify those positions and to renew the spiritual life. This time the revival meetings in the New England states were calm, orderly, and sober, a fact everybody attributed to a genuine work of God, nor of man-made discipline, and clergy and people alike were thankful for this experience which lasted, with interruptions, until about 1830.[104] On the other hand, the camp meetings in the West, on the frontier, were marked by "rampant emotionalism and bodily agitations."[105] Besides, there was a constant competition between the Baptist and the Methodist preachers, and proselytizing was very common.[106] The theological and philosophical outlook of the American people was shaped and directed through the experience of this Second Great Awakening:

> The First Awakening . . . weakened the old doctrine of predestination, and the Second Awakening finally subverted it entirely. The key issues became the role of man and the means he might use (or that God used) to effect the regenerations of the soul. . . . In philosophical terms it meant that if immediate conversion is available by an act of the human will, then, through God's miraculous grace, all things are possible: human nature is open to total renovation in the twinkling of an eye and so, then, is the nature of society. The world is unfettered from tradition, custom, institutions, is unconditioned by history or environment. Society is totally malleable to the power that works in harmony with God's will. It was from this assumption, pervasive in the nation after 1830, that perfectionism and millenial optimism grew to such importance.[107]

But the vision, so bright for a future in prosperity, also narrowed. The prospect of living in a near-perfect society was the destiny of Americans, not of Europeans, not of decadent, superstitious, ignorant, or colored people. The "WASP mentality" took root: only White, Anglo-Saxon, Protestant members of society could be part of the fulfillment of the "American Dream:" the Paradise, the Garden of Eden in the West.[108] The basis for many social problems that were to rise in the following one and a half centuries was laid.

Independent from this Awakening which seems to have had no influence on it,[109] but simultaneously with it, the Episcopal Church, which in 1811 had nearly 15,000

---

[102] Addison, *Episcopal Church*, pp. 76-77. See Ahlstrom, *Religious History*, II, 63-64.

[103] Ahlstrom, *Religious History*, I, 469, sees the beginning of the Second Great Awakening around 1790, whereas McLoughlin, *Revivals*, pp. 10, 98-140, puts the beginning around 1800.

[104] Ahlstrom, *Religious History*, I, 505-07.

[105] Ahlstrom, *Religious History*, I, 525. Cf. pp. 524-28. See Faulkner, *History*, p. 222; McLoughlin, *Revivals*, pp. 126-35.

[106] Ahlstrom, *Religious History*, I, 536.

[107] McLoughlin, *Revivals*, p. 114.

[108] McLoughlin, *Revivals*, pp. 105-06.

[109] Ahlstrom, *Religious History*, II, 63-66, and Edward Clowes Chorley, *Men and Movements in the American Episcopal Church*, The Hale Lectures (1946; rpt. Hamden, CT: Archon Books, 1961), pp. 36-38, 140-

communicants,[110] witnessed in that year the consecration of two of its strongest leaders. Alexander Viets Griswold (1176-1843) was consecrated Bishop for the "Eastern District" (all New England states except Connecticut); John Henry Hobart (1775-1830) was ordained Bishop of New York. Both persons became the strong leaders of church parties whose activities resulted in a renewed vigor and zeal, Griswold directing the Evangelical wing of the church, Hobart the High Church party. The Evangelicals sometimes seemed to almost loose the Anglican distinctiveness in their rapproachment with the other Protestant and Free churches in the states; however, the early Evangelicals in particular treasured the prayer book. Bishop William Meade (1789-1862) of Virginia, a member of this wing, described the *Book of Common Prayer* at the opening of the General Convention in 1838 as "the most perfect of all liturgies" which should "be maintained in its purity and integrity."[111] Bishop Hobart, from the side of the High Churchmen, thought that the prayer book "exhibits the whole system of Evangelical doctrine with unrivalled simplicity, strength, and clearness;" and second only to the Bible it was "the purest source of divine truth and celestial devotion."[112] In those years the 1789 prayer book was open, it seemed, for adoption by both parties, even though they sometimes strongly opposed each other.

The first fifty years of the republic saw not only quite remarkable changes in the political situation, a resurgence of interest in religious questions, and a narrowing outlook on the world for which America was the center; it also saw the emergence of the symptoms and effects of the Industrial Revolution. The United States lagged behind the developments in Great Britain, but by doing so it could also avoid some of the worst effects of social misery of the masses.[113] The factory system cropped up at the end of the eighteenth century, first in the textile industry due to weaving inventions in Great Britain; other production areas were soon to follow. The entire economy, including agriculture, changed gradually but constantly. Whereas human muscles previously had been the movers behind the work, mechanical, steam, and later on electric power were substituted. This could not but affect everyday life in very profound ways. The production of goods shifted from the domestic base to industry, but so did the working places of those earning the living. Factories and industrial production determined the schedule and the basic necessities of life--not the individual home. For the ordinary household, these changes were more important and dramatic than philosophical or intellectual currents, political manoeuvres, or religious questions.

Changes in economics necessitated good and cheap transportation means. Turnpikes between distant places and improved roads were the first attempts since around 1785 to deal with the demand. From 1810 on, canals were built on a grand scale, helped by the progress steamboats had made since 1807.[114] Beginning in 1828, only three years after the first railway opened in Great Britain, railroads were built in the United States. Ten years later, the country could boast of more than 3,000 miles of railroad, forty percent more than the total of Europe. Railroads were playing a major role in the colonization of the West.[115]

56, give no clues as to any direct or indirect visible relation between the Awakening and the resurgence of strong leaders in the Episcopal Church.

[110] Ahlbright, *History*, p. 162.

[111] Chorley, *Men and Movements*, p. 86.

[112] Chorley, *Men and Movements*, p. 191. As to the social and intellectual vision of the High Church party from the early nineteenth century until the Civil War, see Robert Bruce Mullin, *Episcopal Vision / American Reality: High Church Theology and Social Thought in Evangelical America* (London: Yale University Press, 1986).

[113] Faulkner, *History*, pp. 243-60.

[114] May 24 to June 20, 1819, the *Savannah* crossed the Atlantic Ocean (Savannah to Liverpool) as the first steamship, making the passage much more reliable and safe: Richard B. Morris and Jeffrey B. Morris, eds., *Encyclopedia of American History*, Bicentennial ed. (New York: Harper & Row, 1976), p. 602.

[115] In 1803 the size of the United States had more than doubled by the signing of the Louisiana Purchase Treaty in Paris. From 1803 to 1806, Meriwether Lewis and William Clark went on an overland route to the

One of the social results of the Industrial Revolution was the accentuation of class differences. Distinguished classes had existed almost from the beginning of the colonization. But now those with money and a spirit of entrepeneurship could acquire immense wealth by giving work to those who had lost their source of income to the new factories. Before 1835, when a ten hour work limit was instituted, most of the workers labored fourteen hours a day, six days a week, women and children under twelve yers of age not excluded. Modern capitalism was flourishing, and only gradually were some checks against gross misuse introduced.[116]

The first half of the nineteenth century also saw attempts at humanitarian reforms, including the questions around abolishing the slavery system.

The Constitution had been ambiguous about slavery and the rights of both the owners and the slaves.[117] There was a precarious balance of slave-holding and non-slave-holding states, the former in the South, the latter in the North and Northwest. Due to the progress in cotton planting and harvesting and the processing of cotton, there was a growing demand for slaves, and the numbers increased during the first half of the century from nearly 900,000 in 1800 to more than three million slaves in 1850.[118] Slavery found vehement opponents in anti-slavery and abolitionist societies in the North, who were inspired more by the visions of European revolutions and the idea of equality of all humans than by the fate of those suffering from their lot. This abolitionist movement gained momentum in the 1830s. In 1852 Harriet Beecher Stowe published "perhaps the most influential novel ever published,"[119] *Uncle Tom's Cabin*, which was to exercize immense moral pressure upon those advocating slavery, which in turn was matched by increasing intolerance on the side of the slave holders against those attacking them. Adding to the economic problems constituted by the possible abolition of slavery was the moral question of regarding the Blacks as part of the human race. The dominant attitude was one of seeing them as inferior to Whites. The churches "were slow in joining the antislavery cause, but they did most of the pioneering; and as the movement gained momentum the countless auxiliary organizations of mainstream Protestantism became radiating centers of concern and agitation."[120]

There were many more attempts at humanitarian reforms in the first half of the nineteenth century. Prisons, orphanages, and hospitals were converted into institutions where care for the afflicted and humane treatment substituted for leaving the inmates, orphans, and sick to the mercy of their own fate.[121] General and public education for the masses was approved and introduced.[122] From around 1820 on, "women's rights" were advocated. Unlike educational reforms, these demands for a greater role of women in society and in public life met with staunch resistance, especially from Protestant churches. But owing to some influential protagonists of this movement,[123] to a flourishing of ladies' associations in church life which

---

Pacific. In 1834 Nathanael J. Wyeth led an overland expedition from Independence, Missouri, to Fort Vancouver (then Oregon, at present Washington): Morris and Morris, *Encyclopedia*, pp. 602, 607. The gigantic size of the country, seemingly unendable and almost unimaginable, shaped the "American Mind" more than events at the East Coast. "Westwards," "to the Frontier" were cries then. Politicians nowadays invoke the spirit of adventure and of challenge by calling to "New Frontiers." The first massive trek took place in 1842-43 when during the so-called Oregon Fever a great migration to Oregon country took place via the Oregon trail (from Independence, Missouri, to Astoria): Morris and Morris, *Encyclopedia*, p. 608.

116 Faulkner, *History*, pp. 243-60.

117 Constitution, Art. IV,2: Commager, *Documents of American History*, no. 87, p. 144.

118 Wattenberg, *Statistical History*, A 93, p. 14 note 1.

119 J. C. Furnas, *Goodbye to Uncle Tom* (New York: Sloane, 1956), p. 4; quoted in: Ahlstrom, *Religious History*, II, 102.

120 Ahlstrom, *Religious History*, II, 102.

121 Faulkner, *History*, pp. 262-67.

122 Faulkner, *History*, pp. 271-74.

123 See Frances Sizemore Hensley, "Change and Continuity in the American Women's Movement, 1848-1930: A National and State Perspective," Dissertation The Ohio State University 1981.

were an integral part of an active parish, and above all to an increased and better access of women to general and higher education,[124] the crusade gained slow but steady momentum, although it took decades before some of the demands were met. In the meantime, the White Anglo-Saxon Protestant American male poked fun and exhibited anger at the movement which could be described as having an

> intimate connection with all the radical and infidel movements of the day. . . . It is avowedly opposed to the most time-honored proprieties of social life; it is opposed to nature; it is opposed to revelation. . . . In this respect no kindred movement is so decidedly infidel, so rancorously and avowedly antibiblical.[125]

The WASP man thought he could allow himself to be angry at radical women, and to be satisfied with himself. After an economic panic in 1837, the results of which were to be felt until the early 1840s, the following decade was one of the most prosperous and dynamic in the history of the United States. Advancements of the settlement in the West, the migration to Oregon, inventions,[126] and the impact of the gold discovery on January 24, 1848 on the property of Johann Augustus Sutter (1803-1880) which resulted in the famous Gold Rush of 1848/49--all these events resulted in an economic expansion which was unrivaled.[127]

Some of these developments were foressen in an analysis which the French nobleman Alexis de Tocqueville (1805-1859), one of France's foremost historians and political theoreticians, wrote in a diary of his travels throughout the United States in 1831-33; even after 150 years these pages are still a fascinating and superb inquiry into the political and social reality in America.[128]

The years in which De Tocqueville visited the United States saw the rise of the notion that humanity is capable of becoming perfect. The Second Great Awakening had implanted that idea, and it became part of the American understanding of human nature and destiny. Most of the political, economic, and social phenomena could be deducted from this root. De Tocqueville wrote:

> Equality suggests to the human mind several ideas which would not have originated from any other source, and it modifies almost all those previously entertained. I take as an example the idea of human perfectibility, because it is one of the principal notions that the intellect can conceive, and because it constitutes of itself a great philosophical theory, which is everywhere to be traced by its consequences in the conduct of human affairs. Although man has many points of resemblance with the brutes, one is peculiar to himself,--he improves: they are incapable of improvement. Mankind could not fail to discover this difference from the beginning. The idea of perfectibility is therefore as old as the world; equality did not give birth to it, but has imparted to it a new character.
> When the citizens of a community are classed according to rank, profesion, or birth, and when all men are constrained to follow the career which chance has opened before them,

---

[124] In 1821 the first "seminary" for women was opened at Troy, New York; since 1834 Oberlin College was co-educational: Ahlstrom, *Religious History*, II, 85-87; Faulkner, *History*, p. 277. In 1837 the first all-women college at Mount Holyoke was founded. See Tiziana Rota, "Between 'True Women' and 'New Women:' Mount Holyoke Students, 1837 to 1908," Dissertation University of Massachusetts 1983.

[125] *Harper's New Monthly Magazine*, November 1853; quoted in: Faulkner, *History*, p. 277.

[126] On May 24, 1844 a telegraph, which had in principle been developed by Samuel Morse in 1832, was put into operation with a message from Baltimore to Washington, D.C. The era of telecommunication had begun: Morris and Morris, *Encyclopedia*, pp. 608, 794-95.

[127] Carl Landauer, *Sozial- und Wirtschaftsgeschichte der Vereinigten Staaten von Amerika* (Stuttgart: Metzler, 1981), pp. 55-73.

[128] See James Thomas Schleifer, "The Making of Tocqueville's 'Democracy:' Studies in the Development of Alexis de Tocqueville's Work on America with Particular Attention to His Sources, His Ideas and His Methods," Dissertation Yale University 1972.

> every one thinks that the utmost limits of human power are to be discerned in proximity to himself, and no one seeks any longer to resist the inevitable law of his destiny....
>
> In proportion as cases disappear and the classes of society approximate,--as manners, customs, and laws vary, from the tumultuous intercourse of men,--as new facts arise,--as new truths are brought to light,--as ancient opinions are dissipated, and others take their place,--the image of an ideal but always fugitive perfection presents itself to the human mind. Continual changes are then every instant occurring under the observation of every man: the position of some is rendered worse....: the condition of others is improved; when he infers that man is endowed with an indefinite faculty of improvement....
>
> It can hardly be believed how many facts flow from the philosophical theory of the indefinite perfectibility of man, or how strong an influence it exercizes even on those who, living entirely for the purposes of action and not of thought, seem to conform their actions to it, without knowing anything about it.[129]

Again, it was the concept of equality which was responsible for some phenomena that affected the Church's liturgy in general:

> I have shown that nothing is more repugnant to the human mind, in an age of equality, than the idea of subjection to forms. Men living at such times are impatient of figures; to their eyes, symbols appear to be puerile artifices used to conceal or to set off truths which should more naturally be bared to the light of day: they are unmoved by ceremonial observances, and are disposed to attach only a secondary importance to the details of public worship.
>
> Those who have to regulate the external forms of religion in a democratic age should pay a close attention to these natural propensities of the human mind, in order not to run counter to them unnecessarily.[130]

And about "the clergy of every communion" he had the following remark:

> The American ministers of the Gospel do not attempt to draw or to fix all the thoughts of man upon the life to come; they are willing to surrender a portion of his heart to the cares of the present; seeming to consider the goods of this world as important, though secondary, objects.[131]

De Tocqueville's analyses of the underlying ideological currents of his era, of the laws of worship, and of the conduct of clergy can only be marveled at for their depth and their correctness.

The Episcopal Church had steadied. The membership increased from about 12,000 communicants in 1800 to about 30,000 in 1830: one out of every 415 persons in the United States was an Episcopal communicant.[132]

---

[129] *De la démocratie en Amérique*, II, I, viii, éd. Harold Joseph Laski, Oeuvres, papiers et correspondances d'Alexis de Tocqueville, 1,2, 7e éd. (Paris: Gallimard, 1951), pp. 39-40; English translation: *Democracy in America*, abridged and ed. Richard Douglas Heffner, Mentor Book, 2053 (New York: New American Library, 1956), pp. 156-58. For the sake of space and clarity, the reproduction of the French text has been dispensed with in the footnotes dealing with De Tocqueville's travel diary.

[130] II, I, v: *Démocratie en Amérique*, pp. 31-32; English translation: *Democracy in America*, pp. 152-53.

[131] II, I, v: *Démocratie en Amérique*, p. 34; English translation: *Democracy in America*, p. 155.

[132] Piepkorn, "Episcopal Churches," pp. 201, 215; Addison, *Episcopal Church*, p. 74. It represents an increase of 250%, a number roughly equal to that of the general increase of the population (242%). The United States had 5,308,000 residents in 1800, and 12,900,000 in 1830: Wattenberg, *Statistical History*, A 6-8, p. 8.

The Oxford Movement and the Episcopal Church

A year after De Tocqueville had visited the United States, a solemn audience in 1833 listened to a sermon which initiated a movement whose existence and results were to change forever the face and nature of the Anglican Communion. On July 14, 1833 John Keble preached the "Assize Sermon" at St. Mary's, Oxford, concerning what he called "national apostasy," the utter subjection of the Church under the state authorities. The day has commonly been accepted as the birth of the "Oxford Movement."[133]

The time when the movement arose was ripe for an initiative to renew the Church of England; the church leaders, if there were any worthy of that name, had been more or less uninspiring, the worship life dull,[134] and there had been a benign neglect of the moral authority of the Church. Three main roots can be detected for the rise of the Oxford Movement: a constant, albeit sometimes small, current of High Churchmanship in England; the influx of Roman Catholic clergy into Great Britain after the French Revolution; and the English Romanticism which had its first heyday in the 1820s and 1830s.

The last quarter of the eighteenth century and the first quarter of the nineteenth century saw persons who, despite the then current philosophy of Enlightenment, upheld the authority

---

[133] The literature on this movement abounds and is almost impossible to keep up with. A review of the more important literature can be found in German by Teresa Berger, "'Ex umbris et imaginibus...': 150 Jahre Literatur zur Oxford-Bewegung," *Theologische Revue*, 80 (1984), cols. 353-62. The following works are worth of citation here because they have either become standard literature or present notable challenges to commonly accepted interpretations. The account of an eye-witness of, and participation in, the movement has been given by Richard William Church, *The Oxford Movement: Twelve Years, 1833-1845*, introd. and ed. Geoffrey Best, Classics of British Historical Literature (Chicago: University of Chicago Press, 1970). A psychological essay is written by Geoffrey Cust Faber, *Oxford Apostles: A Character Study of the Oxford Movement*, 2nd ed. (London: Faber & Faber, 1974). The theology and liturgical theology of the Tractarians, as they called themselves, is examined from an Anglo-Catholic point of view by Louis Weil, *Sacraments and Liturgy, The Outward Signs: A Study in Liturgical Mentality*, Faith and the Future (Oxford: Blackwell, 1983); from an evangelical standpoint in: Colin Buchanan, ed., *Anglo-Catholic Worship: An Evangelical Appreciation after 150 Years*, Grove Liturgical Study, 33 (Bramcote, Notts.: Grove Books, 1983). Two special items are worthy of mention. The eucharist: Alf Härdelin, *The Tractarian Understanding of the Eucharist*, Acta Universitatis Upsaliensis: Studia Historico-Ecclesiastica Upsaliensia, 8 (Uppsala: Almquist & Wiksells, 1965); the ecumenical outlook: Henry Renaud Turner Brandeth, *Ecumenical Ideas of the Oxford Movement* (London: SPCK, 1947), and Plato Ernest Shaw, *The Early Tractarians and the Eastern Church* (Milwaukee: Morehouse; London: Mowbray, 1930). A short historical and theological introduction in German can be found in Schnitker, "Kirche, Staat und Liturgie," 112-17. A more profound theological and liturgical investigation, from a Protestant point of view, has been written by Teresa Berger, *Liturgie - Spiegel der Kirche: Eine systematisch-theologische Analyse des liturgischen Gedankenguts im Traktarianismus*, Forschungen zur systematischen und ökumenischen Theologie, 52, Dissertation Heidelberg 1984 (Göttingen: Vandenhoeck & Ruprecht, 1986). A thoroughly revisionist history and understanding of the entire movement, which turns out some quite surprising results, has been written by John R. Griffin, "Tractarian Politics," Dissertation Dublin 1972. This thesis has been expanded in several articles in different periodicals; these will be used throughout this section.

[134] Chorley, *Men and Movements*, p. 360, gives an equally dark and amusing picture of the situation in England around 1800: "In England especially the administration of the sacraments was often attended by gross irreverences. On 'Christening Sunday' men and women of the lowest types would hang round the churches ready to act as sponsors in baptism for a pint of beer. Confirmation was seldom administered and was lightly esteemed. A classic story is told of an English bishop who always commenced his address to the candidates by saying, 'This very interesting, and (as I hold it to be) perfectly unobjectionable ceremony in which we have been engaged.' The wife of another bishop, when confirmation was held in the cathedral, always gave a ball as she said: 'It was a pity so many young people should be brought together without having a chance to enjoy themselves,' and an extension of the hours of sale was granted to the beer-shops."

of the Church, maintained a high regard for the liturgy, and supported the notion of catholicity for the Church of England, without any disregard for the other reformed churches. The most prominent among those High Churchmen was Joshua Watson (1771-1855), a lay man. Others included William Jones (1726-1800), a priest; William Stevens (1737-1807), a lay man; Charles Danbeny (1744-1827), an archdeacon; Alexander Know (1757-1831), an Irish lay man; Thomas Sikes (1764-1834), a priest; and William Van Mildert (1765-1836), Bishop of Durham. A special insistence was put on apostolic succession, and the authority of the priesthood; this was regarded as *articulum stantis aut cadentis ecclesiae*.[135]

After the French Revolution, clergymen fled from France to Great Britain to survive the turmoil and slaughter of those years; they gave moral support to the English Roman Catholics and exercized some considerable influence.[136] A wave of sympathy with the Roman Catholic Church and Roman Catholics followed, which in 1791 resulted in the Act for the Relief of Roman Catholics (31 Geo. 3, c. 32) whereby, among other things, it became lawful again to celebrate Mass openly in England.[137] Some time during the early years of the nineteenth century, Charles Lloyd (1784-1829), then Regius Profesor of Divinity at Oxford and later Bishop of Oxford, got acquainted with a group of those French clergymen reciting the breviary at Somers Town, thereby learning of this part of the liturgy. From 1823 on Lloyd held lectures with a private class of divinity students on the history of the *Book of Common Prayer* and its sources. Among those students were John Henry Newman, Robert Wilberforce, Hurrell Froude, and Frederick Oakeley, names which were to become household names some years later as the front line of Tractarianism.[138]

The third and possibly strongest influence on the origin of the Oxford Movement was Romanticism.[139] This was a reaction against the Enlightenment, with its concomitants: deism, which in England was on the descent after 1740, and utilitarianism. The utter death-blow for the Enlightenment philosophy was the terror of the French Revolution, which had been based upon those principles. When the first generation of Romantic poets appeared on the stage in the last fifteen years of the eighteenth century, deism was antiquated. Those English Romantic poets, notably William Blake (1757-1827), William Wordsworth (1770-1850), and Samuel Taylor Coleridge (1772-1834), were violently opposed to deism and rationalism because they shared an enthusiasm for the Bible and John Milton's *Paradise Lost* [1667].[140] God, their conviction was, is not an impersonal principle, reigning untouchable above the world. Humanity is indeed in a sinful state and needs to be redeemed. And the world is not a mechanical instrument running soul-lessly, but with a goal compatible with the divine plan and the final redemption of humanity. Human beings are capable of seeing more than what the eye makes believe. This capacity of perceiving reality is a creation in the sense that human beings create the world in which they live. Transcendental ideas, therefore, are a

---

[135] Francis Warre Cornish, *The English Church in the Nineteenth Century*, A History of the English Church, 8 (London: Macmillan, 1910), I, 62-76.

[136] See Dominic Bellenger, "The English Catholics and the French Exiled Clergy," *Recusant History*, 15 (1981), 433-51.

[137] Moorman, *History*, pp. 312-13; Bernard Clinton Pawley and Margaret Pawley, *Rome and Canterbury through Four Centuries: A Study of the Relations between the Church of Rome and the Anglican Churches 1530-1973* (London: Mowbray, 1974), p. 70.

[138] Pawley and Pawley, *Rome and Canterbury*, pp. 79-80. It is indicated there that Bishop Lloyd expressly acknowledged his acquaintance with the breviary from the French refugee priests, in a speech in the House of Lords, April 2, 1829.

[139] "The historian today, as he looks back upon the movement over more than a century of time, can view it in a larger perspective than either the political or the theological. Seen thus it appears as an aspect of the general cultural renaissance denoted by the word romanticism. Newman himself, in the Apologia [1864], spoke of 'a spirit afloat' thirty years previously.": Bernard M. G. Reardon, *From Coleridge to Gore: A Century of Religious Thought in Britain* (London: Longman, 1971), p. 92.

[140] John Clubbe and Earnest J. Lovell, *English Romanticism: The Grounds of Belief* (DeKalb, IL: Northern Illinois University Press, 1983), pp. 79-80.

part of the world. Creative perception is also ethical: as it transcends visible cognition, it means a sameness and kinship in all human beings. After all, as the Bible and *Paradise Lost* tell, everyone is a fallen creature, in a state of separation and absence of love for others, and in need of redemption but, because of a share in the divine nature, also capable of it. All these aspects, the visual-creative, the ethical, and the resulting religious one, are bound to elicit a response in the persons to be devout or worshipful towards the God who is the guiding spirit behind all nature of which humanity is a part.[141] One of those poets, Samuel Taylor Coleridge, must be mentioned in particular as he was acknowledged as one of the more prominent influences on John Henry Newman and, by the reaffirmation of the sacramentality and divine origin of the Church, as one who prepared the way for the ecclesiology of the Oxford Movement.[142]

The men who in the aftermath of the Assize Sermon on July 14, 1833 came together quickly realized their mission and, by way of the "Tracts for the Times," spread their ideas. These tracts, published between September 9, 1833 and January 25, 1841, were rather small pamphlets in the beginning but grew into lengthy treatises; some were published anonymously, others signed with the author's name. Through 1841, seven volumes appeared under the editorship of John Henry Newman (1801-1890), who from the beginning was regarded as the undisputed leader of the movement; this ended with his conversion to the Roman Catholic Church on October 9, 1845.[143]

The more profound theological purpose of the movement was clearly expressed in the advertisement for the first volume of the collected Tracts which appeared in 1834. Newman, the unacknowledged editor, wrote:

> The following Tracts were published with the object of contributing something towards the practical revival of doctrines, which, although held by the great divines of our Church, at present have become obsolete with the majority of her members, and are withdrawn from public view even by the more learned and orthodox few who still adhere to them.[144]

Those doctrines in mind are the apostolic succession of the bishops and priests and, by implication, the dignity and duty of these offices and those who bear them; and the catholicity of the Church, which includes a deepened insight into the tradition of the Church. These two doctrines were the hinges and the formal principles of the movement out of which all other ideals and deeds flowed.[145] Newman added:

> Had he [the member of the Church] been taught as a child, that the Sacraments, not preaching, are the sources of Divine Grace; that the Apostolic ministry had a virtue in it which went out over the whole Church, when sought by the prayer of faith; that fellowship with it was a gift and privilege, as well as a duty, we could not have had so many wanderers from our fold, nor so many cold hearts within it.[146]

The Church had to fulfill a divine commission, to make visible the presence of the invisible God to His people. But this commission could not be discharged of in a church that was based on erastianism. Fundamental policies of the Church of England were questioned and

---

[141] Clubbe and Lovell, *English Romanticism*, pp. 2-3, 80-82, 148, 150.

[142] John Coulson, "Coleridge, Samuel Taylor," *Theologische Realenzyklopädie* 8, pp. 152-53. See Richard Charles Allen, "The Habits of the Soul: Samuel Taylor Coleridge's Religious Thought and Its Background, 1794-1798," Dissertation University of Notre Dame 1980.

[143] Reardon, *From Coleridge to Gore*, pp. 87-88.

[144] *In Tracts for the Times*, by Members of the University of Oxford, Vol. I for 1833-34 (London: Rivington; Oxford: Parker, 1834), p. iii.

[145] Almost every publication on the movement deals with this premise so that another discussion of these principles here is deemed unnecessary.

[146] "Advertisement," p. iv.

fought against.[147] The Church was catholic, not erastian. And the Church comprised not only the upper-class gentlemen but all laity; therefore, it was the duty of the bishops and priests to care for all members and not for the privileged only.[148]

The catholicity of the Church was the basis, too, for the discussion of liturgical matters, as liturgy could not be severed from a sound understanding of the Church's nature and purpose. In Tract 34, "Rites and Customs of the Church," published on May 1, 1834, Newman applied the principle of the apostolicity and catholicity of the Church to the worship life:

> Rites and Ordinances, far from being unmeaning, are in their nature capable of impressing our memories and imaginations with the great revealed verities; far from being superstitious, are expressly sanctioned in Scripture as to their principle, and delivered to the Church in their form by tradition.[149]

The esteem for the value of those observances and customs, lost in the Church of England, had to be retrieved lest a serious defect remain.[150]

The best expression of the character and value of the liturgy was written by Isaac Williams (1802-1865) in 1840 as Tract 86, titled "Indications of a Superintending Providence in the Preservation of the Prayer Book and in the Changes it has undergone." The worship life of the Church, he said, was ordered with the aid of divine assistance and was conducted in the presence of God; all forms would take their value from this reality:

> If, as St. Augustin [sic] maintains, the same Spirit, which was in the Prophets when they spoke, was in the translators of the Septuagint when they interpreted, expressing the same things differently, in the same manner that He does by different Prophets in Scripture, and omitting, or adding, or altering, as best suited the wisdom of His purpose; so also the omissions and additions and alterations in our own Liturgy, we may reverently trust, were ordered by the same Spirit under whose control the first rites of Catholic worship were ordained. For if the presence of Christ still continues in His Church, in what circumstances can we conceive His divine control to be more exerted than in regulating these changes? For rituals and forms of prayer, however unimportant in human eyes, assume a very high character and value when considered as the appointed means of access from man to God; as methods of approach to Him, which He has Himself provided, and of which we are bound to make use,-- for as individuals we have no choice;--as moreover objects of sacred association to which the

---

147 John R. Griffin, "The Anglican Politics of Cardinal Newman," *Anglican Theological Review*, 55 (1973), 442; John R. Griffin, "Dr. Pusey and the Oxford Movement," *Historical Magazine of the Protestant Episcopal Church*, 42 (1973), 139; John R. Griffin, "The Oxford Movement: A Revision," *Faith and Reason*, 4 (1979), 26, 33; John R. Griffin, "The Social Implications of the Oxford Movement," *Historical Magazine of the Protestant Episcopal Church*, 44 (1975), 157, 165.

148 Newman has been called "the great (and almost solitary) champion of the laity in the nineteenth century.": Griffin, "Anglican Politics," 440. Richard Hurrell Froude (1803-1836), Newman, and other members went so far as to ask of the bishops to accept the ideal of a Church which would identify with the poor, thereby alienating the rich and noble. Froude advocated part-time priests from the lower classes: "The notion that a priest must be a gentleman is a stupid exclusive protestant fancy, and ought to be exploded.": *The Remains of Richard Hurrell Froude*, ed. by Friends (London: Rivington, 1838), I, 373-74. The business of the clergy was to identify with the laity, and especially with the lower classes. This demanded of the clergy a lifestyle of complete poverty as sign of an "apostolic" or genuine vocation, of which celibacy was a part. It was certainly in the intention of these advocates of a social consciousness of the Church that almost all worker-priests in England in the second half of the nineteenth century were avowed adherents of the Oxford Movement.: Ralph William Franklin, "Pusey and Worship in Industrial Society," *Worship*, 57 (1983), 388-89, 393, 397, 402; Griffin, "Anglican Politics," 443; Griffin, "Social Implications," 156, 158-61.

149 In *Tracts for the Times*, by Members of the University of Oxford, Vol. I for 1833-34 (London: Rivington; Oxford: Parker, 1834), Tract 34, p. 7.

150 Newman, "Rites and Customs of the Church," pp. 7-8.

affections of good men will naturally become attached from use, and the more attached the
better they are; as instruments, however mean in man's estimation, which serve as vehicles
through which virtue and healing go forth from Christ to restore our soul's maladies; as
moulds of thought and expression to those suits which, in the majestic words of Hooker, "the
Almighty doth there sit to hear, and angels, intermingled as associates, attend to further."

This consideration will afford a high value and importance to many changes in themselves
apparently trivial; and it must be remembered that the lessons of Divine wisdom are often
written in the very smallest characters, and that it is not from single letters or syllables, but
from the combinationn of them, when carefully put together, that those lessons are to be
understood.[151]

The reforms of the liturgy in the course of the English Reformation were seen as falling short of this high esteem, without, however, extinguishing the divine presence in the life of the Church:

Though in tracing historically these alterations, external circumstances were not such as we
could have wished or approve, yet that notwithstanding there has resided in the Church a
Divine Life, a power of assimilating, and converting, and turning into nourishment, he-
terogeneous, and often hurtful substances. And thence it has happened that notwithstanding
the worldly influences to which she has been subject, the King's Daughter, though she has
passed through the fire, has been in misfortune, and is in captivity, yet, under all changes, is
still "glorious within," and "her clothing of wrought gold." . . .

The first point which I would wish to show is, that through these alterations there runs one
prevailing tendency, to put into our mouths the language of servants rather than that of sons.
Now, though it may be a matter of doubt whether the Reformation was in all respects what the
name imparts, or whether it was brought about in general by motives of sincere repentance,
yet it must be allowed that it was a call to repentance on the part of God, a call to the Church
to return to her first love and repent; and that it was on the part of man a profession of
repentance.[152]

The general tone and spirit of the English prayer book was said to be one of humiliation, repentance, and sinfulness; the American prayer book, in William's view, would be only slightly better. In the offices of the English prayer book, baptism would be characterized by a "deep and humbling tone of mortification." The omission of anointing at baptism and confirmation would run against the "primitive, universal, and, possibly, apostolical" practice.[153]

The tone for the whole Ritualist Movement in the wake of the later Oxford Movement, when matters of liturgical detail dominated the discussion and the ideals of the first generation Tractarians were neglected or abandoned,[154] was set when Williams wrote in Tract 86: "In Christianity there is no such thing as a merely external and significative rite without being in some degree sacramental also."[155]

Edward Bouverie Pusey (1800-1882), who later lent his name to the movement but whose views often did not correspond with the aims of the first generation members,[156] wrote

---

[151] In *Tracts for the Times*, by Members of the University of Oxford, Vol. V for 1838-40 (London: Rivington; Oxford: Parker, 1840), Tract 86, pp. 7-8.

[152] Williams, "Indications of a Superintending Providence," p. 9.

[153] Williams, "Indications of a Superintending Providence," pp. 19-23, 27-29, 57.

[154] When the resistance of the bishops against the Oxford Movement grew, especially after the (in)famous Tract 90 by Newman, the obedience to the bishops was given up by the adherents and followers, a remarkable reversal of the implication of apostolic succession. See Griffin, "Oxford Movement," 121-27.

[155] Williams, "Indications of a Superintending Providence," p. 28.

[156] Pusey differed in theological and political questions with the other members, up to around 1850. On erastianism, episcopacy, and the Reformation he held quite the opposite opinions. Newman later charged him

Tract 67 on "Scriptural Views of Holy Baptism as established by the consent of the ancient Church, and contrasted with the systems of modern schools." In it he argued that justification came by faith, but through baptism. He strongly defended the idea of baptismal regeneration as a new principle of life imparted to us through and in baptism which would be also, at the same time, the incorporation into Christ. But the operation of it would be a mystery and not up to us to know.[157]

The Tracts came to an abrupt end, and the movement was very much discredited in the eyes of most of the spectators, even those who had stood aside or had entertained some sympathy for the cause, when on January 25, 1841[158] Newman published as Tract 90 his "Remarks on Certain Passages in the Thirty-Nine Articles." Fear about the very existence of the Church of England arose, and the protests against his ideas prevented a serious discussion of them. Newman had intended

> to show that, while our Prayer Book is acknowledged on all hands to be of Catholic origin, our Articles also, the offspring of an uncatholic age, are, through God's good providence, to say the least, not uncatholic, and may be subscribed by those who aim at being catholic in heart and doctrine.[159]

The arguments employed by Newman mostly rested on the weak premise that the Thirty-Nine Articles, based on the Forty-Two Articles of 1553 and published in 1563, could be reconciled with the decrees and pronouncements of the Council of Trent, and were all but convincing. He drew some conclusions which would be relevant to liturgical matters too; of course, as the previous discussion by Newman had suffered from his bias, so, too, were the conclusions unbalanced.

> It is a duty which we owe both to the Catholic Church and to our own, to take our reformed confessions in the most Catholic sense they will admit; we have duties towards their framers. In giving the Articles a Catholic interpretation, we bring them into harmony with the Book of Common Prayer, an object of the most serious moment in those who have given their assent to both formularies. . . .
> Anglo-Catholics then are but the successors and representatives of those moderate reformers.[160]

After the debâcle of this last of the Tracts, Newman parted company with the other prominent members of the movement, disillusioned, disappointed, and insulted. His conversion to the Roman Catholic Church on October 9, 1845 was the end of the Oxford Movement.

During the earlier years of the movement there appears to have been little notice of the Tracts in the Episcopal Church. Stimulated by some positive response, however, an American edition was published in 1839 with a surprisingly large circulation.[161] Gradually a party spirit arose, and supporters and opponents of the Tracts rallied together. The Evangelicals strongly rejected the publications and the underlying theology as tendencies to

---

with creating a "party" in the church, something Newman, Froude, Williams, and the others never had had in their minds. See Griffin, "Dr. Pusey," 138, 141, 143, 146, 151.

[157] In *Tracts for the Times*, by Members of the University of Oxford, Vol. II, part II for 1834-35, 4th ed. (London: Rivington; Oxford: Parker, 1842), Tract 67, pp. 20-24. See Weil, *Sacraments and Liturgy*, pp. 45-49. Newman applied even stronger words in the "Catena Patrum. No. II: Testimony of Writers in the Later English Church to the Doctrine of Baptismal Regeneration," in *Tracts for the Times*, by Members of the University of Oxford, Vol. III for 1835-36, new ed. (London: Rivington; Oxford: Parker, 1840), Tract 76.

[158] Again, the highly symbolic feastday of the Conversion of St. Paul.

[159] In *Tracts for the Times*, by Members of the University of Oxford, Vol. VI for 1840-41 (London: Rivington; Oxford: Parker, 1841), Tract 90, p. 4.

[160] Newman, "Remarks on Certain Passages," pp. 80-91.

[161] Ahlbright, *History*, p. 230; Chorley, *Men and Movements*, pp. 195-98.

Romanize the Episcopal Church. These fears gained strength after Tract 90 had appeared, and opposition was very heavy.[162] The supporters of the ideals of the movement scored on one important point: at the General Theological Seminary in New York, erected in 1817 as a supra-diocesan training institution for the clergy, with the House of Bishops as the canonical visitor, the Oxford theology was taken "very seriously;"[163] and only after a close scrutiny of all the faculty members and students did the seminary receive a controversial clean bill of health from the visitors in 1844.

The General Convention of 1844 in Philadelphia devoted four full days to the discussion of Tractarianism, at a time when the quarrels surrounding it were at their height. Both parties had in the meantime set up their own papers and periodicals; and the Evangelicals in particular had tried to strengthen their position by erecting, in addition to the journals, societies for education, and two independent missionary societies. The House of Deputies at that 1844 General Convention put forward a resolution which was adopted almost unanimously:

> Resolved, That the House of Clerical and Lay Deputies, consider the liturgy, offices and Articles of the Church sufficient exponents of her sense of the essential doctrines of Holy Scripture; and that the Canons of the Church afford ample means of discipline and correction for all who depart from her standards; and further, that the General Convention is not a suitable tribunal for the trial and censure of, and that the Church is not responsible for, the errors of individuals, whether they are members of the Church or otherwise.[164]

In essence a judgment on the validity of the Oxford theology was not passed but an irenic note stricken. The bishops, however, spoke out against the adoption of any Romish doctrine, in a Pastoral Letter issued at the same convention.

Naturally there were converts to the Roman Catholic Church, but far fewer left the Episcopal Church than the Church of England. It has been computed that of the 1,976 clergy affected by the controversies, twenty-nine, or one and a half percent, changed their allegiance to the Church of Rome; nineteen of these were ordained in the 1840s. Four of these twenty-nine eventually returned to the Episcopal Church. The most prominent convert was Levi Silliman Ives (1797-1867), a former convert from Presbyterianism who had become Bishop of North Carolina and who left for the Roman Church in 1852.[165]

Gradually ritualism was substituted for a discussion of the underlying principles of the Oxford Movement in the Episcopal Church, too. But the immediate effect within the church was a sharp division along party lines. Essential differences between the High Churchmen and the Evangelicals were clarified and heightened. At the same time, amidst the "open warfare,"[166] increasing tolerance was seen for a variety of interpretations of theological principles as long as they were confined within the acknowledged significance of the Bible, the *Book of Common Prayer*, and the full range of Anglican tradition. "Hereafter there would be less concern about enforcing conformity in either doctrine or practice, and only the attempts of minorities to bend the entire church to their points of view would lead to major crises."[167]

Little by little, some effects could be observed on the liturgy which, due to the sacramental viewpoint of the Tractarians and their followers, gained an increased interest. Holy communion became a weekly instead of an infrequent and irregular celebration. Church buildings were more carefully erected with an eye on the different parts of the Church's liturgy. It is obvious that this could not in many instances happen without heavy opposition.

---

[162] Ahlbright, *History*, pp. 233-36; Chorley, *Men and Movements*, pp. 201-05.

[163] Chorley, *Men and Movements*, p. 206. See Ahlbright, *History*, pp. 236-39; Chorley, *Men and Movements*, pp. 209-17.

[164] Ahlbright, *History*, pp. 239-40. See Chorley, *Men and Movements*, pp. 220-21.

[165] Ahlbright, *History*, pp. 243-44; Chorley, *Men and Movements*, pp. 224-27, 228-34.

[166] Chorley, *Men and Movements*, p. 224.

[167] Ahlbright, *History*, p. 245.

One major consequence of a heightened esteem of the liturgy was a concern for high moral standards among the laity and clergy. Parishes with enriched ritual nearly always succeeded in reaching out to the common working man and were in the forefront of the struggle for social justice for those exploited or taken advantage of in the labor process. They helped to break down "the inherited alliance of wealth and social position with the Episcopal Church."[168]

William Augustus Muhlenberg and the Muhlenberg Memorial

One of the persons influenced by Tractarianism without being a strict adherent to it was William Augustus Muhlenberg (1796-1877), grandson of the "patriarch of American Lutheranism," Henry Melchior Muhlenberg (1711-1787).[169] He combined an esteem for a dignified liturgy with a deeply ecumenical outlook and a profound concern for social responsibility within the Church.

In 1836 Muhlenberg published *Hints on Catholic Union* in which he proposed a plan for a confederation of the major American Protestant churches; this would be achieved through an expanded use of the Apostles' Creed, an ordination formula that would be used by all bodies, the use of common prayers, hymns, and liturgical readings, and a council of common affairs.[170] For three years, from 1851 to 1853, he was the editor of the *Evangelical Catholic*, a weekly, later a monthly, periodical which was devoted to fostering genuine unity among the churches based on an all-encompassing catholicity and the Evangelical principles of the importance of Scripture, faith, and justification.[171]

In 1852 he founded a deaconess society, in 1865 he set up the Sisterhood of St. Mary, with the approval of the diocesan bishop.[172] It was the first religious order for women in the Anglican Communion after the Reformation. In 1857 he founded St. Luke's Hospital in New York, where he became the pastor-superintendent. In these foundations, in his assignments at a boys' school in Flushing, New York, in 1836, and later in the Church of the Holy Communion he established in New York City in 1846, he systematically combined liturgy and social justice. He placed an emphasis on good singing, color, and the church year together with the central position of the weekly Sunday eucharist and daily Morning and Evening Prayer.[173]

---

[168] Ahlbright, *History*, p. 248. Cf. pp. 245-48. For the same phenomenon in Great Britain, see Franklin, "Pusey," 388-90, 393-97.

[169] In 1872 Muhlenberg wrote a statement of his ecclesiastical position in which he declared, among other things, "I was never a High Churchman. Receiving my theology from Bishop White, the Apostolic Succession and Sacramentarian doctrine were alike foreign to my system--if I ever had a system; but I have been claimed by High Churchmen because of my Liturgic, or what would be now called Ritualistic, propensities, or, to use another word--aesthetic. . . . When the 'Tracts for the Times' appeared, I was much interested in them, and still more in Mr. Newman's sermons. These, I must confess, captivated me. I read them frequently in the chapel of St. Paul's College, and frankly acknowledge that for some three years, I might have been classed among the Puseyites. Yet, how radically wanting I was in my system, may be judged from the fact that I never received the doctrine of Baptismal Regeneration. . . . Then I began to see that its logical results were Romanism; and from that, if it were the truth, I would not shrink. . . . Mr. Newman's 'Doctrine of Development,' [1845] fully opened my eyes. I well remember, how, having read half through the book, I tossed it from me, explaining, 'My soul is escaped as a bird from the snare of the fowler.'[Ps 124:6]": Anne Ayres, *The Life and Work of William Augustus Muhlenberg* (New York: Harper, 1881), pp. 171-73.

[170] Ahlbright, *History*, p. 270.

[171] Ayres, *Muhlenberg*, pp. 236-49.

[172] See Mary Sudman Donovan, "Women's Ministries in the Episcopal Church, 1850-1920," Dissertation Columbia University 1985.

[173] Chorley, *Men and Movements*, pp. 257, 362-63.

Unity among Christians, the Church's concern for an outreach to all those entrusted to its care, including the lower half of the social stratum, and care for the significance and celebration of the liturgy were the determining factors in a memorial which he and a number of supporters presented to the bishops at the General Convention of 1853 in New York. In the long run, this so-called Muhlenberg Memorial initiated a new consciousness of the Episcopal Church in ecumenical and liturgical matters. The undersigners observed and asked:

> The actual posture of our church with reference to the great moral and social necessities of the day, presents to the mind of the undersigned a subject of grave and anxious thought. . . . The divided state of our American Protestant Christianity, . . . and . . . the utter ignorance of the Gospel among so large a portion of the lower classes of our population, making a heathen world in our midst, are among the considerations which induce your Memorialists to present the inquiry whether the period has not arrived for the adoption of measures, to meet these exigencies of the times, more comprehensive than any yet provided for by our present ecclesiastical system: in other words, whether the Protestant Episcopal Church, with only her present canonical means and appliances, her fixed and invariable modes of public worship, and her traditional customs and usages, is competent to the work of preaching and dispensing the Gospel to all sorts and conditions of men, and so adequate to do the work of the Lord in this land and in this age?[174]

They proposed the admission to the ordination for those affiliated with other churches, provided these men could be absolved from following all even unessential particulars, including all miniscule liturgical regulations. The Episcopal Church, in other words, was perceived by the memorialists as the ultimately one national Church for all non-Roman Catholics, thus effecting "a Church unity in the Protestant Christendom of our land." The memorial went on:

> This leads your petitioners to declare the ultimate design of their Memorial--which is to submit the practicability, under your auspices, of some ecclesiastical system, broader and more comprehensive than that which you now administer, surrounding and including the Protestant Episcopal Church as it now is, leaving that church untouched, identical with that church in all its great principles, yet providing for as much freedom in opinion, discipline, and worship, as is compatible with the essential faith and order of the Gospel. To define and act upon such a system, it is believed, must sooner or later be the work of an American Catholic Episcopate.[175]

The short-term effect of this memorial was the establishment of a committee to look into the matter and to make recommendations to the next General Convention. When this was held in Philadelphia in 1856, the bishops, acting on the committee's report, approved a resolution concerning liturgical regulations that

---

[174] Ayres, *Muhlenberg*, pp. 263-64; Charles C. Tiffany, *A History of the Protestant Episcopal Church in the United States of America*, The American Church History Series, 7 (New York: Christian Literature Company, 1895), p. 573.

[175] Ayres, *Muhlenberg*, p. 266; Tiffany, *History*, p. 574. See Edward Rochie Hardy, "Evangelical Catholicism: W. A. Muhlenberg and his Memorial Movement," *Historical Magazine of the Protestant Episcopal Church*, 12 (1944), 155-92. The designation of the bishops as "American Catholic Episcopate" seems to have been highly unusual at that time for persons not devoted to Tractarianism. In the immediately preceding paragraph, the bishops were addressed as "your venerable body as a college of *Catholic and Apostolic Bishops*" [emphasis in the original text]. The Memorial was directed to them; therefore, the petitioners would have tried to appeal to those theological qualities the bishops saw as their possession.

on special occasions, or at extraordinary services, not otherwise provided for, ministers may, at their discretion, use such parts of the Book of Common Prayer, and such lesson or lessons from Holy Scripture, as shall, in their judgment, tend most to edification.[176]

This was deemed by the bishops to be sufficient as a response compatible with the urgency of the request, and appropriate for a Church which had grown from a communion membership of 30,000 in 1830 to about 100,000 in 1850.[177]

Social and Ecclesiastical Life in the Second Half of the Nineteenth Century

The 1850s were a decade of extraordinary economic development, due to an expansion of transportation facilities and refined production processes. It was also the decade with the second greatest percentage of increase in the population. In 1850 the United States counted 23,191,000 residents; in 1860 this number had grown to 31,443,000.[178] Of these, around fifteen percent were Blacks.[179] From the mid-1840s to the mid-1850s, moreover, two large immigration waves from Germany and Ireland arrived. Whereas the real causes for the almost a million Germans are unknown, the almost 1,300,000 Irish were driven by the exceptionally poor potato harvests and the consequent devastating hunger.[180]

The following decade saw the first and only civil war in the United States. From April 1861 to May 1865, troops of the Union, the northern and western states, fought against troops of the Confederate States, those states that had withdrawn from the United States and proclaimed themselves the Confederate States on February 4, 1861. The North aimed at the restoration of the Union and, if possible, the freeing of the slaves; the South fought for the recognition of the independence and sovereignty of the Confederacy. During those years most of the churches split along the political lines. From 1861 to 1865, the Episcopal Church in the South was a separate body. But from November 1865 on, all the dioceses represented therein were received, with no punitive action, in the parent body again. There were no long-lasting wounds, unlike circumstances in other churches and denominations.[181]

When the war ended, the losses had been heavy. More than 350,000 soldiers were dead in the Union forces, more than 275,000 wounded. In the Confederate forces, more than 250,000 soldiers had died, and more than 100,000 were wounded. More than one-third of both armies were casualties. It was a triple defeat for the South. The army had lost the war. The Union was restored, and several amendments to the Constitution abolished slavery and all legal inferiority of the Black population in all states of the Union.[182] The result was an economic breakdown in the South, and the social fabric of society had to readjust to the new situation. Work on the cotton and tobacco fields went on, however, after a short slump.[183] Many former slaves now were regular laborers and wage earners. For the economy in the North, the civil war was almost a stroke of luck. The production of clothing and shoes, and later of other products, too, shifted from small manufacturing units to factories. "Business"

---

[176] Quoted in: Addison, *Episcopal Church*, p. 185; Detscher, *Evolution*, p. 227.

[177] There were about 1,500 clergymen in 1850. The ratio of the communicant membership to the entire population in the United States: in 1830: 1 to 415; in 1850: 1 to 235: Piepkorn, "Episcopal Churches," pp. 202, 215.

[178] Wattenberg, *Statistical History*, A 1-5, p. 8. The percentage of increase was 35.6, only 0.3% lower than the highest percentage which was reached in the preceding decade.

[179] Wattenberg, *Statistical History*, A 91-104, p. 14.

[180] Wattenberg, *Statistical History*, C 92, 95, p. 106; Landauer, *Sozial- und Wirtschaftsgeschichte*, p. 75.

[181] Ahlstrom, *Religious History*, II, 116-48; Ahlbright, *History*, pp. 252-59.

[182] Amendments 13-15, attaining legal force in 1865, 1868, and 1870: Commager, *Documents of American History*, no. 87, pp. 147-48.

[183] Wattenberg, *Statistical History*, K 554, 562, p. 518.

became associated with "Big Business," and the 1860s saw an overall capitalist consolidation and large-scale speculation.[184]

The quarter of a century after the civil war was a hectic period of constant change even for the ordinary citizens, as they had to adapt to altered economic conditions, shiftings in production processes, the influence of important technical inventions and innovations, and the mental effects of an ever-increasing standing of the United States as an economic power of the first order. These developments were aggravated by an immigration wave of almost incomprehensible measure.

"Boom" and "prosperity" were the catchwords of the day, and the old as well as new industries (oil, steel) were rapidly expanding. Urbanization was achieved in large steps. Within the four decades 1860-1900, the percentage of those living in urban territory doubled from twenty to about forty percent.[185] Against the exploitation by the factory owners and employers, laborers and workers began to organize, at first with little success, but in 1886 the American Federation of Labor was established.[186] After the civil war, farming and agriculture gradually changed with the introduction of machinery. Some inventions, at first sight of little significance, were bound to have a tremendous impact on the economy. In 1867 the first practical typewriter was developed; in 1876 Alexander Graham Bell invented the telephone, and a year later the first intercity telephone lines were connected. In 1879 Thomas Alva Edison built the first practical incandescent bulb, a product which was to change forever everyday life and the entire economic process in most profound ways. Beginning in the 1880s, electricity was generated on a larger scale. That period also saw the birth and rise of supermarkets and chain stores. At the end of the century, life had changed more drastically during the previous four decades than during the centuries before.

Gradually the frontier in the West was closed. In 1858 mail service was inaugurated to California; in 1861 the first telegraph message from San Francisco was received in Washington; in 1869 California and Nebraska were joined by railroad, and the next year the first transcontinental railroad trip was made from Boston to Oakland; other important railroad links were to follow. In 1890 the Superintendent of the Census pronounced the closing of the frontier, with it one of the greatest forces for molding the American ethics and mind had come to an end.[187]

The latter half of the nineteenth century saw a major challenge to all aspects of life by the influx of more than 16,000,000 immigrants to the United States, more than ninety-five

---

[184] Faulkner, *History*, pp. 360-66; Landauer, *Sozial- und Wirtschaftsgeschichte*, p. 86.

[185] 1860: 19.77%; 1870: 25.68%; 1880: 28.17%; 1890: 35.11%; 1900: 39.68%: Wattenberg, *Statistical History*, A 57-72, pp. 11-12.

[186] Landauer, *Sozial- und Wirtschaftsgeschichte*, pp. 102, 114, 124, 126.

[187] Faulkner, *History*, pp. 430-32; Landauer, *Sozial- und Wirtschaftsgeschichte*, pp. 89-90; Morris and Morris, *Encyclopedia*, pp. 610-13, 615, 794, 796. In 1893 Frederick Jackson Turner read a paper before the American Historical Association on "The Significance of the Frontier in American History." He rejected the common view that American culture and institutions were an extension of European principles and put forth the idea that it was the frontier westwards which in effect had shaped the entire American civilization. Effects of this frontier would be a common nationality, legislation and democratic institutions, paper money, intellectual traits, etc. As to the last category, he said: "To the frontier the American intellect owes its striking characteristics. That coarseness and strength combined with acuteness and inquisitiveness; that practical, inventive turn of mind, quick to find expedients; that masterful grasp of material things, lacking in the artistic but powerful to effect great ends; that restless, nervous energy; that dominant individualism, working for good and for evil; and withal that buoyancy and exuberance which comes with freedom--these are traits of the frontier, or traits called out elsewhere because of the existence of the frontier. . . . He would be a rash prophet who would assert that the expansive character of American life has now entirely ceased. Movement has been its dominant fact, and, unless this training has no effect upon a people, the American energy will continually demand a wider field for its exercise.": Quoted in: Richard Douglas Heffner, *A Documentary History of the United States* (Bloomington: Indiana University Press, 1952), p. 177; the entire paper is excerpted, pp. 169-77. The importance of the frontier experience has been commonly accepted afterwards.

percent from Europe.[188] During this wave the countries of origin gradually shifted from northwestern and central Europe to eastern and southern Europe, a development that was bound to add a peculiarly explosive tint to the responses by some American groups which feared the loss of the WASP identity: White, Anglo-Saxon, Protestant.[189]

During all these years the Episcopal Church faced struggles within its own confines and set landmarks which determined its further cause.

The Oxford Movement had advanced into a second stage in which ritual details, ceremonial, gothic church structure, and cathedrals[190] had taken prominence over theological questions. The controversy surrounding the introduction of many ceremonies which were regarded as Romish threatened to widen the chasm between the High Churchmen and the Evangelicals. The General Conventions of 1868, 1871, and 1874 dealt at length with these problems. Finally a canon was added to the constitution regulating the ceremonial to be used, especially during the celebration of holy communion.[191] But the canon ultimately failed to check the growing adherence to a more elaborate ritual.

Theologically the Evangelicals pressed for more liberty in the use of the prayer book and for the elimination of references to opinions they thought not agreeable to Scripture. In support of their demands mass rallies were held, petitions were signed to the General Conventions, and heavy verbal battles were fought. The major point of strife was the issue of regeneration in the baptismal office. As regeneration was thought of as meaning an instantaneous moral change in the infant at baptism, to which the Evangelicals objected, they demanded liberty to omit references to it while administering baptism, and in general to teach their rejection of regeneration as in agreement with the church position on it. The bishops present at the General Convention in Baltimore in 1871 were forced to issue a statement declaring that in their opinion the word "regenerate" and "regeneration" in the office of baptism of infants "is not there so used as to determine that a moral change in the subject of baptism is wrought in the recipient."[192]

Eventually this issue, together with some others upheld by the Evangelicals, figured as the main reason for a schism in the church and establishment of the Reformed Episcopal Church in 1873. This group adopted the *Proposed Book of Common Prayer* of 1786 as their own because in it all those doctrines they condemned had been left out, and it was, therefore, very much suited to their theology and church policy.[193]

The solution to the problems would have been for both sides to demand a prayer book revision along the lines of their particular predilections and interests. But this seemed to be dangerous, as the losses might have outweighed the gains. The momentum for revision built up by the Muhlenberg Memorial of 1853 had waned. It took another initiative to start the process, and this time it was linked to the name of William Reed Huntington (1838-1909). In the House of Deputies to which he was delegated from 1871 until 1907, he was as bold and courageous a leader as could have been wished for. Like Muhlenberg he had a broad vision of the Church's mission and was active in social, ecumenical, and liturgical fields. In 1871 he sponsored a motion to introduce in the Episcopal Church the order of deaconnesses, which was finally approved at the General Convention in 1889. During his tenure as rector of Grace Church, New York City, from 1883 to 1909, he continued or instituted various social programs specifically destined for an inner-city parish.[194] In 1870 his long public work for

---

[188] Between 1851 and 1900, 16,659,406 immigrants were counted. The following two decades between 1901 and 1920, another 14,531,197 immigrants arrived: Wattenberg, *Statistical History*, C 89-90, pp. 105-06.

[189] Ahlstrom, *Religious History*, II, 330-34.

[190] The first American Episcopal cathedral was that in Chicago, elevated from the rank of a parish church to that dignity in 1861: Ahlbright, *History*, pp. 292-93.

[191] Chorley, *Men and Movements*, pp. 359-92.

[192] Chorley, *Men and Movements*, p. 409.

[193] Ahlbright, *History*, pp. 285-87; Chorley, *Men and Movements*, pp. 405-22.

[194] Ahlbright, *History*, pp. 310, 318.

Christian unity began. He published the first of his major books on that theme. The same year he laid down in a sermon that Christian unity can, and should be, achieved by holding up the four essential principles on which the Church was founded: the Scriptures as the Word of God; the Apostles' and Nicene Creeds as the expression and rule of faith; baptism and the Lord's Supper as the two sacraments ordained by Christ; the episcopate as the key stone of governmental unity. He regarded the acceptance of these four points as sufficient for establishing church unity; no particular form of worship or uniformity was called for in a thus united church. These four points appeared in a report of the Committee on Christian Unity to the House of Bishops at the 1886 General Convention in Chicago. This committee, established after the presentation of the Muhlenberg Memorial of 1853, traced the concern for unity among the Christians to that Memorial. The four points, proposed by Huntington in 1870 and introduced by the committee in 1886, were adopted by the General Convention and became known as the Chicago Quadrilateral.[195]

The Book of Common Prayer 1892

At the 1874 General Convention in New York, William Reed Huntington, who was a delegate for the first time, boldly called for a complete revision of the *Book of Common Prayer*; but this plea failed. At the 1880 General Convention in New York, however, he repeated his proposal that a committee be formed which should consider "certain alterations in the *Book of Common Prayer* in the direction of liturgical enrichment and increased flexibility of use."[196] The appointed committee stood under the leadership of Huntington himself and met three times between 1880 and 1883. It prepared a special edition of the prayer book with the proposed changes to be discussed by the next Convention. This the 1883 General Convention in Philadelphia did; on the last evening it authorized the republication of the proposed book, together with the changes made by the Convention, with the final action to be taken in 1886. When the ensuing book appeared in 1885 it was much critized publicly. Twenty-eight dioceses moved not to accept the proposed book. At the General Convention in 1886 in Chicago, Huntington himself eloquently defended a certain Americanization of the book, reminiscent of the "paradise" tradition in "God's own country:"

> If ... by Americanism ... be meant any departure from that standard of pure and wholesome English set forth to be the perpetual heritage of the people of our blood, in King James' Bible and in the *Book of Common Prayer*, if that be what is meant by Americanism, then I say again I will have no pity on it. ... But if ... by Americanism be meant a keen appreciation of those features of our national life that are confessedly unique, extraordinary and unparalleled, if by

---

[195] Ahlbright, *History*, pp. 271, 347; Hatchett, *Commentary*, p. 558; John F. Woolverton, "W. R. Huntington: *Liturgical Renewal and Church Unity in the 1880s*," Anglican Theological Review, 42 (1966), 187-94. Two years later, the third Lambeth Conference, called as a meeting of all bishops of the Anglican Communion by the then Archbishop of Canterbury, Edward White Benson, slightly revised the text and made it the precondition and sufficient basis for "Home Reunion." Since that time, it has been affirmed over and over again as the Anglican position on this question. The "Lambeth Quadrilateral" of 1888 reads: "That, in the opinion of this Conference, the following Articles supply a basis on which approach may be by God's blessing made towards Home Reunion: (a) The Holy Scriptures of the Old and New Testaments, as 'containing all things necessary to salvation,' and as being the rule and ultimate standard of faith. (b) The Apostles' Creed, as the Baptismal Symbol; and the Nicene Creed, as the sufficient statement of the Christian faith. (c) The two Sacraments ordained by Christ Himself--Baptism and the Supper of the Lord--ministered with unfailing use of Christ's words of institution, and of the elements ordained by Him. (d) The Historic Episcopate, locally adapted in the methods of its administration to the varying needs of the nations and peoples called of God into the Unity of His Church.": *Book of Common Prayer 1979*, pp. 877-78. The Chicago Quadrilateral is printed pp. 876-77.

[196] Quoted in: Detscher, *Evolution*, p. 228.

Americanism be meant sympathy with those longings of the national mind and heart for a better unity, which some think God has planned, which problems some think God has Himself especially solved in this land between the oceans, why, then, I say that the only criticism which can be passed upon the Committee of Revision of the American Common Prayer Book is that it did not lack "Americanism."[197]

The proposed book, however, was defeated, and the committee discharged. A new committee was established, this time without the membership of Huntington. Its report to the 1889 General Convention in New York was accepted; a list of the changes was sent to the dioceses as required by the constitution. After the ratification by the dioceses the new *Book of Common Prayer* was definitely approved at the General Convention in Baltimore on October 21, 1892.[198]

The title of the book, which is identical with the previous one of 1789, is indicative of the fact that only minor changes had been introduced in the liturgy of the Episcopal Church.

The ratification and preface were *verbatim* taken over from the 1789 prayer book.[199] Added to this material was a short section "Concerning the Service of the Church" spelling out the permission first granted at the General Convention of 1856, to use the hitherto joined orders of Morning Prayer, litany, and communion as distinct services, and the repetition of setting forth special forms of worship if necessary.[200]

The "Order for the Administration of the Lord's Supper or Holy Communion" was almost identical to the one adopted in 1789.[201] The decalogue could be limited to recitation once a month only, in this case substituted by the summary of the law. The Nicene Creed was printed within the order at its appropriate place after the gospel. The two long exhortations about the next day of the celebration of holy communion and about the frequency and negligence of receiving it, respectively, needed not be read anymore--after almost three and a half centuries a relief from two tedious and certainly not overly rousing texts. The exhortation about the nature of receiving holy communion needed be recited once a month only.

The "Ministration of Public Baptism of Infants, To be used in the Church" had one rubrical addition about the people remaining standing until the Lord's Prayer; otherwise it was identical with the 1789 rite.[202]

The same was true for the "Ministration of Baptism to such as are of Riper Years and able to answer for themselves." At the end of this order a rubric governing the conditional baptism of a person and the ensuing formula were given.[203]

The "Order of Confirmation, Or Laying on of Hands upon those who are baptized, and come to Years of Discretion" had been amended.[204] A presentation of the candidates, without an individual roll-call, had been added after the initial exhortation about the character and merits of confirmation. It was followed by the reading of Acts 8:14-17, the traditional rationale for the reservation of the administration of confirmation to the bishop. The last rubric about the admittance to communion after confirmation, or the desire for confirmation, was now preceded by another rubric admonishing the minister "earnestly" to move the persons who had been confirmed, to come, "without delay," to communion. Both rubrics together tried to establish a sound eucharistic practice.

---

[197] *The Churchman*, October 16, 1886, p. 456; quoted in: Woolverton, "Huntington," 185.

[198] Addison, *Episcopal Church*, p. 226; Ahlbright, *History*, pp. 296-97; Detscher, *Evolution*, pp. 228-40; Sydnor, *Real Prayer Book*, pp. 61-65; Woolverton, "Huntington," 180-85.

[199] McGarvey, *Liturgiae Americanae*, pp. 6-32.

[200] McGarvey, *Liturgiae Americanae*, p. 34.

[201] McGarvey, *Liturgiae Americanae*, pp. 212-56.

[202] McGarvey, *Liturgiae Americanae*, pp. 258-72.

[203] McGarvey, *Liturgiae Americanae*, pp. 282-96.

[204] McGarvey, *Liturgiae Americanae*, pp. 306-12.

This revision had not been a thorough one which, given the strongly conservative mood of the delegates, it could not be unless old wounds should break open again and new party strife would begin. But at least it relieved the burden of too many exhortations to be read and listened to at too many occasions, thereby giving the celebrations more flow. Making Morning Prayer, litany, and communion distinctive liturgies enabled those attending to appreciate the different nature of each of them. But a certain uneasiness remained whether this new *Book of Common Prayer* was the answer of the Episcopal Church to the demands for more flexibility and concern for the conditions of those the Church was sent to in its mission. These feelings of a shortcoming gradually won the upper hand, and thirty-six years later another revised *Book of Common Prayer* was adopted.

Social and Ecclesiastical Life at the Turn of the Century

On the surface the United States was the epitome of growth without limit, the land of boundless possibilities. The catchword of the day was prosperity. In 1900 the population had increased to 76,094,000 people,[205] forty percent of whom lived in urban territory.[206] Life had become more comfortable for city dwellers due to technical innovations, many of which affected the work at home for the housewives; the conditions of everyday life improved, at least for those belonging to the middle class. They could enjoy rapidly increasing educational facilities; newspapers and magazines were founded.[207] It was in those days that the vast economic empires of such household names as Rockefeller, Vanderbilt, Carnegie, and Mellon were built up or cemented. This could happen because of the "bright sky of laissez-faire capitalism"[208] at the turn of the century. One-tenth of the population owned nine-tenth of the personal wealth, accumulated at the cost of the exploitation of both common labor of the workers and the material resources of the country. The period around the turn of the century was

> an age of aggressiveness, of unbridled acquisitiveness, of coarseness and vulgarity, when concern for the traditional principles of public and private morality had been supplanted by the worship of Mammon. . . . [The] extravagant visions of personal gain [of the business leaders] were seldom beclouded with concern for the welfare of their laborers or the many weaker competitors whom they pitylessly destroyed by fair means or foul.[209]

Bribery of politicians at every level of government was normal. Checks against this monopolization of power by way of legislation or court judgment were rendered impossible. It was a question of "Social Darwinism," of the survival of the fittest, not impeded by anybody or anything but helped by government assistance.

In 1889 Andrew Carnegie (1835-1919) wrote *The Gospel of Wealth*, a publication summarizing with precision and consistency the ideas of those adhering to this "Social Darwinism."

> The contrast between the palace of the millionaire and the cottage of the laborer with us today measures the change which has come with civilization. This change, however, is not to be deplored, but welcomed as highly beneficial. It is well, nay, essential for the progress of the race, that the houses of some should be homes for all that is highest and best in literature and the arts, and for all the refinements of civilization, rather than none should be so.

---

[205] Wattenberg, *Statistical History*, A 6-7, p. 8.
[206] Wattenberg, *Statistical History*, A 57-72, p. 11.
[207] Faulkner, *History*, pp. 471-80.
[208] Faulkner, *History*, p. 548.
[209] Heffner, *History*, pp. 155-56.

....
The price which society pays for the law of competition, like the price it pays for cheap comforts and luxuries, is also great; but the advantages of this law are also greater still, for it is to this law that we owe our wonderful material development, which brings improved conditions in its train. But, whether the law be benign or not, we must say of it, as say of the change in the conditions of men to which we have referred: It is here; we cannot evade it; no substitutes for it have been found; and while the law may be sometimes hard for the individual, it is best for the race, because it ensures the survival of the fittest in every department. We accept and welcome, therefore, as conditions to which we must accommodate ourselves, great inequality of environment, the concentration of business, industrial and commercial, in the hands of a few, and the law of competition between these, as being not only beneficial, but essential for the future progress of the race.

....
One who studies this subject will soon be brought face to face with the conclusion that upon the sacredness of property civilization itself depends--the right of the laborer to his hundred dollars in the savings bank, and equally the legal right of the millionaire to his millions.

....
We might as well urge the destruction of the highest existing type of man because he failed to reach our ideal as to favor the destruction of Individualism, Private Property, the Law of Accumulation of Wealth, and the Law of Competition; for these are the highest results of human experience, the soil in which society so far has produced the best fruit. Unequally or unjustly, perhaps, as these laws sometimes operate, and imperfect as they appear to the Idealist, they are, nevertheless, like the highest type of man, the best and most valuable of all that humanity has yet accomplished.

....
Those who would administer [surplus wealth] wisely must, indeed, be wise, for one of the serious obstacles to the improvement of our race is indiscriminate charity. It were better for mankind that the millions of the rich were thrown into the sea than so spent as to encourage the slothful, the drunken, the unworthy. Of every thousand dollars spent in so-called charity today, it is probable that $950 is unwisely spent; so spent, indeed, as to produce the very evils which it proposes to mitigate or cure.

....
Such, in my opinion, is the true Gospel concerning Wealth, obedience to which is destined some day to solve the problem of the Rich and the Poor, and to bring "Peace on earth, among men Good Will."[210]

To his (partial) exoneration it must be said that Carnegie spent more than 300 million dollars on philanthropic projects (libraries, universities, etc.).

At first some individuals, and then later on churches, ecclesiastical organizations, and interdenominational institutions, raised their voices not against wealth in itself or the advancement of productivity in the industry but against the excesses of the "Gilded Age" of uncontrolled accumulation of riches at the expense of human exploitation. They tried to advance a code of ethics that combined entrepreneurship with Christian social responsibility towards those dependent on the employers. This response has from the beginning been known as "Social Gospel."[211]

---

[210] Andrew Carnegie, *The Gospel of Wealth* (London: Hagen, 1889); excerpted in: Heffner, *History*, pp. 158-65; quotations: pp. 158-59, 160, 161, 164, 165.

[211] Ahlstrom, *Religious History*, II, 250-73. Some literature: Richard B. Dressner, "Christian Socialism: A Response to Industrial America in the Progressive Era," Dissertation Cornell University 1972; Charles Howard Hopkins, "The Rise of Social Christianity in American Protestantism 1865-1912," 2 vols., Dissertation Yale University 1937; William R. Hutchinson, "The Americanness of the Social Gospel: An Inquiry in Comparative History," *Church History*, 44 (1975), 367-81; Susan Curtis Mernitz, "The Disintegration of Faith: The Social

This theological school too had some of its roots in American millenialism. Human nature, it was presupposed, is capable of perfectibility; if the evil forces would be destroyed, God's purpose with humanity could be brought to shine in His chosen people, the Americans. Yet in order to have as many Americans as possible participate in this glory, the social forces that worked against these prospects and against the dignity of human beings would have to be controlled and corrected. Christian ethics had to be directed towards the task of giving everybody, the rich as well as the poor, a share in this hope. And most representatives went further and said, a share also in the material goods of the possessing class. The Social Gospel was at the same time an economic theory, a theological school, and an attempt to transform their own ideas into living reality.

Its moral message consisted almost exclusively in applications, mild or severe, of the idea that the doctrine of laissez faire required Christian modifications. The Iron Law of Wages so dear to classical economics must be qualified by the Great Commandment. Between employer and employee brutality and conflict must yield to compassion and mutual respect.[212]

To this extent a great number of organizations, projects, and publications were launched, but because the vast majority of American Protestants was rather conservative theologically, it took until the first two decades of the twentieth century before the worst grievances were remedied. Particularly powerful in his advocacy of the Social Gospel was Walter Rauschenbusch (1861-1918)[213] who in 1907 published his most famous book *Christianity and the Social Crisis*, which became the standard work for the ideas of this incarnation of Christian ethics. Other outstanding representatives of the Social Gospel were Washington Gladden (1836-1918), Francis Greenwood Peabody (1847-1936), and Josiah Strong (1846-1916). Within the Episcopal Church three organizations were founded between 1887 and 1911 to help bring about an improvement in the lot of the workers. They were later absorbed by official church commissions or other organizational forms.[214]

Even at the end of the first decade of the twentieth century, the average wage for American workers was less than two dollars a day, and more than two-thirds of the adult male workers failed to earn six hundred dollars a year, the living minimum for a family.[215] The astonishing lack of industrial action, strikes, or massive resistance against these inhumane conditions may psychologically have been due to xenophobia, a fear of social climbing by those masses from southern and eastern Europe that constituted more than half of all immigrants far into the second decade of the twentieth century.[216] Thus employers could control those who had the work but no adequate wages; the millions of immigrants, as was known, would take any work they could get.

A hitherto unimaginable economic expansion, technical revolutions, scientific discoveries, xenophobia, a rapidly increasing urbanization, the closing of the frontier--all these were contributing factors to the idea that the traditional "American way of life" was eroding, giving way to something both uncontrollable and dangerous for the society at large

---

Gospel and Modern American Culture," Dissertation University of Missouri-Columbia 1986; Robert Scott Miller, "Business and Labor: The Social Gospel View," Dissertation University of Kentucky 1973; Joseph Howard Walsh, "Protestant Response to Materialism in American Life, 1865-1900," Dissertation Columbia University 1974. The underlying *geistesgeschichtliche* ideas of the Social Gospel have been well described by Janet Forsythe Fishburn, *The Fatherhood of God and the Victorian Family: The Social Gospel in America*, Dissertation The Pennsylvania State University 1978 (Philadelphia: Fortress, 1981).

[212] Ahlstrom, *Religious History*, II, 252.
[213] See David Alan McClintock, "Walter Rauschenbusch: The Kingdom of God and the American Experience," Dissertation Case Western Reserve University 1975.
[214] Ahlbright, *History*, pp. 314-16.
[215] Faulkner, *History*, p. 512; Wattenberg, *Statistical History*, D 739-93, pp. 166-68.
[216] Wattenberg, *Statistical History*, C 89-101, p. 105.

and the individual.[217] The cultural confusion was only thinly drowned by the humming of the factories. But at the core of it lay

> the fear that science (formerly considered the expositor of God's law of creation) had become the enemy of God's law. Evolution and the naturalistic, pragmatic philosophy of the "new social science"--particularly the behaviorist and Freudian psychological theories--seemed to undermine the whole basis of Christian faith as the romantic evangelists understood it.[218]

The revivalists who took up those fears and had a clear-cut answer to it did so by expressing the feelings of Big Business: Fear God, do not complain, work as you are told, and God will bless you--sooner or later. It was not by accident that the big revival meetings of the most prominent preachers in this crusade, Dwight Lyman Moody (1837-1899) and William ("Billy") Ashley Sunday (1863-1935), were financed by businessmen and those who had interest in the soothing message of both preachers. Moody was particularly popular between 1875 and 1885; Sunday had his triumphs between 1905 and 1920. Both were the torchbearers of the old fundamentalism and Protestant work ethics. Their appeal was greatest among the middle-class, and Sunday especially had no problem demanding the closing of most Protestant churches when he was in town so that the congregations could come to the "revival tabernacles" which held 15,000 to 20,000 people at a time. It was a perfect "revival machinery"[219] which turned Christianity into "something dulcet and sentimental."[220]

The answer to the challenges of the traditional faith came from different corners: the liberal theology which had its heyday then in the United States and which was nourished by, and in turn nourished, a historically critical exegesis of the Bible; scientists who tried to explain the real meaning of the discoveries beyond the simplistic and false allegations by Fundamentalists; and the advocates of the Social Gospel. For some churches the reaction to the clash between the traditional belief in creation, in God's omnipotence and purpose, in the inerrancy of the Bible and the scientific, theological, and social developments at the turn of the century was a strife for their own survival, for their adherence to the hitherto accepted answers or the openness for new responses to old questions. The Fundamentalistic induration of some Protestant churches to the present time has its roots in insecurity about their answers to these challenges.[221]

There were no outstanding names around which those trying to reconcile the dilemma could rally, as the solution to the problems came from several angles. But the basic answer was clear:

> The old perfectionism and free will of Romantic Evangelicalism protrayed man as unconditioned by nature, unbound by contingencies of heredity and environment, and capable of miraculous power over all obstacles in personal or social reformation. But the new light of this Third Awakening described God's power as locked into nature's laws. Even with God's help men could not leap over nature or culture to challenge the "realities" of life as it is.[222]

As to the Episcopal Church, two parties proved to be crucial for a relatively smooth acceptance of the new realities and ideas, the Broad Churchmen, and, following the lead by the Tractarians and the social concern they and their disciples showed, the Anglo-Catholics.

---

[217] Again, the basis for this section is McLoughlin, *Revivals*, pp. 141-78. Not every historian agrees with McLoughlin to call this the Third Great Awakening. For example, Ahlstrom, *Religious History*, II, 201-07, speaks of a revival of fundamental middle-class Christian ideas and leaves the dispute between natural sciences and theology out of this context: II, 229-34.

[218] McLoughlin, *Revivals*, p. 146.

[219] McLoughlin, *Revivals*, p. 146.

[220] Ahlstrom, *Religious History*, II, 203.

[221] The infamous "Monkey Trial" of 1925, in which John Thomas Scopes was indicted for teaching evolution contrary to the state laws of Tennessee, is only the most widely known example of Fundamentalist intransigence. See Ahlstrom, *Religious History*, II, 274-97, 395-403, esp. 397-98.

[222] McLoughlin, *Revivals*, p. 156.

The Broad Churchmen saw themselves as embodying the Anglican tradition of comprehensiveness and inclusiveness. "Truth is truth, however and whencesoever obtained, and we can never have occasion to be either afraid of it or unthankful for it," was a programmatic statement William Reed Huntington made at a meeting of the Church Congress, an annual assembly of Broad Churchmen, in 1875.[223] They succeeded in keeping the Church's mind open for the challenges of science and scholarly interpretations and receptive to the problems a rapidly changing world posed for the faithful.

Another serious attempt to cope with these questions and to propose answers happened in 1887 when a book appeared which was bound to stir the Church of England and to a slightly lesser, nonetheless profound, degree the entire Anglican Communion. The writers were "a group of young teachers of theology who felt a common discipleship towards the Tractarian Movement, and a common desire to grapple with the intellectual questions which Christians were having to face at the time."[224] These men tried to offer a solution to the problems technical innovations, scientific discoveries, cultural trends, and political decisions posed, in the light of the central Christian dogma, the Incarnation, the belief in the Logos who was at work in creation and was still present so that even those things that seemed to run counter to the Christian faith could be seen not as inimical to it but as shedding new light on it. The preface to this book, *Lux Mundi*, written by the Anglo-Catholic Charles Gore (1853-1932)[225] outlined the purpose rather modestly:

> to put the Catholic faith into its right relation to modern intellectual and moral problems; . . .
> to present positively the central ideas and principles of religion, in the light of contemporary thought and current problems.[226]

Among the contributions to the book the one essay that became the turning point for the acceptance of modern scholarly investigations by the church was Gore's own article "The Holy Spirit and Inspiration."[227] In it Gore set out that the Holy Spirit was working through the whole of creation as well as upon the Christian society and the individual soul. The revelation made by Christ fulfilled all the foreshadows in natural and human history without having to reject what worth would be in them. Whereas the fullness of truth would be in Christ, insight into truth could be afforded by other positions, too. As to the Old Testament and the question of verbal inspiration, Gore accepted that there were elements of idealism, dramatic composition, and primitive myths in the narratives and the poetry, yet they would not be an obstacle to regarding the Old Testament as revealing God's intentions with His chosen people. Scientific inquiry and literary analysis would not be to the detriment of belief, and there would be no final conflict between matters of faith and the conclusions of knowledge.[228]

To the many critics who had accused him of selling the faith out to reason and science, Gore replied in the preface to the tenth edition of the book in 1888. The object, he wrote, of the essay on the Holy Spirit and the inspiration was "to give to anxious enquirers . . . a freedom in regard to Old Testament problems as wide as the Catholic faith seemed to

---

[223] Quoted in: Ahlbright, *History*, p. 307. Cf. pp. 305-11.

[224] Arthur Michael Ramsey, *From Gore to Temple: The Development of Anglican Theology between Lux Mundi and the Second World War 1889-1939*, The Hale Memorial Lectures of Seabury-Western Theological Seminary, 1959 (London: Longmans, Green & Co., 1960), p. 2.

[225] See Bernard M. G. Reardon, "Gore, Charles," *Theologische Realenzyklopädie* 13, pp. 586-88.

[226] In *Lux Mundi: A Series of Studies in the Religion of the Incarnation*, ed. Charles Gore, 14th ed. (London: Murray, 1895), pp. vii-viii.

[227] Reardon, *From Coleridge to Gore*, pp. 433-44.

[228] "The Holy Spirit and Inspiration," in *Lux Mundi: A Series of Studies in the Religion of the Incarnation*, ed. Charles Gore, 14th ed. (London: Murray, 1895), pp. 230-66.

warrant."[229] As for the New Testament, critical investigation, he said, would be reassuring "in asserting the historical truth of the records on which our Christian faith rests."[230]

The contributors to *Lux Mundi* now became "the dominant influence in Anglican divinity;" more particularly, Charles Gore was the driving force behind the next forty years of theological life of the church.[231]

One year after the publication of *Lux Mundi* which, however, seems not to have featured prominently at the assembly discussions, and four years prior to the adoption of the 1892 *Book of Common Prayer*, the then Archbishop of Canterbury, Edward White Benson, called in 1888 the third Lambeth Conference, a meeting of all bishops of the Anglican Communion. This gathering took up the issue of the prayer book as one of the more prominent subjects. In their Encyclical Letter the bishops recognized the *Book of Common Prayer* as "standard of doctrine and worship alike . . ., the special heritage of the Church of England, and, to a greater or lesser extent, received by all the Churches of our Communion."[232] Among the resolutions adopted by the bishops was one that was more or less openly directed at the then current revision process of the prayer book in the Episcopal Church:

> That, inasmuch as the *Book of Common Prayer* is not the possession of one Diocese or Province, but of all, and that a revision in one portion of the Anglican Communion must therefore be extensively felt, this Conference is of opinion that no particular portion of the Church should undertake revision without seriously considering the possible effect of such action on other branches of the Church.[233]

This resolution was in turn based upon the report of the committee of the conference on mutual relations that had declared:

> The attention of the Committee has been further directed to the danger of important divergencies with regards to matter of doctrine, as well as forms of worship, being introduced amongst the Anglican Churches by the possible assumption on the part of each Province or Diocese of the power of revising the *Book of Common Prayer*. Such divergencies might be injurious to the Church at large, and would certainly interfere with the mutual relations of its different parts.
>
> It is not within the province of the committee to lay down rules as to the powers of the different branches of the Anglican Communion in this matter, or as to the line of action which they ought to follow. This remark applies with especial emphasis to the Episcopal Church of America, though the Committee cannot abstain from remarking with pleasure that recent changes in the Book of Common Prayer by that Church have been rather in the direction of nearer approach to the English Book than of further departure from it.[234]

As the Lambeth Conference has no legislative power on its own and the possible adoption of its proposals and resolutions rests solely in their intrinsic value and/or potential for

---

[229] In *Lux Mundi: A Series of Studies in the Religion of the Incarnation*, ed. Charles Gore, 14th ed. (London: Murray, 1895), p. xiv.

[230] "Preface to the Tenth Edition," in *Lux Mundi: A Series of Studies in the Religion of the Incarnation*, ed. Charles Gore, 14th ed. (London: Murray, 1895), p. xxviii.

[231] Ramsey, *From Gore to Temple*, pp. 11, 13.

[232] Lambeth Conference, *Conference of Bishops of the Anglican Communion, Holden at Lambeth Palace, in July 1888: Encyclical Letter from the Bishops, With the Resolutions and Reports* (London: SPCK, 1888), pp. 18-19.

[233] *Lambeth Conference 1888*, p. 24. The following Resolution has become famous as the "Lambeth Quadrilateral."

[234] *Lambeth Conference 1888*, p. 74. The reference to "recent changes" in the last sentence is rather curious: the changes proposed by the revising committee in 1883 and 1886 were not officially adopted and incorporated into the prayer book yet; and to call the revision of 1789 "recent," after ninety-nine years, simply is wrong linguistic usage.

realization, no legal force was given to the unexpressed underlying idea that the prayer book of each province might be revised only by the authority of the entire Anglican Communion, the 1662 *Book of Common Prayer* of the Church of England being the standard. This relative independence of each province in matters of worship was accepted by the committee on authoritative standards when it declared in its report that the prayer book would not be "an indispensable condition of intercommunion" that should be everywhere accepted in its "original form."[235]

The next Lambeth Conference, presided over in July 1897 by Archbishop Frederick Temple of Canterbury, reaffirmed that

> [t]he *Book of Common Prayer*, next to the Bible itself, is the authoritative standard of the doctrine of the Anglican Communion. The great doctrines of the Faith are there clearly set forth in their true relative proportion.[236]

Within this context of a value system, it was understandable that adaptations would be possible within limits only as the doctrine of the Church would be immediately touched upon.[237] The power of each bishop to adapt prayer book services to local circumstances without affecting "the doctrinal teaching or value of the Service or passage thus affected" was accepted.[238] This possibility was a consequence of the bishops' "ius liturgicum . . . which, by the Common Law of the Church, belongs to their office."[239]

Thirty years before this Conference had assembled, in 1867, the United States had bought Alaska and the Aleutian Islands from Russia. As a consequence an episcopal see was transferred by the Holy Russian Synod from the Alaskan town of Sitka to San Francisco. In 1862 the General Convention of the Episcopal Church had established a "Russo-Greek Committee" which was to seek ways of communication with the Russian Orthodox Church. Subsequent negotiations between the committee and representatives of the Russian Synod brought no final conclusions. In 1868 the Ecumenical Patriarch Gregory VI granted that Anglicans dying in Eastern countries be given a Christian burial by Orthodox clergy and be buried in Orthodox cemeteries. The General Convention of 1871 extended the Russo-Greek Committee.[240] In 1904 the Russian Orthodox Archbishop of North America, Tikhon, made a formal inquiry to the Russian Synod as to the procedure to be followed if and when Episcopal clergymen and congregations wished to be received into the Russian Orthodox Church. He was particularly interested to know whether they might be permitted to continue using the *Book of Common Prayer* for their services. A special commission, appointed by the Russian Synod, looked into the matter and made a detailed analysis of the 1892 prayer book. The findings were published in Russian in 1904.[241] In 1917 an English translation was made available in the prestigious Alcuin Club Tracts series, edited by the famous and very influential liturgiologist Walter Howard Frere, who himself had been a member of a group of Anglican bishops and clergy which accompanied a parliamentary delegation from Great Britain to Russia in 1912. Frere had given lectures on the life of the Anglican Churches during that trip in which he had made an "impressive vindication of the Catholic claims of the

---

[235] *Lambeth Conference 1888*, p. 109. The committee however did not declare what was understood by the "original form," which might be that of 1549 or 1662.

[236] "Encyclical Letter," in Lambeth Conference, *Conference of Bishops of the Anglican Communion, Holden at Lambeth Palace, in July 1897: Encyclical Letter from the Bishops, With the Resolutions and Reports* (London: SPCK, 1897), p. 21.

[237] *Lambeth Conference 1897*, pp. 21-22.

[238] *Lambeth Conference 1897*, pp. 44-45.

[239] *Lambeth Conference 1897*, p. 149.

[240] Georges Vasilievich Florovsky, "The Orthodox Churches and the Ecumenical Movement prior to 1910," in *A History of the Ecumenical Movement 1517-1948*, ed. Ruth Rouse and Stephen Charles Neill (London: SPCK, 1954), pp. 202-05.

[241] Florovsky, "Orthodox Churches," p. 212.

Anglican Communion."[242] The influence of the English version is difficult to assess, as the report seems not to have been quoted in later official reports regarding the prayer book and prayer book revision. Yet it can be assumed that the American liturgists and those concerned with the *Book of Common Prayer* and its revision have certainly read it.

Among other things, the report of the commission of the Russian Synod dealt with the communion service, the ministration of baptism, and the confirmation service.

In the scrutiny of the "Order for the Administration of the Lord's Supper, or Holy Communion,"[243] the epiclesis over the gifts "to bless and sanctify with thy Word and Holy Spirit these thy gifts of bread and wine," and over the communicants "that we receiving them according to thy Son our Saviour Jesus Christ's holy institution, in remembrance of his death and passion may be partakers of his most blessed Body and Blood," were viewed as unsatisfactory expressions of the belief in the change of the elements into the Body and Blood of Christ. The Anglican eucharist also was not regarded as a sacrifice for the living and the dead, according to these observations. The eucharistic doctrine, especially on the change of the elements, of the Episcopal Church as expressed in the *Book of Common Prayer* was seen "as being in variance with the whole Church on this question, and as belonging to a Church which in its symbolic literature and in its catechism confesses a doctrine which is clearly protestant."[244]

The criticism of the "Rite of Ministration of Baptism" dealt with the omission of exorcisms, the permission to omit the signing with the cross on the forehead, the omission of anointing with holy oil, the permission to have the parents serve as sponsors, and the permission to use aspersion as the method of administering the sacrament.[245] All these particulars were disapproved of as nonconsistent with ancient and Orthodox usage. But it was conceded that

> the sufficiency in general and in essence of the Form of the Sacrament of Baptism which is found in the Common Prayer Book is assumed by the fact that the validity of Anglican Baptism is acknowledged by the Orthodox Russian Church.[246]

The "Service of Confirmation"[247] underwent heavy and serious critique due to the lack of the anointing and of the recitation of the ensuing formula:

> This omission of anointing, together with the omission of the Catholic formula, entirely harmonizes with the dogmatic theories of the Anglicans, which deny to confirmation the significance of an effectual sacrament.[248]

According to these observations it was absolutely necessary to introduce the anointing with oil and to advance the administration of this sacrament by the presbyter to a position immediately after baptism, together with infant communion, as in the practice of the Eastern churches.

A prominent place was given to the complaint that the Anglican Services in general, and that of the communion in particular, lacked

> any confession of faith in a living and real bond existing between the earthly and heavenly parts of the Church.... The Common Prayer Book, however, in praying for others, prays only for the living, as though the dead were already beyond the Church's range.[249]

---

[242] Florovsky, "Orthodox Churches," p. 213.
[243] Walter Howard Frere, ed., *Russian Observations upon the American Prayer Book*, trans. Wilfrid J. Barnes, Alcuin Club Tracts, 12 (London: Mowbray; Milwaukee: Young Churchman Co., 1917), pp. 2-7.
[244] Frere, *Russian Observations*, p. 7.
[245] Frere, *Russian Observations*, pp. 21-23.
[246] Frere, *Russian Observations*, p. 21.
[247] Frere, *Russian Observations*, pp. 23-25.
[248] Frere, *Russian Observations*, p. 24.
[249] Frere, *Russian Observations*, pp. 29-30.

The absence of prayers and hymns to the saints ought to be amended by introducing them into the worship in some form or degree.250

The final verdict was a strong-worded statement almost dealing more with Anglicanism in general than with the American prayer book:

> The examination of the "Book of Common Prayer" leads to the general conclusion that its actual contents present very little comparatively that clearly contradicts Orthodox teaching, and therefore would not be admissible in Orthodox worship. But this conclusion comes not from the fact that the book is actually Orthodox, but merely from the fact that it was compiled in a spirit of compromise, and that, while skilfully evading all more or less debateable points of doctrine, it endeavours to reconcile tendencies which are really contradictory. Consequently both those who profess protestantism and their opponents can alike use it with a quiet conscience. But worship which is so indefinite and colourless (in its denominational bearing) cannot, of course, be accepted as satisfactory for sons of the Orthodox Church, who are not afraid of their confession of faith, and still less for sons who have only just joined the Orthodox Church from Anglicanism. If it were, their prayer would not be a full expression of their new beliefs, such as it ought essentially to be.251

The church, at the time when the Observations were originally published in Russian, had grown to a communicant membership of about 800,000, with 5,000 clergymen; in 1910 the membership was more than 930,000. In 1920 the membership was counted not in numbers of communicants but of all baptized persons; the magic number of one million members had been passed, and in 1930 the church counted more than 1,200,000 baptized.252

Social and Ecclesiastical Life from the Turn of the Century to 1928

The years from the turn of the century to 1928, the year of the final acceptance of a new *Book of Common Prayer* of the Episcopal Church, were a period of ever-increasingly rapid changes, elated hopes, troublesome experiences of war, and, in general, a period of most contradictory data.

In 1903 "Kitty Hawk" initiated a new era: Orville and Wilbur Wright succeeded in the first jumps through the air in their aeroplane. Humanity had acquired wings, and flying was added to the means of transportation. In 1906 Reginald A. Fessender introduced an improved model for voice transmitting on the radio. In 1915 telephone connections were installed between New York and San Francisco. At the end of this period two remarkable feats demonstrated the rapid advancement of technology. In 1927 Charles A. Lindbergh went on the first transatlantic nonstop flight. And New York was connected to Washington, D.C. in the first television transmission.253

The United States became an itinerant country. In 1900 8,000 automobiles were registered; in 1910 458,300; in 1920: 8,131,500; and in 1929 21,362,000 cars were owned, which means that one car was registered for almost every five persons in the country.254

A lot of household improvements made life easier for everybody, especially the housewife. The percentage of homes with electric service rose from eight in 1907 to sixty-

---

250 Frere, *Russian Observations*, pp. 30-31.
251 Frere, *Russian Observations*, p. 34.
252 Piepkorn, "Episcopal Churches," pp. 204, 215.
253 Morris and Morris, *Encyclopedia*, pp. 615-16, 797-99.
254 Wattenberg, *Statistical History*, Q 152, p. 716; A 7, p. 8. As of 1900, 76,094,000 people lived in the United States. In 1910 the number had increased to 92,407,000. In 1915 the one hundred million landmark was surpassed: 100,546,000. In 1920 106,461,000 people were estimated. And in 1928 120,509,000 people lived in the United States: Wattenberg, *Statistical History*, A 7, p. 8.

five in 1928,[255] while the percentage in urban areas naturally was vastly higher than in rural areas. The increasing electrification allowed the use of such appliances as the electric light, vacuum cleaner, electric iron, and washing machine.

In dark contrast to these improved living conditions, eighty-three percent of all gainfully employed people still did not earn even $1,000 per year in 1920,[256] whereas $2,000 to $2,500 was the official minimum requirement for maintaining a family of five "at a level of health and decency" for one year.[257] One of the consequences of this lack of adequate financial means was the increasing number of women in the labor force. In 1920 almost a quarter of the total female population was employed; of all married women, nine percent was earning a salary.[258]

One result of the entrance of women into commercial life was the Nineteenth Amendment to the Constitution, which in 1920 gave women the right to vote.[259] Economic power was followed by political power. One more cause for this Amendment was that women had shown that in a time of emergency and crisis they were able to keep the economy and the nation running: on April 6, 1917 the United States had declared War on Germany. In 1918 almost eighteen percent of the toal male population was in arms.[260] When on Armistice Day, November 11, 1918, the First World War was over, more than 53,000 men had died in action; in addition, more than an equal number had died from diseases. More than 204,000 men had been wounded.[261]

In political terms the years after the First World War were spent in grand isolationism. In 1924 the Immigration Act was passed, which severely restricted the flow of immigrants to the United States and established quotas for all countries of origin. Whereas in 1924 more than 700,000 immigrants arrived in the United States, that number sank to less than 300,000 in 1925, the first year of the legal force of the act, and never reached the pre-act numbers again.[262] In foreign affairs, too, the United States stayed aloof.

The big issue of the 1920s certainly was Prohibition which attempted to curb all manufacture, sale, or transportation of intoxicating liquors. An Amendment to the Constitution was ratified and became effective January 16, 1920.[263] The momentum for the prohibition of alcoholic beverages had been building since around the turn of the century.[264] But the "absorbing interest" of the "prohibition experiment"[265] was only for those who obeyed the law; whoever wanted to, could acquire alcohol, albeit for highly inflated prices unless one joined the ranks of home distillers. The main reason for the impotence of prohibition was the failure to generate a mentality toward this topic different from the one before the Amendment became effective.

Five years after the period discussed here, in 1933, the Twenty-First Amendment repealed the Eighteenth Amendment, thereby legally ending the prohibition experiment.

---

[255] Wattenberg, *Statistical History*, S 109, p. 827.

[256] In 1920 the average annual earnings in all industries, including farm labor, was $1,407 per year; excluding farm labor, $1,489: Wattenberg, *Statistical History*, D 779-80, p. 168.

[257] Faulkner, *History*, p. 652.

[258] Wattenberg, *Statistical History*, D 48-60, p. 133.

[259] Commager, *Documents of American History*, no. 87, p. 148.

[260] Of 51,974,000 men, 2,897,167 were in the Armed Forces as of June 30, 1918: Wattenberg, *Statistical History*, A 24, p. 9; Y 904, p. 1141.

[261] Wattenberg, *Statistical History*, Y 879-82, p. 1140. Total death number: 116,516.

[262] Wattenberg, *Statistical History*, C 89, p. 105.

[263] Amendment 18: Commager, *Documents of American History*, no. 87, p. 148.

[264] Ahlstrom, *Religious History*, II, 350-53, 388-91.

[265] Faulkner, *History*, p. 660.

The Book of Common Prayer 1928

The third round of liturgical revision within the Episcopal Church began in 1913, twenty-one years after the adoption of the then legal prayer book of 1892. Both the date of starting this process and the actual results of it show that the modern "Liturgical Movement" did not yet play a role in the deliberations about the shape of the liturgy and the texts produced for this book. Although at the time when the new *Book of Common Prayer* went into legal force the first hints and traces of that Liturgical Movement could be seen, revisions carried out for the 1928 prayer book must be looked at in the light of both the renewed interest in liturgy in the Anglican Communion as a whole[266] and the wish to respond to the changed social and theological circumstances.

The dioceses of California and Arizona presented to the General Convention of 1913 in New York City a memorial asking for the establishment of a Joint Commission of both Houses to consider a revision and enrichment of the prayer book, since, as their spokesman, Edward Lambe Parsons, said, "[t]here are several parts of the Prayer Book which might be revised and enriched whereby it would be better adapted for present use."[267] This commission was established by the resolution

> that a Joint Commission consisting of seven Bishops, seven Presbyters, and seven Laymen be appointed to consider and report to the next General Convention such revision and enrichment of the Prayer Book as will adapt it to present conditions, if, in their judgment, such revision be necessary; Provided, that no proposition involving the Faith and Doctrine of the Church shall be considered or reported upon by the Commission; and Provided, that no proposal to change the Title-page of the Prayer Book or the Name of the Church shall be referred to said Commission.[268]

In its report to the General Convention of 1916 in St. Louis, Missouri, the commission gave an outline of its work. It briefly touched upon the first reserve of the doctrine stated in the resolution of 1913:

> Faith or Doctrine, however, is involved in each expression of worship; and every proposal for revision or enrichment does necessarily touch them. No form of prayer or praise, of intercession or thanksgiving, or of exhortation, could be added to the Prayer Book or taken out of it, or in any degree altered or amended, without involving expressions of what the Church believes or teaches. It has been obvious to the Commission that the General Convention did not instruct them to make no change in the Book, but to make no change in it that would involve a change in the belief or teaching of the Church. To this principle they have adhered.[269]

This statement was a clear indication of both the reluctance to change the most important expression of the Church's faith, and of the problems encountered by a group whose task is a revision of just that expresion of belief, unless the proposed amendments consist in mere trivialities which are not worth the efforts.

The proposed resolution IX on the rite of the public baptism of infants[270] gave permission to administer the sacrament even apart from Morning or Evening Prayer. The exhortation to the congregation was shortened, without any negative statements about all men being

---

[266] Cuming, *History*, pp. 183-90.

[267] Quoted in: Sydnor, *Real Prayer Book*, p. 69.

[268] Episcopal Church, General Convention, *Report of the Joint Commission on The Book of Common Prayer Appointed by The General Convention of 1913* (Boston: Updike, 1916), p. v. The last reserve was an echo of constant efforts, almost from the beginning on, to change the church's name, mostly in a direction to omit the word "Protestant": Shoemaker, *Origin and Meaning*, p. 237.

[269] *Report 1916*, p. x.

[270] *Report 1916*, pp. 87-89.

conceived and born in sin, the impossibility of entering the kingdom of God except through regeneration and new birth, and the grant to the child of that "which by nature he cannot have." The heavily remodeled text was proposed in this version:

> Dearly beloved, let us beseech God the Father Almighty, through our Lord Jesus Christ, that this Child may be baptized with water and the Holy Ghost, and received into Christ's Holy Church, and be made a living member of the same.[271]

Luther's Flood Prayer was proposed for omission without substitution. In the prayer of thanksgiving after the baptism and before the final exhortation to the godparents, the reference to the crucifixion of the old man, the abolishment of the whole body of sin, and the participation in the death of Christ ought to be omitted. All these proposals were adapted for the changes in the order of baptism of adults in resolution XI.[272]

These proposals were a clear indication of the influence of contemporary advanced liberal theology in America, which was a theological outlet of the almost indigenous idea so dear to Americans that humanity would be capable of perfection, that human nature would be more clearly defined by its virtues than by its vices, and that the evil in the world could be conquered. All these notions ran counter to many traditional liturgical texts. The solution to this dilemma, it was proposed, was not the correction of the theological teachings but the abolition or substitution of the liturgical texts.[273]

At the same Convention to which this report was submitted, thirty-nine clergymen went even further in this direction and asked that the revision should be more profound, giving more emphasis to the Church's mission and responsibility, and less emphasis to the fallen nature of humanity. At the same time, more variety within the broader context of the prayer book was asked.[274]

The commission was given renewed authority and was to submit another report to the next Convention.

This Convention of 1919 in Detroit received the second report. As far as the order of baptism was concerned, this proved to be a groundbreaking report in that it proposed the unification of the previously different rites of baptism:

> The three Offices for the Public and Private Baptism of Infants and for the Baptism of those of Riper Years have been combined in one. It will be apparent upon inspection that one form, with appropriate rubrical directions for various conditions, is enough. It is desirable to discourage private baptism where it is not really unavoidable. In the revised formula some of the homiletical parts of the old Offices have been omitted.[275]

Accordingly the new order was given in its entirety in resolution VIII.[276] Basically it was the same text as the one for the public baptism of infants, as it stood at the time the report was submitted, with the insertion of the gospel reading John 3:1-8 or Matthew 28:18-20 as alternatives; the reading of the gospel, however, could be omitted. The formerly long address to the godparents before the interrogatories had become an introduction to the questions. These were asked of the parents and godparents as the persons responsible for teaching the

---

[271] *Report 1916*, p. 88. One wonders whether by omission of hitherto accepted and well-known texts about the nature of unbaptized people the doctrine of the Church has not been heavily touched upon. The commission must have been aware of this fact.

[272] *Report 1916*, pp. 93-95.

[273] The whole history of Christian liturgy can be written as an investigation into the different meanings, emphases, and applications of the ancient axiom "legem credendi lex statuat supplicandi." See Geoffrey Wainwright, *Doxology: The Praise of God in Worship, Doctrine and Life, A Systematic Theology* (London: Epworth, 1980), pp. 218-83.

[274] Sydnor, *Real Prayer Book*, p. 70.

[275] Episcopal Church, General Convention, *Second Report of the Joint Commission on The Book of Common Prayer Appointed by The General Convention of 1913* (New York: Macmillan, 1919), pp. xviii-xix.

[276] *Second Report*, pp. 103-14.

child to renounce the evil, for instructing it in the Christian faith, and for teaching it to live according to God's law. Adults were asked those questions in their own right and had to answer them by themselves. The signing with the cross on the forehead was restored both in ritual and with the ensuing text, although the following rubric once again allowed the omission if it was desired. The first rubric after the actual order permitted, at the discretion of the minister, the saying of the Apostles' Creed immediately after the renunciation and before the second question.

At the next General Convention in Portland, Oregon in 1922, the third report of the commission was "being thoroughly studied . . . section by section, service by service, line by line."[277] The report itself stated that the office of baptism and others

> have been carefully restudied in the light of criticism received by the Commission, and the Offices are presented in a form considerably revised from that of the last Report. This is especially true of the Baptismal Office.[278]

Again the issue of possible changes in the doctrine of the Church was brought up:

> The commission takes this occasion to state that there has been no intention or desire on its part to change the doctrine of the Church. This ought to go without saying. If, in some instances, there has been change of emphasis, it is, in the opinion of the Commission, only where such changed emphasis represents the mind of the whole Church. It will be for the Church to decide whether or not the Commission is justified in this opinion.[279]

Immediately following were some sentences of the principles by which the members of the commission wished to be guided:

> There are, of course, some who would wish to see no changes whatever in our *Book of Common Prayer*. Those who are of this mind are, it is confidently believed, very few. The vast majority of our people desire to see a revision accomplished that will tend to make the Book more helpful in meeting the religious needs of the people in the life and worship of today. It is certainly the unanimous desire of the members of the Commission that no faithful users of the book in the past, whatever their training or school of thought, shall find it when revised in any respect less truly the vehicle of their thought and worship. In other words, the motives of the Commission have been purely liturgical.[280]

In the resolution VIII on the "Ministration of Holy Baptism" the following changes of major importance to the order proposed in 1919 could be found.[281] The invitation to prayer at the beginning had the clauses on the necessity of regeneration and new birth for entering the kingdom of God and the request to grant to the baptizand "that which by nature he cannot have" reinserted into the text. The Apostles' Creed was said after the gospel reading, followed by the minister's recitation of a *cento* of seven verses, partly taken from the Psalms, serving as an introduction to the ensuing prayer of thanksgiving for the faith and petition for the baptizand. The godparents were then spoken to and asked the interrogatories, addressed to themselves in the name of the child. Adults to be baptized were to make answer to the

---

[277] Sydnor, *Real Prayer Book*, p. 72.

[278] Episcopal Church, General Convention, *Third Report of the Joint Commission on The Book of Common Prayer Appointed by The General Convention of 1913* (New York: Macmillan, 1922), p. xi.

[279] *Third Report*, pp. xvi-xvii.

[280] *Third Report*, p. xvi. It may be appropriate to put a question mark behind a "purely liturgical" revision in the context of the utter interdependence of liturgy and faith in the Episcopal Church and, for that matter, in the entire Anglican Communion. To be guided by the principle of a "purely liturgical" revision and not to touch the faith of the Church are two different things. Lacking an institutional *magisterium* proper is tantamount to having a commission on the revision of liturgical texts serve as the interpreter of the Church's faith as expressed in the liturgy.

[281] *Third Report*, pp. 92-105.

questions by themselves. An additional question to the sponsors asked about their willingness to take seriously their teaching office and to make sure that the child would be brought to the bishop for confirmation. The phrase in the thanksgiving after baptism about the death unto sin, the life unto righteousness, and the burial with Christ in his death had been part of the 1919 proposed text and reappeared here. Other prayers taken out of the prayer book might be added after the thanksgiving. Instead of the final exhortation to the godparents, a blessing was proposed modeled after Ephesians 3:15-19. A new rubric was inserted after the order that

> when any such Persons as are of riper years are to be baptized, timely notice shall be given to the Minister; that so [sic] due care may be taken for their examination, whether they be sufficiently instructed in the Principles of the Christian Religion; and that they may be exhorted to prepare themselves, with Prayers and Fasting, for the receiving of this holy Sacrament.[282]

The General Convention, having received this report and discussed it thoroughly, resolved that the commission was to present to the next General Convention no new proposals.[283]

In 1923 a book was published by authority and resolution of the General Convention, outlining the alterations in the prayer book already adopted in 1919 and 1922, as well as a list of the proposals first approved in 1922 and scheduled to be ratified at the next General Convention.[284]

That Convention of 1925 in New Orleans received the fourth report of the commission. Most of the points proposed for resolution regarding the ministration of baptism dealt with the rearrangement of rubrics.[285] Two of those, however, were significant: the questions to the godparents about their willingness to take seriously their duties of teaching and of bringing the child to confirmation were separated from the questions of renunciations and of belief by a space left in the text. Secondly, the prayer for sanctification of the water "to the mystical washing away of sin" had been recast into a Preface, with the respective dialogue before and the proper introduction. The amendments were again printed in a book to serve for ratification in 1928.[286]

The next General Convention, 1928 in Washington, D.C., approved for the second time, and thereby made final, the proposed amendments; on October 9 it accepted the new *Book of Common Prayer*.

The book that was published as the result of this revision process had the same title as its two American predecessors; the ratification text of the 1789 book and its preface also reappeared.[287] The section "Concerning the Service of the Church"[288] was partly new to complement the Canon Law of the Episcopal Church:

> The Order for Holy Communion, the Order for Morning Prayer, the Order for Evening Prayer, and the Litany, as set forth in this Book, are the regular Services appointed for Public Worship in this Church, and shall be used accordingly.[289]

---

[282] *Third Report*, p. 103-04.
[283] Episcopal Church, General Convention, *Fourth Report of the Joint Commission on The Book of Common Prayer Appointed by The General Convention of 1913* (New York: Macmillan, 1925), p. 8.
[284] Detscher, *Evolution*, pp. 250-52; Sydnor, *Real Prayer Book*, pp. 72-73.
[285] *Fourth Report*, pp. 21-24.
[286] Detscher, *Evolution*, p. 253.
[287] *The Book of Common Prayer and Administration of the Sacraments and Other Rites and Ceremonies of the Church according to the use of the Protestant Episcopal Church in the United States of America Together with the Psalter or Psalms of David* ([New York:] Church Pension Fund, [1929]), pp. iv-vi.
[288] *Book of Common Prayer 1928*, p. vii.
[289] *Book of Common Prayer 1928*, p. vii.

Permission was given to add other devotions, even, "when expressly authorized by the Ordinary," in place of Morning and Evening Prayer.

The "Order for The Administration of the Lord's Supper or Holy Communion" evidenced some rather well-done changes compared with the 1892 book.[290] Not only the opening recitation of the Lord's Prayer and the decalogue but also the following collect asking for guidance could be omitted. The dialogue "The Lord be with you. And with thy spirit. Let us pray" was restored before the collect of the day, a return to the 1549 book. The reading section had received more participation of the people by providing the reponses "Glory be to thee, O Lord" after the reading, a possible hymn or anthem afterwards, and the response "Praise be to thee, O Christ" after the gospel. After the creed and announcements to be given, the "Bidding Prayer, or other authorized prayers and intercessions" might be said. The word "militant" had been dropped from the title of the prayer for Christ's Church. A new phrase for the departed had been inserted: that God "grant them continual growth in thy love and service."[291] The customary exhortations to be read after this prayers since 1552 had been omitted for the regular Sunday eucharist; they were to be said, according to a rubric preceding them, on the first Sundays of Advent, and Lent, and Trinity Sunday, and printed after the order as an appendix.[292] Three new Prefaces were provided.[293] The Prayer of Humble Access had been shifted to a position after the Lord's Prayer, which was advanced to the end of the eucharistic prayer, as the more natural place. Therefore, the otherwise unchanged "Prayer of Consecration" immediately followed the Preface. Even considering the increase in communion frequency in this century in the Episcopal Church, the fact is very felicitous that the rubric was left untouched which required that for a consecration of more eucharistic matter, be it bread or wine, if either one had been spent, the entire text of the post *Sanctus*, the institution narrative, the anamnesis, and the epiclesis were to be said.

As a whole, most of the exhortatory and rather tedious material had been done away with or limited to a few times per year. The shift in the positions of several texts had brought the service closer to the medieval and pre-Reformation order. An outline of the possible variations in, and the general scope of, the celebration will help clarify what was officially to be done after the 1928 prayer book had become the source for celebrating the eucharist:[294]

    The Lord's Prayer
The collect for purity
Decalogue and/or summary of the law
    Kyrie
    Concluding collect

---

[290] *Book of Common Prayer 1928*, pp. 67-89.

[291] This formula is curious in that it asks for actual increase of something the departed might have for God. There are no explanations for this rather unorthodox formula given other than an acknowledgement of the peculiar character of it for the American prayer book: "The thought of 'growth' in the life beyond is characteristic of the newer prayers for the departed in the American book;" and a reference is given to two more prayers whose thrust goes in the same direction: Massey Hamilton Shepherd, *The Oxford American Prayer Book Commentary* (New York: Oxford University Press, 1950), *ad* pp. 74-75. And Hatchett, *Commentary,* p. 341: "In 1928, amid great controversy, a petition for the departed was restored to the prayer for the church, 'beseeching thee to grant them continual growth in thy love and service.' The idea of growth in the life beyond, which is hardly typical of traditional prayers for the departed, was characteristic of those which made their way into the 1928 Book."

[292] *Book of Common Prayer 1928*, pp. 85-89.

[293] The first of the three new texts, the Preface for Epiphany and seven days after, could also be found, slightly varied, in the 1928 Proposed English prayer book and others. It refers to Christ's glory in our flesh and the light we are brought into out of our darkness. The Preface for Purification, Annunciation, and Transfiguration alludes to the Word made flesh and rephrases 2 Cor 4:6. The Preface for All Saints is based on Hebr 12:1 2: Shepherd, *Prayer Book Commentary, ad* pp. 77-79.

[294] The indented elements were subject to provisions for less than regular or weekly use.

Salutation
Collect of the day
Epistle
    Hymn or anthem
Gospel
Nicene or Apostles' Creed
Announcements
    Bidding prayer
Sermon
Scriptural words at the offertory
    Hymn or anthem
    Secret intercessions
Prayer for the whole state of Christ's Church
The exhortations (thrice a year)
General confession
Absolution
Comfortable Words from the Scripture
Preface
Prayer of Consecration with oblation and invocation
The Lord's Prayer
Prayer of Humble Access
    Hymn
Ministration of the communion
Postcommunion prayer
Gloria in excelsis
Blessing

    The result of this revision of the service was "the shaping of the entire eucharistic rite into closer accord with ancient and more universal patterns," so that "the American service of Holy Communion now had a general similarity to the Roman Mass,"[295] a summary which ought to be taken *cum grano salis* but which at the same time points in the direction of the process for the years to come.
    The most obvious novelty in the "Ministration of Holy Baptism" was the realization of the proposal by the committee preparing the prayer book that the formerly different offices of baptism had been united into one.[296] The private baptism of children was strongly discouraged in the first rubric. The textual version was left as proposed. The reference to the entrance into God's kingdom by regeneration, and the petition to grant to the baptizand "that which by nature *he* cannot have" were readmitted to the first exhortation. Luther's Flood Prayer was left out. Three different gospel texts were given.[297] The thanksgiving for grace and faith, and the petition for the baptizand were said by the minister and people together. The interrogatories of renunciation and belief were asked of the godparents to be answered "in the name of this Child;" the two questions about their willingness to adhere to their duties were answered on their own behalf. At the baptism of adults the interrogatories were to be answered by the baptizands on their own behalf and by themselves. The petitions for the baptismal grace to be given to the person to be baptized, and the benediction of the water, cast into the form of a Preface, followed. After the immersion or affusion, the signing with the cross, and invitation to thanksgiving, the Lord's Prayer to be said by all, and a final thanksgiving for the regeneration and incorporation into the Church, and the petition for a life according to the baptismal grace, followed. The benediction concluded the service.

---

[295] Porter, "Unofficial History," p. 105. As this commentary was made after the most recent revision, it too does not suggest an influence of the Liturgical Movement on the 1928 book.
[296] *Book of Common Prayer 1928*, pp. 273-82.
[297] Mk 10:13 16; John 3:1 8; Mt 28:18 20.

The "Order of Confirmation Or Laying on of Hands upon Those that are Baptized, and come to Years of Discretion" had been streamlined in that the initial exhortation had been dropped. A second question, following the one about the willingness to ratify the baptismal promises, had been added, asking whether the candidates would promise to follow Christ as their Lord and savior. The remaining service had been left as it stood.[298]

This revision, still rather conservative by nature,[299] yet not without daring breaks with the post-Reformation tradition,[300] was to a great extent influenced by the experience of a pastoral situation in a post-World War I era which demanded more than a miniscule change of letters. Adaptation to this situation became necessary. The answer to the questions, and the response to this urgency, were taken mostly from pre-Reformation, even ancient, liturgies. Nonetheless, within the context of a book that contained the rites of the Church in general, but was still exclusively denominational in outlook and use, the liturgy of the Episcopalians was yet easily recognizable as Anglican.

---

[298] *Book of Common Prayer 1928*, pp. 296-99.
[299] Suter and Cleaveland, *American Book of Common Prayer*, p. 65.
[300] See, for example, the prayers for the deceased, "a drastic repudiation of postreformation standards, but where pastoral need and the desire to restore ancient usage went hand in hand, Episcopalians in America unhesitatingly parted company with more conservative Anglicans in other lands.": Porter, "Unofficial History," p. 104.

The Prayer Book of 1979

Social and Ecclesiastical Life between 1928 and 1950

Almost exactly a year to the day after the 1928 *Book of Common Prayer* had been accepted, the "Roaring Twenties" came to a disastrous end when the boom cycle of the economy collapsed between October 24 and 29, 1929. Nobody has yet come up with a convincing explanation of the exact reasons for the ruin of the economy around that time.[1] Within a short period firms went bankrupt, the financial basis of millions of people broke down, and the country was in a depression the likes of which it had never seen. The frenzy of speculation with stocks, bonds, and savings that had caught even the masses had taken its toll. The downslide continued until 1932/33, with ever-increasing speed. The gross national product, the sum of the value of all goods produced and services provided, sank from $103 billion in 1929 to $55.6 billion in 1933. It declined steadily up to 1936. The index of wholesale prices declined by almost one-third between 1929 and 1932. From 1929 to 1933, more than 10,000 banks went out of business. The number of unemployed persons rose from 1,550,000 in 1920 to 12,830,000 in 1933, which constituted more than twenty-five percent of the civilian labor force. The rate of suicides increased from 13.9 per 100,000 people in 1929 (1928: 13,5) to 17.4, the highest ever, in 1932.[2]

> Statistics provide the only way to tell the national story of the first years of the depression. But they tell us nothing about the depression in human terms, and it was people, not numbers, that suffered through the era. There are no words to describe the whole calamity adequately.[3]

For those affected--more than the civilian labor force only, as family members and dependent people also endured the ordeal--the basics of everyday life often broke down. A great many people had difficulties getting food; malnutrition and even starvation were not uncommon. There were schools where almost all children were underweight. Another problem was housing, as soon as the rent could not be paid any longer. On vacant lots in the cities and on the outskirts so-called "Hoovervilles" arose, tents made from cardboard boxes or wood. "Okies" were on the move to the Southwest, the Promised Land, especially California--people who had lost everything except their bare life.[4] At least to some degree, all strata of American society were affected, and for most people the toll of the Depression was horrible.[5]

The winner of the 1932 presidential election was the then governor of New York, Franklin Delano Roosevelt (1882-1945). Within a week after his inauguration (March 4, 1933), he called a special session of Congress to initiate and enact the first phase of a grand relief and recovery program for the whole economy. The New Deal, as this program was called, was nothing less than a total reversal of the economic and financial policy of the state, although the First New Deal in 1933/34 was a "shotgun approach" to the problems with no underlying systematic theory.[6] The economy, up to now led by liberal capitalist ideas, was subjected to a close federal supervision; the state now participated in it. The Agricultural Adjustment Act (May 1933), the National Industry Recovery Act (June 1933), and the Social Security Act (August 1935) were milestones in readjusting the economy. A balance of

---

[1] Landauer, *Sozial- und Wirtschaftsgeschichte*, p. 165.

[2] Wattenberg, *Statistical History*, F 1, p. 224; F 31, p. 226; E 23, p. 199; X 580, p. 1019; D 8-9, p. 126; D 85-86, p. 135; H 980, p. 414.

[3] David A. Shannon, *Between the Wars: America, 1919-1941*, Houghton Mifflin Books in American History (Boston: Houghton Mifflin, 1965), p. 112.

[4] Shannon, *Between the Wars*, pp. 112-14.

[5] See Nigel Gray, *The Worst Of Times: An Oral History of the Great Depression* (Aldershot, Hants.: Wildwood House, 1985).

[6] Shannon, *Between the Wars*, pp. 153-54.

interest between producer and consumer, employer and employee was intended, and a social net was constructed for the "underdogs," those who, for different reasons, had to rely on welfare and were otherwise not able, particularly in emergency situations, to secure a human standard of living. The many laws and measures represented more, however, than relieving the populace of inhumane living conditions. What made these programs different was that, firstly, they intended to guarantee that every American would have at least a minimum standard of living, and, secondly, it would be a right, not a matter of charity, to receive this help. By these actions the individualism and laissez-faire mentality of the former decades gave way to a social and collective action.[7] It was the state, no longer the individual or the employer, who took responsibility for the welfare of the citizens. From 1934 on the statistics showed that productivity increased again, unemployment went down, albeit slowly, and the economy recovered somewhat from the Great Depression that had followed the crash of the stock market in 1929.

After the 1938 presidential elections the era of the New Deal was over. Prosperity, however, had not returned to such a degree that it would measure up to the pre-Depression period. Only because of, and during, the War was the economy able to recover completely and to make substantial gains.[8]

There was a distinctly conservative reaction in some church quarters, however, which condemned the New Deal policies as socialist-inspired, the ongoing social and entertainment trends as devilish, and the repeal of Prohibition as a blow to an integral Christian, especially Protestant, life. There were even strong flirtations not only with Anticommunism but also with Facism.[9]

Five weeks after the invasion of Poland by the German army, Albert Einstein and others told Roosevelt, who had been triumphantly reelected in 1936, on October 11, 1939 of the possibilities of developing an atomic bomb. The previous year Otto Hahn had for the first time probed nuclear fission. Until December 7, 1941, the date of the attack by the Japanese army on the naval base at Pearl Harbor, the United States had declared itself neutral but was leaning heavily towards the United Kingdom and France, who received weaponry from the United States. On December 8, 1941 War was declared on Japan, and on December 11 on Germany and Italy. On April 12, 1945 Roosevelt died and was succeeded by Harry S. Truman (1884-1972). On May 7, 1945 the German army surrendered unconditionally. On July 16 the first atomic bomb was exploded in a test at Alamogordo, New Mexico. On August 6 an atomic bomb was dropped on the Japanese city of Hiroshima, followed three days later by another bomb on Nagasaki. On August 15 the Japanese army surrendered. The Second World War was over.[10] The cost: the lives of more than 55 million people, troops as well as civilians. The consequences were a complete redrawing of the world map, especially in Europe; a sharp division between the "East" dominated by the Soviet Union, and the "West" dominated by the United States and, to a lesser degree, the United Kingdom and France; and the desperate attempt to prevent the repetition of such a slaughter on a worldwide scale by founding the United Nations on June 25, 1945 in San Francisco. The gravest consequence: the constant threat of complete self-destruction of the human race by the atomic bomb and the nuclear weaponry theater built up by several countries after the Second World War.

The United States had more than 16 million people in the Army and the other military forces. Seventy-three percent of these troops served overseas. More than 405,000 troops

---

[7] William E. Leuchtenberg, *Franklin D. Roosevelt and the New Deal: 1932-1940*, The New American Nation Series (New York: Harper & Row, 1963), pp. 332, 340.

[8] Shannon, *Between the Wars*, p. 182. Leuchtenberg, *Roosevelt*, p. 347, attributes the recovery almost completely to the results of the New Deal.

[9] Ahlstrom, *Religious History*, II, 414-21.

[10] Morris and Morris, *Encyclopedia*, pp. 429-80.

were killed, of which 291,000 in battle and 114,000 through wounds, sickness, in captivity or otherwise. More than 670,000 military personnel were wounded.[11]

The years following the Second World War were characterized by a steady growth of the economy and a relatively calm social environment. The population had increased from 123,188,000 in 1930 to 132,122,000 in 1940 and to 151,684,000 in 1950. The gross national product rose by more than one-third, from $211.9 billion in 1945, to $284.8 billion in 1950. The index of wholesale prices rose almost fifty percent during the same period. The number of unemployed people rose slightly over one million people in 1945 to 3.2 million in 1950, from 1.9% of the civilian labor force to 5.3%; but contrary to the years of the Great Depression those unemployed were cared for, at least for a certain period, by the federal and state unemployment and welfare schemes set up in the New Deal legislation. The average annual earnings of employees, which had fallen from $1,405 in 1929 to slightly over $1,000 in 1933, climbed from $2,190 in 1946 to $2,992 in 1950.[12]

The unemployment and social distress of the Great Depression had had the cleansing effect for the churches of taking superficiality and sentimentality out of the religious life. The wartime period had led to a rediscovery and reaffirmation of the national spirit and religious heritage. The dynamics of a growth economy and a heavy migration to the cities presented new challenges to the churches. Together with the new external enemy, Communism, and the threat of human extinction by the atomic bomb, the spiritual insecurity resulted in a steady rise of institutional affiliation with churches and denominations.[13] The heightened awareness of religious life, without which human life was thought impossible, was the reason for a surge in books seeking to relieve Americans of the anxiety, distress, and emptiness of their lives, mostly by blending Freudian psychological insights, common sense attitudes, and some theological vision (often of the soothing kind). On the other hand, renewed revivalist vigor was the result of the crusade of William Franklin ("Billy") Graham (born 1918) and others, appealing more to conservative constituencies than to mainstream Protestant denominations.[14]

The frailty of human nature, so apparent during the Great Depression and the Second World War, became a prominent feature in what was called "neo-orthodox" theology, a movement of "complex development,"[15] in reaction against liberal theology which had been in vogue in the first decades of the century. It was a blend of a renewed emphasis on the sovereignty and transcendence of God and the reality of sin in human life, and an acceptance of modern biblical scholarship and liberalism as far as social policy was concerned. God, Christ, Trinity, Church--these realities became reasserted and the focus of Christian life again.[16] The most prominent representatives of this theological school were Karl Barth (1886-1968),[17] Paul Tillich (1886-1965),[18] and the Niebuhr brothers, Reinhold (1894-1970)[19] and H. Richard (1894-1962).[20]

---

[11] Wattenberg, *Statistical History*, Y 856-82, p. 1140.

[12] Wattenberg, *Statistical History*, A 6, p. 8; F 1, p. 224; E 23, p. 199; D 85-86, p. 135; D 722, p. 164.

[13] Ahlstrom, *Religious History*, II, 448, while acknowledging the "notoriously inaccurate" church membership statistics, nonetheless gives the results of surveys which showed that from 1930 to 1950 the percentage of the people who declared themselves affiliated with a church increased from forty-seven to fifty-five. As a corrollary, the sum spent on post-war church construction, too, leaped from $26 million in 1945 to $409 million in 1950: p. 448.

[14] Ahlstrom, *Religious History*, II, 451-57.

[15] Robert Theodore Handy, *A History of the Churches in the United States and Canada* (Oxford: Oxford University Press, 1979), p. 394.

[16] Ahlstrom, *Religious History*, II, 425-43, 458-59; Handy, *History of the Churches*, pp. 393-97.

[17] See Eberhard Jüngel, "Barth, Karl," *Theologische Realenzyklopädie* 5, pp. 251-68.

[18] See Charles W. Kegley, *The Theology of Paul Tillich* (New York: Macmillan, 1952).

[19] See Bertrand de Margerie, *Reinhold Niebuhr: Théologien de la communauté mondiale*, Museum Lessianum: Section théologique, 64 (Paris: Desclée de Brouwer, 1969).

[20] See Libertus A. Hoedemaker, *The Theology of H. Richard Niebuhr* (Boston: Pilgrim Press, 1970).

The neo-orthodox theology was supported in its central positions by the Liturgical Movement, which had rediscovered a fuller understanding of the nature of the Church and which also involved churches from the Reformation, and in turn inspired it.[21]

The Liturgical Movement within the Episcopal Church

In the Anglican Communion interest in the liturgy began to reemerge in the nineteenth century just as in the Roman Catholic Church.[22]

Although the protagonists of the Oxford Movement regarded themselves as theologians rather than persons occupied with the minutiae of ritual detail, they nonetheless saw the liturgy as expressing in human terms the truth revealed in the Incarnation and as being conducted in the presence of God; from these realities the forms of the liturgy would take their ultimate value.[23]

The so-called Ritualists shifted the emphasis from the theological foundation of the liturgical matters, the Church and its catholicity, to questions of the right conduct of the rites and to borrowings from medieval or modern Roman Catholic ceremonies, as they regarded these superior to the liturgy of the *Book of Common Prayer*.

> What the Anglo-Catholics of a hundred years ago were able to borrow from the Catholics of the time were precisely those features which now appear to Catholics to be amongst the

---

[21] Ahlstrom, *Religious History*, II, 457-58; Handy, *History of the Churches*, p. 395.

[22] This cannot, and does not pretend to, be a monograph-like account of the Liturgical Movement in the Episcopal Church or the Anglican Communion, let alone in all so-called liturgical churches. The purpose of this section is to outline some major influences upon the liturgical life of the Episcopal Church, the understanding of the liturgy, and the revision process of the 1928 *Book of Common Prayer*. The history of the Liturgical Movement in the Roman Catholic Church must be taken for granted; abundant bibliographical material is available on it. It is true: "Liturgiology of itself... does not produce a liturgical movement. One cannot recount the history of the modern liturgical movement merely by way of a bibliographical guide to liturgical studies. Some of the most learned liturgiologists have had little concern about the practical applications of their historical findings.": Massey Hamilton Shepherd, "The History of the Liturgical Renewal," in *The Liturgical Renewal of the Church: Addresses of the Liturgical Conference, Held in Grace Church, Madison, May 19-21, 1958*, ed. Massey Hamilton Shepherd (New York: Oxford University Press, 1960), p. 27. Dom Gregory Dix, for example, admittedly one of the greatest and certainly most influential liturgists of this century in all churches, was known for not caring about a reconciliation of his private way of celebrating Mass in the manner of the old Latin Low Mass (at his abbey in Nashdom, England, the monks never used the *Book of Common Prayer* but only the Latin books for the Roman Rite of the Mass, and the Benedictine Divine Office) with his liturgical theology. When once asked about a reconciliation of his mumbling the entire service, so that hardly anybody could hear anything, with his published works, he answered: "I don't make any attempt to." (Communication in letters to the author received from Massey H. Shepherd, Jr., April 14, 1986, p. 2; July 12, 1986, p. 2). But the correctness of the above-quoted statement by Shepherd admitted, a more bibliographical approach will nonetheless have to suffice here for the purpose of the research and due to a lack of publications which could otherwise be consulted.

[23] See Donald Gray, *Earth and Altar: The Evolution of the Parish Communion in the Church of England to 1945*, Alcuin Club Collections, 68 (Norwich: Canterbury, 1986), pp. 9-15. The members of the Oxford Movement knew about the ideas of the founder and first abbot of Solesmes, Dom Prosper Guéranger (1805-1875), from the beginning of his literary activity on: Ralph William Franklin, "Guéranger and Variety in Unity," *Worship*, 51 (1977), 397 note 30. No written evidence is available, however, of an acquaintance of Guéranger's with the ideas of the Oxford Movement. Cuthbert Johnson does not even mention the movement as a possible influence, albeit indirect: *Prosper Guéranger (1805-1875): A Liturgical Theologian, An Introduction to His Liturgical Writings and Work*, Studia Anselmiana, 89: Analecta Liturgica, 9 (Roma: Pontificio Ateneo San Anselmo, 1984).

weakest points in their recent liturgical practice. For example, a preference for low Mass (as private as possible) rather than a public celebration; the high Mass carried out so as to do without Communion or any participation at all by the faithful; and, above all, an enthusiasm for Benediction of the Blessed Sacrament which tended to make it, rather than the Mass itself, the focus of congregational worship.[24]

On the other side the Ritualists were successful in reaching out to social classes otherwise mostly unattended; they made the struggle for social justice their own and tried to reconcile the "common man in the pew" through sensible means they were able to understand with the nucleus of the Christian gospel.

The Ritualists also succeeded in heightening awareness of the demands of more contemporary needs of worship (without a rigidly enforced uniformity). They also fostered a deepened study of liturgiology. Around the turn of the century England especially abounded with liturgists of the first rank. In 1890 the Henry Bradshaw Society was founded for publishing important liturgical texts from all eras. The names of Frank Edward Brightman (1856-1932), successively Bishop of Chichester, of Ely, and of Winchester,[25] John Dowden (1840-1910), Bishop of Edinburgh,[26] Walter Howard Frere (1863-1938), Bishop of Truro,[27] and John Wickham Legg (1843-1921)[28] have to be mentioned here. Their study of the history of the *Book of Common Prayer* and of the liturgy in the Middle Ages was crucial in establishing the view that the liturgy according to the *Book of Common Prayer* was anything but "incomparable" and "incorrigeable." The fact itself that the *Book of Common Prayer* was revised in the United States in 1789 and 1892 made clear that contemporary needs carried more weight than the preservation of the literal integrity of the 1662 *Book of Common Prayer*.

In the 1920s several activities focused attention on the renewal of the Church's liturgy, either as a direct results of attempts to revise the *Book of Common Prayer*, or as a byproduct of ecumenical interests because persons were involved in both ecumenical dialogues and the Liturgical Movement.

In several of the member churches of the Anglican Communion, revisions of the then legal *Book of Common Prayer* were carried out. In Canada, Ireland, Scotland, and South Africa the books were revised,[29] just as the Episcopal Church received its new prayer book in 1928. But if by Liturgical Movement anything more is meant than an exchange of words and (slightly) greater flexibility of the rubrical frames, then these processes were not yet influenced by the deeper theological issues of the movement. The two abortive attempts at altering the English 1662 prayer book, due to the defeat in the House of Commons in 1927 and 1928, generated (besides a ridiculous situation because the defeat had been due to non-

---

[24] Louis Bouyer, *Liturgical Piety* (Notre Dame: University of Notre Dame Press, 1955), p. 48; quoted in: Shepherd, "Liturgical Renewal," p. 48. For the situation in England, see Moorman, *History*, pp. 365-67, 401-03; for the situation in the United States, see Chorley, *Men and Movements*, pp. 359-92.

[25] A bibliography of the works written or edited by Brightman can be found in [Walter Howard Frere,] "Memoir of F. E. Brightman," *Journal of Theological Studies*, 33 (1931/32), 337-40.

[26] See his *Further Studies in the Prayer Book* (London: Methuen, 1908); *The Workmanship of the Prayer Book: In Its Literary and Liturgical Aspects*, The Churchman's Library (London: Methuen, 1899); and his editions, among others, of *The Annotated Scottish Communion Office: An Historical Account of the Scottish Communion Office, and of the Communion Office of the Protestant Episcopal Church in the United States of America* (Edinburgh: Grant, 1884); and *The Scottish Communion Office, 1764*, new ed. by Henry Albert Wilson (Oxford: Clarendon, 1922).

[27] A bibliography of the works written or edited by Frere can be found in John Henry Arnold and Edward Gerald Penfold Wyatt, eds., *Walter Howard Frere: A Collection of His Papers on Liturgical and Historical Subjects*, Alcuin Club Collections, 35 (Oxford: Oxford University Pres; London: Milford, 1940), pp. 230-32.

[28] The titles of the works written or edited by Legg can be found in Sidney Leslie Ollard, "Legg, John Wickham," *Dictionary of National Biography* (1927), pp. 330-31.

[29] Cuming, *History*, pp. 184-90.

Anglican members of the House) a healthy shock and much soul-searching about the nature of the Church, of the liturgy, and of the principles to be followed.[30]

An event whose impact is difficult to assess yet which linked the Ecumenical and Liturgical Movements was the Malines Conversations which on the invitation of Cardinal Désiré Mercier (1851-1926) were held at his mansion in Malines. Since 1908 Mercier held a deep friendship with Dom Lambert Beauduin (1873-1960) and had encouraged Beauduin in his pursuit of the liturgical apostolate on which he had embarked in 1909. Mercier chaired the talks with representatives of the Archbishop of Canterbury. The conversations themselves had been officially approved by the Apostolic See of Rome. Among the representatives of the Archbishop were Howard Frere and Charles Gore, who at that time had acquired high acclaim as theologians in the Church of England and beyond. Mercier asked Beauduin in October 1924 to write a paper on the significance of the pall and the role it could play in reunion with the Anglicans, an issue that had been raised at the second round of talks March 14-15, 1923. Beauduin's proposal "L'Eglise anglicaine unie non absorbie" was read by Mercier at the fourth conversation, May 19-20, 1925. It centered on the extension of a patriarchate for the Archbishop of Canterbury and a group reunion. The authorship of this much-discussed proposal was revealed by the successor to Mercier and participant in the Conversations, Cardinal Joseph Ernest van Roey (1874-1961). After the death of Mercier, the Apostolic See forbade any further conversations, and the dialogue abruptly ended. Besides Beauduin, Frere, and Mercier, a fourth person to link the Ecumenical and Liturgical Movements was Monsignor Pierre-Henri Battifol (1861-1929), who was called upon when the need for historical expertise was obvious.[31]

By the end of the 1920s Romano Guardini (1885-1968), Odo Casel (1886-1948), Pius Parsch (1884-1954), and Ildefons Herwegen (1874-1946) were fully engaged in supporting and furthering the cause of the Liturgical Movement in the Roman Catholic Church. The publications were in German and for the most part not yet translated into English; but liturgists and theologians in England and the United States kept themselves nonetheless informed.[32] One particularly helpful tool for the spread of developments in Germany as well as other countries (Belgium, France) was the periodical *Orate fratres* that was published since 1925 by the Liturgical Press which had been established at St. John's Abbey in Collegeville, Minnesota, and was edited by Virgil Michel (1890-1938). Michel had studied in Rome in 1924/25 and had followed classes in liturgiology under Beauduin.[33]

In England two books became the most crucial in the advance of the Liturgical Movement in the 1930s: one written by Father Arthur Gabriel Hebert (1886-1963) of the (Anglican) Society of the Sacred Mission, and the other edited by him.

In 1935 Hebert wrote *Liturgy and Society* which showed in its subtitle that it was about *The Function of the Church in the Modern World*. The publication centered on the Christian

---

[30] Cuming, *History*, pp. 162-83. See Gray, *Earth and Altar*, pp. 50-67; Robert F. Schmidt, "Prayer Book Revision in the Church of England, 1906-1929: Liturgy, Doctrine, and Ecclesiastical Discipline," Dissertation Miami University 1984.

[31] Moorman, *History*, p. 422; Pawley and Pawley, *Rome and Canterbury*, pp. 281-98; Sonya A. Quitslund, *Beauduin: A Prophet Vindicated* (New York: Newman, 1973), pp. 56-79.

[32] Only two books by Guardini were published in English in 1930 by Sheed & Warden, London: *Vom Geist der Liturgie* as *The Spirit of Liturgy*, and *Von heiligen Zeichen* as *Sacred Signs*. Gray, *Earth and Altar*, p. 196, stresses that despite some literary contact with publications of Roman Catholic authors, there was no particular influence of the Liturgical Movement on the Continent upon the development of the Parish Communion in the Church of England. He sees the roots rather in the Christian Socialist Movement and other socially concerned groups within the Church of England--which themselves had part of their roots in the Oxford Movement and with the later Ritualists.

[33] Jeremy Hall, "The American Liturgical Movement: The Early Years," *Worship*, 50 (1976), 472-81; Quitslund, *Beauduin*, pp. 302-03 note 13. See Jeremy Hall, *The Full Stature of Christ: The Ecclesiology of Virgil Michel O.S.B.* (Collegeville, MN: Liturgical Press, 1976).

mystery of the Incarnation as "the manifestation of the Divine Goodness in the flesh, in Jesus as the Son of God first, and then through the Holy Spirit in the members of His mystical Body."[34] The Church's inner life would be the central point of a Christian living and the underlying interest of all renewal movements, including the Liturgical Movement.[35] The Liturgical Movement, of which a short history within the Roman Catholic Church was given,[36] would be at its core not a ritualistic hobby but a theological revival of the first order.[37] Hebert agreeingly quoted the theological platform of the *Semaine liturgique*, June 12-16, 1932, at Namur, Belgium:

> It is a matter of the conception of the living Church, and of the unity in a catholic and common life of worship, dominated by the Christian mystery, which is the translation into liturgy of the Divine work of redemption, and the means whereby that redemption continues as a living power in us and for us. From a practical point of view this doctrinal aspect is the most important of all. . . .
> It is the theology of the life of the Church as a supernatural organism, of which we form a part, of the life of the Church in which the mystery of redemption finds its continuation and accomplishment; . . . the corollary of sacramentalism, the unalienably corporate character of worship, by which it is attached to a system of rites and symbols, whose reality, independent of the worthiness of the ministers, makes on the faithful an imperious and urgent demand for conscious participation, by which it attains in them its full glory--the selflessness of voluntary self-surrender which forms its basis, in virtue of the object which it seeks and the motives which control it. "The Church fulfils in worship a threefold aim: she unites, she sanctifies, and she adores. But she unites only in order to sanctify, and she sanctifies only in order better to adore." . . .
> Christianity is above all a Mystery: that is, a Divine Action through which God wills to save mankind and every individual, and to exalt us to a participation in His Divine Life.[38]

Passages like this one, as well as positive quotations of publications by monks of Maria Laach, including its abbot Ildefons Herwegen,[39] showed that Hebert approved of the mystery theology of Odo Casel and others, and the emphasis on ecclesiological principles was not

---

[34] Arthur Gabriel Hebert, *Liturgy and Society: The Function of the Church in the Modern World* (London: Faber & Faber, 1935), pp. 94-95.

[35] Hebert, *Liturgy and Society*, pp. 11-126.

[36] Hebert, *Liturgy and Society*, pp. 127-28.

[37] Gray, *Earth and Altar*, p. 201: "For Hebert the value of the liturgy was that it leads to worship, not to the realm of speculation, but to the heart of the saving work of Christ, and that worship is not individualistic but within the fellowship of the Body of Christ in the Holy Eucharist."

[38] "Es handelt sich um die Lehre von der lebendigen Kirche und von der Einheit im katholischen und gemeinsamen kultischen Leben, zuhöchst beherrscht vom 'Mysterium', der wesentlichen Transponierung der Erlösung, die sich darin durch uns und für uns fortsetzt. Ja, vom streng praktischen Standpunkt aus gesehen ist diese Lehrbewegung sogar das Wichtigste. . . . [E]s ist die Theologie vom Leben der Kirche als eines übernatürlichen Organismus, von dem wir einen Teil bilden, vom Leben der Kirche, durch das das Mysterium der Erlösung sich fortsetzt und vollendet; . . . der infolge der Sakramentalität unveräußerliche Gemeinschaftscharakter des Kultes, der ihn an ein System von Riten und Symbolen bindet, dessen Wirksamkeit unabhängig von dem moralischen Stand seiner Diener mit ehrfurchtgebietender Dringlichkeit von den Gläubigen eine aktive und bewußte Teilnahme fordert, damit er in ihnen seinen vollen Glanz erreicht; die Uneigennützigkeit und die Freiwilligkeit, die seine Basis bilden durch das Objekt, das er erstrebt, und die Motive, die ihn dazu treiben. 'Die Kirche erfüllt im Kult eine dreifache Aufgabe: sie vereinigt, sie heiligt und sie betet an; aber sie vereinigt nur, um zu heiligen, und sie heiligt nur, um besser anzubeten.' . . . [D]as Christentum ist vor allem Mysterium, d.h. ein göttlicher Akt, durch den Gott die Menschheit und jeden einzelnen retten und zur Teilhabe an Seinem göttlichen Leben erheben will.": D. A. Robeyns, "Die religiöse und theologische Bedeutung der liturgischen Erneuerung," *Liturgische Zeitschrift*, 5 (1932/33), 2-4; English translation: Hebert, *Liturgy and Society*, pp. 131-32.

[39] Hebert, *Liturgy and Society*, pp. 64-65, 83-84, 207-08.

surprising. As to the revision of the *Book of Common Prayer*, he pleaded for those forms of prayer which would best meet the needs of the modern world: those that would be truly universal. If those old prayers were given a modern application, they would be preferable to "spurious modernity" which would be trivial and shallow.[40]

The second book highly influential after its publication was a book of essays called *The Parish Communion*; Hebert edited it in 1937. The book was concerned with the Sunday Parish Eucharist at or around 9 o'clock in the morning, not with questions of the arrangement but, again, with a deepened understanding of the eucharist and of the Church.[41]

In the first article written by Hebert himself on the "Parish Communion in Its Spiritual Aspect," the real issue was "a movement of return to the Sacraments and the Liturgy, as the sacramental expression of our redemption through Christ and of the nature of the Church as His mystical Body."[42] The proposal at the end of the article, however, well-intended though it was, seems to have been slightly out of tune with the conditions of modern life: in order to increase the reverence for the sacrament, a fast should be observed on the morning of the celebration. This advice has not met with much success.

A second article in this book foreshadowed a monumental work that was to appear eight years later. Dom Gregory Dix, O.S.B. (1901-1952), of Nashdom Abbey, gave hints in his essay on "The Idea of 'The Church' in the Primitive Liturgies" of his famous "four-action shape" of the eucharistic liturgy taken from the pre-Nicene eucharistic settings: the offertory, the Prayer of Thanksgiving, the fraction, and the communion, which he took as normal and normative for the eucharist.[43] He went on to a somewhat sentimental description of a "Pre-Nicene Eucharist" taken from Hippolytus' *Apostolic Tradition*, which he had edited the same year; thereby he had made available to the English-speaking market an attempt at a critical text edition. But the important message he, too, conveyed, was:

> The Eucharist is unmistakably the action and the offering, not of the celebrant, but of the whole Church in its hierarchical unity.... The "Liturgical Movement" ... seeks to return behind the mediaeval "clerical" distortion of the eucharist to the truer and deeper conception of the Church of the Martyrs, only because it has first recovered a more authentic notion of what is involved in the doctrine that the Church is the mystical Body of Christ, that the sovereign Spirit of the Risen Life of Jesus is the very breath of her life.[44]

In January 1945 appeared the book written by Gregory Dix which has been repeatedly hailed as "the greatest piece of liturgical writing of an Anglican this century."[45] It was his classical *The Shape of the Liturgy*. His point of departure for the discussion of the topic was:

> It is the sequence of the rite--the Shape of the Liturgy--which chiefly performs the eucharistic action itself, and so carries out the human obedience to the Divine command 'Do this'. It is the phrasing of the prayers which chiefly expresses the meaning attached to that action by the

---

[40] Hebert, *Liturgy and Society*, p. 226.

[41] Arthur Gabriel Hebert, "Preface," in *The Parish Communion: A Book of Essays*, ed. Arthur Gabriel Hebert (London: SPCK; New York: Macmillan, 1937), pp. v-vi.

[42] "The Parish Communion in Its Spiritual Aspect, with a Note on the Fast before Communion," in *The Parish Communon: A Book of Essays*, ed. Arthur Gabriel Hebert (London: SPCK; New York: Macmillan, 1937), p. 7. See Gray, *Earth and Altar*, pp. 205-06.

[43] In *The Parish Communion: A Book of Essays*, ed. Arthur Gabriel Hebert (London: SPCK; New York: Macmillan, 1937), pp. 99-100.

[44] Dix, "Idea of 'The Church,'" pp. 105-06.

[45] Kenneth W. Stevenson, *Gregory Dix - Twenty-Five Years On*, Grove Liturgical Study, 10 (Bramcote, Notts.: Grove Books, 1977), p. 23. Stevenson stands at the Evangelical side in the Church of England. In 1982 the book was republished with thirteen pages of additional notes by Paul V. Marshall (New York: Seabury). The reviewer of that edition, too, calls the book "the single most influential book on liturgical history ever written in English.": Columba Stewart, review of *Gregory Dix, The Shape of the Liturgy*, ed. with additional notes by Paul V. Marshall, *Worship*, 57 (1983), 88.

theological tradition of the church. Both are essential parts of eucharistic worship. But they have an independent history, even though they are always combined in the tradition of the liturgy.[46]

Dix proceeded to unfold his basic thesis about the eucharistic action. Whereas the Last Supper was defined by a "seven-action scheme" of the rite (Jesus took bread, gave thanks over it, broke it, distributed it with words of explanation, took a cup, gave thanks over it, handed it over with words of explanation), the liturgical shape of the eucharist was a drastic modification of that scheme into a four-action shape:

> With absolute unanimity the liturgical tradition reproduces these seven actions as four: (1) The offertory; bread and wine are 'taken' and placed on the table together. (2) The prayer; the president gives thanks to God over bread and wine together. (3) The fraction; the bread is broken. (4) The communion; the bread and wine are distributed together.
>
> In that form and in that order these four actions constituted the absolutely invariable nucleus of every eucharistic rite known to us throughout antiquity from the Euphrates to Gaul.[47]

Dix went on to develop his argument in the consistency and changes, including additions and accretions as well as drastic transformations in the time of the Reformation, of the four-action shape.[48] This basic thesis about the shape of the eucharistic liturgy has been accepted both by scholars and in subsequent liturgical revisions.[49]

The other rather influential topic taken up by Dix was his contrast of the eschatological orientation of the pre-Nicene liturgy to the historical direction of the post-Nicene worship. He traced this shift in emphasis from "the eternal consequences of the redemption" and the transformation of the participants into the realm of the kingdom of God and the world to come to "the historical process of redemption" and the rising weight of the celebration of historical events in the liturgical year, the calendar, and--together with an increase of the anamnesis--in the eucharistic prayer.[50] Again, scholars and liturgical revisions have taken up the insistence on the basically eschatological character of the Christian liturgy and have followed Dix in this respect.[51]

In the same year *The Parish Communion* appeared in England (1937), two American liturgists published *The American Prayer Book: Its Origins and Principles*. The authors were Edward Lambe Parsons (1868-1960) and Baynard Hale Jones (1887-1957). Parsons was Bishop of California and member of the Standing Liturgical Commission while Jones taught liturgics at Sewanee from 1939 on where Massey Hamilton Shepherd came in contact with him.[52] The book itself did not present any major surprises or advancements but gave a good history of the *Book of Common Prayer* and made available the data English people could find in Frere's update of Procter's *New History of the Book of Common Prayer*. The Reformation was seen by Parsons and Jones as the expression of individualism and spiritual, political, and

---

[46] Dix, *Shape of the Liturgy*, p. 2.

[47] Dix, *Shape of the Liturgy*, p. 48.

[48] Dix regarded Cranmer as a consistent Zwinglian, and the 1549 *Book of Common Prayer* as "a mere ballon d'essai" for the doctrinally purer 1552 book: *Shape of the Liturgy*, pp. 640-56, 658.

[49] Stevenson, *Dix*, p. 23 note 7, p. 24 notes 5-6; Geoffrey Wainwright, "Recent Eucharistic Revision," in *The Study of Liturgy*, ed. Cheslyn Jones, Geoffrey Wainwright, and Edward Yarnold (London: SPCK, 1978), p. 284.

[50] Dix, *Shape of the Liturgy*, pp. 303-96.

[51] Stevenson, *Dix*, p. 27.

[52] Urban Tigner Holmes, "Education for Liturgy: An Unfinished Symphony in Four Movements," in *Worship Points The Way: A Celebration of the Life and Work of Massey H. Shepherd, Jr.*, ed. Malcolm C. Burson (New York: Seabury, 1981), p. 121. As will be seen in the progress of this chapter, Shepherd is the key person behind the *Book of Common Prayer* 1979.

social freedom and so, by implication, a movement not to be discarded.[53] Yet in matters liturgical they believed that

> [t]here is good ground for the assertion that we need liturgical experiments. There is excellent ground for the judgment that the Prayer Book with all its values is neither as complete nor as permanent as our forefathers used to think it.[54]

Parsons was later to be involved in the revision process that began in 1949.

A book that was bound to have more impact, both because of the author himself and the contents, was *Prayer Book Interleaves*, published posthumously in 1942, by William Palmer Ladd (1870-1941). Ladd, as dean of the Berkeley Divinity School in New Haven, Connecticut, was "the principal catalyst for the liturgical awakening in the Episcopal Church."[55] He was familiar with Maria Laach and its role in the Liturgical Movement and thought highly of the monks' "invaluable service to the whole Church."[56] He was very much hostile to the influence, as he saw it, of the Oxford Movement on the liturgical developments in the Anglican Communion which he thought "almost wholly bad," "ghastly," their efforts a "procrustean bed" and an attempt "to appease the pope."[57] On the other hand, he saw as the aim of the Liturgical Movement "to encourage the laity to understand and take their part in liturgical worship."[58] Although "our *Book of Common Prayer* is the best in the world,"[59] yet he acknowledged the need for revision and proposed ten suggestions as to how "our incomparable Prayer Book" might be perfected.[60] In them he advised revision, enrichment, simplification, and adaptation of the communion service to the needs of the day so that the eucharist would be the chief service on every Sunday in every parish. The calendar and lectionary should be revised; psalms should be included in the service; the offering should be separated from the Prayer for the Church; intercessions should be made more lively; and long wait during communion should be avoided by communion in one kind.[61] He set forth an outline of "The Holy Eucharist Simplified" which was closely structured after a Roman Catholic Mass, with its main feature the abolishment of the exhortatory texts, and a Prayer of Consecration which was a severely abridged version of that in the 1928 prayer book.[62] Ladd's greatest contribution may prove to have been the influence he had on Shepherd. The relationship was acknowledged by Ladd's widow[63] and by others who knew both persons.[64]

---

[53] Edward Lambe Parsons and Baynard Hale Jones, *The American Prayer Book: Its Origins and Principles* (New York: Scribner, 1937), p. 28.

[54] Parsons and Jones, *American Prayer Book*, p. 296.

[55] Holmes, "Education for Liturgy," p. 120.

[56] William Palmer Ladd, *Prayer Book Interleaves: Some Reflections on How the Book of Common Prayer Might Be Made More Influential in Our English-Speaking World*, 2nd ed. (New York: Oxford University Press, 1943), p. 22.

[57] Ladd, *Prayer Book Interleaves*, pp. 20-21. Cf. pp. 24, 166.

[58] Ladd, *Prayer Book Interleaves*, p. 22.

[59] Ladd, *Prayer Book Interleaves*, p. 107.

[60] Ladd, *Prayer Book Interleaves*, pp. 107-09, 155-57.

[61] This last proposal makes one wonder whether Ladd did not fall into the same trap as he saw the representatives of the Oxford Movement and the Ritualists in; if it were not an anachronism for that time one might have the irreverent idea that the era of spiritual fast food had arrived. Fortunately enough, the realization of this last proposal did not gain any ground.

[62] Ladd, *Prayer Book Interleaves*, pp. 180-83.

[63] Ladd, *Prayer Book Interleaves*, p. vi.

[64] Sherman Elbridge Johnson, "Massey Shepherd and the Episcopal Church: A Reminiscence," in *Worship Points The Way: A Celebration of the Life and Work of Massey H. Shepherd, Jr.*, ed. Malcolm C. Burson (New York: Seabury, 1981), pp. 9-10: "Dean Ladd greatly influenced Shep's thinking and his liturgical style." Holmes, "Education for Liturgy," p. 121: "Shepherd and Ladd were very close. . . . There is no question of the impact of the personality and thought of Ladd upon the guiding spirit of liturgical reform in the Episcopal Church."

Massey Hamilton Shepherd (born 1913) was active in teaching graduate students around the country, and as a member of the Standing Liturgical Commission of the Episcopal Church since 1946. In addition, he was a member of the Commission on Ways of Worship of the World Council of Churches, one of the Anglican observers at the Second Vatican Council in 1964, an Observer at the Consilium for the Implementation of the Constitution on the Sacred Liturgy from 1966 to 1969, a member of the Commission on Worship of the Consultation on Church Union (1965-1968), and of the International Consultation on English Texts.[65] In 1950, when he was already established as a first-rank liturgist, he published *The Oxford American Prayer Book Commentary* which became the standard commentary and reference work to the 1928 *Book of Common Prayer*.[66] Describing himself as a convinced Platonist with a predilection for formal, liturgical worship, he acknowledges the influence Guardini, Casel, and Ladd had on him.[67] As his name will be frequently mentioned in the course of the most recent revision process of the prayer book, there is no need here to add to the statement that "it is impossible to name another single person who has played a larger part in (the) development and acceptance" of the 1979 *Book of Common Prayer*.[68]

A fruit of the Liturgical Movement in the English-speaking world was the liturgy that was devised for the Church of South India. This church was formed from the Anglican, Methodist, Congregationalist, and Presbyterian churches in South India in 1947 and issued, in the course of the years, forms of worship and liturgical texts and rites. These showed on the one hand the parentage of the formerly separate churches, but on the other hand tried to incorporate both ancient Syrian and Indian elements, and findings and ideas (especially on the eucharist) that had emerged in the years when the Liturgical Movement had begun to make its influence show in the perception of liturgy and in the way it was celebrated.[69]

There is a certain ambiguity about the Christian initiation in this church's liturgy. In a former edition of *An Order for Holy Baptism* (1955) it was stated in the introduction

> that Baptism, Confirmation, and first Communion are parts of one process of entry into the Church, and by a provision for the combination of these in one continuous rite, if desired, in the case of adolescent and adult candidates.[70]

Yet in *The Book of Common Worship* of that Church, the different stages are headed: "Holy Baptism. I. The Baptism of Persons Able to Answer for Themselves. II. The Baptism of Infants." "An Order of Service for the Reception of Baptized Persons into the Full Fellowship of the Church Commonly Called Confirmation."[71] Both the baptism and the confirmation services resemble the respective order in the 1928 *Book of Common Prayer* of the Episcopal Church; they were expanded with Scriptural texts, addresses to the congregation and the candidates, and litanies. In the first address to the candidates for confirmation, the minister tells them that they have come "to ratify the solemn covenant then [at baptism] made, to

---

[65] Johnson, "Massey Shepherd," pp. 9-16 (slightly corrected).
[66] See Ronald V. Glens, "A Select Bibliography of the Writings of Massey Hamilton Shepherd, Jr.," in *Worship Points The Way: A Celebration of the Life and Work of Massey H. Shepherd, Jr.*, ed. Malcolm C. Burson (New York: Seabury, 1981), pp. 273-83.
[67] Massey Hamilton Shepherd, "The Berakah Award: Response," *Worship*, 52 (1978), 300-01.
[68] Johnson, "Massey Shepherd," p. 16.
[69] Cuming, *History*, pp. 195-98; Thomas Samuel Garrett, *Worship in the Church of South India*, Ecumenical Studies in Worship, 2 (London: Lutterworth, 1958), pp. 12-16; Hatchett, *Commentary*, p. 11.
[70] Quoted in: Garrett, *Worship*, pp. 36-37.
[71] *The Book of Common Worship As Authorized by the Synod 1962* (London: Oxford University Press, 1963), pp. 102-30. The Baptism of Infants and the Confirmation are reprinted in: Jagger, *Christian Initiation*, pp. 304-14. At the end of the confirmation service a "membership card" is given to the newly confirmed persons: *Book of Common Worship*, p. 130; Jagger, *Christian Initiation*, p. 314, no. 35.

profess your faith the Lord Jesus, to consecrate yourselves to him, and to receive the gifts which he is waiting to bestow."[72]

Not so much in the question of the Christian initiation as in the order of the eucharist has there been an influence of the worship of the Church of South India upon the liturgical revisions of other churches. The liturgy of that church "went behind the patristic developments after Constantine to the more primitive models of Justin Martyr and Hippolytus in the age when the Church was without help, without protection, without privilege."[73]

Currents of Life between 1950 and 1979

In retrospect the distinction between the first fifteen years of the period between 1950 and 1979 and the second half of it could not have been clearer. Whereas the 1950s and the first half of the 1960s are nowadays sometimes transfigured as the "good old times," with the social fabric seemingly intact, growth in the economy, and an everyday life undisturbed by geopolitical or domestic turmoil--or so it was perceived; any spots staining this image tend to be forgotten--, the second half of the 1960s and the 1970s were indeed "traumatic years;"[74] the morals of the nation underwent heavy strains and, after the apparently harmonious and *petit-bourgeois* 1950s, sank to low tides.

The population grew from 151,684,000 in 1950 to 180,671,000 in 1960, and to 204,879,000 in 1970. In this period the gross national product jumped from $284.8 billion to $977.1 billion. The average annual earnings of employees rose from $2,992 in 1950 to $7,564 in 1970. An ever-increasing number of women were gainfully employed in the labor force; the percentage rose from 31.4 of the total female population in 1950 to 42.6 in 1970. Of all the married women in the labor force, more than thirty percent of the participation rate in 1970 had children under six years.[75]

The "home" of the people became ever more widespread figuratively through the use of the cars and the influx of telecommunications. In 1950 more than 40 million cars and 8.5 million trucks were registered; in 1970 these figures had increased to almost 90 million cars and more than 18 million trucks. In 1950 fifty-two percent of the families owned one car, and fifteen percent owned two or more; in 1970 fifty-four percent owned one car, but twenty-eight percent owned two or more. In 1950 61.8 percent of all households had a telephone; in 1970 90.5 percent. The radio had became standard equipment in households by 1950: ninety-four percent owned a set (in 1970 almost ninety-eight percent). The increase in the number of television sets, however, was spectacular in this period. Whereas in 1950, almost nine percent owned a set, this number had grown to eighty-six percent of all households in 1960, and to nearly ninety-four percent in 1970.[76] Whatever happened in the world could be seen at home, and people could be informed if they wanted to. Major events no longer took place "somewhere" and "somehow" but were transmitted live into every home.

Another war, albeit undeclared, marked the beginning of this period. From 1950 to 1954, American soldiers fought in Korea. When these five years had ended, more than 5.7 million military personnel had been involved, fifty-six percent of whom served overseas. More than

---

[72] *Book of Common Worship*, p. 124; Jagger, *Christian Initiation*, p. 311, no. 10.

[73] Shepherd, "Berakah Award," 307.

[74] Sydney Eckman Ahlstrom, "The Traumatic Years: American Religion and Culture in the '60s and '70s," *Theology Today*, 36 (1980), 504-22.

[75] Wattenberg, *Statistical History*, A 6, p. 8; F 1, p. 224; D 772, p. 164; D 58, p. 133.

[76] Wattenberg, *Statistical History*, Q 153-55, p. 716; Q 176-77, p. 717; R 3, p. 783; R 104-05, p. 796, combined with A 288, p. 41.

54,000 soldiers had died, 33,629 in battle and 20,617 from other sources. More than 103,000 were wounded.[77]

Parallel with the last two years of the Korean conflict was the spectacle of daily live radio and television broadcasts from the hearings of the Senate Committee on Un-American Activities. Chaired by Wisconsin senator Joseph McCarthy, this committee was set to a grand-scale witchhunt on everybody who did not conform to its own perception of a good and typical American and therefore was suspicious of "pink" or "leftist" inclinations. University professors, writers, journalists, artists, and member of other groups which possibly disseminated "Un-American" ideas were subject to sharp, hypocritical, and biased scrutinies; the result often was devastating for the further career, even of those who were cleared of the charges.

The Montgomery Bus Boycott on December 1, 1955 by the Black population of that city is often taken as the beginning of the institutionalized Civil Rights Movement of the Black people. As leader of that movement emerged the Baptist pastor Dr. Martin Luther King, Jr. The next ten years were marked by riots, often brutal force, a resurgence of heavy racial tensions above all in the South, often backed by high-ranking politicians, attempts to regulate by legislation (Civil Rights Act 1964; Voting Rights Act 1965), and court judgments. The grievances and defects that had sparked the movement, the desegregation of schools and public facilities, and a gradual escalation of the impact of the movement culminated in the 1963 March on Washington and the 1965 convergence on Birmingham and Selma. A big moral boost for the non-violent change of society, advocated by Martin Luther King, was the Nobel Peace Prize he was awarded in 1964.

It came as a shock to may Americans when they learned that the incarnation of Godlessness and Sin, the Soviet Union, had succeeded in beating them in the race to outer space: on October 4, 1957 the first artificial satellite, Sputnik I, circled the globe. On April 12, 1961 the first manned spaceship, Wostok I, orbited the earth with the Soviet cosmonaut Yuri Gagarin aboard; two weeks later the first American, Alan B. Shephard, Jr., flew on a parabolic curve through space; only a year later the first American astronaut, John H. Glenn, circled the earth three times. The Sputnik crisis led to an increased effort in the United States to make education in basics and natural sciences more efficient in school and to concentrate on better learning.

Another watershed was reached when on November 8, 1960 the young and charismatic, but above all Roman Catholic, John Fitzgerald Kennedy was elected thirty-fifth President of the United States. After the complacent years of the Eisenhower era the new President, twenty-seven years younger than his predecessor, invigorated the self-esteem of the population. Although during his tenure the world stood on the brink of a new war twice, during the Berlin Wall crisis in the summer of 1961 and during the Cuban Missile crisis October 22 to November 20, 1962, he tried to seize on the mood of the day through his goal of the "New Frontier," a renewal program for society which under his successor, Lyndon Baines Johnson, became the "Great Society" program, the policy for equality and prosperity for all Americans. The assassination of President Kennedy on November 22, 1963 in Dallas was a tremendous shock.

Spiritually the 1950s and the beginning of the 1960s were marked by a "surprising and almost unsolicited increase in church membership."[78] In 1950 fifty-seven percent were affiliated with a church; in 1960 sixty-three percent; in 1965 sixty-four percent.[79] The trend was marked: religion was a part of the "American way of life," and this up to the upper echelons of the government. President Eisenhower is quoted as having remarked: "Our

---

[77] Wattenberg, *Statistical History*, Y 856-82, p. 1140.

[78] Ahlstrom, "Traumatic Years," 508.

[79] Wattenberg, *Statistical History*, H 793, p. 391, combined with A 6, p. 8. It is notoriously difficult to assess and compare church membership statistics since the churches have different definitions of their own membership which often does not depend solely on baptism. Ahlstrom, *Religious History*, II, 488, gives different and even more provocative figures: 1950 55%; 1960 69%.

government makes no sense unless it is founded on a deeply felt religious faith--and I don't care what it is."[80] The Pledge of Allegiance to the Flag was rephrased as referring to one nation "under God" in 1954. Two years later the phrase on the coins and bills, "In God We Trust," became the official motto of the United States.[81] These were constitutionally risky pieces of legislation as they came close to "an establishment of religion" specifically forbidden by the First Amendment to the Constitution, but the prevalent mood of the country showed no sign of restraint of the people's piety. The 1950s especially were heydays of the so-called "civil religion,"[82] "a collection of beliefs, symbols, and rituals with respect to sacred things and institutionalized in a collectivity."[83] A cycle of patriotic days (Independence Day, Veterans' Day, Memorial Day), family-oriented days (Mother's Day, Father's Day, Halloween, Thanksgiving, and, to a certain extent, Christmas), and national "saints" days (Washington's Birthday, sometimes Lincoln's Birthday, and, since 1986, Martin Luther King's Birthday) gives to the people a pattern of semi- or quasi-festive collective rituals of remembering persons or facts constitutive of the social fabric of the nation.

Up to the early 1960s it was American to believe in (a) God, to be affiliated with a church, and to be a good patriot by showing this and by joining in the nation's own quasi-religious festivities.

By contrast, the picture for the second half of the 1960s and the 1970s could not be darker. The prevalent mood was one of gloom, challenge, breakdown of traditional value systems, and, in general, an overflow of questions with but few answers.

The Vietnam War from 1961 to 1974 was unpopular and drained a vast amount of political energy, human lives, and economic resources. The ongoing struggle for equality and against unjustice due to race, sex, color, origin, or sexual orientation demanded an entirely new mentality for everybody who did not belong to these suppressed or underprivileged sections of the population. The assassinations of President Kennedy on November 22, 1962, of Dr. Martin Luther King, Jr., on April 4, 1968, and of Robert F. Kennedy on June 6, 1968 made many Americans question whether they were rather dominated by greed, envy, selfishness, and disrespect for the most sacred property--life itself. The break-in at the Democratic Party headquarters at the Watergate complex in Washington, D.C., on June 17, 1972 and its gradual disclosure, culminating in the disreputable resignation of Richard M. Nixon from the Presidency on August 9, 1974, left a credibility gap for politics and politicians. Even the presidency, 1977 to 1981, of Jimmy [James E.] Carter, who had advocated a greater transparency of government and higher ethics in office, could not restore this trust in the nation itself and its representatives. The seizure of American hostages in Iran on November 4, 1979 showed the impotence of a world power against the force of an inimical mob abroad to protect the integrity of life of its citizens.

They were years of protest, challenge, and withdrawal. The Beat and Rock music of the young people was the revolt against their parents' cultural values. "Flower Power" and "Woodstock" (1969) stood for both a revolt against brutal forces and a withdrawal from the real problems of society. The demonstrations against the Vietnam War and the students' protests were expressions of anger at a system which was not as just and as benevolent as it ought to be, and they showed growing dissatisfaction with the complacence of those in authority.

The only bright spot in these years which gave the people a moment of relief was the first landing on the moon by a human being; on July 20, 1969 Neill A. Armstrong and his crew

---

[80] *Christian Century*, 71 (1954); quoted in: Ahlstrom, *Religious History*, II, 450, and "Traumatic Years," 508.

[81] Ahlstrom, *Religious History*, II, 450-51.

[82] This term was coined in 1967 by Robert N. Bellah in his article "Civil Religion in America," *Daedalus* (1967), 1-21.

[83] Bellah, "Civil Religion," 8; quoted in: Richard L. Eslinger, "Civil Religion and the Year of Grace," *Worship*, 58 (1984), 372.

touched down and set foot on an extraterrestrial body. This "giant leap for mankind" showed the potential the United States could unleash if it had a goal worth striving for.

If there is one common denominator for all the struggles and the emotional turmoil the people experienced, then it was the realization that the order by the Constitution, to "establish Justice" and to "promote the general Welfare," was still unfinished. The tumults of these years showed that the issues were

> a full-scale critique of the American way of life: both the social injustices of the system itself and the ideological, philosophical, and theological assumptions that have justified and legitimized the existing social order.[84]

One attempt to cope with the apparent erosion of puritan values and the failure of traditional social ethics was a rapid increase and militancy of Fundamentalism and evangelical religion in the second half of the 1970s. Although this phenomenon affected the so-called liturgical churches (Roman Catholic, Lutheran, Episcopal) less than churches from the Reformed tradition and other Protestant denominations, the protagonists of this resurgence of Fundamentalism began to wield considerable influence in public in general and in politics, trying to undo the social progress of the 1960s and 1970s which they regarded as the source of the evil state of the nation's stature and morale.

Liturgical revisions are often necessitated by a breakdown of the social order in which the texts and rites were formerly devised. But it is always a risky enterprise to embark on a revision process during a time of social stress, turmoil, and disorder.

Preliminaries to the Revision Process, a Lambeth Conference, and the Second Vatican Council

The revisions of the *Book of Common Prayer* in some of the member churches of the Anglican Communion which were carried out in the first quarter of this century had given a sense of the historical relativity of the *Book of Common Prayer* to the members of the 1928 General Convention, which finally approved the definite prayer book for the Episcopal Church. Besides, it was undesirable to keep the General Convention busy with miniscule detail. On the other side, the Convention could not avail itself of an institutionalized group of persons interested in liturgical matters, unless expressly established by the Convention. Therefore in 1928 it established a liturgical commission as a Standing Commission of the church with the resolution that

> there be appointed a Standing Liturgical Commission, consisting of eight Bishops, eight Presbyters, and eight Laymen, to be appointed by the Chairmen of the two Houses, to which Commission may be referred, for preservation and study, all matters relating to the Book of Common Prayer, with the idea of developing and conserving for some possible future use, the liturgical experience and scholarship of the Church.[85]

This bulky commission was in 1946 reduced to two bishops, five presbyters (later six, the Custodian of the Standard Book having been made an *ex officio* member), and two lay persons.

---

[84] Ahlstrom, "Traumatic Years," 512.
[85] Episcopal Church, General Convention, *Journal of the General Convention of the Protestant Episcopal Church in the United States of America Held in the City of Washington, D.C. From October Tenth to October Twenty-Fifth, inclusive, in the Year of Our Lord 1928* (New York: Abbot Press, 1929), p. 352. See Albright, *History*, p. 357; Detscher, *Evolution*, p. 255; Sydnor, *Real Prayer Book*, p. 80.

In 1943 the Standing Liturgical Commission first asked the General Convention, meeting in Cleveland, Ohio, to mark the four hundredth anniversary of the first *Book of Common Prayer* in 1949 by being allowed

> to prepare a systematic Revision of the Book of Common Prayer, which shall be admitted to the Church for study not later than the Autumn of 1949; and that the commission then consider any further suggestions, and all criticisms of such Proposed Book, and submit its completed work for action by a later General Convention.

The reason for this proposal was "suggestions for Prayer Book revision which are notable for their number and their cogency" and which the commission had received in the course of the previous years.

> With a realization of the rich stores of liturgical knowledge contributed by recent research, and benefitting by the experience of other Churches of the Anglican Communion with Prayer Books which have appeared since our 1928 revision, we feel that the time is ripe for a more systematic and complete revision than has been possible heretofore.[86]

Without calling it by that name, the Liturgical Movement had begun to make an impact on the church's liturgy and the way it was perceived by the members, especially those interested in the matter. The House of Bishops voted that the whole question be referred back to the Standing Liturgical Commission.[87]

The same rationale, the fourth centennial of the first *Book of Common Prayer*, and the same reason for a revision, "a far higher level [of] liturgical knowledge and interest . . . than at any previous centennial," were quoted in the report of the Standing Liturgical Commission to the General Convention, held in Philadelphia in 1946, to ask for an eventual revision of the prayer book, which was deemed "inevitable." This time, however, a different approach was proposed along the lines of some kind of trial use of material which would from time to time appear in a series of Prayer Book Studies. Each issue would deal with one office or feature of the church's liturgy.[88] Again, this proposal was voted down by the General Convention.

In 1949 the Standing Liturgical Commission reported to the General Convention in San Francisco that two studies for inclusion in a series of Prayer Book Studies had been completed and that others were in an advanced state of preparation. The Convention was asked to secure the publisher, the Church Hymnal Corporation, against any financial losses in the course of the undertaking. This contingency fund was appropriated as a guarantee for any loss to the publisher.[89]

The first of the booklets to appear in this Prayer Book Studies series was the one on baptism and confirmation, with a study on the liturgical lectionary under the same cover; it was published in 1950. The Standing Liturgical Commission stated in the preface that "there is a widespread and insistent demand for a general revision of the Prayer Book." Nonetheless, the booklet was handed out for study purposes only, not for any revision proposal or for liturgical use. It was hoped that the balance in doctrine seen in the prayer

---

[86] Episcopal Church, General Convention, *Journal of the General Convention of the Protestant Episcopal Church in the United States of America Held in Cleveland, Ohio From October Second to October Eleventh, inclusive, in the Year of Our Lord 1943* (n.p.: Printed for the Convention, 1943), p. 434. As to the revisions of the *Book of Common Prayer* in the different churches, see Cuming, *History*, pp. 183-95.

[87] *General Convention 1943*, p. 60.

[88] Episcopal Church, General Convention, *Journal of the General Convention of the Protestant Episcopal Church in the United States of America Held in Philaelphia, Pennsylvania From September Tenth to Twentieth, inclusive, in the Year of Our Lord 1946* (n.p.: Printed for the Convention, 1947), pp. 439-40.

[89] Episcopal Church, General Convention, *Journal of the General Convention of the Protestant Episcopal Church in the United States of America Held in San Francisco, California From September Twenty-Sixth to October Seventh, inclusive, in the Year of Our Lord 1949* (n.p.: Printed for the Convention, 1949), pp. 434-35, 270.

book would be maintained in the studies and publications.[90] The commission attempted, as stated in the introduction to the first part of the study, "to answer the constant demand that the structure and meaning of the initiatory rites of Baptism and Confirmation be simplified and clarified, and, where necessary, be enriched in content."[91] The difficulties arising from the separation of the one original baptismal rite into two distinct rites, baptism and confirmation, were seen, yet the commission naturally could not abolish the dichotomy. The proposed changes in the baptismal services went in three directions: the length of the service, the clarification of rubrics, and the simplification of the text.

The "Ministration of Holy Baptism" was given in its entirety, with all the proposed alterations printed continuously.[92] The opening rubrics stressed the public character of baptism; it might also be administered after the proclamation of the gospel during the communion service. The requirements for the sponsors were strengthened regarding their own church life and the prebaptismal instructions.

The first exhortation made a theological reinterpretation, despite the disclaim of the commission's intention, when it changed the phrasing "that *he* may be baptized with water and the Holy Ghost, and received into Christ's holy Church"[93] into the wording "that *he*, being baptized, may be received into Christ's holy Church,"[94] thereby clarifying--and definitely putting to rest the grievances of the puritans of the sixteenth century--that the reception into the Church would be made by being baptized, not in a sign or ceremony distinct from it. The text accompanying the signing with the cross after the washing remained unchanged, however, reading again "We receive this Child (Person) into the congregation of Christ's flock" instead of a possible "We have received." The word "regeneration" ws given as the English "spiritual birth," although the commission was eager to point out that "this simplification of phrase does not imply any weakening whatsoever of the Church's adherence to the doctrine of Baptismal Regeneration."[95] The possible reading of John 3:1-8 was dropped. The following invitation to prayer and the ensuing prayer were dropped, and the service continued after the gospel reading with the baptismal interrogatories, called promises. The question for belief was rephrased so as to specifically ask about the three divine Persons. If a child was to be baptized, additional questions were asked of the sponsors about their willingness to live up to their duties. A new set of suffrages asking for divine assistance for the baptizands, and a new prayer petitioning for these persons a life according to their baptism, were added. In the blessing of the font the allusion to Christ shedding water and blood on the cross was replaced by a phrase that he suffered death, was buried, and rose "that we might live unto thee in newness of life by the power of his Resurrection." Water baptism and signing with the cross were headed by the title "The Baptism." The final thanksgiving had received some phrases from the omitted prayer by all after the gospel proclamation. A new prayer was proposed, asking for grace for the sponsors.

The final rubric allowed that an adult would be baptized and confirmed in one continuous celebration, the baptismal service ending with the signing of the cross, and the confirmation service immediately beginning with the central part after the renewal of the baptismal vows--a felicitous addition pointing in the direction of a return to the original inclusive rite.

The service in general had received a good streamlining without sacrificing theologically sound or necessary ideas.

The confirmation service had been given both a grand enrichment at the beginning of the celebration, and, in the very heart of the rite, a heavy theological reinterpretation.

---

[90] Episcopal Church, Standing Liturgical Commission, *Baptism and Confirmation; The Liturgical Lectionary*, Prayer Book Studies, 1; 2 (New York: Church Pension Fund, 1950), pp. vi-vii.
[91] *Baptism and Confirmation*, p. 3.
[92] *Baptism and Confirmation*, pp. 24-30.
[93] *Book of Common Prayer 1928*, p. 274.
[94] *Baptism and Confirmation*, p. 25.
[95] *Baptism and Confirmation*, p. 17.

In order to make the service more suitable for the solemn occasion, and as it was not necessarily linked to any other regular worship (Morning or Evening Prayer, communion service), the entire "Order of Confirmation"[96] was preceded by a possible introduction with reading Acts 1:8, setting the tone for interpreting the confirmation as strength for Christian witness, Psalm 27:1,4f,7-11,13,15f, the reading of Ezekiel 36:25-28 (the clean water), a hymn, the Apostles' Creed, and a prayer by the minister asking for light and strength from the Holy Spirit. The minister for this preparation would not be the bishop but a presbyter. In the presentation of the candidates a question by the bishop to the minister about previous examination and readiness of the confirmands had been inserted. The invitation to a renewal of the baptismal confession had been rephrased to stress the duty of a Christian life; the interrogatories were the same as in the proposed baptismal order, so as to show the connection of the two services. In the following prayer by the bishop and in the confirmation formula ensuing, the sacramental action had been drastically reinterpreted. Where the bishop was to say, according to the confirmation rite in the *Book of Common Prayer*, "Strengthen them, we beseech thee, O Lord, with the Holy Ghost, the Comforter, and daily increase in them thy manifold gifts of grace," and in the formula accompanying the laying on of hands, "Defend, O Lord, this thy Child with thy heavenly grace,"[97] now it was proposed that the bishop would ask in the prayer, "Send into their hearts, we beseech thee, O Lord, thy Holy Spirit, and daily increase in them thy manifold gifts of grace;" and the formula was to read, "Confirm, O Lord, this thy Child with thy heavenly grace."[98] It is not difficult to regard this double rephrasing not only as a turning back to the 1549 rite but also as a stronger emphasis of the Western perception developed as a consequence of the early medieval interpretation of the gift of the Holy Spirit in confirmation, to the detriment of the action in baptism.[99] The second concluding prayer was omitted, and the blessing was broadened to include a dismissal.

This study, the first in a series of twenty-nine that appeared from 1950 to 1976, did not wield much influence or meet widespread critique. The first booklet to awaken a lot of response was Prayer Book Studies 4: *The Eucharistic Liturgy*, published in 1953. As the House of Bishops had--contrary to the constitution of the church--approved trial use of this liturgy, provided that all who participated in celebrations according to the proposed format would mail their comments to the Standing Liturgical Commission, a large amount of correspondence was generated. The result was a broader interest by the church members in the further publications of the commission.[100]

Eight years after the appearance of Prayer Book Studies 1, the bishops of the Anglican Communion convened for their ninth Lambeth Conference. Judged by the sheer number of pages in the official documents, the 1958 Lambeth Conference was the one that has been most concerned about the *Book of Common Prayer*, its revision, and theological and practical statements about the sacraments. It is always captious and dangerous to attribute certain developments to the dictum that the time was "ripe for it" and the *zeitgeist* rendered a discussion of the points both inevitable and fruitful for the growth of the community involved. The Liturgical Movement in the Roman Catholic Church had advanced to a stage beyond mere official toleration; papal encouragement and reforms, even of the center of the liturgical year, the Paschal Triduum (1951/55), had shown that a thorough revision of the liturgy was

---

[96] *Baptism and Confirmation*, pp. 31-35.
[97] *Book of Common Prayer 1928*, p. 297.
[98] *Baptism and Confirmation*, p. 34.
[99] The classical study on the development of the rite (and later of the theology) of confirmation in the West is John Douglas Close Fisher, *Christian Initiation: Baptism in the Medieval West*, Alcuin Club Collections, 47 (London: SPCK, 1965).
[100] Communication in a letter received from Massey H. Shepherd, Jr., April 14, 1986, p. 3.

possible and necessary.[101] Groundbreaking literature had been published in the past thirty years on the history and theology of the liturgy both in English and in other languages. And increasingly developments in one church brought about some reaction in another in the era of the Ecumenical Movement. Without being able to point to one particular reason for the deliberations and statements of the Lambeth Conference, the mere fact that the heart of the Church's life, the liturgy, was a prominent feature on the agenda showed that the nature of worship was indeed regarded as a question of life or death for the Church--as it was also shown a few years later by the assembly of Roman Catholic bishops at the Second Vatican Council. All three different types of pronouncements issued by the members of the Lambeth Conference dealt with the liturgy.

The Encyclical Letter of the bishops hailed the fact that through a growing knowledge of biblical teaching and of the apostolic and ancient liturgy a greater unity was achieved among the different traditions within the Anglican Communion.[102]

In the resolutions adopted, the bishops focused on the features in the prayer book which were regarded as essential to the unity within the Communion: the canonical Scriptures and creeds, baptism, confirmation, holy communion, and the ordinal, and they urged

> that a chief aim of Prayer Book revision shold be to further that recovery of the worship of the Primitive Church which was the aim of the first Prayer Books of the Church of England.[103]

Furthermore the report of the sub-committee on the *Book of Common Prayer* was recommended for study by all members of the Anglican Communion.

This report dealt with prayer book revision in general, and with different parts in the prayer book. The *Book of Common Prayer*

> is the public expression of the worship of God in the Anglican Communion, and it is on the worship of God, creation's secret force, that all human activity depends. It is only in worship that all the Church can learn the will of God and receive wisdom and power to do it. . . .
> Worship then is the first concern of the Church, and it must be the worship of the whole Church, priests and people together bringing to God every human interest and activity and problem and conflict to be taken into his will and used for his purposes.
> It is with this end in view that the sub-committee has approached its task of considering the prayer books of the Anglican Communion, and their continuing suitability as the instrument of the worship of the Church in the world as it is to-day.[104]

The 1662 prayer book was seen as one among many, and the right of every church to change or adapt the prayer book to its own conditions was underlined. The aim of the reformers

---

[101] From an insider's point of view, the different stages and developments of the liturgical reform in the Roman Catholic Church have been authoritatively told by Annibale Bugnini, *La riforma liturgica (1948-1975)*, Biblioteca "Ephemerides Liturgicae" "Subsidia," 30 (Roma: CLV Edizioni Liturgiche, 1983).

[102] Lambeth Conference, *The Lambeth Conference 1958: The Encyclical Letter from the Bishops Together with the Resolutions and Reports* ([London:] SPCK; [Greenwich, CT:] Seabury, 1958), p. 25.

[103] *Lambeth Conference 1958*, p. 47. It is worth noting that the bishops themselves spoke of the recovery of the worship of the primitive Church as the aim of the Anglican reformers; clearly, the bishops suggested hereby, they had not succeeded in achieving this goal. As to "the first Prayer Books of the Church of England," one might ask which ones these were, and whether the 1662 *Book of Common Prayer*, still the legal prayer book in the Church of England, had in the eyes of the bishops not this aim of recovering the worship of the primitive Church, let alone achieving this end. But in this resolution, too, this same aim was demanded of any prayer book revision.

[104] *Lambeth Conference 1958*, p. 78. The plural "prayer books" in the last sentence clearly indicated that "the *Book of Common Prayer*" had in the mind of the sub-committee lost its identity as being the one book used for the worship. That included an acknowledgment that different editions within the Anglican Communion at the same time are indications of different expressions of the one faith--or, in the worst case, of faith different from church to church.

themselves from 1549 on, to pattern the worship according to the models of the primitive Church, would itself be a reason for further revision.

> We might ask what elements in the Book of Common Prayer are due to the sixteenth and seventeenth century misunderstanding of what is "primitive" in public worship, and what elements need to be substituted or added in order to make Prayer Book services truer to the ideal towards which Cranmer was feeling his way.[105]

On a practical level eight features were given "which are most effective in maintaining the traditional doctrinal emphasis of the worship and witness of the Anglican Communion." Among those features were worship in the vernacular, as totally common prayer, services that would be easy to follow and not with too many seasonal variations, and the importance of, and balance among, word and sacrament. Among the suggestions for further recovery of elements that originated in the worship of the primitive Church were shorter and fewer exhortations; the "people's prayers," the intercessions, at the eucharist; the link between the offertory and the prayer of consecration; and an extension of the motives of thanksgiving in the eucharistic prayer beyond Calvary, but for all "mighty works of God," especially the resurrection, ascension, and coming again of Christ.[106] For the communion service the subcommittee hoped

> that it is now possible to work towards a liturgy which will win its way throughout the Anglican Communion. The Committee would not suggest a return to the rigid and legalistic ideas of uniformity which prevailed for some centuries. It recognizes that even in the Sacrament of Unity there is a place for variations of rite to meet local situations and needs.[107]

Old Testament readings, corresponding to the epistle or gospel, were proposed at the principal eucharist on Sundays; the responsorial psalm might be reintroduced between the readings; and the *Gloria in excelsis* was suggested for reinsertion in the introductory part of the Sunday eucharist.

In the matter of Christian initiation the report of the Committee on Baptism and Confirmation and the ensuing resolutions of the previous Lambeth Conference of 1948 were confirmed, and Prayer Book Studies 1 of the Standing Liturgical Commission of the Episcopal Church was, among other books, recommended for study. Adult baptism, closely related to the confirmation, culminating, according to ancient patterns, in the first communion, should be a concern of the Church. Twelve elements were suggested for incorporation in any baptismal service:

1-- The reading of Scripture concerning baptism
2-- A renunciation of the former way of life
3-- A profession of faith with the reciting of the baptismal creed
4-- Promises of a Christian life style
5-- Blessing of the water, possibly in litany form
6-- Baptism with water in the threefold Name
7-- The signing with the cross
8-- [The acknowledgment of] the reception of the baptized into the   Church
9-- Thanksgiving for the seal of the Holy Spirit for ever
10-- Prayer for growth in the Christian life
11-- An exhortation to the congregation about its duty towards the newly baptized
12-- An exhortation to the newly baptized to live the new life.[108]

The committee once again endorsed that adult baptism, confirmation, and first communion should be combined so that these three different stages could be seen as one process of initiation.

---

[105] *Lambeth Conference 1958*, p. 80.
[106] *Lambeth Conference 1958*, p. 80.
[107] *Lambeth Conference 1958*, p. 81.
[108] *Lambeth Conference 1958*, pp. 86-87.

The documents of the ninth Lambeth Conference, with their far-seeing visions, can in retrospect be regarded as having come at the right time, encouraging liturgical revision and at the same time giving some guidelines. It has been made clear that the time of strict and enforceable uniformity would now be part of history, not of present age, of the Anglican Communion, and more than ever adaptation to the urgencies of the modern time was demanded. The best way to adapt, however, was seen to be in going back to ancient patterns and ideas, and the liturgy in accordance with the primitive Church remained the ideal.

Around this time the Roman Catholic Church too was undergoing an invigoration and opening up, the likes of which it had not seen for centuries, when the realization broke through that the Second Vatican Council, announced by Pope John XXIII on January 25, 1959, would try to reconcile the church with the realities of the modern world. Although these high expectations were bound to be dashed by the disappointment when the final documents were made known, the first fruit of the Council (held from 1962 until 1965), the Constitution on the Sacred Liturgy, had the most-felt impact on the believers' church life. This document, the only remaining one from the original schemes introduced and dealt with in the conciliar hall, was approved by the Council Fathers and promulgated on December 4, 1963. The text laid the groundwork and set the tone not only for concrete liturgical reforms spelled out in the course of the document, but also for the theological understanding of the liturgy, its ecclesiological dimension, and its pastoral nature. As such the Constitution was bound to have an impact far greater than the revision of liturgical rites within the Roman Catholic Church. Its influence was felt in other churches too, in their understanding of liturgy and in the results of the revisions of their liturgical books. This could be all the more so as both in the conciliar hall and, from 1966 until the close of its work, during the work of the Consilium for the Implementation of the Constitution on the Sacred Liturgy (whose duty it was to carry out the reforms of the liturgical rites), representatives of other churches were present. And although they did not have the right to take the floor or to vote, their mere presence was a stimulus for openness towards the other churches. One of the observers for the Anglican Communion was Massey H. Shepherd, Jr., first at the Council itself and later, from 1966 to 1970, at the Consilium (together with Canon Ronald Jasper, chairman of the Church of England's Liturgical Commission).[109]

In his commentary on the Constitution Shepherd pointed out three characteristics of the document.[110]

The paschal mystery is the unitive pattern for the understanding of the foundation of the Church and liturgy and the door to a new practice of worship which transcends the polemic between the churches on the nature and conduct of the liturgy; the paschal mystery is the origin and heart of the liturgy.[111] The Constitution stressed the corporate, responsible

---

[109] It should not be forgotten that of all churches and denominations arising from the Reformation only the Anglican Communion has been mentioned by name by the documents of the Second Vatican Council as occupying "locum specialem" among those bodies "in quibus traditiones et structurae catholicae ex parte subsistere pergunt": Decretum de oecumenismo "Unitatis redintegratio," no. 13: Alberigo, *Conciliorum Oecumenicorum Decreta*, p. 915. See David John Bird, "'The Anglican Communion Occupies a Special Place': An Examination of the Background, Development and Reception in the Roman Catholic Church of the Text on the Special Place of the Anglican Communion in 'Unitatis Redintegratio'," Dissertation Duquesne University 1987.

[110] Massey Hamilton Shepherd, "The Liturgy," in *The Second Vatican Council: Studies by Eight Anglican Observers*, ed. Bernard Clinton Pawley (London: Oxford University Press, 1967), pp. 158-64.

[111] In this context he acknowledged the "fruitful insights" of the "Mystery-theology" of the Benedictines of Maria Laach, and especially of Odo Casel whose work has been the binding, if unacknowledged, thread of the Constitution: Shepherd, "Liturgy," p. 161; see his "Berakah Award," 304. Casel's work on the "Kultmysterium" was published in English in 1962 as *The Mystery of Christian Worship and Other Writings* (Westminster, MD: Newman). His classical definition of the liturgical mystery "Das Mysterium ist eine heilige kultische Handlung,

participation by the entire liturgical assembly which includes laity and clergy. This thrust is at the same time a point of departure for, and the result of, a new and clearer vision of the Church which is both visible and invisible, human and divine, temporal and eschatological; it includes the corporate priesthood of all believers; and manifests this priesthood of all believers in the full active participation of all.[112] The Roman Catholic Church has relinquished the idea of strict uniformity in its liturgy, "a principle so dear to the sixteenth century, both in the Roman Catholic and the Anglican churches." Substituting for it is "the quest for unity without uniformity."[113]

Shepherd foresaw that the liturgies of both the Roman Catholic and the Anglican churches would be "bound to exert influence upon the other--in structure, in language, and in the perspective of a commonly shared Biblical theology of the 'Paschal Mystery.'"[114] This prophecy did prove to be true on the Anglican side when the Episcopal Church embarked on a new prayer book revision in 1964.

The Standing Liturgical Commission of the Episcopal Church had concluded by 1960 at the latest that, as pressure for serious prayer book revision had begun to mount, the method to be followed should be that of trial use of the office or feature of the prayer book under discussion for a certain period, as the Roman Catholic Church (for example, the reform of the Paschal Vigil) and other Anglican churches had experienced already, before any definite action would be taken. To support this instrument of decision-making, Shepherd was asked to draft *The Problem and Method of Prayer Book Revision*, which was published well before the 1961 General Convention as Prayer Book Studies 15.

At the General Convention (September 18-29, 1961) in Detroit itself, the Standing Liturgical Commission through a speech by Shepherd (who had not been elected as a deputy but was nonetheless given the floor in the House of Deputies to address the assembly on this point for ten minutes)[115] proposed an amendment to the church's constitution--which until that time forebade any use of unauthorized prayer book services--to the effect that trial use of the rites issued by the commission might be made useful; the matter passed both Houses.[116]

The following General Convention (October 12-23, 1964) in St. Louis affirmed the decision of the previous Convention. It was said that the Prayer Book Studies had made available to the church "the results of sound scholarship and reasonable proposals for the revision of the Book of Common Prayer in whole or in part;" a joint commission was to propose to the next Convention a plan of revising the prayer book, "with a special view to

---

in der eine Heilstatsache unter dem Ritus Gegenwart wird; indem die Kultgemeinde diesen Ritus vollzieht, nimmt sie an der Heilstat teil und erwirbt sich dadurch das Heil." (Odo Casel, *Das Kultmysterium*, 4. durchgesehene und erweiterte Aufl., hrsg. Burkhard Neunheuser [Regensburg: Pustet, 1960], p. 79) is translated in English as: "The mystery is a sacred ritual action in which a saving deed is made present through the rite; the congregation, by performing the rite, takes part in the saving act, and thereby wins salvation.": *The Mystery of Christian Worship*, p. 54; quoted in: Burkhard Neunheuser, "Odo Casel in Retrospect and Prospect," *Worship*, 50 (1976), 494-95. This view is reflected in articles 2, 6, 7, and 48 of the Constitution on the Sacred Liturgy.

[112] Shepherd, "Liturgy," pp. 162-63. These aspects are found in articles 2, 7, 14, and 41 of the Constitution.

[113] Shepherd, "Liturgy," p. 164.

[114] Shepherd, "Liturgy," p. 164. The only point at which he saw the Constitution at variance with the theology of the *Book of Common Prayer* is the text in article 104: "eorumque [Sanctorum] meritis Dei beneficia [Ecclesia] impetrat,": ALberigo, *Conciliorum Oecumenicorum Decreta*, p. 838. But he pointed out that the Anglican churches are in communion with the Old Catholic churches and the Philippine Independent Church which subscribe to this doctrine: Shepherd, "Liturgy," p. 159.

[115] Communication of this background (also for the previous section) in a letter received from Massey H. Shepherd, Jr., April 14, 1986, p. 4.

[116] Episcopal Church, General Convention, *Journal of the General Convention of the Protestant Episcopal Church in the United States of America Held in Detroit, Michigan From September Eighteenth to Twenty-Third, inclusive, in the Year of Our Lord 1961* (n.p.: Rand McNally, 1961), pp. 559-62.

making the language and the form of the services more relevant to the circumstances of the Church's present ministry and life."[117] This resolution was adopted. At the same time *The Liturgy of the Lord's Supper* was authorized for trial use, a form of the eucharistic liturgy which was in 1966 published as Prayer Book Studies 17.

In order to assess the direction the church would be going, and the acceptance of this rite more fully, the Standing Liturgical Commission mailed questionnaires on trial use (of which over 1,500,000 were distributed for "the man in the pew,"[118] and over 10,000 for the clergy). The commission decided after the evaluation of the returns that there would be need for two rites (with more or less the same structure, yet one in traditional language, the other in contemporary vernacular English) for the daily office, the eucharist, and the burial liturgy.

A new round of prayer book revision had begun.

The Revision Process of the Book of Common Prayer

Three years later the Standing Liturgical Commission recalled, when it submitted its report to the General Convention of 1967, that the Episcopal Church, in an age of ever-closer ecumenical agreements especially on the pattern and form of the eucharist, would not want to fall into the background, particularly as the prayer book had set

> the highest standards for Christian worship in the English-speaking world. The Church would not wish to settle for any lower standard of excellence at a time when a greater body of knowledge and experience is available in the field, and when new studies and constructive co-operation are achieving such favorable results.[119]

In view of all requirements the commission did not see a period of revision shorter than at least nine years, above all as prayer book revision

> is a difficult and delicate process, calling for spiritual depth, theological balance, literary beauty, and pastoral practicability. It requires the best knowledge, talent, and experience that the Church can command.[120]

To carry out the task adequately, not only an increase in membership of the commission would be necessary, but also the appointment of about two hundred consultants from all groups and geographical areas of the church, some of whom would subsequently be appointed to drafting committees which would each be responsible for a single service or section of the prayer book; these committees would be headed by a member of the Standing Liturgical Commission.

The drafts of the different services could be approved for a three years' trial use in 1970 and adopted in 1973; drafts not recommended for trial use in 1970 would be returned to the particular committee for reworking and submission in 1973 for a trial use from 1973 to 1976.

---

[117] Episcopal Church, General Convention, *Journal of the General Convention of the Protestant Episcopal Church in the United States of America Held in St. Louis, Missouri From October Twelfth to Twenty-Third, inclusive, in the Year of Our Lord 1964* (n.p.: Printed for the Convention, 1964), pp. 348-49.

[118] The Episcopal Church had by 1966 grown to its peak membership of about 3,647,297 baptized persons; afterwards the membership declined somewhat. For 1979 a membership of 3,095,080 baptized, with 12,978 clergypeople, is recorded: David E. Sumner, *The Episcopal Church's History: 1945-1985* (Wilton, CT: Morehouse-Barlow, 1987), p. 199.

[119] Episcopal Church, General Convention, *Journal of the General Convention of the Protestant Episcopal Church in the United States of America, Otherwise Known as The Episcopal Church, Held in Seattle, Washington From September Seventeenth to Twenty-Seventh, inclusive, in the Year of Our Lord 1967* (n.p.: Printed for the General Convention, 1967), Appendix p. 23.4.

[120] *General Convention 1967*, Appendix p. 23.5.

The Standing Liturgical Commission would proceed to unify the separate drafts into one volume, which would be presented to the General Convention for adoption as the *Draft Revised Book of Common Prayer*. This could be done by 1973 or 1976, so that three years later the revision process would be completed.[121] The necessary resolutions enabling the process to take place as scheduled were adopted by both Houses.[122]

It might occur to some that the church had come a long way from the sudden, rapid, and unprepared introduction of the first prayer book of 1549 to the long and public revision process the Episcopal Church initiated in 1964 and outlined in 1967. At the same time, given the almost ever-present experience that such an enterprise carried out by so many different groups within the church in most instances exceeded stated deadlines by years, it is in retrospect almost miraculous that the new prayer book became the standard one as originally scheduled, in 1979.

When the Standing Liturgical Commission resumed its work after the 1967 Convention, one of the drafting committees that were created was that on Christian initiation.[123] This committee prepared a draft of a rite of Christian initiation which was distributed to the consultants, the chairmen of the diocesan liturgical commissions, and the bishops; it was published in early 1970 and became the first study to be completed according to the 1967 revision plan. This booklet, Prayer Book Studies 18, has been hailed as "the bravest and most consistent with scholarship of all the Prayer Book Studies;" on the other hand, "its recommendations were more than the bishops of the Episcopal Church could fathom. They had been out of seminary too long and were too threatened; so it never came to be."[124] The proposed rite of "Holy Baptism with the Laying-On-of-Hands" was "a sharp break with traditional Anglican practice."[125]

The introduction served, among other things, as a theological outline of the meaning and practice of baptism, the practice and problems of confirmation, and unification of the entire rite of Christian initiation.

> The basic principle of this proposal is the reunion of Baptism, Confirmation, and Communion into a single continuous service, as it was in the primitive Church. Thus, the entire liturgy will be recognized as the full reception of the candidate into the family of God by the power of the Holy Spirit: beginning with the acceptance, through faith, of forgiveness of sins and redemption in Christ--of burial with Christ in the water in order that we may rise in him to newness of life; followed by the conferring of the gifts of the Spirit by the Laying-On-of-hands; and ending with participation in the holy meal at which the entire family is united, nourished, and sanctified.
>
> This proposed rite avoids both the practical disadvantage of delaying Confirmation, and the theological problem of attributing to Confirmation seperately, some necessary aspects of Christian initiation that belong to the very beginning of our Christian life. It will make possible a proper understanding of the priesthood of all believers, which the baptized are to exercize in the worship of God and the service of man.[126]

The bishop was seen as the chief minister of his diocese; when visiting a parish he would preside over the entire administration of Christian initiation. In his absence, the priests would

---

[121] *General Convention 1967*, Appendix pp. 23-6-7.

[122] *General Convention 1967*, pp. 481-82.

[123] From this point on, some material of the drafting committee on Christian initiation, that is kept at the Archives of the Episcopal Church in Austin, Texas, and not available to the public, has been used with the required discretion especially with regard to persons.

[124] Holmes, "Education for Liturgy," p. 133.

[125] Charles P. Price, *Introducing the Proposed Book of Common Prayer*, rev. ed. of Prayer Book Studies, 29 (New York: Seabury, 1977), p. 61.

[126] Episcopal Church, Standing Liturgical Commission, *Holy Baptism with the Laying-On-of-Hands*, Prayer Book Studies 18 on Baptism and Confirmation (New York: Church Pension Fund, 1970), p. 19.

act in his stead, even for the laying on of hands. Early admission to communion was advocated.

In the rite itself, the opening rubrics provided for a participation of all ministries, and of lay persons.[127] Sponsors were to be instructed about baptism and their duties.

The entire service was to be the chief service of Sunday or any other feast. Therefore, the setting was that of the eucharist, no longer that of Morning or Evening Prayer. After an entrance song, opening versicles (Ephesians 4:4-6a), greeting, and either the collect of the day or a special collect asking that those baptized into Christ's death might also live with him, the ministry of the word would take place with the readings from the ordinary three years' cycle or with special readings.[128] After the sermon all those concerned, ministers, candidates, and sponsors, might go to the font, by their movement marking the beginning of the new part. The candidates would be presented to the bishop by their sponsors. Three questions about a Christian life style, one question of renunciation, and the questions of belief would be asked of all persons present, including, of course, the congregation. The questions of belief would be asked by means of indicating the divine Persons ("Do you believe in . . ."), and the response would be given by all through a recital of the entire respective part of the Apostles' Creed. Six short litany petitions would be said for the candidate(s), the people responding with the usual "Lord, hear our prayer." The following blessing of the water, said by the bishop or in his absence by the priest, was a remarkable piece of a new liturgical prose hymn in the form of a Preface.[129] The first verse gave thanks to the Father for the gift of water in creation, in the exodus, and in the baptism of Jesus who through his death and resurrection led us from the bondage of sin to everlasting life. The second verse gave thanks for the water of baptism in which we were buried in Christ's death that we might share in his resurrection, and were renewed by the Holy Spirit. The commandment to baptize all nations was then alluded to. The third verse was the epicletical dimension of the prayer, the petition to sanctify the water by the power of the Holy Spirit so that the baptized might continue in the risen life of Christ. If chrism was to be used, the bishop, by laying his hands on the vessel, would bless it by alluding to Christ's anointment by the Holy Spirit to be servant of all and by asking that those anointed with this consecrated oil might share in Christ's ministry.[130] The next and

---

[127] *Holy Baptism with the Laying-On-of-Hands*, pp. 31-43.

[128] For the first reading: Ez 36:24-28; for the second reading: 2 Cor 5:17-20, or Rom 8:14-17, or Rom 6:3-5; for the gospel: Mark 1:9-11, or John 3:1-8, or Mark 10:13-16. A responsorial psalm had not yet been provided at this stage of the revision.

[129] It was drafted by Leonel L. Mitchell and Margaret Mead, the former being a capacity in his own right on baptismal liturgy, the latter having been one of the leading anthropologists. The text itself reads: "We thank you, heavenly Father, for the gift of water. Over it the Holy Spirit moved in the beginning of creation. Through it you led the children of Israel out of the bondage of Egypt into the land of promise. In it your Son Jesus received the Baptism of John and was anointed by the Holy Spirit as the Messiah, the Christ who would lead us by his death and resurrection from the bondage of sin into everlasting life. / We thank you, heavenly Father, for the water of Baptism, in which we are buried with Christ in his death that we may share in his resurrection, and through which we are renewed by the Holy Spirit. In joyful obedience, therefore, to your Son, we make disciples of all nations and baptize them in the Name of the Father, and of the Son, and of the Holy Spirit. / Now sanctify this water, we pray you, by the power of your Holy Spirit, that those who here are cleansed from sin may be born again, and continue for ever in the risen life of Jesus Christ, our Savior; / To him, to you, and to the Holy Spirit, be all honor and glory, now and for ever." "*Amen.*": pp. 37-38.

[130] "Eternal Father, whose Son Jesus Christ was anointed by the Holy Spirit to be the servant of all men, we pray you to consecrate this oil, that those who are sealed with it may have a share in the ministry of our great High Priest and King; who lives and reigns with you and the Holy Spirit, one God for ever and ever." "*Amen.*": *Holy Baptism with the Laying-On-of-Hands*, p. 38. Episcopal Church, Standing Liturgical Commission, *Holy Baptism: together with A Form for Confirmation or the Laying-On of Hands by the Bishop with the Affirmation of Baptismal Vows as Authorized by the General Convention of 1973*, Prayer Book Studies, 26 (New York: Church Hymnal Corporation, 1973), p. 15, reads "servant of all" instead of "servant of all men" and "may share in" instead of "may have a share in." The final version in the *Book of Common Prayer 1979*, p. 307, has slightly

central section was titled "The Baptism and Laying-On-of-Hands." The water rite would be administered through immersion or aspersion. The bishop or in his absence the priest would then say a prayer over the newly baptized and over the candidates for confirmation, thanking God for the forgiveness of sins and the rise to new life of grace by water and the Holy Spirit, and invoking the gifts of the Holy Spirit:

> Strengthen and confirm *them*, O Lord, with the riches of your Holy Spirit: an inquiring and discerning spirit, a spirit of purpose and of perseverance, a spirit to know and to love you, and a spirit of joy and wonder in all your works.[131]

After this prayer the bishop or in his absence the priest would lay his hands on each of the candidates by signing them on their forehead with the cross, with chrism if desired, and saying, "*Name*, you are sealed by the Holy Spirit."[132] The sealing would be followed by a text, said by all present, which addressed the newly baptized and confirmed with a reception into God's household and wished for a life of grace.[133] The exchange of the Peace between ministers and people concluded the rite. The bishop or the priest would continue to preside over the eucharist for which a special Preface might be used if no other one was provided.[134] Should there be no communion, the Lord's Prayer, a prayer of thanksgiving for the incorporation into the Church, and the share in the inheritance of the saints in light, additional prayers, if wished for, and a blessing would conclude the service.

Some additional directions and suggestions for a proper carrying out of the rites and the eucharist were added; for example, if processions to or from the font would be necessary.[135] The ministration of baptism by deacon(esse)s was outlined, and emergency baptism by a baptized lay person in the absence of a clergyman was directed, the latter including the signing with the cross, the Lord's Prayer, and possible other prayers.[136]

---

rephrased the prayer: "Eternal Father, whose blessed Son was anointed by the Holy Spirit to be the Savior and servant of all, we pray you to consecrate this oil, that those who are sealed with it may share in the royal priesthood of Jesus Christ; who lives and reigns with you and the Holy Spirit, for ever and ever." "*Amen*."

[131] *Holy Baptism with the Laying-On-of-Hands*, p. 39. This prayer is, of course, a good paraphrase of the one provided in the Gelasian sacramentary, "Deus omnipotens, pater domini nostri Iesu Christi": Leo Cunibert Mohlberg, Hrsg., *Liber Sacramentorum Romanae aeclesiae ordinis anni circuli (Cod. Vat. Reg. lat. 316 / Paris Bibl. Nat. 7193, 41/56) (Sacramentarium Gelasianum)*, Rerum Ecclesiasticarum Documenta: Series maior, Fontes, 4, 3. Aufl., verbessert und ergänzt von Leo Eizenhöfer (Roma: Herder, 1981), p. 74, no. 451.

[132] *Holy Baptism with the Laying-On-of-Hands*, p. 39. In all probability the compilers of this rite were inspired by the same text which is used since 1971 at the Confirmation in the Roman Catholic Church, the "Sphragis doreas Pneumatos hagiu" of the Byzantine chrismation--a happy instance of a turn to an ecumenically accepted confirmation text. And in this case the rite of confirmation would have lost all ambiguity with which it was burdened in the Anglican tradition.

[133] "We receive you into the Household of God, that you may confess the faith of Christ crucified, and share with us in his eternal priesthood. May the Lord arm you with his heavenly grace, that you may daily increase in his favor all the days of your life. Amen.": *Holy Baptism with the Laying-On-of-Hands*, p. 40. *Holy Baptism: together with A Form for Confirmation*, p. 16, changed the text: "We receive you into the household of God. Confess the faith of Christ crucified, proclaim his resurrection, and share with us in his eternal priesthood." The formerly last sentence, a rephrasing of the confirmation formula in the *Book of Common Prayer 1928*, p. 297, was dropped without any substitute and reappeared in longer form as a prayer over the newly confirmed: p. 26. The *Book of Common Prayer 1979*, p. 308, retains the text of Prayer Book Studies 26.

[134] "Because in Jesus Christ our Lord you have received us as your children, made us citizens of your kingdom, and given us the Holy Spirit to guide us into all truth; Therefore, etc.": *Holy Baptism with the Laying-On-of-Hands*, p. 40. The final version in the *Book of Common Prayer 1979*, p. 381, substitutes "as your sons and daughters" for "your children," otherwise adopting it.

[135] *Holy Baptism with the Laying-On-of-Hands*, pp. 42-43.

[136] *Holy Baptism with the Laying-On-of-Hands*, pp. 44-45. Obviously (emergency) baptism by a lay person had by now lost its controversial nature and was accepted. The *Book of Common Prayer 1928*, p. 281,

The authors of this unified rite certainly were aware that criticism and severe bewilderment would follow the publication of this trial use; the reactions were heavy once the booklet reached the members of the church concerned.[137] In general, the laity was very responsive, because of their greater share of participation and involvement in the celebration. Bishops began to complain that confirmation had been taken from them and given to the presbyters. The presbyters sometimes felt that baptism had been taken from them and given to the bishops.

It might justly be assumed that the adoption of this unified rite was not (yet) possible; anything to the contrary would not have been other than a real miracle. The mere fact, however, that the Standing Liturgical Commission of the Episcopal Church dared to publish a truly revolutionary rite was a sign of both the insight that the present dealing with confirmation was anything but satisfactory, and of the quality of the proposal.[138]

A Special General Convention[139] was held August 31 to September 5, 1969, in South Bend, Indiana. Although the bishops had been given their copies of Prayer Book Studies 18, this issue was not an official subject of the meeting. The Standing Liturgical Commission once again outlined the advantages of the time-consuming, yet necessary process of revising the prayer book by means of trial use as adopted by the 1961 and 1964 General Conventions:

> The purpose of trial use . . . is to remove the process of liturgical revision from the realm of purely theoretical discussion and to provide a basis of judgment in terms of actual experience; trial use makes it possible to subject a proposed rite to the test of responsible and controlled experimentation over a period of time sufficient to reveal both its merits and its shortcomings; and, finally, trial use provides an opportunity for every member of the Church to voice his reaction, thus minimizing the risk that a relatively small number of revising "experts" or powerful committee leaders would dominate the course and results of the process of revision.[140]

Measures taken by the Standing Liturgical Commission included, according to the report, the co-operation with the diocesan liturgical commissions and the assistance of 260 consultants from all groups of the church, plus fourteen non-Episcopal reader-consultants from other churches, plus, of course, general correspondence. Taken together, these efforts meant an unrivalled integration of the whole church into the process; the "democratization" of the church, at least in respect to liturgical revision, had taken roots.

The Special General Convention also passed a resolution which encouraged the Standing Liturgical Commission

---

had provided for the administration of baptism by "any baptized person" "in cases of extreme sickness, or any imminent peril, if a Minister cannot be procured."

[137] Frank Currer Quinn, "Contemporary Liturgical Revision: The Revised Rites of Confirmation in the Roman Catholic Church and in the American Episcopal Church," Dissertation Notre Dame 1978, pp. 412-15.

[138] Bishop Frederick B. Wolf of Maine, himself a member of the committee on Christian initiation since 1971, gives a good survey of all possible misconceptions about the confirmation (still) in vogue in large parts of the church: "Christian Initiation," in *Prayer Book Renewal: Worship and the New Book of Common Prayer*, ed. Hayden Barry Evans (New York: Seabury, 1978), pp. 36-39.

[139] The word "Special" refers to the fact that this General Convention had been convoked not three, but two years after the prior one. The next General Convention was held according to the regular triennial pattern, as computed from the 1967 Convention, in 1970.

[140] Episcopal Church, General Convention, *Journal of the Special General Convention of the Protestant Episcopal Church in the United States of America, Otherwise Known as The Episcopal Church, Held in South Bend, Indiana From August Thirty-First to September Fifth, inclusive, in the Year of Our Lord 1969* (n.p.: Printed for the Convention, 1970), p. 325.

to explore and take advantage of all opportunities for collaboration, on both the national and international levels, by consultations and otherwise, with comparable bodies related to other Christian communions that are likewise working for liturgical reform; and to seek agreement with the aforementioned groups in respect of those essential structures and basic formularies of sacramental and liturgical rites which are shaped in common, whether deriving from Holy Scripture or from the universal tradition of the Church.[141]

In theory this resolution meant that anything specifically and exclusively Anglican could be sacrificed in favor of a common structure in the liturgy--the reversal of an unwritten tradition that nothing of the individual church heritage might be given up.[142]

The next Convention, in the regular pattern, met October 11-22, 1970 in Houston, Texas. A great many liturgical issues were discussed.

In its report the Standing Liturgical Commission briefly acknowledged the influence of the liturgical revisions in all branches of the Anglican Communion and in all other major churches. Advances in scholarship and in ecumenical contacts also posed a challenge to the church in adjusting its formularies and forms of worship to contemporary demands. A diminution, however, of the fundamental theology and the characteristically Anglican style of the heritage was not contemplated.[143]

Some of the drafting committees for the different parts of the prayer book had in the meantime completed their tasks by producing the respective booklets in the Prayer Book Studies series. These booklets were proposed for adoption by the General Convention in order to make them officially available for trial use. Some of the material in the studies was presented in both a traditional and a contemporary version as far as the wording was concerned.[144] The situation of Christian initiation, after Prayer Book Studies 18 had appeared, was the subject of one of these paragraphs. The new proposed rite was regarded as a return to the practice of the early undivided Church. Practical problems with the underlying theological ideas and the implementation of the rite had been anticipated, however; therefore, an ad-hoc committee had been set up to study all those difficulties. Nonetheless this service, "nothing more than the product of the private cogitations of a handful of scholars and experts," was recommended for trial use in the report and in the ensuing resolutions proposed.[145] The resolution called not only for authorization of the rite for trial use, but also

---

[141] *Special General Convention 1969*, p. 335. The mandate mentioned in this text was carried out through personal contacts and representation in both inter-church task forces (Commission on Worship of the Consultation on Church Union; International Consultation on English Texts) and denominational commissions on liturgical reform (for example, the Roman Catholic Consilium for the Implementation of the Constitution on the Sacred Liturgy; the Inter-Lutheran Commission on Worship). Johnson, "Massey Shepherd," p. 15; Geoffrey Wainwright, "'E pluribus unum': Questions of Unity and Diversity on the Ecumenical and Liturgical Scene in the USA," in *Communio Sanctorum: Mélanges offerts à Jean-Jacques von Allmen* (Genève: Labor et Fides, 1982), pp. 291-96; Geoffrey Wainwright, "Il rinnovamento liturgico nelle chiese dell'America del Nord," *Rivista Liturgica*, 68 (1981), 400-06.

[142] It would be worth the effort of a thorough phenomenological, historical, and theological research to show the interdependence of liturgical rites, and thereby, at least to a certain extent, of the expression of faith, of the major American "liturgical" churches, up to a point that collaboration with other American churches receives precedence over the allegiance to, and links with, the mother churches in Europe. This cooperation concerns, among other projects, the eucharist, a common eucharistic lectionary, and a common liturgical psalter.

[143] Episcopal Church, General Convention, *Journal of the General Convention of the Protestant Episcopal Church in the United States of America, Otherwise Known as The Episcopal Church, Held in Houston, Texas From October Eleventh to Twenty-Second, inclusive, in the Year of Our Lord 1970* (n.p.: Printed for the Convention, 1970), p. 491.

[144] *General Convention 1970*, pp. 494-502. The double versions were for the same material as in the finally adopted *Book of Common Prayer* 1979.

[145] *General Convention 1970*, p. 499.

requested each bishop to visit the parishes in his diocese, beginning with Easter Eve 1971, so that he himself could inaugurate the trial use of the rite in each parish. Furthermore, specific licenses were to be issued, according to the proposed resolutions, under the bishop's signature and seal to the priest authorized to perform the rite. Persons having received the laying on of hands under these circumstances were to be given certificates by the diocesan bishop, indicating that he or she had received "the Apostolic Rite of the Laying-on-of-Hands (or Confirmation)" at the hands of a priest acting under the bishop's license. In addition, each bishop was requested in this resolution to visit at least once a year every parish where the priest had thus been authorized; at this occasion he himself was to be the chief minister of the rite.[146]

On October 21 the trial use of the rite of baptism with the laying on of hands was authorized. Several specific guidelines were attached to this resolution, which in fact cut so deeply into the substance of the proposed rite that the intentions of the Standing Liturgical Commission and of the drafting committee on Christian initiation must be regarded as having failed:

> 1) That the Baptismal Section of the same be authorized for trial use, subject to the direction and guidance of the Ordinary;
> 2) That children be admitted to Holy Communion before Confirmation, subject to the direction and guidance of the Ordinary;
> 3) That the Rite entitled, "Holy Baptism with the Laying-On-of-Hands," be authorized for trial use, with a Bishop as the Officiant, provided that no children under the present age normal for Confirmation shall receive the Laying-on-of-Hands during this trial-use-period;
> 4) That the document entitled, "Holy Baptism with the Laying-On-of-Hands," be referred to the Anglican Consultative Council at its meeting in Keny in February-March 1971, for its consideration and counsel;
> 5) That in the period following the adjournment of this General Convention, the Bishops shall arrange a period of intensive study of, and instruction in, Prayer Book Studies 18 in their several Dioceses.[147]

In other words: only bishops could use this rite in its entirety if the initiands were of proper age; in all other cases, parts of the rite had to be omitted. The attempt to restore for the Episcopal Church what the compilers of the rite had seen as the normative practice of the early Church had failed.

Because of the authorization by the General Convention, the initiatiatory rites were reprinted *verbatim*, but without the introduction and together with the other rites that were approved by the Convention, in a book published in 1971, *Services for Trial Use*, which were authorized alternatives to prayer book services for the period from January 1, 1971 to December 31, 1973.

In the fall of 1971 the House of Bishops met in Pennsylvania to discuss an official statement on the importance of confirmation, defending a particular rite basically on the merits that the commitment to a Christian life had to be received of a person mature enough for issuing it, by the bishop representing the whole Church:

> We do not wish to see the meaning of a public, mature decision for Christ lost in this Church. . . . For many of us infant baptism can only be defended when at a later date a person makes his own personal decision for Jesus Christ.[148]

---

[146] *General Convention 1970*, pp. 499-500.

[147] Quoted after the reprint of the resolution immediately prior to the text of the rite in: Episcopal Church, Standing Liturgical Commission, *Services for Trial Use: Authorized Alternatives to Prayer Book Services* (New York: Church Hymnal Corporation, 1971), p. 21.

[148] "Pocono Statement," *Anglican Theological Review*, 54 (1972), 119.

The uneasiness of the bishops with both the current situation concerning confirmation of persons baptized as infants and the proposed rite, apparently being viewed as a threat to their role in the Church, is felt throughout the statement.

While in 1971 and 1972 the drafting committee on Christian initiation was studying the comments received on Prayer Book Studies 18 and preparing major amendments to the rite, which in turn would be subject to scrutiny by the Standing Liturgical Commission and its consultants, the commission itself met on April 19-21, 1972 in Chicago with the doctrine and worship committee task force on Christian initiation of the Anglican Church of Canada. In the joint sessions, there was general agreement on three propositions:

> 1. Baptism is a complete act of Christian initiation.
> 2. Holy Baptism, the Laying-on-of-Hands, and the Eucharist form one continuous action.
> 3. The recognition of the intimate relationship of the act of initiation with the Paschal mystery is crucial.[149]

In October-November 1972, a special meeting of the House of Bishops was held in New Orleans, in part to cover the prayer book revision. The Standing Liturgical Commission was requested to submit a report about this item.[150] After a repetition of the official task of the commission regarding the revision, a schedule for completion of this process was proposed, asking for the second and final adoption of the revised prayer book by 1979. The reaction to trial use from the total membership of the church was termed "very mixed."

> The pressures on all sides are no different in character from those that attended our American revisions of 1789, 1892, and 1928. What is different about this revision is that the entire Church has been invited and encouraged to engage in the process by active participation, through live acts of corporate worship.[151]

The right of the Church to revise the liturgy was once again stressed. A flexibility in different styles of language was regarded as possible and necessary; the twentieth century had the same right as the sixteenth.

> We must accept the fact that the Age of Uniformity is over, whether by acts of parliament or by canons of General Convention. Uniformity in worship was an integral aspect of a period of absolute monarchies, both secular and ecclesiastical, when conformity to prescribed words and actions was regarded as the test of a subject's loyalty to kings and popes. The end of the Age of Uniformity corresponds to the end of all explicit or implicit political establishment of the Church in modern society....
> We believe that to try to enforce a return to the older ideal of uniformity will alienate both those who prefer customary, and those who prefer more innovative modes of praise and prayer in common worship....
> We cannot understand Prayer Book revision apart from this vast context of historical development.[152]

Prayer book revision and liturgy in general were thereby clearly seen as not being the same in the sixteenth and seventeenth centuries and in the present era. The word "uniformity" nowhere occurs in the 1979 *Book of Common Prayer*.

The paschal mystery was described as the "unitive principle" in Christian worship, the one fundamental sacrament which would find expression in different sacramental celebrations, in the celebration of the Christian initiation as well as in others. The trial use

---

[149] Minutes of the Standing Liturgical Commission, April 19-21, 1972, p. 21.

[150] Episcopal Church, General Convention, *Journal of the General Convention of the Protestant Episcopal Church in the United States of America Held in Louisville, Kentucky From September Thirtieth to October Eleventh, inclusive, in the Year of Our Lord 1973* (New York: Seabury, 1973), pp. 1099-104.

[151] *General Convention 1973*, p. 1101.

[152] *General Convention 1973*, pp. 1102-03.

rite of baptism, therefore, would be "an honest attempt to restore the unity and integrity of the Paschal Mystery in simplicity and dignity."[153] The recovery of this central mystery in the liturgy was regarded as the precondition for a true renewal of the Church's worship. Because of all the importance of the "primary and indispensable work of the Church"--the worship--haste in, and shortcutting of, the revision of the prayer book was seen as being dangerous to the integrity and position of both the present and the future prayer books.

The bishops who had received this report were given on the next day the opportunity for a question-and-answer session with Bishop Chilton Powell of Oklahoma, chairman of the Standing Liturgical Commission, and Massey H. Shepherd, Jr., its vice-chairman, on the proposed draft for a revised service of baptism.[154] They knew the seriousness of prayer book revision in general--as well as that of Christian initiation in particular--and the role they had to take in it in order to live up to their office.

At the request of the House of Bishops, a joint session of the theological and the prayer book committees with the Standing Liturgical Commission was held to study the issue of Christian initiation again. A report or study document was to be submitted to the bishops. The result of this meeting on December 6-9, 1972 in Dallas was both a "Statement on Agreed Positions" and the draft of the rites for baptism and confirmation that were to be submitted to the General Convention in 1973. One paper that served as an extended theological commentary on baptism and Christian initiation, prepared and presented at the meeting by Daniel Stevick, was later published separately; this will be discussed after the rites according to Prayer Book Studies 26. As the Agreed Positions are "fundamental"[155] to understanding both the rites in Prayer Book Studies 26 and in the finally adopted *Book of Common Prayer*, they are given here in their entirety:

> A. Concerning Baptism.
>
> 1. There is one, and only one, unrepeatable act of Christian initiation, which makes a person a member of the Body of Christ.
> 2. The essential element of Christian initiation is baptism by water and the Spirit, in the Name of the Holy Trinity, in response to repentance and faith.
> 3. Christian initiation is normatively administered in a liturgical rite that also includes the laying-on of hands, consignation (with or without Chrism), prayer for the gift of the Holy Spirit, reception by the Christian community, joining the eucharistic fellowship, and commissioning for Christian mission. When the Bishop is present, it is expected that he will preside at the rite.
>
> B. Concerning a post-baptismal Affirmation of Vows.
>
> 1. An act and occasion of (more or less) mature personal acceptance of promises and affirmations made on one's behalf in infancy is pastorally and spiritually desirable.
> 2. Such an act and occasion must be voluntary; but it should be strongly encouraged as a normal component of Christian nurture, and not merely made available.
> 3. It is both appropriate and pastorally desirable that the affirmations should be received by a Bishop as representing the Diocese and the world-wide Church; and that the Bishop should recall the applicants to their Christian mission, and, by a laying-on of hands, transmit his blessing, with a prayer for the strengthening graces.
> 4. The rite embodying such affirmations should in no sense be understood as being a "completion of Holy Baptism", nor as being a condition precedent to admission to the Holy

---

[153] *General Convention 1973*, p. 1103.
[154] *General Convention 1973*, p. 1105.
[155] Price, *Introducing the Proposed Book*, p. 64.

Communion, nor as conveying a special status of Church membership.

5. The occasion of the affirming of baptismal vows and obligations that were made by godparents on one's behalf in infancy is a significant and unrepeatable event. It is one's "Confirmation Day."

6. The rite itself, however, is suitable, and should be available, for other occasions in the lives of Christian people. For example, (1) when a person who has been baptized in some other fellowship of Christians wishes to become a member of The Episcopal Church, it is desirable and appropriate that this person be presented to the Bishop, as representing the world-wide episcopate, and that the new relationship be blessed with the laying-on of hands and a recommissioning to Christian service; and (2) when a person whose practice of the Christian life has become perfunctory, or has completely lapsed, awakes again to the call of Christ and desires to signalize his response publicly, and to receive a strengthening gift of the Spirit for renewal.[156]

These positions went back to the inherited ambiguity about the meaning of the part of the church's liturgy that is called confirmation. Whereas Prayer Book Studies 18 was a clear-cut ritual expression of the integrity of Christian initiation which consisted of the administration of the water, the laying-on of hands with the consignation as the expression of the gift of the Holy Spirit in this initiation, and the first admission to communion, the "Agreed Positions" watered down this integrity. This was not done so much by taking away elements of the "Baptism," which in the former proposal as well as in Prayer Book Studies 26 and in the finally adopted *Book of Common Prayer* still retains the water rite, the consignation and the sealing by the Holy Spirit, and--implicitly--the admision to communion, as by revaluing the medieval and Reformation idea of an affirmation office which retains the title "Confirmation." The ambivalence which was expressed in this text and with which the Episcopal Church has to live lies in the fact that theologically everything that Christian initiation in its different ritual parts stands for has been restored to "Baptism:" the water bath of remission of sins and new life, the gift of the Holy Spirit, and the admission to communion, or, in traditional parlance, baptism, confirmation, and first communion. Yet the word "Confirmation" remains standing not for the gift of the Holy Spirit but an affirmation office. It is clear that this rite is not a part of the initiation process but a ritualized assent to what has been done in infancy. It is illogical that such a rite of the affirmation of baptismal vows and obligations should be an "unrepeatable event" by virtue of being called "Confirmation Day." It is expressive of the unclear state of mind of the bishops that the rite itself, even with the laying on of hands, should be used for other occasions, too. Only because this laying on of hands is not called "Confirmation," it can be repeated. In all these cases, "Confirmation," reception into the Episcopal Church, and reaffirmation of Christian commitment, the strengthening gift of the Holy Spirit is invoked.

It is a confusing and irritating concept of Christian initiation that was expressed in these Agreed Positions.

The next General Convention took place September 30 to October 11, 1973 in Louisville, Kentucky.

In its report to the Convention[157] the Standing Liturgical Commission pointed out that, in general, the reactions to the trial use of all the rites had been positive, and that the questionnaires returned showed some consistent, yet sometimes mutually exclusive, tendencies: a desire to preserve the traditional language of the 1928 prayer book; a desire to modernize the language used in the liturgy; and a desire to introduce more flexibility, spontaneity, and greater participation by lay persons. The commission would, therefore, propose a

---

[156] *Holy Baptism: together with A Form for Confirmation*, pp. 3-5; also in: *General Convention 1973*, p. 625; Price, *Introducing the Proposed Book*, pp. 64-65.
[157] *General Convention 1973*, pp. 608-40.

revised prayer book which would contain more than one authorized form for the regular services.

A timetable of the further revision process, corresponding to that adopted by the bishops at their meeting in October 1972 in New Orleans, was proposed, calling for completion of all revision work by the commission by September 1975, the publication of a *Proposed Book of Common Prayer* by April 1976, the first constitutional action to be taken by the Convention in September 1976, and the second and final one in September 1979. The ensuing resolution was adopted.[158]

The section on the experiences with Prayer Book Studies 18 reported that the baptismal part of that service was "very well received." Due to the misgivings about the nature and theology of confirmation and about the role of the bishops in the initiation process, the history of the past two years was recalled, and the Agreed Positions of the joint meeting in 1972 were reprinted. Of Prayer Book Studies 26, which was proposed for authorization for trial use, it was said that it "embodies a significant consensus, reached after a long and thorough process of study and consultation."[159] The ensuing resolution calling for authorization of the rites contained in that booklet was proposed and, with some changes in the wording of its text, passed.[160]

The two rites thus authorized were "Holy Baptism"[161] and "A Form for Confirmation or the Laying-On-of-Hands by the Bishop with the Affirmation of Baptismal Vows."[162] The double title itself tells the story of the continuation of the uncertainty about, and separation of, those two parts of Christian initiation.

The opening rubrics of the baptismal rite envisioned the sacrament administered within the chief Sunday or feastday service, the eucharist. The bishop, if present, was to preside over both celebrations. Other clergymen and lay persons were to assist the presiding minister. One or more sponsors (without any further qualifications) were required for each baptizand, parents fittingly being included among those of their children. The parents and godparents were to be instructed about baptism, their duties, and their responsibilities. These rubrics were a modest revision of those of Prayer Book Studies 18 and essentially the same as those in the final prayer book.

In the celebration itself, the opening and the ministry of the word were the same as in the previous book.[163] After the sermon and the procession to the font, if possible, the candidates would be presented. If they could answer for themselves, they would be asked about their desire to be baptized. For infants, the parents and godparents would be asked about their readiness to be responsible for the child's Christian faith and life, and about their Christian help for the infant. The congregation would be asked about its support for the baptizands. The three questions of renunciation in a more contemporary version immediately followed, answered by the candidates who could speak for themselves, as well as the parents and godparents on behalf of the infants. In the following "Profession of Faith and Commitment," four questions would be asked about the willingness to lead a life patterned after Christ. Should there be persons who want, in the presence of the bishop, to make a special affirmation of their baptismal vows and to receive the laying on of hands, the bishop would invite all to renew their baptismal covenant. The four preceding questions would be omitted in this case. The minister would ask about the belief in the three divine Persons, and the respective part of the Apostles' Creed would be said by all present. Four more questions were added, addressed to, and answered by, all the people: about their willingness to continue in the apostles' teaching and fellowship, in the breaking of bread, and in prayers; to proclaim, by

---

158 *General Convention 1973*, pp. 614-15, 617, 441.
159 *General Convention 1973*, pp. 625-26.
160 *General Convention 1973*, pp. 626, 454-55.
161 *Holy Baptism: together with A Form for Confirmation*, pp. 8-19.
162 *Holy Baptism: together with A Form for Confirmation*, pp. 21-27.
163 The only change: instead of John 3:1-8, only verses 1-6 were proposed as one of the gospel readings.

word and example, the gospel of Christ; to seek and serve Christ in all persons, and to love the neighbor as oneself; and to strive for justice and peace among all people, and to respect the dignity of every human being.[164] Six short petitions, the same as in the 1970 draft, would be said for the candidates, the litany being led by a person appointed for it. The blessing of the water, said by the bishop or in his absence by the priest, would follow, introduced by the Preface dialogue, without *Sursum corda*. The text was almost the same as in Prayer Book Studies 18, but with the subordinate clauses being broken up into short principal clauses. In the second verse a reference to our looking for Christ's coming again as Lord of all the nations had been inserted; this was dropped in the final version of the prayer book. If the bishop were present he might now bless the chrism. The next and central section, "The Baptism," consisted of the water rite by immersion or aspersion, with the ensuing Trinitarian formula, to which the people would respond, "Amen." The bishop or in his absence the priest would then pray over the newly baptized the prayer of thanksgiving for the grace of baptism and of petition for the gifts of the Spirit. In place of "Strengthen and confirm *them*, O Lord, with the riches of your Holy Spirit," it would now be asked, "Sustain *them*, O Lord, with the riches of your Holy Spirit." The signing with the cross on the forehead, with chrism if desired, was accompanied not with the effectual formula, as in 1970, of: "You are sealed by the Holy Spirit," but with the prolix and long-winded text: "*Name*, child of God, inheritor of the Kingdom of heaven, by the water of Baptism you have been sealed by the Holy Spirit and marked as Christ's own for ever."[165] After the greeting of the newly baptized by the minister (without any proposed wording) he and the people would receive the baptized into the household of God: "Confess the faith of Christ crucified, proclaim his resurrection, and share with us in his eternal priesthood."[166] The exchange of the Peace would lead up to the continuation of the eucharist with the intercessions or the offertory. Those having been baptized would be allowed to receive communion.

If there were any persons who were presented to the bishop for a special affirmation of their baptismal vows, this would be done before the exchange of the Peace; in this case the celebration would continue with the "Dedication to Mission" which was printed in the "Confirmation" section. Should there be no eucharistic celebration, the service would end with the Lord's Prayer, the thanksgiving for the grace of baptism, and the blessing, as had been proposed in Prayer Book Studies 18.

Provisions were made for conditional and emergency baptism, the latter being possible by any baptized person.[167] In the section on additional directions and suggestions[168] it was proposed that the administration of baptism would be "especially appropriate" at the Paschal Vigil, on Pentecost Sunday, the first Sunday after Epiphany being The Baptism of Our Lord Jesus Christ, and All Saints' Day, or the Sunday thereafter being a possible additional observance of that feast. Baptisms were to be reserved, if possible, for these days, or when the bishop would be present. The choice of these days was a chance to open up the otherwise exclusive fixation of the theology of baptism on the paschal mystery, in favor of other possible and traditional interpretations or accents of the event, as, for example, the incorporation into the communion of saints, or the adoption in His Son as a child of God by the Father. In place of Ezekiel 36:24-28, any other Old Testament reading for the Paschal

---

[164] This question-and-answer part of the service had a certain ambiguity: it is praiseworthy that the social aspects of Christian life were emphasized, something all too often forgotten in the context of baptism; yet, if there would be no candidates for a reaffirmation of their baptismal vows, at least the adult baptizands would have to answer fourteen questions of renunciation, commitment, and faith. The centrality of the questions answered with the recitation of the Apostles' Creed could easily be overshadowed by the sheer number of questions, and by the apparently more dramatic nature of the other questions.

[165] *Holy Baptism: together with A Form for Confirmation*, p. 15.

[166] *Holy Baptism: together with A Form for Confirmation*, p. 16.

[167] The qualification "in the absence of a clergyman," still in *Holy Baptism with the Laying-On-of-Hands*, had been dropped.

[168] *Holy Baptism: together with A Form for Confirmation*, pp. 18-19.

Vigil was allowed for use. Suggestions were given for the insertion of suitable psalms, canticles, and hymns. The architectural arrangement of the church was to be taken into account for the several parts of the celebration. Other clergymen were allowed to assist in administering the water rite. A candle, lighted from the paschal candle, could be given after baptism to the newly baptized or the godparents. Baptized persons were allowed to receive holy communion.

A comparative table of the administration of baptism in Prayer Book Studies 18, Prayer Book Studies 26, and the finally adopted *Book of Common Prayer* may show the congruences and divergencies among those three forms:

Prayer Book Studies 18	Prayer Book Studies 26	*Book of Common Prayer*[169]
The opening of the eucharist	The opening of the eucharist	The opening of the eucharist
The lessons	The lessons	The lessons
The sermon	The sermon	The sermon
The Presentation and Affirmation	*Presentation of the Candidates*	*Presentation and Examination of the Candidates*
	Presentation of adults and older children	Adults and older children
	Presentation of infants	Infants and younger children
4 questions	4 questions	3 questions
1 question of renunciation	3 questions of renunciation	3 questions of renunciation
	Profession of Faith and Commitment	
	4 questions	3 questions
		Presentation of other candidates to the bishop
		3 questions

---

[169] *Book of Common Prayer 1979*, pp. 299-311.

		The Baptismal Covenant
3 questions of belief	3 questions of belief	3 questions of belief
	4 questions about Christian life	5 questions about Christian life
Prayers for the candidates (litany)	Prayers for the candidates (litany)	Prayers for the candidates (litany)
The Blessing of the Water	*Blessing of the Water*	Thanksgiving over the Water
(The Blessing of Oil)	*(Blessing of the Chrism)*	(Consecration of the chrism)
The Baptism and Laying-On-of-Hands	*The Baptism*	*The Baptism*
Trinitarian formula	Trinitarian formula	Trinitarian formula
Prayer over the newly baptized	Prayer over the newly baptized	Prayer over the newly baptized
Signing with the cross:	Signing with the cross: "Child of God, inheritor of the Kingdom of heaven, by the water of Baptism	Signing with the cross:
"You are sealed by the Holy Spirit"	you have been sealed by the Holy Spirit	"You are sealed by the Holy Spirit in Baptism
	and marked as Christ's own for ever."	and marked as Christ's own for ever." "*Amen.*"
	Greeting of the newly baptized	
Reception of the newly sealed person	Reception of the newly baptized person	Reception of the newly baptized person
The exchange of	The exchange of	The exchange of

the Peace	the Peace[170]	the Peace[171]
Intercession or offertory of the eucharist	Intercession or offertory of the eucharist	The prayers of the people or the offertory of the eucharist

The "Form for Confirmation or the Laying-on-of-Hands by the Bishop with the Affirmation of Baptismal Vows"[172] is a rather curious text in that neither in the opening rubrics nor in any of the texts said during the celebration did the word "Confirmation" appear; yet, this form was clearly seen as bestowing on the candidates that which the bishops wanted to retain as their privilege, and what in traditional terminology is called "Confirmation." The form itself could, and was supposed to, be used for three different circumstances, only the first of which would be the traditional "Confirmation."

The short opening rubrics stated the nature and purpose of this rite:

> Holy Baptism is full initiation by water and the Holy Spirit into Christ's body the Church.
> The bond which God establishes in Baptism is indissoluble.
>   In the course of their Christian development, baptized members of the Church are expected, as a normal component of their Christian nurture, to reaffirm their baptismal promise in the presence of the Bishop. Such Affirmation should be made by:
> - Those who are ready, and have been duly prepared, to make a mature public affirmation of their faith and commitment to the responsibilities of their Baptism;
> - Those who wish to return to the Christian life and mission after having neglected or abandoned it;
> - Those who have come into the Bishop's jurisdiction from another Church.[173]

If the service were to take place within the context of the administration of baptism, the entire first part up to the "Dedication to Mission" would be omitted.

The eucharist during which confirmation is to be administered would begin in the regular pattern. The collect and lessons on Sundays and feastdays would be those of the day; otherwise, the collect would commemorate the turning away from the old life of sin by baptism into the death and resurrection of Christ and ask for a renewal in the Holy Spirit and a life in righteousness and holiness. The first reading would be Jeremiah 31:31-34, the second Ephesians 4:7,11-16, and the gospel reading would be John 14:15-21. The sermon would follow. The service proper consisted of two parts: the "Profession of Faith and Commitment," and the "Dedication to Mission." Those who wanted to make the special affirmation of their baptismal vows would be presented to the bishop who would ask them about their willingness to profess the faith in the words of the baptismal creed. The ensuing three questions of belief, answered by the common recitation of the appropriate part of the Apostles' Creed, and the four questions about Christian life were the same as in the baptismal service. The "Dedication to Mission" would begin with the invitation by the bishop to those who had renewed the covenant of their baptism, to renew the "individual commitment to proclaim by word and deed his [Christ's] message of reconciliation, hope, and love," to which the candidates would respond that they would follow Christ and "work and pray and give for the spread of the kingdom."[174] The bishop would then pray over the whole group that, as God had sealed us by His Spirit to His service, so He might renew the covenant with the

---

[170] The Peace is exchanged here if the form for the affirmation of baptismal vows is not to follow.

[171] The Peace is exchanged here if confirmation, reception, or the reaffirmation of baptismal vows is not to follow.

[172] *Holy Baptism: together with A Form for Confirmation*, pp. 21-27.

[173] *Holy Baptism: together with A Form for Confirmation*, p. 22.

[174] *Holy Baptism: together with A Form for Confirmation*, p. 26.

candidates, and send *them* in the power of His Spirit to do the tasks He had set for *them*. He would then lay his hand on the head of each person and say, "Strengthen your servant, *Name*, with the riches of your Holy Spirit; sustain *him* and empower *him* for your service."[175] After this commission the bishop would continue with the text that was used as the proper confirmation formula in the 1928 prayer book, that God might defend the persons with His grace so that *they* might be His for ever, and increase more and more in the Holy Spirit.[176] All would respond to this dedication prayer by saying, "Amen." The Peace would then be exchanged, and the service would continue with the intercession of the eucharist. The bishop might bless the chrism to be used at susequent baptisms, with the prayer provided for in the baptismal service. Should there be no eucharist, the Lord's Prayer, and other prayers at the bishop's discretion, would be said.

The set-up of this service, and the texts used, clearly indicated a preference by those who had been responsible for arranging the rite for an understanding of the laying on of hands as the strengthening for giving witness, ideally to the faith and implications of the baptism the confirmed person had received probably years ago. Prayer Book Studies 26, therefore, stood in a line quite different from that of Prayer Book Studies 18: Whereas the latter understood the laying on of hands simply in terms of a gesture appropriate for expressing the riches of Christian initiation which cannot be comprehended in just one symbol, that of immersion or aspersion, the former regarded the laying on of hands as an additional "service" to equip the candidates with better means and strength for their Christian life. Besides, nothing in the form provided by Prayer Book Studies 26 suggested that the confirmation would be unrepeatable, as was clearly the case with the post-baptismal laying on of hands in the earlier draft since it was an integral part of baptism itself and, therefore, cannot be repeated. Even the use of the same gesture and text for all three occasions outlined in the opening rubrics indicated the contrary.

Obviously, more work had to be done on this part of the prayer book services.

For the discussion during the joint meeting of the Standing Liturgical Commission and the prayer book and theological committees of the House of Bishops in December 1972, Daniel Stevick had prepared, at the request of the Standing Liturgical Commission, an essay outlining the theological and practical implications and problems of Christian initiation today. The commission gave Stevick the opportunity to publish under his own name a revision of his paper as a supplement to Prayer Book Studies 26.[177]

The author immediately pointed to the central crucial problems for prayer book revision in general, and the reform of Christian initiation in particular:

Anglican rites have characteristically stood as vehicles of the liturgical actions of the church without any official, binding, definitive rationale. The tradition of liturgies and the tradition of explanation of liturgies have been distinct. The two interact, of course, and especially so at times when liturgies are undergoing change. But the two are not identical.[178]

The dichotomy of what would be the ideal (the closely bound up rites of baptism, confirmation, and first communion, being the rites of Christian initiation) and what is the

---

[175] *Holy Baptism: together with A Form for Confirmation*, p. 26.

[176] *Book of Common Prayer 1928*, p. 297.

[177] Although the commission wanted to have the supplement understood "not as its own official rationale or statement of position," and the author himself claimed that "it is not the Commission's official account of the rite being proposed," it is nonetheless safe to conjecture that this essay would not have been published in the Prayer Book Studies series as an accompaniment to number 26 if the commission had not agreed with the positions taken by the author, especially since the commission, "after a careful reading, has commended it as an introduction to the thinking that produced the rites in Prayer Book Studies 26.": Daniel B. Stevick, *Holy Baptism: together with A Form for the Affirmation of Baptismal Vows with the Laying-On of Hands by the Bishop also called Confirmation*, Supplement to Prayer Book Studies, 26 (New York: Church Hymnal Corporation, 1973), pp. 6-7.

[178] Stevick, *Holy Baptism*, pp. 7-8.

present situation (the dissatisfaction with the way the different parts were understood and administered) was clearly seen. Rites shaped, to a great extent, in the sixteenth century could not be identified with patterns of the early Christian centuries as far as some prominent features were concerned, as adaptation of these rites of Christian initiation to the demands of the present time would be required. With this in mind, Stevick gave an outline of the historical development of the initiation rites, of the present-day situation, of particular question areas (infant baptism, confirmation, first communion), anthropological and psychological ideas on initiation, and a commentary on the principles and the actual version of the proposed rite.[179] The present situation of the breakdown of "Christendom" as an ubiquitious phenomenon, and even predominance or precondition of society, would be a *kairos*, an opportunity, not a loss. The church would have to respond to this challenging moment in history also by reevaluating its rites of initiation.[180] Infant baptism was, in its theology as well as practice, "less secure than is sometimes realized." For the English reformers, the Church of England and the realm of England had been the same community with different names; to be born in England had meant to be baptized in the Church of England. Today, indiscriminate baptism would only add numbers of nominal, not really alive, members. And even the argument of the pre-eminence of God's initiative to the response by human beings was "a new theological account of infant baptism; it has no history prior to the modern era," and was as much a later theological support for existing church practice, as earlier theological ideas by, for example, St. Augustine. Yet, the abandonment of infant baptism on a wholesale basis would not be the solution, either, regarding the crises those churches undergo which favor "believer's baptism." But any new rite of initiation would have to take into account these developments and have to be open for possible new ways.[181]

As to confirmation, there had been a lack of clarity throughout the history of Anglicanism as to its meaning and function, and many concepts had been thrown together to make up what was then announced in the parishes as "Confirmation." This confusion dated from the time the Anglican pattern had been shaped with the patristic laying on of hands carried out in the liturgy, and the catechetical dimension stressed by the reformers. The former had been an unrepeatable rite, the latter had served as the end of a long educational and nurturing process and, in essence, had been repeatable. In the technological world of today, it would be wrong to assume that there would be a fixed point for representing growth into adulthood. This might not demand the same answer for two persons at the same age, and the response to the baptismal reality might look different for everyone involved.[182]

Despite a heavy and unfortunate break in the sequence of Christian initiation, the author felt most for first communion at an early age so that children, fully initiated through baptism, as the opening rubric of the confirmation rite in Prayer Book Studies 26 had said, would be admitted into the full sacramental practice of the Christian life and later might not remember a time when he or she had not been receiving at the Lord's table.[183]

The new proposed rites could, in the words of the commentator, best be described as separating the functions that up to now had been combined in confirmation as the prayer book had provided for. The signing with the cross as the post-baptismal blesing would immediately follow this immersion or aspersion. This unified baptismal rite, then, would be the full initiation and could (and should ideally) lead to the first communion of the baptized person in that same celebration. The catechetical and educational aspect of confirmation had been made a separate service to be used when the occasion would ask for it, in response to the

---

[179] One area the author unfortunately did not mention, is the discussion of the right (and duty) of the Church to baptize infants, which was heatedly going on in Europe at the time of the revision process of the *Book of Common Prayer*, particularly in the late '60s and early '70s.

[180] Stevick, *Holy Baptism*, p. 39.

[181] Stevick, *Holy Baptism*, pp. 40-47, a very thought-provoking chapter which has not received as much publicity and attention as it deserves.

[182] Stevick, *Holy Baptism*, pp. 48-70.

[183] Stevick, *Holy Baptism*, pp. 71-77.

unrepeatable starting point of baptism. All these reflections would lead to the realization that neither rite is a *rite de passage*: The baptismal rite would not be attached to birth or infancy, even if it could be used for such an age, nor would the confirmation rite be linked to puberty or adolescence but was intended as a mature response to the baptismal event.

> The unified rite of baptism, consignation, and eucharist is here set forth as the standard. Whenever the rite is administered (except in emergency situations) and to whomever, all of it should be administered. It is not liturgically fragmented or theologically ambiguous. The prayer for the gift of the Spirit is restored to the rite of Baptism, not because it supplies something otherwise lacking in Baptism, but because it expresses something that is part of the meaning of Baptism, but which seems to be less clear if left implicit.[184]

Baptism, however, was set in a perspective of response and becoming, of a faith-at-start. The proposed "Form for the Affirmation of Baptismal Vows" would serve as a solemn renewal of the baptismal covenant.

> This renewal of baptismal promises made before the Bishop is not associated with any one designated moment of life; it can be used at any age; and it can be used more than once. No special status or privilege attaches to it; thus it should not create an elite within the fellowship. It imposes little and allows for much.[185]

The decision by the Standing Liturgical Commission to accompany Prayer Book Studies 26 with a profound and sometimes thought-provoking commentary certainly was a good one. It has helped in understanding the mind of those proposing the rites and in educating the bishops and the church at large in the dignity and integrity of Christian initiation.

The rites most frequently used in the Church's daily life and previously authorized for trial use were published in 1973 in one volume called *Authorized Services*. The preface stressed the provisional character of this edition in that not all permissible trial use services had been included, and in its reaffirmation that the 1928 prayer book still remained the official *Book of Common Prayer*. The study of Prayer Book Studies 26, which was *verbatim* reprinted in this volume, as well as that of the supplement written by Stevick, was once again recommended to the bishops and clergymen.[186]

Despite all efforts by the Standing Liturgical Commission to find agreement on the character and rites of Christian initiation, there was still much dissatisfaction, and the House of Bishops dealt with the situation again at its meeting in the fall of 1974. A paper was issued consisting of five points concerning initiation: baptism is the full initiation; confirmation is an unrepeatable sacrament;[187] confirmation should not be conferred on infants but only on those who can affirm their baptismal promises; chrismation is part of baptism, not of confirmation; a repeatable rite is desired whereby adults may affirm their faith.[188]

The Standing Liturgical Commission itself felt the need to revise Prayer Book Studies 26 once more to take into account the criticisms and suggestions; this final version was published in 1975 and authorized for trial use in 1975-76. Several changes could be noted.

The revision placed the express presentation of the candidates for confirmation, for reception into the Episcopal Church, and for a reaffirmation of their baptismal vows behind the profession of faith and commitment in the baptismal part; the question to the congregation

---

[184] Stevick, *Holy Baptism*, p. 88.

[185] Stevick, *Holy Baptism*, p. 92.

[186] Episcopal Church, Standing Liturgical Commission, *Authorized Services 1973* (New York: Church Hymnal Corporation, 1973), pp. vii-xiii, esp. p. ix. The rites proposed in *Holy Baptism: together with A Form for Confirmation* were reprinted pp. 2-23.

[187] Further theological comment was not given.

[188] Quinn, "Contemporary Liturgical Revision," pp. 419-21.

for support of these persons in their Christian life was asked after this presentation. The litany of petitions for the candidates, after the Apostles' Creed and the questions about a Christian life, was now ended with a collect which was a revision of the collect used at the entrance of the eucharist. The "Blessing of the Water" was retitled "Thanksgiving Over the Water;" the "Blessing of the Chrism" had become "Consecration of the Chrism." In the prayer over the newly baptized after the immersion or aspersion, the phrase "Sustain *them*, O Lord, with the riches of your Holy Spirit" now read "Sustain *them*, O Lord, in your Holy Spirit." The lengthy formula of the laying on of hands (with chrismation) was shortened to "*N.*, you are sealed by the Holy Spirit in Baptism and marked as Christ's own for ever," to which the people would respond "Amen."[189]

At the confirmation, reception, or reaffirmation of the baptismal vows, the prayer for the Spirit over the candidates was somewhat enlarged. The revision provided a separate formula for the actual laying on of hands for each of the three groups, so that there would be no confusion about the "efficacy" of the rite for each one concerned.[190]

The General Convention of 1973 had accepted a resolution calling for publication of a draft proposed prayer book half a year prior to the next Convention. The Standing Liturgical Commission complied with this directive when on February 2, 1976 it published *The Draft Proposed Book of Common Prayer and Administration of the Sacraments and Other Rites and Ceremonies of the Church According to the use of the Protestant Episcopal Church in the United States otherwise known as The Episcopal Church Together with The Psalter or Psalms of David.* It was "Presented to the General Convention of 1976 by the Standing Liturgical Commission in compliance with the directions of the General Convention of 1973."[191] The contents corresponded to both the proposed book and the final prayer book.[192]

The next Convention was held in Minneapolis, September 11-23, 1976.

In its report to the Convention the Standing Liturgical Commission announced that it had completed the work on the draft proposed prayer book in July 1975, and that it would recommend the adoption of the book which would thereby be issued and authorized as "The Proposed Book of Common Prayer."[193] A theological commentary on the draft proposed book, serving as "an authoritative and invaluable guide" to the study of it, would be published

---

[189] "Holy Baptism," pp. 9, 12-13, 14, in Episcopal Church, Standing Liturgical Commission, *Holy Baptism; A Form for Confirmation, for Reception, and for the Reaffirmation of Baptismal Vows*, Prayer Book Studies 26, rev. (New York: Church Hymnal Corporation, 1975).

[190] "A Form for Confirmation, for Reception, and for the Reaffirmation of Baptismal Vows," pp. 7-8, in *Holy Baptism.*

[191] (New York: Church Hymnal Corporation, 1976), title page, flyleaf.

[192] As to baptism in this Draft Book, see Marion Josiah Hatchett, "Draft Proposed Prayer Book," *Worship*, 50 (1976), 220-23; for confirmation, 231.

[193] Episcopal Church, General Convention, *Journal of the General Convention of the Protestant Episcopal Church in the United States of America, Otherwise Known as The Episcopal Church, Held in Minneapolis, Minnesota From September Eleventh to Twenty-Third, inclusive, in the Year of Our Lord 1976* (Ambler, PA: Trinity Press, 1976), pp. AA-271-305, esp. AA-271-83.

and made available.[194] A part of the continuing program of the commission would be an increased contact with other churches both within and outside the Anglican Communion.

> Since *The Draft Proposed Book of Common Prayer* is the first major revision of an Anglican Prayer Book, incorporating many new liturgical principles, recovering much of the historical tradition common to all Christian churches, and to Anglican churches in particular, and aiming towards the greatest possible comprehensiveness, it is only natural to expect intensive interest on the part of churches that find themselves at different stages of the same process.[195]

And, finally, the commission expressly stated that its task when it was established in 1928 had been to collect and collate material bearing upon future revisions of the prayer book, and that it intended to take this mandate seriously by presenting "at reasonable intervals of, say, fifteen or twenty years" major suggestions for further prayer book revision.

On September 7 the House of Bishops voted on resolution A-104 adopting the draft proposed book, referring it to the next Convention for final adoption. By a large majority the book was adopted[196] and authorized for use for a period of three years, beginning on the first Sunday of Advent 1976.[197] The bishops also approved the book;[198] the amendments were considered and authorized,[199] and the Standing Liturgical Commission directed to prepare and edit the thus adopted book.[200]

In January 1977 the ensuing book was published: *Proposed The Book of Common Prayer and Administration of the Sacraments and Other Rites and Ceremonies of the Church*

---

[194] This was done by publishing the booklet by Charles D. Price, a member of the Standing Liturgical Commission, *Introducing the Draft Proposed Book*, Prayer Book Studies, 29 (New York: Church Hymnal Corporation, 1976), a copy of which was made available to each bishop and delegate of the Convention prior to the meeting. After the convention the booklet was republished as *Introducing the Proposed Book: A Study of the Significance of the Proposed Book of Common Prayer for the Doctrine, Discipline, and Worship of the Episcopal Church*, Prayer Book Studies, 29, rev. (New York: Church Hymnal Corporation, 1976). This booklet is identical with the normal book edition in 1977 of Price, *Introducing the Proposed Book*. It was regarded by the Standing Liturgical Commission to be the "authoritative guide" on the proposed book, and, therefore, also on the *Book of Common Prayer 1979*. Among the programs identified in the report, one was described as "the completion of a study identifying the sources of the various liturgical formularies included in The Draft Proposed Book:" *General Convention 1976*, p. AA-273. This had been done on a private basis by Hatchett; when the commission learned about this endeavor it decided not to pursue this project further but to entrust it to that author.

[195] *General Convention 1976*, p. AA-274. These churches were not specified. It was said, however, that scholars of the Lutheran, Roman Catholic, Presbyterian, and Methodist churches had cooperated in establishing the text of Eucharistic Prayer D in Rite Two. In 1978 the *Lutheran Book of Worship* adopted the version of the psalms as in the *Proposed Book of Common Prayer* 1976.

[196] Clergy: Yes 107, No 3, Divided 3; Laity: Yes 90, No 12, Divided 3: *General Convention 1976*, pp. D-75-76, D-79, D-83-87.

[197] Clergy: Yes 111, No 2, Divided 1; Laity: Yes 101, No 6, Divided 5: *General Convention 1976*, p. D-93.

[198] *General Convention 1976*, p. B-113.

[199] *General Convention 1976*, p. C-26. Two changes of the *Draft Proposed Book* are noteworthy. In Holy Eucharist, Rite Two, the Standing Liturgical Commission had left the *filioque* out of the Nicene Creed (p. 361; it had been retained in the traditional version of the creed in Holy Eucharist, Rite One, p. 330). The House of Deputies voted down an attempt to restore the *filioque* (General Convention 1976, p. C-12), the House of Bishops voted to restore it (pp. B-106, C-17, C-23), the House of Deputies again voted it down (pp. C-24, D-121, D-131). Officially the text of the Nicene Creed in the published *Proposed Book* would have left out the *filioque* as there was no canonical action for its inclusion. Massey H. Shepherd, Jr., assumes that the actual inclusion has been an editorial action for the publication of the *Proposed Book* after the Convention (Letter received from him, July 12, 1986, p. 3). The second change was the elimination of the Reproaches in the Good Friday liturgy (*Draft Proposed Book*, pp. 281-83). The House of Deputies voted to omit those (*General Convention 1976*, p. C-14), the House of Bishops did not take any action.

[200] *General Convention 1976*, pp. AA-278, C. 26.

Together with the Psalter or Psalms of David According to the Use of The Episcopal Church.[201] This book served as an official alternative to the 1928 *Book of Common Prayer* until the next General Convention in 1979.

In between these two Conventions, attention was for a moment directed to the eleventh Lambeth Conference held in 1978.

Two resolutions of this body concerned the liturgy. In the first, the adoption of a common structure for the eucharist was welcomed and commended "as an important unifying factor in our Communion and ecumenically;" the second drew attention to the experience of those churches that had adopted the three years' eucharistic lectionary of the Roman Catholic Church.[202]

Two texts of this conference deserve further mentioning. In a recommendation for ministry in rural churches it was said:

> In some places the traditional practice of confirmation places a heavy burden on bishops, therefore it is recommended that each province of the Anglican Communion should re-examine the theology and practice of initiation with particular reference to the bishop's role.[203]

A statement on liturgy and the *Book of Common Prayer* commended the developments in the Anglican Communion concerning renewal of worship and adaptation:

> There has been a welcome growth in the understanding that worship is a corporate activity in which all members of the Body of Christ have their proper share. To each is given by the Holy Spirit, as St Paul teaches, his or her own gift to be used for the building up of the Body of Christ. . . .
>
> In the past, the Book of Common Prayer was an important unifying factor in Anglican worship. The development of regional Prayer Books in the twenties and thirties and of more thorough-going revisions of the services in recent years has altered the situation. Nevertheless, worship remains an important unifying force, as is evidenced by the remarkable agreement on the structure of the eucharist that has developed in recent years, not only among the provinces of our own communion but also ecumenically. We believe this unity in structure can rightly co-exist with flexibility in content and variety in cultural expression.[204]

Within the life of the Episcopal Church, the next, the sixty-sixth, General Convention took place September 9-20, 1979 in Denver. Its primary and most important task was the constitutionally required second adoption of the new prayer book and, thereby, the finalization of this revision process.

In its submitted report the Standing Liturgical Commission told of widespread use of the proposed book and of considerable educational efforts around the rich variety of resources available.[205] The proposed book, used in the schedule of regular worship at the Lambeth

---

[201] The short title of the Church was adopted as the only one to appear on the title page, at the 1976 Convention: *General Convention 1976*, p. C-26. The contents of the proposed prayer book were the same as in the final one. A further discussion of it seems therefore unnecessary.

[202] Lambeth Conference, *The Report of the Lambeth Conference 1978* (London: Church Information Office, 1978), p. 47.

[203] *Lambeth Conference 1978*, pp. 85-86. It is difficult, having in memory the year-long struggle of the Episcopal Church and its bishops with the theological proper of the confirmation and the involvement of the bishops in Christian initiation, not to regret that this recommendation came at least one Lambeth Conference too late, and not to smile about the very existence of this text.

[204] *Lambeth Conference 1978*, pp. 94-95.

[205] Episcopal Church, General Convention, *Journal of the General Convention of the Protestant Episcopal Church in the United States of America, Otherwise Known as The Episcopal Church, Held in Denver, Colorado*

Conference the year before, was said to have been widely recognized as "a landmark in Prayer Book revision" and as "a significant model" to be looked upon by other churches engaged in revising their liturgy. However, considerable reaction against the proposed book and for the complete retention of the 1928 prayer book was also noted;[206] the Presiding Bishop of the Church and the Standing Liturgical Commission had prepared a set of draft guidelines for the implementation of the new prayer book, taking into consideration the 1928 *Book of Common Prayer*.

On the Convention floor itself, the House of Bishops discussed the proposed book on September 11.

> The Bishop of Utah, Chairman of the Committee on the Prayer Book and Liturgy, requested the Rt. Rev. Chilton Powell, former Chairman of the Standing Liturgical Commission, to come to the platform for the purpose of moving Resolution A-133:
> Resolved, the House of Deputies concurring, That the *Draft Proposed Book of Common Prayer and Administration of the Sacraments and other Rites and Ceremonies of the Church, together with the Psalter or Psalms of David, the forms of making, ordaining, and consecrating Bishops, Priests, and Deacons, the form of Consecration of a Church or Chapel, and the office of institution of ministers, and Historical Documents of the Church, including the Articles of Religion*, published on February 2, 1976 by the Church Hymnal Corporation, as amended by the Sixty-Fifth General Convention, is hereby adopted and declared THE BOOK OF COMMON PRAYER of this Church pursuant to Article X of the Constitution. The motion was seconded by the Bishop of Dallas. After discussion, the motion carried. Resolution adopted.[207]

The next day, September 12, the House of Deputies concurred with the resolution.[208] The proposed prayer book thereby became *The Book of Common Prayer according to the use of The Episcopal Church.*

As the establishment of the new prayer book had been constitutionally secured, some guidelines for congregational worship could be issued.[209] In the resolution necessary for authorizing them, the 1928 prayer book was called "a rich part of the liturgical heritage of this Church;" texts from that book might be used under the authority of the bishop and subject to the guidelines. However, this permission in no way "sanctions the existence of two authorized *Books of Common Prayer* or diminishes the authority of the official Liturgy of this Church as established by this Convention." The guidelines themselves declared that the 1979 prayer book was the liturgical norm. The book would have to be continuously studied; a worship committee ought to be established in the parishes, working with and advising the rector; and the congregation should make itself familiar with music composed for the new book. Congregations using the 1928 book ought to use the calendar and lectionaries of the

---

From September Ninth to Twentieth, inclusive, in the Year of Our Lord 1979 (New York: Episcopal Church Center, 1979), pp. AA-150-71, esp. AA-150-58.

[206] For an account of the activities of the "Society for the Preservation of the Book of Common Prayer," see Holmes, "Education for Liturgy," pp. 133-35. See also (as rationales by two of the members of that society) Margaret Doody, "Our Fathers, Often Faithless Too," in *No Alternative: The Prayer Book Controversy*, ed. David Martin and Peter Mullen (Oxford: Blackwell, 1981), pp. 36-56; Dorothy Mills Parker, "The Issue of the American Prayer Book," in *No Alternative: The Prayer Book Controversy*, ed. David Martin and Peter Mullen (Oxford: Blackwell, 1981), pp. 141-61. See Marion Josiah Hatchett, Review of *No Alternative: The Prayer Book Controversy*, ed. David Martin and Peter Mullen, *Worship*, 57 (1983), 463-64.

[207] *General Convention 1979*, p. B-28. Four bishops requested to go on record for having cast negative votes on the prayer book resolution; one request was withdrawn the following day: pp. B-28, C-10.

[208] Clergy: Yes 107, No 1, Divided 2; Laity: Ywes 99, No 2, Divided 6: *General Convention 1979*, p. D-55.

[209] Quoted in: Detscher, *Evolution*, p. 367 note 272; the draft of the guidelines proposed by the Standing Liturgical Commission: *General Convention 1979*, pp. AA-167-68.

1979 book, make copies of the new book available for congregational study and worship, and make provisions for the regular and frequent use of the 1979 book.

Conclusions

This process of revision resulting in the 1979 prayer book lasted for twelve years, 1967 to 1979, or even twenty-nine years, if the publication of the first booklet within the Prayer Book Studies series is taken as the initial step. In this period, the emphasis shifted from a revision of the prayer book within the context of the history of the *Book of Common Prayer* to a reform of the church's liturgy which did not hesitate to refuse the adoption of entire parts of the 1928 prayer book if they did not seem to be sufficient in clarity, theology, and liturgical expression.

The three categories: uniformity, apostolic liturgy, and adaptation, received a total redistribution of their importance during this revision process.

The constitution of the Episcopal Church as it stood in 1950 and until 1964 made no references to the use of material not contained in the prayer book, unless occasions asked for special services authorized by the bishop. Insofar as the official liturgy was concerned, uniformity was demanded in adhering to the duly established prayer book. When the General Conventions of 1961 and 1964 changed the constitution so as to allow the trial use of services under circumstances determined by the Convention, the idea of uniformity was laid aside, if not in theory, then at least in practice. A congregation of the Episcopal Church did not need to use the prayer book texts and adhere to the prayer book rubrics in order to celebrate the liturgy that was recognized as the church's proper one.

Uniformity also presupposes the existence of an authority strong enough to enforce the provisions and to dictate its own view on the subjects. Trial use, in direct contrast, gives the subjects the chance to tell the authority what they want, and whether or not they are ready to accept what the authority determines. Trial use, therefore, is more than an efficient means to learn the reality in the congregations and to test the willingness to go along with the proposals of a commission or committee; it is a radically different church model in that the people, those "below," determine the church's liturgy. Given the great respect for the *Book of Common Prayer* and its significance for not only the worship, but also the doctrine and discipline of the church, it is noteworthy to what large extent church policy and, to a certain extent, orthodoxy are co-determined by a more or less democratic process. The test case for this phenomenon would have come if, say, the congregations had accepted the liturgy of Christian initiation as proposed in Prayer Book Studies 18 with the laying on of hands by either the bishop or a priest in his absence. To specify who would have had the authority to make the laying on of hands the theological equivalent to the Anglican confirmation would have been a difficult task, to say the least. The House of Bishops, the House of Deputies, the Standing Liturgical Commission, and the congregations, all could have claimed that mandate.

After the establishment of the 1979 prayer book as the official and constitutional prayer book of the church, permission was given for a limited further use of the 1928 book. The General Convention saw itself confronted with the refusal to follow a new line of uniformity, which is outlined in the different patterns of celebration provided for most of the prayer book services and in the many rubrics, leaving the decision to use different texts to the local situation and/or the discretion of the presiding person. Is it conceivable that in using, for example, the texts of the 1928 prayer book for the celebration of the eucharist or of the Christian initiation, different expressions of the faith in the same reality are coexisting in the church; or are they actually different faiths?

> Their [the members of the Society for the Preservation of the Book of Common Prayer] interest was in the rhetoric of the trial use, true; but even more they were concerned for the

theology. They were correct when they said, as they did repeatedly and sometimes abrasively, that the theologies of the 1928 *Book of Common Prayer* and [*Services for Trial Use*] were different. The [Standing Liturgical Commission] probably was strategically wise in not affirming this too loudly, but its members knew that the [Society for the Preservation of the Book of Common Prayer] was correct. There is a clear theological change.[210]

Uniformity in matters liturgical often was an outward adherence to regulations pressed upon the church by the appropriate authorities. Loosening this connection created an opportunity to achieve a profound unity in the expression of faith, the liturgy. All care had to be taken that this would not be lost as well.

The Episcopal Church has succeeded in its liturgy in regaining many ideas the Anglican reformers wanted to pursue when they talked about the reintroduction of a liturgy that would correspond to the ideals of the primitive Church. A certain fascination with the early and patristic eras of the Church can be detected in the revision process. When, for example, it was said that Prayer Book Studies 18 on baptism and confirmation had been written by a drafting committee with E. C. Whitaker's *Documents of Baptismal Liturgy* in one hand and M. J. Hatchett's master thesis, "Thomas Cranmer and the Rites of Christian Initiation" in the other,[211] it is obvious that the texts of the former were consulted and used more often than those of the latter. The decision to take seriously the intention of the Anglican Reformers, and not only the texts of the prayer book, came with the promulgation of the Constitution on the Sacred Liturgy by the Second Vatican Council; the guidelines laid down there, especially those pointing in a direction of return to the apostolic sources of the liturgy, were the turning point for the revision process in the Episcopal Church.[212] The closest the Episcopal Church in its initiation rites ever came to this ideal was Prayer Book Studies 18. It is truly regrettable, yet with human compassion understandable, that this trial rite was never given a fair chance to live (or die) in the liturgical life of the congregations. Fear of having gone too far and fear of the loss of the dignity and integrity of their own pastoral office prevented the bishops from taking this step. Fortunately, the step back, in Prayer Book Studies 26, was not a wholesale return to the Reformation period.[213]

The involvement of the church at large in the revision process signified from the beginning that not only would the local circumstances of the congregations be taken into account, but also that the rites proposed and subsequently adopted by the General Conventions would be a framework "only," which would have to be adapted by the parishes according to their pastoral needs. Uniformity and adaptation are mutually dependent upon each other: The less the uniformity in worship is stressed and enforced, the more the possibilities of adaptation can come to the fore, and the more responsibility is laid on those preparing and participating in the actual services. In this regard the later trial use services required more adaptation than the former ones. It is a point of special reference that the 1978 Lambeth Conference extended the possibility of adaptation even to formerly sacred traditions and theological convictions in Anglicanism by leaving it to the different provinces to determine the bishop's role in administering the confirmation. "Flexibility in content and variety in actual expressions" even border not only on adaptation of certain fixed patterns of liturgy to the local requirements, but on the development of different traditions in worship matters within the Anglican Communion. Since the 1979 prayer book of the Episcopal Church is the first completely revised one within that Communion, it serves as a major example of adapting the liturgy to the genius of the country and will no doubt be followed by others.

---

[210] Holmes, "Education for Liturgy," p. 134.
[211] Holmes, "Education for Liturgy," p. 133.
[212] Oral communication on September 3, 1981 in Berkeley, California, by Massey H. Shepherd, Jr.
[213] Leonel Lake Mitchell, "Revision of the Rites Christian Initiation in the American Episcopal Church," *Studia Liturgica*, 10 (1974), 33-34.

The Church's Liturgy according to the 1979 Book of Common Prayer

The prayer book resulting from this most recent revision process merits close examination both on some peculiarities that set it apart from revised liturgical books of other Christian churches both within and outside the Anglican Communion, and on the offices of Christian initiation, including the order of "Confirmation" and of the eucharist. This examination will show show how close to or how far from the English Reformation of the sixteenth century and other major Christian churches the Episcopal Church is as it uses this authorized *Book of Common Prayer*.

Special Features of the 1979 Prayer Book

Rather than giving an account of the successive orders in the book, the following outline is intended to specify some points which clarify the position of the prayer book in the vastly increasing library of liturgical agendas, and which servce as a means for comparing this book, and its advantages and disadvantages, with those of other churches.

The Book for the Liturgy

The *Book of Common Prayer* legally and intentionally comprises all liturgical services which are, or can be, held in the Episcopal Church, with all the texts and rubrics necessary for a proper, full participation by all persons concerned.
In all services, the entire Christian assembly participates in such a way that the members of each order within the Church, lay persons, bishops, priests, and deacons, fulfill the functions proper to their respective orders, as set forth in the rubrical directions for each service.[1]
The liturgical offices of each order are clearly defined both in general ways, as well as for each service. The bishop or priest is the presider at the worship. Deacons can preside at the liturgy of the word in the daily Office and, in the absence of a bishop or priest, in the form provided in the eucharist. At other sevices, the functions of deacons are subject to the directions for those liturgies. Lay persons may officiate at the liturgy of the word, too.[2] The *Book of Common Prayer* is the "script" for all liturgical functions.[3]
All regular services are given in the book. The diocesan bishop may authorize special devotions from the prayer book or from the Scripture according to the needs of the congregations. If special occasions for worship which are not covered by the contents of the prayer book are appointed by civil or church authorities, the bishop may also set forth those

---

[1] "Concerning the Service of the Church:" *Book of Common Prayer 1979*, p. 13.
[2] "Concerning the Service of the Church:" *Book of Common Prayer 1979*, pp. 13-14.
[3] The reader at the eucharist, at the daily Office, and at the other liturgies, has to take the readings from the Old and New Testaments from a Bible version authorized for use in the liturgy; the same holds true for the reading of the gospel by a deacon or other clergy person. The authorized versions of the Bible are specified in Title II, canon 2 of the constitution. Printing all the readings of the three years' cycle of Sundays and festdays and the readings at the daily office in the two years' cycle according to all the authorized versions would go beyond the limits of lectionaries.

forms.[4] But the *Book of Common Prayer* remains the standard also for those services, and they have to conform to the pattern and liturgical spirit of it.

The principle of establishing a liturgy that in enriched form covers the entire worship life of the church, except in extraordinary and unforeseeable services, resulted in three more semi-official books accompanying the *Book of Common Prayer*.

"Numerous requests from the clergy and a Resolution of the 65th Convention"[5] resulted in revision of a book of which there had been previous editons in 1940, 1949, and 1960. This former book, *The Book of Offices*, subjected to scrutiny and major updating by a committee under the chairmanship of Marion J. Hatchett,[6] became *The Book of Occasional Services*. The intent for choosing this title was to specify more accurately the contents of the book, and to avoid confusion with the daily Office.[7] The material inserted (after having been drafted by sub-committees approved by the committee responsible for the book, considered by the Standing Liturgical Commission, sometimes submitted to diocesan liturgical commissions, and then emended) covers more than 1800 years of liturgical history by instituting or reinstituting, for liturgical use, services which the Standing Liturgical Commission deemed helpful for congregations which want to add to the worship life by including services not provided for in the prayer book. All the material, however, is optional and not required.[8] The contents are classified into three main sections: services in connection with the church year;[9] "Pastoral Services" which include material in relation to members of the congregation, to the sacraments and sacramental rites, and to the church building;[10] and "Episcopal Services," covering some occasions in which the bishop's ministry comes to the fore, concerning either the bishop's own person, or other persons, or the consecration of chrism.[11] The renewed emphasis on baptism, noticeable throughout the prayer book, leaves its traces also in the *Book of Occasional Services*. The "Pastoral Services" segment contains a section on the catechumenate of adults with proposals for the liturgical celebration for the admission of catechumens, prayers to be said at the end of each session of formal instruction during the candidacy, a celebration of the enrollment of candidates for baptism, normally on the first Sunday of Lent, and special prayers and blessings for the following Sundays.[12] If the bishop's visitation is the occasion of a baptism, or if there are other reasons, a vigil on the eve of the baptismal day can be observed. This order is somewhat patterned after the Great Vigil of Easter in that it consists of a *lucernarium*, collect, three or more readings, a prayer in litany form over the candidates, a blessing, and the dismissal.[13] Even the feast of the Baptism of the Lord is provided with the vigil for the eve of the Sunday.[14]

The fact that this book has been included in the revision process and has been given the status of a semi-official extension of the prayer book is an indication that the

---

[4] "Concerning the Service of the Church:" *Book of Common Prayer 1979*, p. 13.

[5] *General Convention 1979*, p. AA-150.

[6] *General Convention 1979*, pp. AA-160-61; Preface: *The Book of Occasional Services* (New York: Church Hymnal Corporation, 1979), p. 6.

[7] Preface: *Book of Occasional Services*, p. 5.

[8] *General Convention 1979*, p. AA-150; Preface: *Book of Occasional Services*, pp. 5-6.

[9] *Book of Occasional Services*, pp. 8-108.

[10] *Book of Occasional Services*, pp. 109-206.

[11] *Book of Occasional Services*, pp. 207-32.

[12] *Book of Occasional Services*, pp. 112-25. The catechumenate is considered to be so important a part of the life of the congregation, not in the least instance of the worship life, that a section "Concerning the Catechumenate" is prefixed to the liturgical orders, outlining the different stages and their meaning (pp. 112-14). As to the catechumenate in the Episcopal Church, see Robert Brooks, "The Catechumenate: A Case Study," in *A Kingdom of Priests: Liturgical Formation of the People of God*, ed. Thomas J. Talley, Alcuin / GROW Liturgical Study, 5 (Bramcote, Notts.: Grove Books, 1988), pp. 15-19.

[13] *Book of Occasional Services*, pp. 126-30.

[14] *Book of Occasional Services*, pp. 49-50.

comprehensiveness of the prayer book has come to its limits; the worship life of the church can in its entirety no longer be covered by one book only.

The Standing Liturgical Commission had proposed to the 1964 General Convention that a book entitled *The Calendar and the Collects, Epistles and Gospels for the Lesser Feasts and Fasts and for Special Occasions*, which had been published the year before, be authorized for trial use for three years;[15] this edition in turn had been based on Prayer Book Studies 11, *The Calendar*, prepared by Massey H. Shepherd, Jr.[16] The extension of the trial use was proposed, in 1967 and 1970, for another three years.[17] In 1973 a revision was set before the General Convention, based on the reactions to trial use of the previous edition, with collects in both contemporary and traditional versions, and the indication of suitable readings, for the lesser feasts and Lenten weekdays, together with responsorial psalms. This second edition was authorized for a triennial trial use in 1973 and 1976.[18] In 1979 a third edition was presented to the General Convention, with revised collects, readings, psalms, biographical material, which had been included in the second edition, too, and the addition of collects and readings for the Easter season.[19] The result of authorization by the General Convention for optional use was *The Proper for the Lesser Feasts and Fasts together with The Fixed Holy Days*.

> The purpose of the revision of the Collects for the Lesser Feasts was to ensure that each Collect be distinctive of the person commemorated, or of that aspect of the Church's life to which that person contributed most significantly.[20]

An intercession by the saint on behalf of those saying or using the collect is, of course, not expressed; therefore, the collects of the renewed Roman sacramentary could serve only as inspiring models, not as texts to be adopted for use; on the other side, the proposed lectionary for the Forty and Fifty Days is identical with the Roman readings of the Lenten and Easter seasons.[21] Biographical material which the Standing Liturgical Commission thought fit for teaching purposes and homiletic value has been added.[22]

This book greatly enhances the celebration of the eucharist on weekdays so that the same collects and readings from the Common of Saints[23] need not be repeated again and again, if the persons are to be commemorated liturgically.

The Standing Liturgical Commission envisioned, in its schedule for the time after the definitive adoption of the proposed prayer book in 1979, that a complete and definitive edition of the altar book would be worked on.[24] This edition, conforming to the *Book of Common Prayer*, was edited under the title *The Altar Book*.[25] It contains in larger print all

---

[15] *General Convention 1964*, p. 669.

[16] Preface: *The Proper for the Lesser Feasts and Fasts together with The Fixed Holy Days*, 3rd ed. (New York: Church Hymnal Corporation, 1980), p. v.

[17] *General Convention 1967*, Appendix p. 23-15; *General Convention 1970*, p. 503.

[18] *General Convention 1973*, p. 630; *General Convention 1976*, p. AA-279.

[19] *General Convention 1979*, pp. AA-150-51.

[20] Preface: *Lesser Feasts and Fasts*, p. iv. Some of the collects are of great literary beauty. See, for example, the collect for St. Augustine, August 28 (in traditional language): "O Lord God, who art the light of the minds that know thee, the life of the souls that love thee, and the strength of the hearts that serve thee: Help us, following the example of thy servant Augustine of Hippo, so to know thee that we may truly love thee, and so to love thee that we may fully serve thee, whom to serve is perfect freedom; through Jesus Christ our Lord, who liveth and reigneth with thee and the Holy Spirit, one God, now and for ever." "Amen." (p. 305)

[21] Preface: *Lesser Feasts and Fasts*, p. iv.

[22] Preface: *Lesser Feasts and Fasts*, p. v.

[23] "Collects: Traditional," The Common of Saints: *Book of Common Prayer 1979*, pp. 195-99; "Collects: Contemporary," The Common of Saints: pp. 246-50; "Lectionary," The Common of Saints: pp. 925-27.

[24] *General Convention 1979*, p. AA-156.

[25] *The Altar Book containing The Holy Eucharist Rites One and Two* (New York: The Church Hymnal Corporation, 1980).

texts necessary for the presider at the eucharist. For convenience, portions from some other rites that can be combined with the eucharist have been inserted *in situ* so that they, too, are available. All texts lending themselves to it, or requiring it, are foreseen with melodies, mostly in an adaptation of the Latin chant.[26] Included, too, are the proper liturgies for special days and the collects of the prayer book, both in traditional and contemporary versions. This edition does not contain any texts not to be found in the prayer book; it is a resource for a dignified fulfillment of the presider's ministry.

Because the Episcopal Church is not limited to the United States but also has dioceses and provinces in other continents,[27] the 1979 *Book of Common Prayer* has been translated into Spanish and French for use in those areas where not English but either one of the other languages is the "tongue understood of the people." The phenomenon of translating the prayer book into living languages is not new; it began with the first *Book of Common Prayer*, which was translated into French for Edward VI's subjects in Calais and the Channel Islands; in 1552 this translation was amended along the lines of the second prayer book. The Elizabethan book of 1559 was translated into Welsh in 1567; the prayer book of 1604 appeared in Irish for the first time in 1608.[28]

Both versions of the 1979 book, the Spanish one of 1982[29] and the French one of 1983,[30] are faithful renditions of the American *Book of Common Prayer*. Except for the "Penitential Order" and the "Holy Eucharist" in the French book, which are given in the two forms found in the American book,[31] all prayers and rites are given in one translation only which linguistically corresponds to the contemporary version in the *Book of Common Prayer*. The Spanish book contains the translation only of the "Penitential Order: Rite Two" and the "Holy Eucharist: Rite Two."[32] The translations in both books have borrowed from the Roman Catholic liturgical books whenever the sources for the texts are the same, such as for the collects of the church year, but are nonetheless independent renderings of apparent literary beauty. As far as translations common for all major churches in one language exist, such as for the ordinary texts of the eucharist or for some frequently used prayers, these are taken over in the prayer book translations. As to the psalter, the French translation has employed the version of the *Psautier Oecuménique*.[33] The only parts missing in both books are the lectionary and the daily Office lectionary.

---

[26] The two exceptions most obvious are the absence of a melody for the Preface of Eucharistic Prayer C, and a highly elaborate chant, adapted from the Mozarabic liturgy, for the Preface of Eucharistic Prayer D. As this latter one is a revision of the fourth eucharistic prayer of the Roman sacramentary with its invariable Preface singing about the creation and ministry of angels, the "countless throngs of angels" are dramatized by no less than fourteen notes on the first syllable of this phrase.

[27] It has missionary districts in Central and Southern America, in Africa, and Asia; there is also the Convocation of the American Churches in Europe. Each of these bodies, plus the Convention of the American Churches in Europe, is a full member of the Episcopal Church and, according to the constitution, Art. I,4, entitled to representation in the General Convention equal to the dioceses in the United States.

[28] Frere, *History*, p. 1256.

[29] *El Libro de Oración Común: Administración de los Sacramentos y otros Ritos y Ceremonias de la Iglesia Junto con el Salterio o Salmos de David Conforme al uso de La Iglesia Episcopal* (New York: Church Hymnal Corporation, 1982).

[30] *Le Livre de la Prière Commune de l'Administration des Sacrements et des autres rites et cérémonies de l'Eglise avec le Psautier, ou les Psaumes de David selon l'usage de L'Eglise Episcopale* (New York: Church Hymnal Corporation, 1983).

[31] "Rite pénitentiel I:" *Livre de la Prière Commune*, pp. 227-29; "Sainte Eucharistie: Rite I:" pp. 231-50; "Rite pénitentiel II:" pp. 253-55; "Sainte Eucharistie: Rite II:" pp. 257-83.

[32] "Orden Penitencial:" *Libro de Oración Común*, pp. 241-43; "La Santa Eucaristía:" pp. 245-73.

[33] *Psautier Oecuménique: Texte officiel* (Paris: Cerf, 1977).

The Role of the Laity in the Celebration of the Liturgy

All the services presuppose that they are held in the presence of, and with active participation by, lay persons. "Private" liturgies, answering the devotional desire of a clergy person only, are not authorized. Care is taken that the central formulas at the sacramental celebrations are answered by all persons with "Amen." Throughout the book there is a noticeable intention to reduce, by way of shifting the emphasis in liturgical theology, the influence of devotional forms derived from the Middle Ages or modern times especially in Mediterranean countries and introduced into the practice of many Anglican parishes by the followers of the Oxford and ritualist movements (for example, Benediction with the Blessed Sacrament, Low Mass, special devotions to the Sacred Heart). Instead, the changes favor making each service a "celebration," a worshipping act of the entire congregation with as much ritual expression of the liturgical reality as possible and/or necessary. A section entitled Additional Directions after most of the services given in the prayer book specifies possibilities for executing the rubrics, and the general guidelines given in the section Concerning the Service ensure the full participation of all people.

Some of the prayer book services may be presided over by lay persons in their own right, as sharing "in the royal priesthood of Jesus Christ:"[34] the daily Office of Morning and Evening Prayer, at noonday, and at compline, and the Great Litany.[35] In the absence of a bishop, priest, or deacon, they may preside over the liturgy of the word in the form provided in the order of the eucharist, over the Good Friday liturgy, and over the burial as far as no eucharist is celebrated. No difference is made between lay men and lay women: all have the same right in the liturgy.

Even in the presence of the bishop, priest, or deacon, it is always assigned to lay persons to serve as readers of the non-Gospel readings at the eucharist and to pronounce the petitions at the prayer of the people. The representatives of the congregation bring the gifts of bread and wine, and other offerings, to the deacon or presider at the eucharist. Lay persons are part of the presenters of candidates for ordination to the ordaining bishop,[36] including the presentation of a bishop-elect of a diocese. The responsibility of the laity for the church, therefore, does not only find expression in the lay representation at the House of Deputies of the General Convention, but also liturgically in presenting, together with priests, to the Presiding Bishop that person for ordination whom they, together with the priests, have elected to be their bishop.[37] The intimate connection in this particular instance of all members in the church is consonant with, and expressive of, a broadened vision of the nature both of the ministry of the Church and of liturgy.[38] It is the result of a renewed understanding of the sacramentality of the Church for the world in which it exercizes through all its members its ministry of grace and reconciliation, and of the expression of that sacramentality in the liturgy in which all members in their different functions are equipped with the means to carry out their tasks.[39] In the catechism appended to the 1979 *Book of Common Prayer* this view is expressed in three questions and answers about the Church (the first two) and the Ministry (the last one):

---

[34] "Holy Baptism," Consecration of the Chrism: *Book of Common Prayer 1979*, p. 307.

[35] This is a revision of the litany that was introduced in the Church of England by Archbishop Cranmer in 1544.

[36] "Ordination of a Bishop," Presentation: *Book of Common Prayer 1979*, p. 513; "Ordination of a Priest," Presentation: p. 526; Ordination of a Deacon," Presentation: p. 538.

[37] Representation of laity in the House of Deputies: constitution, Art. I,4; election of the bishop by presbyters and lay persons: constitution, Art. II,1.

[38] The 1928 Book of Common Prayer did not have any such provisions in its ordination rites: p. 552.

[39] Weil, *Sacraments and Liturgy*, pp. 63-67.

How does the Church pursue its mission?
The Church pursues its mission as it prays and worships, proclaims the Gospel, and promotes justice, peace, and love.
Through whom does the Church carry out its mission?
The Church carries out its mission through the ministry of all its members.
Who are the ministers of the Church?
The ministers of the Church are lay persons, bishops, priests, and deacons.[40]

Comprehensiveness and Adaptation

One of the most striking features of the new prayer book is the provision of "Rite One" and "Rite Two" services for Morning and Evening Prayer, penitential order, eucharist, and burial. Rite One services are those 1928 orders which underwent a revision without being unrecognizable; Rite Two services are creations of contemporary orders. To the extent necessary, Rite One services have been synchronized in pattern with the Rite Two orders so that both rites complement rather than exclude each other. "Rite I connects us to our Anglican past, and Rite II connects us to our Anglican and ecumenical present and future."[41] The Standing Liturgical Commission adopted this form in order to meet the requirements both of congregations strongly attached to the traditional Anglican worship, and of congregations and communities which prefer contemporary forms. Rite One gives the opportunity to retain texts more or less unaltered, which in the course of time have become endeared to persons and have left an imprint even on the private devotional life; Rite Two opens up the vast realm of creativity in liturgical forms, with much the same right as the early centuries and the Reformation period possessed. Even in Rite One, however, most of the texts used, and all of the rubrics governing the different participation of persons carrying out their functions, are the same as in Rite Two; no theological difference can be made out of the choice of either rite. The use of Rite One or Two is often a question of preference for customary or contemporary language.

Rite One of the Morning and Evening Prayer, of the penitential order preceding, as an option, the celebration of the eucharist, of the eucharist, and of the burial are kept in the traditional language pattern of addressing God as "thou," and of adding endings to the verbs where applicable. The rhythm and flow of sixteenth century English prose could in most of these instances be kept intact, collects translated by Archbishop Cranmer could be retained, and the integrity of Rite One for the specific services could be better served. All collects and Prefaces of the church year are given both in the traditional and the contemporary versions.[42] Collects, Prefaces, and other prayers written in contemporary style during the last revision process were "retranslated" into the traditional version. The psalter is in its entirety kept in the contemporary style, although "so that the psalms may be congruent with the services in traditional language, the vocabulary has been largely restricted to that available to Coverdale."[43] The "Prayers and Thanksgivings"[44] have been retained in their original idiom, be it traditional or modern, but in most traditional cases pronouns and verbs have been put in

---

[40] "An Outline of the Faith," The Church: *Book of Common Prayer 1979*, p. 855; The Ministry: p. 855.

[41] Price, *Introducing the Proposed Book*, p. 28.

[42] "Collects: Traditional:" *Book of Common Prayer 1979*, pp. 159-210; "Collects: Contemporary:" pp. 211-61; "Holy Eucharist: Rite One," Prefaces: pp. 344-49; "Holy Eucharist: Rite Two," Prefaces: pp. 377-82. See also Leonel Lake Mitchell, "The Collects of the Proposed Book of Common Prayer," *Worship*, 52 (1978), 138-45.

[43] Hatchett, *Commentary*, pp. 557-58.

[44] *Book of Common Prayer 1979*, pp. 814-41.

italics to facilitate rendering them into a contemporary version. The "Great Litany" also has been kept in the traditional style.[45] It is permitted to conform to traditional language any of the texts in the proper liturgies for special days (Ash Wednesday, Palm Sunday, Maundy Thursday, Good Friday, Holy Saturday, and The Great Vigil of Easter) and in other prayer book services that are celebrated in a Rite One setting (Morning and Evening Prayer, eucharist).[46]

An entirely new feature, and something which deserves to be closely watched in its execution, is the provision of "An Order of Worship for the Evening;"[47] "An Order for Celebrating the Holy Eucharist;"[48] "An Order for Marriage;"[49] and "An Order for Burial."[50] Common to all these four forms is the fact that they provide not an entire set of texts, rubrics, and ritual directions for the respective services, but give outlines only of the essential parts of the worship, with most of the texts and other features of the celebration to be filled in at the discretion of the participants after careful preparation.

The worship order for the evening is basically a *lucernarium* rite with a short thanksgiving for the light, the *Phos hilaron*, and a continuation of the service with the Evening Prayer, the entire eucharist from the salutation and the collect of the day on, a meal or *agapé*, or with a selection of traditional features for an evening office: psalms, readings, canticles, prayers, blessing, and/or dismissal. This service can be presided over by a lay person (excluding, of course, the possible eucharistic celebration) or a clergy person, and is very suitable for worship with groups.

The order for celebrating the eucharist requires extremely careful preparation by the presiding priest and all participants. "It is not intended for use at the principal Sunday or weekly celebration of the Holy Eucharist."[51] The outline is given that priest and people "gather in the Lord's Name, Proclaim and Respond to the Word of God, Pray for the World and the Church, Exchange the Peace, Prepare the Table, Make Eucharist, Break the Bread, Share the Gifts of God."[52] It is the basic pattern of the eucharist according to Rites One and Two which is outlined here. For the eucharistic prayer the specification is given that it is said by the priest in the name of those gathered, in the words of one of the eucharistic prayers provided in the prayer book; all people respond by saying "Amen." Two additional forms for the "Great Thanksgiving," the eucharistic prayer, are given, in which the Preface, the post-*Sanctus* part, in which God is praised "for the salvation of the world through Jesus Christ our Lord," and, in form two, the intercessions, are to be filled in extempore.[53] The epiclesis over the gifts, institution narrative, anamnesis, and epiclesis over the communicants are abbreviated versions of those provided elsewhere in the prayer book or in the renewed Roman sacramentary.[54] This order is a daring experiment in the art of being together as God's people to hear His word, to respond to it, and to celebrate the redemption wrought for us. If successful, more than 1500 years of liturgical history would be bridged backwards, and the ideal of an "apostolic liturgy" would have been approached.

The order for marriage gives the guidelines for celebrating the wedding. Due to the specific situation in the United States with reference to the civil law, special provisions have to be made, but the liturgy of the word, the exchange of the vows, the declaration of the union of man and woman as husband and wife, prayers, and, if presided over by a bishop or priest, a

---

[45] *Book of Common Prayer 1979*, pp. 148-55.
[46] "Concerning the Service of the Church:" *Book of Common Prayer 1979*, p. 14.
[47] *Book of Common Prayer 1979*, pp. 108-14.
[48] *Book of Common Prayer 1979*, pp. 400-05.
[49] *Book of Common Prayer 1979*, pp. 435-36.
[50] *Book of Common Prayer 1979*, pp. 506-07.
[51] "An Order for Celebrating the Holy Eucharist:" *Book of Common Prayer 1979*, p. 400.
[52] "An Order for Celebrating the Holy Eucharist:" *Book of Common Prayer 1979*, pp. 400-01.
[53] "An Order for Celebrating the Holy Eucharist:" *Book of Common Prayer 1979*, pp. 402-05.
[54] Hatchett, *Commentary*, pp. 415-16.

blessing, are always included. Only the actual version of the vows is written out. If the eucharist is celebrated, this is done according to either Rite One or Two, or according to the order for celebrating the holy eucharist.

The order for burial likewise gives guidelines only, without the proposal of any text. Elements of the service are the reception of the body; anthems, psalms, or hymns; prayers for the bereaved; readings; a homily, and possibly the Apostles' Creed; prayer for the deceased and the participants; commendation of the deceased, and committal of the body to the grave. A note is appended to the extent that the liturgy for the dead is an Easter liturgy; yet the sympathy with those who mourn ought not to be forgotten as this would be unchristian.

Since by definition these orders forego any uniformity in their execution, they may be regarded as the triumph of flexibility over stiffness, and as the death knell of any kind of monolithic liturgy.

The Reverence for Tradition

Although the new prayer book in essence begins a tradition of its own by the sometimes radical revisions it contains, still the emphasis is consistently on the tradition of the Church catholic. "Your heritage is the faith of patriarchs, prophets, apostles and martyrs, and those of every generation who have looked to God in hope."[55] The calendar of the church year has been greatly enriched both with feasts of the Lord and with commemorations of saints and heroes of the faith. Whereas the 1928 prayer book knew a liturgical celebration of the apostles and evangelists, St. John the Baptist, St. Stephen, the Innocents, St. Michael and all Angels, and two feasts of Mary (Purification and Annunciation), the new prayer book provides for the celebration of saints throughout all centuries, from the first through the twentieth centuries.[56] The Sunday has almost absolute precedence over all other fests, except All Saints' Day, Christmas Day, The Holy Name (January 1), Epiphany, The Presentation, and The Transfiguration; except during Advent, Lent, and Easter, the feast of the dedication of a church and the feast of its patron or title may be celebrated on a Sunday.[57]

The deliberate inclusion of texts from the English prayer books, both in Rites One and Two of the services, and in the many prayers and thanksgivings, witnesses the fact that the 1979 *Book of Common Prayer* is used in a church which is

> a constituent member of the Anglican Communion, a Fellowship within the One, Holy, Catholic, and Apostolic Church, of those duly constituted Dioceses, Provinces, and regional Churches in communion with the See of Canterbury, upholding and propagating the historic Faith and Order as set forth in the Book of Common Prayer.[58]

Despite all ecumenical relations,[59] the celebration, for example, of "Saint Mary the Virgin, Mother of Our Lord Jesus Christ" on August 15, which is a major holy day in the Episcopal Church, nowhere expresses the dogma of the assumption, with body and soul, of Mary.[60] For the period from the Reformation through the twentieth century, only those

---

[55] "Ordination of a Bishop," The Examination: *Book of Common Prayer 1979*, p. 517.

[56] There are five persons who died in the twentieth century and who are listed in the calendar. March 27: Charles Henry Brent, Bishop of the Philippines, and of Western New York, 1929; July 27: William Reed Huntington, Priest, 1909; August 18: William Porcher DuBose, Priest, 1918; September 2: The Martyrs of New Guinea, 1942; October 15: Samuel Isaac Joseph Schereschewsky, Bishop of Shanghai, 1906.

[57] "The Calendar of the Church Year," 2. Sundays: *Book of Common Prayer 1979*, p. 16.

[58] Preamble of the constitution.

[59] See Sumner, *Episcopal Church's History*, pp. 131-53.

[60] The collect: "O God, you have taken to yourself the Blessed Virgin Mary, mother of your incarnate Son: Grant that we, who have been redeemed by his blood, may share with her the glory of your eternal kingdom.":

persons have been adopted for inclusion in the calendar who belonged to one of the churches of the Anglican Communion. The section entitled "Historical Documents of the Church"[61] prints, among other things, the preface to the 1549 *Book of Common Prayer*; the Articles of Religion, a revision in 1801 of the Thirty-Nine Articles of the Church of England; and the Chicago-Lambeth Quadrilateral 1886, 1888, on Christian reunion. The *Book of Common Prayer* is still a book of the Episcopal Church.

Prior to the 1892 revision of the prayer book, the history of its subsequent revisions could account only for an ever-further cutback of proper liturgies for special days. The 1928 prayer book had provided ordinary texts for those special days marked, in earlier times, by extraordinary liturgical actions. The 1979 *Book of Common Prayer* restores those special days to their ancient dignity.

Ash Wednesday is provided with a penitential section within the liturgy of the word, with an option imposition of ashes.[62]

Palm Sunday is an occasion where the "Liturgy of the Palms" is celebrated by going in procession, with hymns, psalms, and anthems sung.[63]

Maundy Thursday has received a rubric allowing for the optional ceremony of the washing of feet.[64]

The old proper liturgy for Good Friday is restored with the readings, the solemn collects, an optional veneration of the cross, and a possible administration of the communion from the reserved sacrament, the eucharistic species having been consecrated at the Maundy Thursday liturgy.[65]

Holy Saturday, a day with no celebration of the eucharist, has been given an optional liturgy of the word.[66]

The Great Vigil of Easter has been restored to all its splendor and grand standing.[67] The bishop, when present, is the chief presider; the priests share in the reading of the collects after each lesson and assist at baptism and the eucharist. It is the deacon's "prerogative" to carry the paschal candle and to chant the *Exsultet*. Lay persons carry out their functions of readers and singers.[68] The service itself consists of the traditional four parts: the lighting of the paschal candle, with *Exsultet*; the liturgy of the word with nine readings from the Old Testament, of which at least two have to be read; the baptismal liturgy, with baptism and confirmation to be administered, if there are candidates, or else the renewal of baptismal vows; and the eucharist, beginning with a canticle and the collect of the night.

As far as these proper liturgies are concerned, the Reformation of the sixteenth century has come to an end. As they are "sensitive Anglican adaptations of important traditional liturgical substance,"[69] they are more than a restoration of pre-Reformation material; they are ritual expressions of that unifying factor for Church and world which has become the central "theme" of the Church's liturgy: the paschal mystery.

"Collects: Contemporary," Saint Mary the Virgin: *Book of Common Prayer 1979*, p. 243; the traditional version: p. 192.

[61] *Book of Common Prayer 1979*, pp. 863-78.

[62] *Book of Common Prayer 1979*, pp. 264-69.

[63] *Book of Common Prayer 1979*, pp. 270-73.

[64] *Book of Common Prayer 1979*, pp. 274-75.

[65] *Book of Common Prayer 1979*, pp. 276-82.

[66] *Book of Common Prayer 1979*, p. 283.

[67] *Book of Common Prayer 1979*, pp. 284-95.

[68] "The Great Vigil of Easter," Concerning the Vigil: *Book of Common Prayer 1979*, p. 284.

[69] Price, *Introducing the Proposed Book*, p. 59. Nothing, however, corroborates his opinion that "[i]t is important to observe . . . that the use of none of these Proper Liturgies is required." (p. 59) Some of the optional material may not be included in the services of some parishes, and, in general, these liturgies require a thorough preparation where those questions will be answered. But there is no rubric, or any other indication, in the 1979 *Book of Common Prayer* that these liturgies in their entirety are optional or not "required."

Social Concern and the Adoption of Contemporary Ideas

The 1979 *Book of Common Prayer* has two special features which make it of particular interest to scholars and church people elsewhere.

There is an attempt throughout the prayer book to employ what is called inclusive language: verbal expressions that are as broad as possible to include all circumstances and elements of human society. This ist most obvious in the effort by the Standing Liturgical Commission to avoid as much as possible the word "man" and "men" so as to forego any possibility of misunderstanding the respective sentences or rubrics in a way that would exclude women. Generic terms are often eliminated by using words like "people," "they," and others. The psalter, as "a body of liturgical poetry,"[70] is subject to the same regulation; and Psalm 1, for example, which is titled *Beatus vir qui non abiit*, includes happy and wicked women, too, by reading "Happy are they who have not walked."[71] But whenever messianic allusions are obvious or have been seen in the respective verse in the course of history, there has been no change.[72] In other liturgical texts, all words referring to a person addressed, or concerning a person referred to in a prayer, are printed in italics so as to make it immediately clear that these phrases have to be adapted to the situation. By employing inclusive language the Episcopal Church has been sensitive to the complaints and demands by those groups who in traditional church parlance have been all too easily left out of the recognition they deserve and have been all too often discriminated against. The struggle against this injustice, which was one of the reasons for the social unrest in the 1960s and 1970s, has left its mark on the vocabulary used in the liturgy, too.[73]

On September 20, 1976 the House of Bishops voted, in General Convention, on a history-setting amendment to the constitution: the ordination of women to become priests and bishops (the ordination to the diaconate had been permitted earlier).[74] In response to this development, appropriate changes had to be made in the *Proposed Book of Common Prayer*: the pronouns had to be italicized; the rubrics had to be amended; and some textual changes had to be made.[75] Throughout the entire book, the terms "the bishop," "the priest," "the deacon," "the celebrant," "the officiant," "the minister" are repeated where otherwise "he" would have sufficed. As to the presidency in the liturgy, there are no restrictions for women priests, and they share to the full extent in the ministry.

---

[70] "The Psalter," Concerning the Psalter: *Book of Common Prayer 1979*, p. 582.

[71] "The Psalter," Psalm 1: *Book of Common Prayer 1979*, p. 585. See Wainwright, "'E pluribus unum,'" pp. 302-03.

[72] For example, Ps 8:5-7 read: "What is man that you should be mindful of him? the Son of man that you should seek him out? You have made him but little lower than the angels; you adorn him with glory and honor; You give him mastery over the works of your hands; you put all things under his feet.": "The Psalter," Psalm 8: *Book of Common Prayer 1979*, p. 592. See the provocative article by Gail Ramshaw Schmidt, "De Divinis Nominibus: The Gender of God," *Worship*, 56 (1982), 117-31.

[73] For an introduction to the use of inclusive language as far as women are concerned, see L. Clark, "The Politics of Liturgical Change," in *Image-breaking, Image-building*, ed. L. Clark, M. Ronan, and E. Walker (New York: Pilgrim Press, 1981), pp. 83-89; Sharon Emswiler and Thomas Neufer Emswiler, *Woman and Worship: A Guide to Non-Sexist Hymns, Prayers, and Liturgies*, rev. and enlarged ed. (San Francisco: Harper & Row, 1984); *Language and Sex: Difference and Dominance*, ed. Barrie Thorne and Nancy Henly (Rowley: Newbury House, 1975).

[74] Sumner, *Episcopal Church's History*, pp. 12-30.

[75] *General Convention 1976*, pp. B-106-07, C-48-52. See Detscher, *Evolution*, p. 359.

The Eucharist as the Central Liturgy

Whereas an, albeit unintentional, by-product of the Reformation of the sixteenth century was a diminution of the appreciation of the eucharistic celebration, this prayer book makes clear that not a liturgy of the word or a homily is the principal worshipping act but the celebration whose climax is the Great Thanksgiving and the communion of all:

> The Holy Eucharist, the principal act of Christian worship on the Lord's Day and other major Feasts, and Daily Morning and Evening Prayer, as set forth in this Book, are the regular services appointed for public worship in this Church.[76]

This reassessment is consistent with the rediscovery of the centrality of the Sunday in the life of a Christian congregation. The fact that the order for celebrating the holy eucharist is provided shows that it is reckoned with more than the one Sunday eucharist.[77] Many more parishes of the Episcopal Church now have weekday eucharists than have regular or even daily Morning and Evening Prayer. As much as the reinstallation of the eucharist in its old rights and prerogatives is to be welcomed and supported, the danger should not be overlooked; the balance tips in the direction of an exclusiveness of the eucharist, to the detriment of other services of thanksgiving for the creation, redemption, and hope of glory, especially the Morning and Evening Prayer.[78]

Due to the increased awareness of the centrality of the eucharist, this present prayer book provides that, except for the reconciliation of a penitent, all other liturgical rites can be or must be celebrated within the context of a eucharist. For the ordinations, the celebration of a new ministry, the dedication and consecration of a church, and the burial, no other settings are given but within the eucharist; all other sacraments and liturgical actions are preferably done in a eucharist. The rubrics for baptism, for example, govern that "Holy Baptism is appropriately administered within the Eucharist as the chief service on a Sunday or other feast."[79] Daily Morning and Evening Prayer may precede the eucharist which then commences with the (exchange of the Peace and the) offertory. The role that in former prayer books was held by Morning and Evening Prayer as the regular services within which the other actions take place, if possible, has been taken over by the eucharist.

Variety and Flexibility

The different services are marked by the frequent appearance of the words "or," "may," and "if," to indicate the various options those engaged in the liturgical act may choose. This applies both to texts sung or said, and to rubrics followed or disregarded. Within the setting of one celebration, so many possible variations have to be taken into account that one may be left with the impression of different actions. To help those carrying out a special liturgical ministry to find the most appropriate ways of dealing with this hitherto unknown level of

---

[76] "Concerning the Service of the Church:" *Book of Common Prayer 1979*, p. 13.

[77] *Book of Common Prayer 1979*, pp. 400-05.

[78] A church that knows eucharistic celebrations only has lost its sound liturgical life. The celebrations can no longer respond to the requirements of real celebrations due to the inflation of occasions when they are to be held; and this one service is not balanced by other liturgical acts. There is, above all, the danger that the eucharist, in this case, has to take over all the other by-purposes of worship, for example, educational or devotional intentions. It is to be hoped that the Episcopal Church will be spared in this matter the (disastrous) experience of the Roman Catholic Church.

[79] "Holy Baptism," Concerning the Service: *Book of Common Prayer 1979*, p. 298.

flexibility, most of the services are provided with a section preceding the entire rite, called Concerning the Service, in which theological guidelines and pastoral implications of the ensuing rite are given. In Additional Directions following the rite, suggestions of a more practical and ceremonial nature are given. The time of a straight-jacketed service which could be read from the beginning to the end is definitely over, and careful preparations are asked instead.

The factor which determines the actual composition and form is the congregation gathered to celebrate Christ's mystery in the liturgical action. "A congregation is assured considerable latitude in setting its own liturgical use, although necessary guidelines have been established."[80] This freedom to determine its own liturgy is not a liberty to do according to one's own wishes or predilections; education in the art of liturgical celebration is necessary; or rather: the congregation is to be a community which is aware of its own mission, and which continues "in the apostles' teaching and fellowship, in the breaking of bread, and in the prayers."[81] More than ever, this prayer book makes it clear that the Episcopal Church, like other churches, is not a monolith but consists of communities which have unalienable rights. Congregations which prefer, for example, to celebrate the eucharist according to Rite One in an outline which makes it almost indistinguishable from the form prescribed and provided by the 1928 prayer book, are part of it, just as are congregations which celebrate the eucharist according to Rite Two in a fashion which makes it difficult to see the difference from a eucharist celebrated in a Roman Catholic church.

All these special features outlined here will be encountered again when it comes to considering the reformed rites of Christian initiation, set in their prayer book context. It was inevitable that a certain preliminary confusion might arise concerning the many options and varieties. But celebrations rarely are straightforward events; and the riches of the initiation cannot be limited to required exhortations being listened to, or to the execution of what is "essentially necessary" for the validity of the rite.

Holy Baptism

The liturgy of baptism[82] is printed after the section on proper liturgies for special days[83] and before the holy eucharist.[84] The insertion of baptism in the Easter vigil liturgy and in regular Sunday eucharistic celebrations, as well as the theological necessity of being baptized before being administered the communion, rightly justify the position in the book.

Seven paragraphs in the preliminary section Concerning the Service establish theological and pastoral principles without which the nature and liturgy of baptism cannot rightly be understood.[85]

The first paragraph has been taken over *verbatim* from the same section of "A Form for Confirmation or the Laying-on of Hands" in Prayer Book Studies 26,[86] but has a more proper and eminent place before baptism. It states that baptism "is full initiation by water and the Holy Spirit into Christ's Body the Church. The bond which God establishes in Baptism is indissoluble." The first sentence clearly replies to the questions and criticisms concerning the

---

[80] Price, *Introducing the Proposed Book*, p. 28.
[81] "Holy Baptism," The Baptismal Covenant: *Book of Common Prayer 1979*, p. 304.
[82] "Holy Baptism:" *Book of Common Prayer 1979*, pp. 298-314.
[83] "Proper Liturgies for Special Days:" *Book of Common Prayer 1979*, pp. 264-95.
[84] "The Holy Eucharist:" *Book of Common Prayer 1979*, pp. 316-82.
[85] *Book of Common Prayer 1979*, p. 298.
[86] "A Form for Confirmation," Concerning the Service: *Holy Baptism: together with A Form for Confirmation*, p. 22.

extent of Christian initiation and the perfection of baptism. At the same time, the operation of the Holy Spirit who works in the administration of the water is acknowledged. The second sentence establishes the unrepeatability of baptism in the life of a Christian.

The second paragraph requires that baptism be administered within the eucharist as the chief service on a Sunday or other feast. This, too, is a theological principle, as the intrinsic relation between baptism as the requirement for participation in the eucharist, and the eucharist as the end toward which baptism is directed, is pronounced. Furthermore, the connection between baptism and the liturgical year is safeguarded, the different seasons and feasts offering an interpretation of the several aspects of the paschal mystery. The Additional Directions recommend in the first paragraph what days are particularly appropriate for the administration of baptism.[87] As the central liturgical celebration of the year, the Easter Vigil has preeminence. Together with the reading Romans 6:3-11,[88] it highlights in ritual action the death and resurrection theme of the paschal mystery. The Day of Pentecost, as the old second occasion for baptism, emphasizes the role of the Holy Spirit in baptism. All Saints' Day, or the Sunday after that feast,[89] signifies the incorporation into the "household of God,"[90] "that we are very members incorporate in the mystical body of thy Son, the blessed company of all faithful people."[91] The Feast of the Baptism of the Lord speaks about the adoption as sons and daughters, and the anointment with the Holy Spirit. The other occasion directed in these guidelines is the visitation of the bishop. Being the chief minister of the diocese, it is the holder of this ministry, as the third paragraph of the section Concerning the Service states, who is the celebrant[92] of baptism; this includes the preaching and presiding over both sacraments. The bishop's prerogative is to officiate over the presentation and examination of the candidates; to say the thanksgiving over the water; to consecrate the chrism if desired; to say the prayer over the newly baptized; and to preside over the rites that follow. All of this, except for the consecration of the chrism, is to be done by a priest if the bishop is absent, as the fourth paragraph directs.

The three remaining paragraphs concern the number and duties of sponsors, of which one or more must accompany each candidate for baptism. Sponsors of adults and older children must have known the candidate for an appropriate length of time, for it is required that, in presenting their candidates, they endorse them; at the same time they pledge their support of the candidates by prayer and a Christian life. Sponsors of infants, among whom the parents of the child fittingly are included, must have undergone instruction in the meaning of baptism, in their duties towards the children regarding their Christian life, and in their responsibilities as members of the Church. All this, previously communicated in long, verbose, and unchangeable exhortations within the administration of baptism, now precedes the actual service, to the advantage of the nature of the celebration. Sponsors of infants present their

---

[87] *Book of Common Prayer 1979*, pp. 312-13.

[88] "The Great Vigil of Easter," At the Eucharist, Epistle: *Book of Common Prayer 1979*, p. 295.

[89] The Episcopal Church, curiously, knows two proper celebrations of that feast which is one of the seven Principal Feasts observed, taking precedence over any other day or liturgical celebration: the day proper of November 1, and the Sunday following that date, in addition to its observance on the fixed date. Although Ascension Day and The Epiphany are counted among these Principal Feasts, too, no such provision has been made for them, possibly for theological reasons (the unity of the Fifty Days not to be interrupted, and the Feast of the Baptism of the Lord as one of the Epiphany mysteries celebrated on the Sunday following). Neither one of these three feasts is a legal holiday in the United States, of course. "The Calendar of the Church Year," 1. Principal Feasts: *Book of Common Prayer 1979*, p. 15.

[90] "Holy Baptism," The Baptism, Reception into the congregation: *Book of Common Prayer 1979*, p. 308.

[91] "Holy Eucharist: Rite One," The Breaking of the Bread, Postcommunion prayer: *Book of Common Prayer 1979*, p. 339.

[92] Choice of words can be unintentionally revealing: despite the claim that it is the congregation with all its members that celebrates the liturgy, with some of the members carrying out their special liturgical ministry, all too often the 1979 prayer book still speaks about "the Celebrant" when it refers to the person presiding over the liturgy. It is in details like this that a mentality still lives on.

candidates, make the promise "in their own names," and take the vows on behalf of their candidates.

A slightly different pattern of the opening rites of the eucharist is followed,[93] with a set of four special versicles said after the opening acclamation, taken from Ephesians 4:4-6a. The *Gloria in excelsis* might be sung here, if desired.[94] The following collect is properly that of the day. When the bishop is the presider, and for sufficient reason on other occasions, the special collect may substitute for that of the day.[95] This collect "At Baptism" speaks about our baptism into the death and resurrection of Christ, and a turn from the old life of sin, and asks that, as we have been reborn to new life in Christ, we may live in righteousness and holiness all our days.[96] The readings, too, are normally taken from the day. Subject to the same direction as for the collect, one or more readings provided for use at baptism may be substituted for the regular ones.[97] After the gospel the sermon is given, unless it is prefered to have it preached after the exchange of the Peace at the end of the following sacramental rites.

The presentation and examination of the candidates is a trialogue:[98] the presider asks for the candidates to be presented; those who can speak for themselves are individually presented by their sponsors and asked each by the presider about their desire to be baptized, to which they give a response; infants and younger children are then individually presented by their parents and godparents. After the presentation these are asked whether they are willing to care for the child's Christian faith and life, and whether they will help, by prayers and witness, to assure that the child grows into the full stature of Christ; both of these questions are answered by the parents and godparents. The following three renunciations of all evil and wicked forces, powers, and desires,[99] and the three questions of adherence to Christ as savior, to his grace and love, and following him as Lord (an enlargement of the one question in the 1928 book)[100] are answered by those who can speak for themselves in their own names, and by the parents and godparents on behalf of the infants and younger children.

---

[93] "Holy Baptism:" *Book of Common Prayer 1979*, pp. 299-301.

[94] "Holy Baptism," Additional Directions: *Book of Common Prayer 1979*, p. 312.

[95] "Holy Baptism," Additional Directions: *Book of Common Prayer 1979*, p. 312.

[96] "Collects: Traditional," Various Occasions, no. 10, At Baptism: *Book of Common Prayer 1979*, p. 203; "Collects: Contemporary," Various Occasions, no. 10, At Baptism: p. 254. The collect proposed in *Holy Baptism with the Laying-On-of-Hands*, p. 34, and *Holy Baptism: together with A Form for Confirmation*, p. 9, is shifted in the 1979 *Book of Common Prayer* to conclude the litany, the Prayer for the Candidates: p. 306.

[97] "Holy Baptism," Additional Directions: *Book of Common Prayer 1979*, p. 312. "The Lectionary," Various occasions, no. 10: p. 928, provides as readings from the Old Testament: Ez 36:24-28; as reading from the New Testament: Rom 6:3-5; or Rom 8:14-17; or 2 Cor 5:17-20; as gospel reading Mark 1:9-11; or Mark 10:13-16; or John 3:1-6. These provisions are the same as in *Holy Baptism: together with A Form for Confirmation*, p. 9; *Holy Baptism with the Laying-On-of-Hands*, p. 34, had John 3:1-8 instead of 3:1-6. As responsorial psalms, optionally following either reading before the gospel, are given: 15; or 23; or 27; or 42:1-7; or 84; or canticle 9, The First Song of Isaiah, 12:2-6 ("The Daily Office," Daily Morning Prayer: Rite Two, The Lessons, Canticle 9: *Book of Common Prayer 1979*, p. 86). Permission is given to substitute the rading Ez 36:24-28 by any of the Old Testament readings from the Easter Vigil. Those are: The Story of Creation (Gen 1:1--2:2); The Flood (Gen 7:1-5,11-18; 8:6-8; 9:8-13); Abrahams sacrifice of Isaac (Gen 22:1-18); Israel's deliverance at the Red Sea (Ex 14:10--15:1); God's presence in a renewed Israel (Is 4:2-6); Salvation offered freely to all (Is 55:1-11); [A new heart and a new spirit (Ez 36:24-28);] The valley of dry bones (Ez 37:1-14); The gathering of God's people (Zeph 3:12-20): "The Great Vigil of Easter," The Liturgy of the Word: *Book of Common Prayer 1979*, pp. 288-91.

[98] *Book of Common Prayer 1979*, pp. 301-03.

[99] *Holy Baptism with the Laying-On-of-Hands*, p. 35, had one such question, after the questions of adherence to Christ. This was changed in *Holy Baptism: together with A Form for Confirmation*, p. 11, to the present form.

[100] "Holy Baptism:" *Book of Common Prayer 1928*, p. 278.

If in this liturgy the bishop at the same time administers the "Confirmation," or receives persons into the Episcopal Church, or accepts the reaffirmation of baptismal vows by other persons, these are now presented and asked whether they reaffirm their renunciation of evil and their commitment to Christ.[101] At the end of this part of the liturgy, the congregation comes to the fore again by being asked by the presider whether they will do all in their power to support the candidates in their Christian life. The question is affirmed by the congregation in the plural: "We will."[102] An invitation to join the candidates and to renew their own baptismal covenant leads up to the following section.

The baptismal covenant is divided into two parts.[103] The first is a threefold question about the three divine Persons, asked by the presider and answered by everybody with the respective part of the Apostles' Creed. The restoration of the full text of the baptismal creed to the American prayer book, which had reduced it to one simple question about the articles of the Christian faith as they are contained in this creed, is very much to be welcomed and agreeable to the ancient dignity of this text.[104]

The second part consists of five questions that concern the consequences of baptism for a Christian life: the continuation in the apostles' teaching and fellowship, in the breaking of bread and in the prayers; the perseverance in resisting evil, and the intention to repent when fallen into sin; the proclamation of the gospel by word and example; the Christian love of the neighbor as oneself; and the strife for justice and peace among all people, and the respect for the dignity of every human being.[105] These five questions replace the one question in all prayer books since 1662 about keeping God's will, and walking in it all the days.

A prayer for the candidates of baptism, and of the laying on of hands if there are any, follows in the form of seven short petitions, asked by a person appointed for it who might be one of the sponsors,[106] and answered by the congregation with the acclamation "Lord, hear our prayer." The intercessions ask for perseverance of the candidates in what they have promised, and for the fullness of God's peace.[107] The concluding prayer, the former collect of the baptismal eucharist, prays that all who are baptized into Christ's death may live in the power of his resurrection and look for him to come again in glory--the final eschatological note a welcome extension of the meaning of baptism, which is otherwise lacking in the texts.

The thanksgiving over the water follows, immediately preceded, where practicable, by a filling of the font with clean water.[108] It consists of three parts. The first is a thanksgiving for

---

[101] The *Draft Proposed Book of Common Prayer* still had these two questions combined as one, with one answer by the candidate affirming that he/she will follow Christ as Savior and Lord: "Holy Baptism," Presentation and Examination of the Candidates: p. 305.

[102] The discovery of the congregation as having rights and duties independent of those of individual members had led the churches in the revision of their liturgies to acknowledge this fact by having the congregation respond as "we," instead of a multiple "I." *Holy Baptism with the Laying-On-of-Hands* lacks this question; *Holy Baptism: together with A Form for Confirmation*, p. 11, puts it between the presentation of the candidates for baptism and the renunciation.

[103] *Book of Common Prayer 1979*, pp. 304-07.

[104] The former American prayer books assumed that baptism would be administered in the context of Morning or Evening Prayer which contained, as an integral part, the Apostles' Creed so that the text itself was said during the service. But it was a part of the daily Office, not of baptism.

[105] *Holy Baptism with the Laying-On-of-Hands*, p. 35, had two only which are the fourth and fifth now, asked before the renunciation. *Holy Baptism: together with A Form for Confirmation*, p. 12, had four of them, after the Apostles' Creed, lacking what is now the second one (resisting evil, and repenting).

[106] "Holy Baptism," Additional Directions: *Book of Common Prayer 1979*, p. 312.

[107] Both *Holy Baptism with the Laying-On-of-Hands*, pp. 36-37, and *Holy Baptism: together with A Form for Confirmation*, p. 13, have six petitions; the one asking that the candidates be filled with God's holy and life-giving Spirit is lacking in either revision. The concluding prayer, too, is missing in both Studies as it served as the collect of the eucharist.

[108] "Holy Baptism," Additional Directions: *Book of Common Prayer 1979*, p. 313.

the water itself. Allusions are made to the creation, to the exodus through the Red Sea, and to Christ's own baptism and anointing with the Holy Spirit as the Christ who would lead us, through his own death and resurrection, to a life free from the bondage of sin, to everlasting life. The second part is a thanksgiving for the water of baptism in which we share in Christ's death and resurrection and are reborn by the Holy Spirit. Obedient to Christ's commandment, those who have come to him are brought into his fellowship and baptized in the name of the Trinity. The third part is an epiclesis over the water during which the presider touches the water. The sanctification of this water by the power of the Holy Spirit is asked so that those who here are cleansed from sin and born again may live for ever in the risen life of Christ. A doxology concludes this blessing.

The bishop who is present to preside over the liturgy may now consecrate chrism by placing a hand on the vessel of oil and praying that this oil may be consecrated so that those who are sealed with it may share in the royal priesthood of Christ, who was anointed by the Holy Spirit to be the savior and servant of all.[109]

The central section of the liturgy, itself called The Baptism, immediately begins after the thanksgiving over the water, or after the consecration of the chrism is done.[110] Each candidate is presented by name to the presiding priest or to an assisting priest or deacon, who immerses or pours water upon the candidate by using the name of the person and the Trinitarian formula for baptism, to which is responded *"Amen."*[111] After each candidate is baptized, either the prayer over the newly baptized is said by the bishop or the priest presiding, or the signing with the cross is done after the administration of the water.

The prayer over the baptized is a thanksgiving that by water and the Holy Spirit God has bestowed upon the baptized the forgiveness of sins and has raised them to the new life of grace, and a request for a sustention in the Holy Spirit, with all his gifts to be given.

The signation with the cross on the person's head, with chrism if desired, is done by the bishop or presiding priest to each one with the formula "*N.*, you are sealed by the Holy Spirit in Baptism and marked as Christ's own for ever." *"Amen."*[112]

The reception into the congregation, rather the affirmation of the incorporation into the Church that happened in the water administration, is expressed after the invitation to welcome the newly baptized, by everybody saying that the new members are received into the

---

[109] The consecration of chrism can also take place at a bishop's visitation, in connection with "Confirmation," if there are no candidates for baptism: "Confirmation," last rubric: *Book of Common Prayer 1979*, p. 419. Chrism so consecrated would be used in that parish for the signation after baptism, if the use of chrism is desired.

[110] *Book of Common Prayer 1979*, pp. 307-11. Actually, this section also comprises the *ritus continuus* of confirmation, reception, or reaffirmation, and the continuation of the eucharist. The present part, The Baptism, extends to the end of the actual rite of baptism, excluding confirmation and the other parts. The page reference, therefore, is *Book of Common Prayer 1979*, pp. 307-08.

[111] The "Amen" is italicized (p. 307) which always means a response of this kind by some other person or group, or by the entire congregation. It is not clear who would be the proper entity to say "Amen" in this instance. Hatchett opines that it is "to be said by the congregation as indication of their consent and authorization, and as affirmation of their pledge to support the newly baptized in their life in Christ:" *Commentary*, p. 278. *Holy Baptism with the Laying-On-of-Hands*, p. 39, had it said by the minister baptizing; *Holy Baptism: together with A Form for Confirmation*, p. 15, had a rubric: "The people say, AMEN." The Additional Directions provide that the celebrant, if possible, should face the people across the font at the administration of baptism, with the sponsors being so grouped that the entire congregation has "a clear view of the action:" *Book of Common Prayer 1979*, p. 313.

[112] "Holy Baptism," The Baptism, sealing formula: *Book of Common Prayer 1979*, p. 308. In this instance it is even more difficult to say who is to respond "Amen" than in the case of the administration of the water. *Holy Baptism with the Laying-On-of-Hands*, p. 39, and *Holy Baptism: together with A Form for Confirmation*, p. 15, did not print any "Amen;" Hatchett, *Commentary*, pp. 278-81, esp. p. 281, is silent about this word, too.

household of God, and by expressing the wish that they confess the crucified Lord, proclaim his resurrection, and share with the congregation in his eternal priesthood.[113]

If the "Confirmation," reception into the Episcopal Church, or reaffirmation of baptism vows does not follow immediately, the exchange of the Peace is done now.

The three services reserved for a bishop, "Confirmation," reception, or reaffirmation, are preferably to be part of a baptismal service.[114] In this case, the candidates have, at this point, been presented already, so that the bishop, after an invitation to pray for these candidates, says a prayer over them. It begins with a thanksgiving for the victory over sin and the closeness to God through the death and resurrection of Christ,[115] and for the service through the sealing of the Holy Spirit,[116] and it continues with asking for a renewal of the covenant God has made with the candidates at their baptism, and that they be sent in the power of the Spirit to do the service set before them. The immediately following action is the central part of this rite.

For the "Confirmation" two formulas are given, accompanying the laying on of hands upon each candidate. The first one[117] reads:

> Strengthen, O Lord, your servant N. with your Holy Spirit; empower *him* for your service; and sustain *him* all the days of *his* life. Amen."[118]

The second one is the form used since the 1552 prayer book:

> Defend, O Lord, your servant *N*. with your heavenly grace, that *he* may continue yours for ever, and daily increase in your Holy Spirit more and more, until *he* comes to your everlasting kingdom. Amen.[119]

For reception into the communion of the Episcopal Church, an affirmative formula with a blessing is given:

---

[113] Some inconsistency has crept into the rite at this point. The prayer of consecration of chrism asks "that those who are sealed with it may share in the royal priesthood of Jesus Christ:" *Book of Common Prayer 1979*, p. 307. This formula implies that by being signed and sealed with the cross, whether or not done with chrism, the person is enabled to, and effectually does, share in Christ's priesthood. To express as a wish to come true what has a moment before been effected and has come true is a theological underhandedness which ought to be revised. *Holy Baptism with the Laying-On-of-Hands*, p. 40, added to this wish said by the congregation to the new members: "May the Lord arm you with his heavenly grace, that you may daily increase in his favor all the days of your life. Amen." This is the second part of the old confirmation formula in the former prayer books ("Defend, O Lord").

[114] *Book of Common Prayer 1979*, pp. 309-10.

[115] *Holy Baptism: together with A Form for Confirmation*, p. 26, spoke of the cross only, without referring to the resurrection.

[116] Whereas the signation formula after the administration of water speaks of being sealed "by the Holy Spirit in Baptism" (p. 308), this prayer sees the Holy Spirit as object of the sealing: "that by the sealing of your Holy Spirit you have bound us to your service:" *Book of Common Prayer 1979*, p. 309.

[117] It was drafted by Urban Tigner Holmes: Hatchett, *Commentary*, p. 282.

[118] *Holy Baptism: together with A Form for Confirmation*, p. 26, had a slightly different version: "Strengthen your servant, *Name*, with the riches of your Holy Spirit; sustain *him* and empower *him* for your service."

[119] The former prayer books read "this thy child" instead of "your servant." This rephrasing takes into account that the "Confirmation," in the words of the Agreed Positions of 1972, is "an act and occasion for (more or less) mature personal acceptance of promises and affirmations made on one's behalf in infancy." This formula served as the concluding part of the confirmation prayer within which the laying on of hands took place, in *Holy Baptism: together with A Form for Confirmation*, p. 26.

> *N.*, we recognize you as a member of the one holy catholic and apostolic Church, and we receive you into the fellowship of this Communion. God, the Father, Son, and Holy Spirit, bless, preserve, and keep you. *Amen.*

The formula provided for those persons who had neglected their Christian life and have come to reaffirm their baptismal vows reads:

> *N.*, may the Holy Spirit, who has begun a good work in you, direct and uphold you in the service of Christ and his kingdom. *Amen.*

The prayer said by the bishop after these individual actions is the petition that God's fatherly hand be always with those who have just undergone the episcopal action, that they may be so led in the knowledge and obedience of God's word that they may serve Him in this life, and in the life to come may dwell with Him.

The Peace is exchanged now between the bishop and the people.

As baptism is expected to be administered within the chief eucharist on a Sunday or feast day, the celebration now continues with the prayers of the people, or the offertory; the bishop, when present, is the presider over the eucharist.[120] The bread and wine may be presented by the newly baptized or their godparents.[121] Except on the seven principal feast days[122] the proper Preface of baptism may be used. This prose hymn sings about the effects of baptism: adoption as sons and daughters, citizenship in God's kingdom, and the gift of the Holy Spirit for guidance in all truth.[123]

Should there, for some reason, not be a eucharist as the proper setting of baptism, the service concludes with the Lord's Prayer and a thanksgiving by the presider for the effects of baptism: adoption as God's own children, incorporation into the Church, and a share in the inheritance of the saints. Alms may be given, other prayers may be added; and the final blessing, based on Ephesians 3:14-19 and adopted for the baptismal rite in the 1928 prayer book, is bestowed.

Guidelines not mentioned in the preceding paragraphs concern the appropriate minister of the rites and some proposals for actions and processions.[124]

On the four special baptismal occasions (Easter Vigil, Pentecost, All Saints', Baptism of the Lord) a deacon may be authorized to preside over the rites in the absence of a bishop or priest. In this case, the postbaptismal rites and prayers are omitted. These portions may be administered at a subsequent public baptism over which a bishop or priest presides.

---

[120] *Book of Common Prayer 1979*, pp. 310-11.

[121] "Holy Baptism," Additional Directions: *Book of Common Prayer 1979*, p. 313.

[122] In addition to the days referred to above (All Saints' Day, Ascension, Epiphany), these are Easter Day, The Day of Pentecost, Trinity Sunday, and Christmas Day: "The Calendar of the Church Year," 1. Principal Feasts: *Book of Common Prayer 1979*, p. 15.

[123] "Holy Eucharist: Rite One," Proper Prefaces, Prefaces for Other Occasions: *Book of Common Prayer 1979*, p. 348; "Holy Eucharist: Rite Two," Proper Prefaces, Prefaces for Other Occasions: p. 381. Some of the Prefaces for the Principal Feasts contain references to the sacrament of baptism and/or its effects: Incarnation: "that we might be delivered from the bondage of sin, and receive power to become your children:" "Holy Eucharist: Rite Two," Proper Prefaces, Prefaces for Seasons: *Book of Common Prayer 1979*, p. 378; Pentecost: "uniting peoples of many tongues in the confession of one faith, and giving to your Church the power to serve as a royal priesthood, and to preach the Gospel to all nations:" p. 380; All Saints' Day: "For in the multitude of your saints you have surrounded us with a great cloud of witnesses, that we might rejoice in their fellowship:" Prefaces for Other Occasions: p. 380. Cf. "Holy Eucharist: Rite One," Proper Prefaces, Prefaces for Seasons: pp. 345, 347; Prefaces for Other Occasions: p. 347.

[124] "Holy Baptism," Additional Directions: *Book of Common Prayer 1979*, pp. 312-13.

If there are no candidates for baptism on those four days, the renewal of baptismal vows for all present may be substituted for the Nicene Creed at the eucharist.[125]

Two processions are proposed. The first, if the presentation of the candidates does not take place at the font, should take place before or during the prayers for the candidates so that everybody concerned has arrived at the font for the thanksgiving over the water. At a formal procession, Psalm 42, a hymn or anthem may be sung. The second procession is proposed for the prayer following baptism (and signation, if it is done before the prayer). Psalm 23, a hymn or anthem may be sung.[126]

After baptism (without any further specification), a candle, possibly lighted from the paschal candle, may be given to each newly baptized or to a godparent.[127]

Guidelines for conditional baptism and emergency baptism follow.[128]

"Confirmation"

As the signation is restored to baptism, which is regarded as bestowing the Holy Spirit on the candidates, the "Confirmation" as it is outlined in the 1979 prayer book[129] is actually that part of the former confirmation services which required a certain knowledge, and was given as a rite for children of competent age brought to the bishop to be confirmed. The initiation part of the confirmation, in other words, is contained in the baptismal rite. Therefore, the third and concluding part of the Christian initiation, the first joning of the eucharist and reception of communion, no longer is linked to the administration of this "new" confirmation, but to baptism. The rite itself is given among the "Pastoral Offices."[130]

The rationale for the reception of confirmation is given in unmistakable terms in the first two paragraphs of the section Concerning the Service:[131]

> In the course of their Christian development, those baptized at an early age are expected, when they are ready and have been duly prepared, to make a mature public affirmation of their faith and commitment to the responsibilities of their Baptism and to receive the laying on of hands by the bishop.
>
> Those baptized as adults, unless baptized with laying on of hands by a bishop, are also expected to make a public affirmation of their faith and commitment to the responsibilities of their Baptism in the presence of a bishop and to receive the laying on of hands.[132]

---

125 "Holy Baptism," Additional Directions: *Book of Common Prayer 1979*, p. 312.
126 "Holy Baptism," Additional Directions: *Book of Common Prayer 1979*, pp. 312-13.
127 "Holy Baptism," Additional Directions: *Book of Common Prayer 1979*, p. 313.
128 "Holy Baptism:" *Book of Common Prayer 1979*, pp. 313-14.
129 *Book of Common Prayer 1979*, pp. 412-19.
130 *Book of Common Prayer 1979*, pp. 411-507. These contain the "Confirmation," "A Form of Commitment to Christian Service," Marriage rites, "Thanksgiving for the Birth or Adoption of a Child," "Reconciliation of a Penitent," "Ministration to the Sick," "Ministration at the Time of Death," Burial rites. It is curious that, with all the emphasis given in the revision process by different groups to the "Confirmation" as being a rite that can be administered by a bishop only, the confirmation service appears among these offices which can all be presided over by a priest (or even a lay person), and not among the "Episcopal Services" (pp. 509-79) which contain the ordination rites, the "Celebration of a New Ministry," and the consecration o a new church or chapel. Is this a bow before tradition, or an indication that, albeit as yet in liturgical theology only, a priest might do in this case what now has been reserved for a bishop, as *Holy Baptism with the Laying-On-of-Hands* had tried?
131 *Book of Common Prayer 1979*, p. 412.
132 *Book of Common Prayer 1979*, p. 412. The second paragraph borders on liturgical and theological nonsense. Who or what is to be "confirmed" when adults follow this requirement and are presented for

The setting of this service appropriately is within the baptismal rite; otherwise, the form given under the special heading "Confirmation" is to be followed. As the administration of this confirmation is done within a eucharist, it is appropriate that the newly confirmed present the bread and the wine.[133]

At the confirmation service,[134] all the texts, except the collect and the readings, are taken from those provided for the celebration of baptism. The special collect which might, at the discretion of the bishop, be said, is very closely linked to that given for the baptismal service:

At baptism	At confirmation
Almighty God, by our baptism into the death and resurrection of your Son Jesus Christ, you turn us from the old life of sin:	Grant, Almighty God, that we, who have been redeemed from the old life of sin by our baptism into the death and resurrection of your Son Jesus Christ,
Grant that we, being reborn to new life in him, may live in righteousness and holiness all our days.[135]	may be renewed in your Holy Spirit, and live in righteousness and true holiness.[136]

The readings, just as the collects, are "properly" those of the day. One or more of the special readings may be substituted.[137]

"Confirmation:" the adults who in baptism have made just such a public affirmation of their faith; or the affirmation itself; or--the Holy Spirit given in baptism? And exactly what episcopal imposition of hands is meant here that dispenses from the "Confirmation," the one immediately after the administration of the water which is the bishop's prerogative, if present, to perform ("Holy Baptism," Concerning the Service: *Book of Common Prayer 1979*, p. 298), or the one which is intended as the "Confirmation" even for adolescents and other adults, which would mean that adult candidates for baptism would undergo a *ritus continuus* with the confirmational imposition of hands right after "The Baptism." If a person baptized as adult and afterwards lapsing from Christian life and service wishes to renew his or her commitment, this can best be done with the episcopal laying on of hands and the reaffirmation formula. The idea arises that the provision discussed here comes dangerously close to a denial of the once-and-for-all decision of baptism.

[133] "Confirmation," Concerning the Service: *Book of Common Prayer 1979*, p. 412. The other paragraphs allow the optional insertion of the *Gloria in excelsis* after the opening versicles and before the salutation, and provide that the Nicene Creed is not used at this service.

[134] *Book of Common Prayer 1979*, pp. 413-19.

[135] "Collects: Traditional," Various Occasions, no. 10, At Baptism: *Book of Common Prayer 1979*, p. 203; "Collects: Contemporary," Various Occasions, no. 10, At Baptism: p. 254.

[136] "Collects: Traditional," Various Occasions, no. 11, At Confirmation: *Book of Common Prayer 1979*, p. 203; "Collects: Contemporary," Various Occasions, no. 11, At Confirmation: p. 254.

[137] "The Lectionary," Various Occasions, no. 11: *Book of Common Prayer 1979*, p. 929, provides as readings from the Old Testament Is 61:1-9; or Jer 31:31-34 (the one proposed in *Holy Baptism: together with A Form for Confirmation*, p. 24); or Ez 37:1-10; from the New Testament Rom 8:18-27; or Rom 12:1-8; or Gal 5:16-25; or Eph 4:7,11-16 (as in *Holy Baptism: together with A Form for Confirmation*, p. 24); as gospel reading Mt 5:1-12; or Mt 16:24-27; or Lk 4:16-22; or John 14:15-21 (the one provided in *Holy Baptism: together with A Form for Confirmation*, p. 24). Conspicuously absent is the reading Acts 8:14-17, the traditional, if theologically not convincing, rationale for the reservation, in the Western Church, of the confirmation to the bishop; see Geoffrey Wainwright, "The Rites and Ceremonies of Christian Initiation: Developments in the Past," *Studia Liturgica*, 10 (1974), 5-6. As responsorial psalms, optionally following either reading before the gospel, are given 1; or 139:1-9.

The two major sections of the service proper of the confirmation, the Presentation and Examination of the candidates, and The Baptismal Covenant, are *verbatim* the same, both in rubrics and in texts, as in the baptismal service.[138] After the affirmation of adherence to Christ, and the baptismal promises, the prayers for the candidates are said, preferably the same as in baptism. After that litany, the bishop continues with the prayer over the candidates, the application of the ensuing formula to each candidate according to the purpose of the presentation, with the laying on of hands upon each candidate for confirmation, and the concluding prayer; these texts, too, are the same as in the baptismal service. After the exchange of the Peace the eucharist continues with the prayers of the people, or the offertory. Should there, for some reason, not be a celebration of the eucharist, the service ends with the Lord's Prayer "and other such devotions as the bishop may direct."[139] In this same service, the bishop may consecrate chrism for use at baptism in this parish or congregation, with the prayer provided for in the baptismal section. This is done immediately after the postcommunion prayer and before the bishop's blessing and dismissal.[140]

The Holy Eucharist

The eucharistic celebration according to the *Book of Common Prayer* 1979 has received both a new name and a double pattern.[141] Whereas the 1928 prayer book called the service "The Order for The Administration of the Lord's Supper or Holy Communion,"[142] the new prayer book brings both essential elements into focus by naming it "The Holy Eucharist: The Liturgy for the Proclamation of the Word of God and Celebration of the Holy Communion."[143] The double pattern is expressed in the provision that the eucharist can be celebrated according to a rite very similar to the previous prayer book services, and a rite that has emerged as a common structure for the eucharistic celebration in most major churches within and outside the Anglican Communion, including the Roman Catholic Church. The theological principles, however, are the same for both rites.

A section Concerning the Celebration precedes the print-out of the liturgy.[144] The naming of this section alone makes known that what is done is more than the administration of a sacrament, or a service held; it is a celebration of all who have gathered for that purpose, with all the structures and patterns necessary and possible.

All the ministries and their functions are told. It is the "prerogative" of the bishop to preside over the entire celebration and to give the sermon. Priests "appropriately" concelebrating with the bishop or another priest stand at the altar and have their share in the consecration of the gifts, the breaking of the bread, and distribution of communion.[145] The deacon's ministry is to read the gospel; the prayers of the people may also be led. The altar is prepared by bread and wine being placed on it. In the distribution of communion the

---

[138] *Book of Common Prayer 1979*, pp. 415-19. The section on the infants in the presentation of the candidates is of course dropped.
[139] "Confirmation:" *Book of Common Prayer 1979*, p. 419.
[140] "Confirmation:" *Book of Common Prayer 1979*, p. 419; "Consecration of Chrism apart from Baptism," Initial Rubrics: *Book of Occasional Services*, p. 209.
[141] "Holy Eucharist: Rite One:" *Book of Common Prayer 1979*, pp. 323-49; "Holy Eucharist: Rite Two:" pp. 355-82.
[142] *Book of Common Prayer 1928*, pp. 67-89.
[143] *Book of Common Prayer 1979*, p. 315.
[144] "Holy Eucharist: Rite One:" *Book of Common Prayer 1979*, p. 322; "Holy Eucharist: Rite Two:" p. 354.
[145] There are no further indications of the concelebrants' duties and parts in the actual texts. For the distribution of the communion, some suggestions are given in the section Additional Directions: *Book of Common Prayer 1979*, pp. 406-09.

deacon's function is the administration of the chalice. As these are not duties proper to the presiding priest, they should be done, if there are no deacons, by assisting priests. Lay persons should "normally" read the lessons from the Old and New Testaments; they too may lead the prayers of the people.

Everything preceding the Peace and the offertory can be substituted by Morning and Evening Prayer; in this case a reading from the gospel is to be included, and the intercessions have to conform to the directions given for the prayers of the people.

Rubrical directions themselves are not given in this section; they are printed within the rites and in the section Additional Directions. These paragraphs concern the principle of a celebration by the entire people of God whether they serve as the congregation gathered or in a special function.[146]

In order both to clarify the structure of both rites and to avoid getting lost in too many details, an outline of the pattern of both rites for the Sunday liturgy is given here, with the rite of the Lord's Supper of the 1928 prayer book as comparison.[147] A commentary on the eucharistic prayers follows.

Book of Common Prayer 1928	Rite One	Rite Two
	THE WORD OF GOD	THE WORD OF GOD
	A hymn, psalm, or anthem	A hymn, psalm, or anthem
The Lord's Prayer	Opening versicles	Opening versicles
Collect for Purity	Collect for Purity	Collect for Purity
Ten Commandments, or the Summary	Ten Commandments, or the Summary	

---

[146] In this context, the change in the catechism is significant and self-explanatory. The 1928 *Book of Common Prayer* knew two Offices of Instruction in which the catechism, in a slightly revised version, was rehearsed between the minister and the people; these served as a preparation for confirmation. In the second Office, the question was asked: "What orders of Ministers are there in the Church? Answer: Bishops, Priests, and Deacons; which orders have been in the Church from the earliest times:" p. 294. Specific questions about the offices of a bishop, a priest, and a deacon, were then asked. The present prayer book has in its catechism a section The Ministry: *Book of Common Prayer 1979*, pp. 855-56. The first two questions here read: "Q. Who are the ministers of the Church? A. The ministers of the Church are lay persons, bishops, priests, and deacons. Q. What is the ministry of the laity? A. The ministry of the lay persons is to represent Christ and his Church; to bear witness to him wherever they may be; and, according to the gifts given them, to carry on Christ's work of reconciliation in the world; and to take their place in the life, worship, and governance of the Church:" p. 855. Specific questions are then asked about the ministry of a bishop, of a priest or presbyter, and of a deacon. The last question concerns all members of the Church again: "Q. What is the duty of all Christians? A. The duty of all Christians is to follow Christ; to come together week by week for corporate worship; and to work, pray, and give for the spread of the kingdom of God:" p. 856.

[147] The texts of the rites themselves, without proper Prefaces: "Holy Eucharist: Rite One:" *Book of Common Prayer 1979*, pp. 323-44; "Holy Eucharist: Rite Two:" pp. 355-77. Indented lines in the chart indicate that the particular item is optional. This is mostly printed as "may" or "when (if) appointed" in the text. The two main parts of the eucharist in the *Book of Common Prayer 1979* are given in capitals here, the elements that are printed in boldtype in the book are italicized in this sketch.

of the Law	of the Law	
Lord, have mercy	Lord, have mercy, or Kyrie, or Trisagion	Lord, have mercy, or Kyrie, or Trisagion
Collect for Guidance		
	Glory be to God on high	Glory to God in the highest[148]
	The Collect of the Day	The Collect of the Day
Salutation	Salutation	Salutation
Collect	Collect	Collect
	"Amen"	"Amen"
	The Lessons	*The Lessons*
	Reading	Reading
	Silence Psalm, hymn, or anthem	Silence Psalm, hymn, or anthem
Epistle	Reading	Reading
	Silence Psalm, hymn, or anthem	Silence Psalm, hymn, or anthem
Hymn, or anthem		
Gospel	Gospel Acclamation	Gospel Acclamation
	The Sermon	*The Sermon*
Nicene, or Apostles' Creed	*The Nicene Creed*	*The Nicene Creed*
Announcements Bidding Prayer		
Sermon		
Offertory Sentences		
Prayer for the whole state of Christ's Church	*The Prayers of the People*	*The Prayers of the People*

---

[148] *The Gloria in excelsis* is given in the first place as to be sung or said when appointed; "on other occasions" the Lord, have mercy, or *Kyrie, or Trisagion* is used: *Book of Common Prayer 1979*, p. 356.

	Confession of Sin	Confession of Sin One of the sentences from the Penitential Order
Exhortation	Invitation or Exhortation	Invitation
	Silence	Silence
General Confession Proclamation of forgiveness	General Confession Proclamation of forgiveness	General Confession Proclamation of forgiveness
Comfortable Words	Comfortable Words	
	The Peace	*The Peace*
	THE HOLY COMMUNION	THE HOLY COMMUNION
	One of the Offertory Sentences	One of the Offertory Sentences
	Hymn, psalm, or anthem	Hymn, psalm or anthem
	Bringing of bread and wine and money or other gifts	Bringing of bread and wine and money or other gifts
	The Great Thanksgiving	*The Great Thanksgiving*
Dialogue	Dialogue	Dialogue
Preface	Proper Preface	Proper Preface
Holy, Holy, Holy	Holy, Holy, Holy Blessed is he	Holy, Holy, Holy Blessed is he
Prayer of Consecration "Amen"	Eucharistic Prayer "Amen"	Eucharistic Prayer "Amen"
The Lord's Prayer	The Lord's Prayer	The Lord's Prayer
	The Breaking of the Bread	*The Breaking of the Bread*
	Silence	Silence

	Breaking versicle (1 Cor 5:7b,8a)	Breaking versicle (1 Cor 5:7b,8a)
	Lamb of God	Lamb of God
Prayer of Humble Access	Prayer of Humble Access	
Hymn		
	Invitation to Communion	Invitation to Communion
Reception of the Communion with words of administration	Reception of the Communion with words of administration	Reception of the Communion with words of administration
	Hymns, psalms, or anthems	Hymns, psalms, or anthems
Postcommunion prayer	Postcommunion prayer	Postcommunion prayer
Glory be to God on high		
Blessing of the People	Blessing of the People	Blessing of the People
	Dismissal of the People	Dismissal of the People

It is obvious that the Standing Liturgical Commission has tried to establish in Rite One a liturgy which can be used in the direction of both an approachment to the 1928 eucharistic rite, and a near-identical celebration to that of Rite Two. Both purposes are achieved by using some of the optional material corresponding to the respective rite while leaving out other texts.

At the same time, both Rite One and Rite Two are patterned after what Gregory Dix has made famous as "the fourfold shape:"[149] taking the gifts, giving thanks over them, breaking them, and giving them, although the printed rites do not suggest this in the way the headings are given.

Of particular interest are the six eucharistic prayers given for the celebration of the eucharist, two for Rite One,[150] and four for Rite Two.[151] All of them show an identical structure: Preface, with *Sanctus*; christological part (except Prayer C); institution narrative;

---

[149] Dix, *Shape of the Liturgy*, pp. 78-82, 103-40.

[150] "Holy Eucharist: Rite One," The Holy Communion, The Great Thanksgiving, Eucharistic Prayer I: *Book of Common Prayer 1979*, pp. 333-36; Alternative Form of the Great Thanksgiving: Eucharistic Prayer II: pp. 340-43.

[151] "Holy Eucharist: Rite Two," The Holy Communion, The Great Thanksgiving, Eucharistic Prayer A: *Book of Common Prayer 1979*, pp. 361-63; Alternative Forms of the Great Thanksgiving: Eucharistic Prayer B: pp. 367-69; Eucharistic Prayer C: pp. 369-72; Eucharistic Prayer D: pp. 372-75.

anamnesis, with oblation; epiclesis over the gifts; epiclesis over the communicants; intercessions; concluding doxology. These elements, however, are not marked as such in the print; the title of the entire action, "The Great Thanksgiving," is given before the dialogue of the Preface. It continues through the "Amen" of the congregation.

Eucharistic Prayer I is the text used, as the only one, in the 1928 prayer book and dating ultimately back to the (1637 and) 1764 Scottish revision of the prayer book.

Eucharistic Prayer II is an abridgment, and at the same time an enrichment, of Eucharistic Prayer I.[152] In the christological part, references to the creation of heaven and earth, and to our creation "in thine own image" are inserted. The anamnesis has received a phrase extending it to the "looking for his coming again with power and great glory." In addition to the epiclesis over the communicants, it is asked that the whole Church may be made one body with Christ.

Eucharistic Prayer A, the one given in the context of the celebration according to Rite Two itself, is said to be "a shorter, modern adaptation" of Eucharistic Prayer I;[153] yet its phrasing suggests a rather newly drafted prayer along some of the theological lines of Eucharistic Prayer I. The redemption, through incarnation and cross, from sin and death, and the sacrificial aspect of the cross are the themes of the christological part. After the institution narrative, the memorial acclamation is given; this has become a standard feature of the eucharistic prayers in the major liturgical churches in the United States, including the Roman Catholic Church: "Christ has died. / Christ is risen. / Christ will come again."[154] Of this whole action it is said in the anamnesis that "we celebrate the memorial of our redemption in this sacrifice of praise and thanksgiving;" and by "recalling his [Christ's] death, resurrection, and ascension, we offer you these gifts."[155] An express epiclesis of the Holy Spirit over the gifts is said, and an epiclesis over the congregation included. Due to its concentration on the central subjects of the eucharistic prayer and to its relative brevity, this prayer seems to be well suited for regular use, in particular if the eucharist is celebrated on weekdays.

Eucharistic Prayer B is an adaptation of the prayer given by Hippolytus, though filled in with elements and ideas lacking there. The christological part[156] is preceded by a thanksgiving for the creation, for making Israel God's people, and for the word spoken by the prophets. The memorial acclamation is given in a different version: "We remember his death, / We proclaim his resurrection, / We await his coming in glory," which is immediately taken up by the presiding priest by saying, "And we offer our sacrifice of praise and thanksgiving to you, O Lord of all; presenting to you, from your creation, this bread and this wine."[157] An express epiclesis of the Spirit over both the gifts and the people is prayed, for the latter being asked that they be united to Christ in his sacrifice. The prayer flows into an eschatological outlook, and it ends with a reference to Christ, "the firstborn of all creation, the head of the Church, and the author of our salvation."[158]

Eucharistic Prayer C is a liturgical text which is remarkable in more than one way. This as well as the following eucharistic prayer have a fixed Preface which cannot be exchanged according to season or occasion.[159] Of the sixty-three lines in which this eucharistic prayer is printed from the dialogue before the Preface to the final "Amen," no less than sixteen lines, or one-fourth of the text, are arranged to be said by the people. Responses and acclamations run

---

[152] Hatchett, *Commentary*, pp. 373-74.

[153] Hatchett, *Commentary*, p. 374.

[154] Eucharistic Prayer A: *Book of Common Prayer 1979*, p. 363.

[155] Eucharistic Prayer A: *Book of Common Prayer 1979*, p. 363.

[156] Unlike in the Roman sacramentary, the christological part has not been remodeled to become the Preface of the eucharistic prayer, but it serves as the post–*Sanctus* verse.

[157] Eucharistic Prayer B: *Book of Common Prayer 1979*, p. 368.

[158] Eucharistic Prayer B: *Book of Common Prayer 1979*, p. 369.

[159] Although there are proper Prefaces provided for Sundays as well as the liturgical seasons, there is no prohibition of using the eucharistic prayers with invariable Prefaces on those days.

especially through the Preface. The prayer, as the only among the six, has the epiclesis over the gifts before the institution narrative. Particularly noteworthy is the phraseology of this prayer. The second stanza of the Preface gives thanks for the creation: "At your command all things came to be: the vast expanse of interstellar space, galaxies, suns, the planets in their course, and this fragile earth, our island home."[160] The thanksgiving is extended, too, for bringing forth the human race, blessed with memory, reason, and skill. The christological section, also within the Preface, is rather short compared to both the theme of creation, and to the same section in the other eucharistic prayers. Reference is made to the incarnation in order "to open for us the way of freedom and peace." A special mention is made, in the very short post-*Sanctus* part (four lines), of baptism, as we have been "made a new people by water and the Spirit."[161] The logical sequence of an offering made by recalling the paschal mystery has been reverted; the anamnesis here reads: "Remembering now his work of redemption, and offering to you this sacrifice of thanksgiving, We celebrate his death and resurrection, as we await the day of his coming."[162] The transformation of "us," the people, into "one body, one spirit in Christ" is attributed, not to the operation of the Holy Spirit, but to "the grace of this Holy Communion."[163] This indeed is a thought-provoking eucharistic text.[164]

The last version of the Great Thanksgiving, Eucharistic Prayer D, is a milestone in liturgical history. It is by far the longest of all prayers and is based on the eucharistic prayer of the Liturgy of St. Basil. The actual arrangement of the text and the translation is the work of a committee of American Roman Catholic, Episcopal, Presbyterian, Lutheran, and Methodist scholars, chaired by Marion J. Hatchett;[165] the fourth eucharistic prayer of the Roman sacramentary served as the draft. The Basil anaphora, or slight variations of it, might therefore be the one that is the most wide-spread among Christianity.[166] Differing from the fourth eucharistic prayer of the Roman sacramentary, the epiclesis of the Holy Spirit over the gifts is placed in this version behind the anamnesis and contracted with that over the congregation. Immediately preceding this text is an acclamation which is of a more general phraseology of praise.[167] The more specific intercessions for the ministers of the Church, for

---

160 Eucharistic Prayer C: *Book of Common Prayer 1979*, p. 370.

161 Eucharistic Prayer C: *Book of Common Prayer 1979*, p. 371.

162 Eucharistic Prayer C: *Book of Common Prayer 1979*, p. 371. At the same time, the second part of the anamnesis, beginning with "We celebrate," serves as the memorial acclamation.

163 Eucharistic Prayer C: *Book of Common Prayer 1979*, p. 371. The entire, very short, section after the anamnesis uses imagery which might be said to be prone, or close, to indoctrination: "Lord God of our Fathers; God of Abraham, Isaac, and Jacob; God and Father of our Lord Jesus Christ: Open our eyes to see your hand at work in the world about us. Deliver us from the presumption of coming to this Table for solace only, and not for strength; for pardon only, and not for renewal. Let the grace of this Holy Communion make us one body, one spirit in Christ, that we may worthily serve the world in his name. [Acclamation of the people:] Risen Lord, be known to us in the breaking of the Bread.": p. 371.

164 It does not seem to be accidental that the altar edition of the prayer book does not contain any melodies for either the Preface or any other part of this eucharistic prayer.

165 *General Convention 1976*, p. AA-289.

166 Hatchett himself writes that this prayer is adopted in America by the Inter-Lutheran Commission on Worship and by the Committee on Word and Table of the United Methodist Church; it is, at the same time, proposed for use by the Committee on Worship of the Consultation on Church Union: *Commentary*, p. 377. See also Leonel Lake Mitchell, "The Alexandrian Anaphora of St. Basil of Caesarea: Ancient Source of 'A Common Eucharistic Prayer,'" *Anglican Theological Review*, 58 (1976), 194-206.

167 It follows the anamnesis, with oblation: "Recalling Christ's death . . .; and offering to you, from the gifts you have given us, this bread and this cup, we praise you and we bless you. [Acclamation:] We praise you, we bless you, we give thanks to you, and we pray to you, Lord our God.": Eucharistic Prayer D: *Book of Common Prayer 1979*, pp. 374-75. See Wainwright, "'E pluribus unum,'" p. 295. Noticeable, too, is the fact that this acclamation is directed towards the addressee of the eucharistic prayer, the Father, and not to Christ, as is the case in the other memorial acclamations of the eucharistic prayers.

persons to be named, and for the departed, are bracketed, as are the mention of Mary, the patriarchs, prophets, apostles, and martyrs. These lines can be pronounced or left out, at the discretion of the presiding priest. The language of so difficult and significant a piece of primordial liturgical theology is dignified, yet simple, easy to listen to and to read, yet marking a prose hymn in its own right.

The two fragmentary eucharistic prayers given in the order for celebrating the eucharist[168] are elements borrowed from Eucharistic Prayer A to D. They concern mainly the anamnesis and the epiclesis over the gifts and over the people, in addition to the institution narrative.

Rubrics and guidelines clarifying points which could not be dealt with in the section Concerning the Celebration or in the order of the eucharist itself are given in the Additional Directions.[169] Even here the principle of a common celebration is evident.

When there are persons in the congregation whose mother tongue is other than English, the gospel may be read in that language by a reader appointed by the presider, either in place of, or in addition to, the gospel in the English language.[170] The exchange of the Peace is highly emphasized. Among individuals, any appropriate words of greeting may be used. The Peace may be shifted to a position before or after the sentence of invitation to the communion.[171]

It is in this context of the communion between the members of the one congregation, too, that measures should be taken that during the Great Thanksgiving, from the Preface of the eucharistic prayer to the breaking of the bread, only one chalice be on the altar; if necessary, a flagon of wine may be added from which the other chalices necessary for the distribution of communion may be filled.[172]

Provisions are made for the case that either one of the consecrated material does not suffice for the number of communicants. The presiding priest is then to return to the altar and consecrate more of either one or both. This can happen with the recital of the text:

> Hear us, O heavenly Father, and with thy (your) Word and Holy Spirit bless and sanctify this bread (wine) that it, also, may be the sacrament of the precious Body (Blood) of thy (your) Son Jesus Christ our Lord, who took bread (the cup) and said, "This is my Body (Blood)."
> Amen.[173]

---

[168] "An Order for Celebrating the Holy Eucharist," At the Great Thanksgiving: *Book of Common Prayer 1979*, pp. 402-05.

[169] *Book of Common Prayer 1979*, pp. 406-09.

[170] Additional Directions: *Book of Common Prayer 1979*, p. 406.

[171] Additional Directions: *Book of Common Prayer 1979*, p. 407.

[172] Additional Directions: *Book of Common Prayer 1979*, p. 407.

[173] Additional Directions: *Book of Common Prayer 1979*, p. 408. The italicized "*Amen*" indicates that this text is to be spoken aloud, so that the consent of the people can be given--a provision which might not be in line with the eucharist as a festal gathering with a communion procession and hymns to be sung. A lack of insight into liturgical theology is shown when Price writes about this brief prayer that "in the simplest way possible (it) identifies the new bread or wine with the same intentions which were expressed over the old. It is a gain in simplicity, practicality, and confidence that 'God knows our needs before we ask:'" *Introducing the Proposed Book*, p. 85. In his investigation into the concept of supplementary consecration, Richard F. Buxton distinguishes between two patterns. The first is what he calls a "memorialist view of the eucharistic sacrifice, a real receptionist view of the presence, and the view that consecration is effected by a prayer that must include the institution narrative." This view finds its expression in the *Book of Common Prayer* 1662 and its permission of a supplementary consecration of either one of the eucharistic elements spent: Brightman, *English Rite*, II, 703. The second derives from the Scottish rite of 1764 (ultimately, of 1637) ands says that "the eucharist is an objective Godward pleading of Christ's sacrifice, . . . the essential consecratory part of the eucharistic prayer is the institution narrative-oblation-epiclesis sequence, and . . . there is an objective and permanent real presence associated with the elements and brought about by the Holy Spirit making the bread and wine to be in power,

If both elements have to be consecrated again at the same time, the presiding priest is to say the eucharistic prayer again from the post-*Sanctus* through the epiclesis.[174]

If there is no eucharistic celebration but a liturgy of the word, everything from the beginning of the first part of the normal eucharistic celebration through the prayers of the people may be said. A hymn or anthem follows, and the offerings of the people are received. The service is concluded with the Lord's Prayer, and with either the "Grace," 2 Corinthians 13:13, or with a blessing, or with the exchange of the Peace. Except for the blessing, all this can be said, in the absence of a priest, by a deacon, or, if neither one is present, by a lay person.[175]

"Disciplinary Rubrics," as all prayer books had known them,[176] are added, dealing with the treatment of persons who live "a notoriously evil life" or who "have done wrong to their neighbors and are a scandal to the other members of the congregation," yet intend to receive communion. These persons are to be talked to by the priest and not allowed to proceed until clear proof of repentance and restitution of the wrong is given. The same procedure holds true for any hatred between members of the congregation. The bishop is to be notified about the reasons for refusing the communion.[177]

A renewal of the communion in both directions, the community of the congregation and the adherence to the Lord of the Church, has been attempted by the revision process of the prayer book. Both communions affect each other: if the worship life of the congregation is defective, the members cannot fulfill their Christian duties; if the unity among the members of the congrgation is lacking, the liturgy of the Church is not a corporate worship.[178] If, however, the congregation lives up to the standard the prayer book sets before it, the liturgy is a vast treasure and a nourishment on the spiritual journey of the parish and the individual members and offers riches which penetrate the entire existence of baptized persons.

---

virtue, and effect the body and blood of Christ." In this view, supplementary consecration of only one kind is not permitted, and both elements are to be prayed over: Richard F. Buxton, *Eucharist and Institution Narrative: A Study in the Roman and Anglican Tradition of the Consecration from the Eighth to the Twentieth Centuries*, Alcuin Club Collections, 58 (Great Wakering: Mayhew-McCrimmon, 1976), pp. 220-21. According to this distinction, the provisions for supplementary consecration in the *Book of Common Prayer 1979* are a hybrid form: the permission to consecrate either one of the species derives from the 1662 book, the wording is the extreme abbreviation of the theological concept of the 1764 concept. The following provision for supplementary conecration of both kinds is the continuation of the full-fledged Scottish tradition which, in a strictly theological perspective, is very much preferable to the skeleton of the short text.

[174] If Eucharistic Prayer C (pp. 369-72) has been used, this provision concerns the one post-*Sanctus* sentence, the following short epiclesis, and the institution narrative, without the anamnesis: Additional Directions: *Book of Common Prayer 1979*, p. 408. Obviously it is left to the discretion of the presiding priest to decide what to do with both the memorial acclamation of the congregation, and with such texts as Eucharistic Prayer D, the respective recital of which (from the post-*Sanctus* through the epiclesis) runs over forty-six lines.

[175] Additional Directions: *Book of Common Prayer 1979*, pp. 406-07.

[176] Brightman, *English Rite*, II, 638-39; Gibson, *Prayer Books*, pp. 217, 377; McGarvey, *Liturgiae Americanae*, pp. 212-14; *Book of Common Prayer 1928*, pp. 84-85.

[177] Additional Directions: *Book of Common Prayer 1979*, p. 409.

[178] "An Outline of the Faith," The Ministry: *Book of Common Prayer 1979*, pp. 855-56; Prayer and Worship: pp. 856-57.

The Mystery of Initiation: The Newness of Life

A celebration of genuinely Christian liturgy is self-explanatory; the flow of its movement towards the climax needs no interpretation or comment from outside.[1] Since liturgy by definition is a living entity and not just letters in a book, the divine life that is communicated through it to the celebrants can properly be understood only in the setting of the liturgy. If nonetheless an interpretation of the liturgy of Christian initiation according to the *Book of Common Prayer* is attempted here, the purpose is not to give a historical account of its origins or some material to systematic theologians for a dogmatic treatise of baptism, but to take up the pieces of the liturgy of Christian initiation and to let their intrinsic coherence be apparent also to those who do not have the opportunity to join in its celebration.

The Setting: Paschal, Doxological, and Eucharistic

The setting in which baptism is placed indicates living in its totality: the transforming and all-renewing power of the paschal mystery, the response by those transformed, in the praise of God, and the celebration of and participation in the banquet with the heavenly food of the new creation.[2]

---

[1] This chapter is not devoted to the history of baptism; that has been described sufficiently by Georg Kretschmar, "Die Geschichte des Taufgottesdienstes in der Alten Kirche," in *Der Taufgottesdienst*, Vol. V of *Leiturgia: Handbuch des evangelischen Gottesdienstes*, hrsg. Karl Ferdinand Müller und Walter Blankenburg (Kassel: Stauda, 1970), pp. 1-348, and Alois Stenzel, *Die Taufe: Eine genetische Erklärung der Taufliturgie*, Forschungen zur Geschichte der Theologie und des innerkirchlichen Lebens, 7/8 (Innsbruck: Rauch, 1958). Neither is it a compendium of texts related to baptism; those can be found in Whitaker, *Documents*; and Edward Yarnold, *The Awe-Inspiring Rites of Initiation: Baptismal Homilies of the Fourth Century* ([Slough:] St. Paul Publications, 1972). It is rather an attempt to lead the reader to some spiritual mines and treasures hidden in the initiatory rites of the *Book of Common Prayer* 1979 (including the confirmation, although it does not belong to the sacramental initiation). In order to adhere to non-discriminatory and inclusive language in this chapter, too, preference is given to speaking about "the baptized" and "the faithful." According to the provisions of the liturgy of the Episcopal Church, candidates from the time of their admission on enjoy the name and dignity of being a "Christian:" "Concerning the Catechumenate:" *Book of Occasional Services*, p. 113. But they are not yet called "faithful" or "baptized," according to the tradition of the Church as attested to, among others, by Augustine, Tractatus in Iohannis evangelium xliv,2, in *Sancti Aurelii Augustini in Iohannis evangelium tractatus CXXIV*, ed. Radbodus Willems, Corpus Christianorum Series Latina, 36 (Turnholti: Brépols, 1954), p. 382. This language pattern is observed here. See Michel Dujarier, "Sur le statut du catéchumène dans l'Eglise," *La Maison-Dieu*, 152 (1982), 143-73.

[2] "Caro abluitur, ut anima emaculetur; caro unguitur, ut anima consecretur; caro signatur, ut [et] anima muniatur; caro manus inpositione adumbratur, ut [et] anima spiritus inluminetur; caro corpore et sanguine Christi uescitur, ut et anima de deo saginetur.": Tertullian, *De resurrectione mortuorum* viii,3, ed. J. G. Ph. Borleffs, in *Opera montanistica*, Vol. II of *Quinti Florentis Septimi Tertulliani opera*, Corpus Christianorum Series Latina, 2 (Turnholti: Brépols, 1954), p. 931; English translation: Whitaker, *Documents*, p. 10. It is bad theology to build a case of "discussing" a sacrament in a systematic, canonistic, or ecumenical treatment by asking only what would be absolutely necessary for the "validity" of the sacrament. Such a question, and therefore the answer, is missing the point and does injustice to both the sacrament (if there can be any abstraction from the celebration at all) and the persons who are involved.

The tradition of baptism being administered in the Great Vigil of Easter, so prominent in the first centuries,[3] has been restored to the church's liturgy in the *Book of Common Prayer*. The celebration of the Easter Vigil is "the Passover of the Lord, in which, by hearing his Word and celebrating his Sacraments, we share in his victory over death."[4] The lessons read in the liturgy of the word at the Vigil are regarded as foreshadows of the salvation given in baptism.[5] Even the entire Easter Vigil, except for the first part, the Service of Light, is a celebration more of the dying and rising of the baptizands with Christ than of triumph over death by Christ; this latter mystery is featured more in the solemn eucharist of Easter Day. The night highlights the fact that through the paschal mystery "we are buried with Christ by Baptism into his death, and raised with him to newness of life."[6] This baptismal character of the Great Vigil of Easter and the paschal character of baptism is "the key not only to Baptism but to the totality of the Christian faith itself."[7] The "community of fate" of Christ and his believers, the transition from death to new life, is communicated to the Church and to the baptizands in that nightly celebration in which we make the memorial of his victory. "The Passover provides the day of most solemnity, for then was accomplished our Lord's passion, and into it we are baptized."[8]

The three other "especially appropriate"[9] days for baptism share in the splendor of the Easter Vigil; their dignity also derives from the new life of the Head and the members. On the Day of Pentecost God "opened the way of eternal life to every race and nation by the promised gift of (his) Holy Spirit:"[10] an echo of the "sign for us of the salvation of all nations by the water of Baptism."[11] Christ's Spirit, by whom the baptized are sealed, renews and perfects "the earth," the creation which was "cast down" and is "raised up," which had "grown old" and is "made new."[12] All Saints' Day gives the Church the opportunity to rejoice that of those who served God on earth a number have already "come to the joy of that heavenly

---

[3] Hansjörg Auf der Maur, *Feiern im Rhythmus der Zeit I: Herrenfeste in Woche und Jahr*, Gottesdienst der Kirche, 5 (Regensburg: Pustet, 1983), pp. 72-73; Kretschmar, "Geschichte," pp. 138-40; K. W. Noakes, "Initiation: From New Testament Times until St. Cyprian," in *The Study of Liturgy*, ed. Cheslyn Jones, Geoffrey Wainwright, and Edward Yarnold (London: SPCK, 1978), p. 91; Edward Yarnold, "Initiation: The Fourth and Fifth Centuries," in *The Study of Liturgy*, ed. Cheslyn Jones, Geoffrey Wainwright, and Edward Yarnold (London: SPCK, 1978), pp. 97, 100.

[4] "The Great Vigil of Easter," Address to the congregation at the beginning: *Book of Common Prayer 1979*, p. 285.

[5] Jean Daniélou, *Bible et liturgie: la théologie biblique et des fêtes d'après les Pères de l'Eglise*, Lex orandi, 11, 2e éd. revue (Paris: Cerf, 1958), pp. 50-76, 97-173.

[6] "The Great Vigil of Easter," Address to the congregation before the Renewal of Baptismal Vows: *Book of Common Prayer 1979*, p. 292.

[7] Alexander Schmeemann, *Of Water and the Spirit: A Liturgical Study of Baptism* (Crestwood, NY: St. Vladimir's Seminary Press, 1974), p. 37.

[8] "Diem baptismo sollemniorem pascha praestat cum et passio domini in qua tinguimur adimpleta est.": Tertullian, *De baptismo* xix,1, ed. J. G. Ph. Borleffs, in *Opera Catholica*, Vol. I of *Quinti Septimi Florentis Tertulliani opera*, Corpus Christianorum Series Latina, 1 (Turnholti: Brépols, 1954), p. 293; English translation: Whitaker, *Documents*, p. 19.

[9] "Holy Baptism," Additional Directions: *Book of Common Prayer 1979*, p. 312.

[10] Collect at the Day of Pentecost: *Book of Common Prayer 1979*, p. 227.

[11] "The Great Vigil of Easter," Collect after the fourth lesson (Ex 14:10--15:1): *Book of Common Prayer 1979*, p. 289. The basis is the collect "Deus, cuius antiqua miracula:" Mohlberg, *Sacramentarium Gelasianum*, no. 435. (Hatchett, *Commentary*, p. 247.)

[12] "The Great Vigil of Easter," Collects after the sixth (Is 55:1-11) and ninth (Zeph 3:12-20) lessons: *Book of Common Prayer 1979*, pp. 289, 290. The basis for the first of these is an earlier composition by Harry Boone Porter, for the latter is the collect "Deus inconmutabilis uirtus:" Mohlberg, *Sacramentarium Gelasianum*, no. 432. (Hatchett, *Commentary*, pp. 247-48.)

Jerusalem, where all tears are wiped away and where your saints for ever sing your praise."[13] The petition at the Easter Vigil: "for the glory of your Name multiply, by the grace of the Paschal sacrament, the number of your children,"[14] is seen fulfilled on that day of joy. The Feast of the Baptism of Our Lord, the fourth such privileged day, rather emphasizes the aspect of Christ's proclamation as Son and his anointment with the Holy Spirit. The Holy Spirit, who is his by right, is ours by grace, the "Spirit of adoption which is given to us in Baptism."[15] Our adoption as sons and daughters constitutes "the hope of our glorious resurrection" in Christ[16] which has in a mystical and proleptic way happened as "through the Paschal mystery we are buried with Christ in Baptism into his death, and raised with him to newness of life."[17]

As God grants new life in the baptism into the death and resurrection of Christ, the proper response by those transformed in this mystery is a life corresponding to the grace they have received. It is a life that is characterized above all as "doxological living," a life style based on, and expressing, the thankfulness for what has been done: the salvation given to the baptized, a life consisting in the praise of Him from whom every good thing comes.[18] The acknowledgment of God's great and saving deeds is the openness by which "the plan of salvation" can be carried out and all things can be "brought to their perfection."[19] The pattern of life is that of admiring adoration, praise, and thanksgiving which those, who are redeemed, owe to their Creator and Redeemer:

> At the heart of ordinary Christian life is the recognition of the love of God. All creation is a work of God's love. Jesus Christ is God's giving of himself in love to restore and fulfil all creation. The Holy Spirit is the pouring out of this love in endless transformation and fresh creativity. Praise of God recognises all this and first of all enjoys and celebrates it. Praise is therefore an attempt to cope with the abundance of God's love.[20]

To celebrate this praise of God in the liturgy is an ability given in baptism; tradition has coined this privilege and obligation of the baptized the "deputation to divine worship."[21]

This acknowledgment also serves as the fundament for the renewed liturgy of baptism. The entire liturgy begins with a benediction of the Trinity, thereby setting the tone for the

---

[13] "The Great Vigil of Easter," Collect after the fifth lesson (Is 4:2-6): *Book of Common Prayer 1979*, p. 290. The basis is an earlier composition by Harry Boone Porter. (Hatchett, *Commentary*, p. 247.)

[14] "The Great Vigil of Easter," Collect after the third lesson (Gen 22:1-18): *Book of Common Prayer 1979*, p. 289. The basis is the collect "Deus fidelium pater summe:" Mohlberg, *Sacramentarium Gelasianum*, no. 434. (Hatchett, *Commentary*, pp. 246-47.)

[15] "The Great Vigil of Easter," Collect at the eucharist, II: *Book of Common Prayer 1979*, p. 295. The basis is the collect "Deus, qui hanc sacratissimam noctem gloriosae dominicae resurrectionis inlustras:" Mohlberg, *Sacramentarium Gelasianum*, no. 454. (Hatchett, *Commentary*, p. 179.)

[16] "The Weekdays of Easter Season," Collects from Monday after 2 Easter until 4 Ester, no. 7: *Lesser Feasts and Fasts*, p. 60. The basis is the collect "Semper exsultet," composed of different sources: *Missale Romanum*, Missale Romanum ex decreto Sacrosancti Oecumenici Concilii Vaticani II instauratum auctoritate Pauli Pp. VI promulgatum, ed. typica altera ([Romae:] Typis Polyglottis Vaticanis, 1975), p. 300.

[17] "The Great Vigil of Easter," Address to the congregation before the Renewal of Baptismal Vows: *Book of Common Prayer 1979*, p. 292.

[18] See Teresa Berger, "Lex orandi - lex credendi - lex agendi: Auf dem Weg zu einer ökumenisch konsensfähigen Verhältnisbestimmung von Liturgie, Theologie und Ethik," *Archiv für Liturgiewissenschaft*, 27 (1985), 427.

[19] "The Great Vigil of Easter," Collect after the ninth lesson (Zeph 3:12-20): *Book of Common Prayer 1979*, p. 290. The basis is the collect "Deus inconmutabilis uirtus:" Mohlberg, *Sacramentarium Gelasianum*, no. 432. (Hatchett, *Commentary*, p. 248.)

[20] Daniel W. Hardy and David F. Ford, *Jubilate: Theology in Praise* (London: Darton, Longman & Todd, 1984), p. 1.

[21] For example, Thomas of Aquino, *Summa theologiae* III, 63, 1-6.

whole service: "Blessed be God: Father, Son, and Holy Spirit. And blessed be his kingdom, now and for ever. Amen."[22] This is a far cry from the first words in the Ministration of Holy Baptism as provided by the 1928 *Book of Common Prayer*: "Has this Child (Person) been already baptized, or no?", followed by an address to the congregation.[23] Within the renewed service the major prayers are molded in the cast of a thanksgiving prayer[24] or have their anamnetic address to God translated into praise and thanksgiving.[25] The doxology finds its climax in the Thanksgiving over the Water, which is patterned after the Preface of the eucharistic prayer. In it His Name is called, and He deigns to appear and to work--for His own glory and the redemption of His people.[26] The setting for the baptismal liturgy is a constant renewal and source of the doxological living.

The liturgy of the Church mediates the new life but also meditates it. It is the primary theology of the Church, a speaking to God about Himself in adoration and praise. The Church's liturgy is doxological theology.[27] All speaking about God has its beginning here, in speaking to God, and it leads back to this source. The words and rites used in the liturgy of baptism are not all that can be taken to speak about redemption and Christian living, and a secondary theology is not completely expressed here: liturgy is not a dogmatic treatise. The service, by definition, is a communal rite in which salvation is given. There is, therefore, communication in the service with the source of salvation; and there is, therefore, adoration, praise, and thanksgiving to the Trinity: doxology.[28]

The third setting is closely linked with the first two yet adds another vital dimension. "Holy Baptism is appropriately administered within the Eucharist as the chief service on a Sunday or other feast."[29] The eucharist is "the principal act of Christian worship on the

---

[22] This eulogy is an adaptation from the Byzantine rite of the Liturgy of St. John Chrysostom (Hatchett, *Commentary*, p. 318): "Eulogemene he basileia tu Patros kai tu Hyiu kai tu hagiu Pneumatos nyn kai aei kai tus aionas ton aionon. Amen.": Frank Edward Brightman, ed., *Liturgies Eastern and Western: Being the Texts Original or Translated of the Principal Liturgies of the Church*, Vol. I (1896; rpt. Oxford University Press, 1965), p. 363.

[23] "The Ministration of Holy Baptism:" *Book of Common Prayer 1928*, pp. 273-74.

[24] "Holy Baptism," Thanksgiving over the Water: *Book of Common Prayer 1979*, pp. 306-07. See Leonel Lake Mitchell, "Thanksgiving over the Water in the Baptismal Rite of the Western Church," in *The Sacrifice of Praise: Studies on the Themes of Thanksgiving and Redemption in the Central Prayers of the Eucharistic and Baptismal Liturgies, in honour of Arthur Hubert Couratin*, ed. Bryan D. Spinks, Bibliotheca "Ephemerides Liturgicae" "Subsidia," 19 (Roma: CLV Edizioni Liturgiche, 1981), pp. 229-44.

[25] "Holy Baptism," Prayer for the Gifts of the Spirit: *Book of Common Prayer 1979*, p. 308. The basis for this text is the prayer "Deus omnipotens, pater domini nostri Iesu Christi:" Mohlberg, *Sacramentarium Gelasianum*, no. 451. Prayer for the persons presented for Confirmation, Reception, or Reaffirmation: p. 309. The prayer is based on a draft by Bonnell Spencer. Prayer at the Alternative Ending after the Lord's Prayer: p. 311. The prayer is an abridged and adapted version of the post-Confirmation prayer in the *Books of Common Prayer* 1549, 1552, 1662: Brightman, *English Rite*, II, 796-97. (Hatchett, *Commentary*, pp. 278-79, 282, 283.)

[26] Odo Casel, *Das christliche Opfermysterium: Zur Morphologie und Theologie des eucharistischen Hochgebetes*, hrsg. Viktor Warnach (Graz: Styria, 1968), pp. 175-76, 179-93.

[27] Wainwright, *Doxology*, pp. 20-21 and note 32, pp. 468-69. "The language of worship mediates the substance on which theologians reflect; without that substance, theological talk whould have no referent.": p. 21.

[28] See Teresa Berger, "'Liturgy--a forgotten Subject-matter of Theology?'" in *Gratias agamus: An Ecumenical Collection of Essays on the Liturgy and Its Implications*, ed. Wiebe Vos in cooperation with Geoffrey Wainwright, Studia Liturgica, 17 (Rotterdam: Liturgical Ecumenical Center Trust, 1987), pp. 10-18; Maria Judith Krahe, "'Psalmen, Hymnen und Lieder, wie der Geist sie eingibt:' Doxologie als Ursprung und Ziel aller Theologie," in *Interdisziplinäre Reflexion*, Bd. II von *Liturgie und Dichtung: Ein interdisziplinäres Kompendium*, hrsg. Hansjakob Becker und Reiner Kaczynski, Pietas Liturgica, 2 (St. Ottilien: Eos, 1983), pp. 923-29, 950-56.

[29] "Holy Baptism," Concerning the Service: *Book of Common Prayer 1979*, p. 298.

Lord's Day and other major Feasts."[30] It is the supreme service of adoration, praise, thanksgiving, and intercession of the Church.

It is also the liturgy which, together with baptism, has the closests links with the paschal mystery. Baptism, the incorporation into Christ's death and new life wrought "through the paschal mystery,"[31] is celebrated within the eucharist which is "the memorial of our redemption . . . in this sacrifice of praise and thanksgiving."[32] The administration of baptism within the eucharist is not artificial as if due to the interpretation that "the two great sacraments given by Christ to his Church are Holy Baptism and the Holy Eucharist."[33] It is rather done because both celebrations are representations of the central saving mystery of Christ's death and resurrection.

Baptism is the precondition for the eucharist. As much as the eucharist is the spiritual nourishment for the Church to continue as Church and to remain in this grace, baptism is the washing and sealing so that the community becomes the Church; the grace is given to be "a new people by water and the Spirit."[34] In order to be constantly reminded of this common dignity, baptism is celebrated within the eucharist before the Great Thanksgiving is said and the Bread and the Cup are given.[35] Baptism, in other words, is the entrance to the kingdom of God.

Baptism means to become the People of God; to this People in the eucharist the Gifts of God are given.[36] The communion is the goal towards which baptism is directed: the sacramental union of the Head with his members. It is the heavenly food of the new creation for those "being reborn to new life in him."[37] It is the nourishment for a life according to the baptismal promises and the Sprit given in the sealing. All these aspects: incorporation into the Church, sprritual food for those belonging to "that holy fellowship," and a life based on the dignity of being baptized, are unsurpassably well summarized in the postcommunion prayer in the traditional version of Holy Eucharist Rite One, a prayer originally composed by Archbishop Cranmer for the 1549 *Book of Common Prayer:*

> Almighty and everlasting God, we most heartily thank thee for that thou dost feed us, in these holy mysteries, with the spiritual food of the most precious Body and Blood of thy Son our Savior Jesus Christ; and dost assure us thereby that we are very members incorporate in the mystical body of thy son, the blessed company of all faithful people; and are also heirs, through hope, of thy everlasting kingdom. And we humbly beseech thee, O heavenly Father, so to assist us with thy grace, that we may continue in that holy fellowship, and do all such

---

30 "Concerning the Service of the Church:" *Book of Common Prayer 1979*, p. 13.

31 "The Great Vigil of Easter," Address to the congregation before the Renewal of Baptismal Vows: *Book of Common Prayer 1979*, p. 292.

32 "Holy Eucharist: Rite Two," The Great Thanksgiving, Eucharistic Prayer A, Anamnesis: *Book of Common Prayer 1979*, p. 363.

33 "An Outline of the Faith," The Sacraments: *Book of Common Prayer 1979*, p. 858.

34 "Holy Eucharist: Rite Two," The Great Thanksgiving, Eucharistic Prayer C, Post-*Sanctus: Book of Common Prayer 1979*, p. 371.

35 It is most unfortunate that the catechumens may stay, after the Liturgy of the Word of God, for the Celebration of the Holy Communion, not for the sake of some artificially restored arcane discipline but as a vivid expression of the dignity of those who have been initiated and are invited to share the Bread and the Cup. See *Book of Occasional Services*, pp. 117, 124, 125.

36 "Holy Eucharist: Rite Two," The Breaking of the Bread, Invitation to Communion: *Book of Common Prayer 1979*, p. 364. This is based on the *Sancta sanctis* of the Byzantine Liturgy of St. John Chrysostom: "Ta hagia tois hagiois:" Brightman, *Liturgies*, p. 393.

37 "Collects: Contemporary," Various Occasions, no. 10, At Baptism: *Book of Common Prayer 1979*, p. 254. The basis for this collect is a draft of the Standing Liturgical Commission's subcommittee on Christian initiation. (Hatchett, *Commentary*, p. 211.)

good works as thou hast prepared for us to walk in; through Jesus Christ our Lord, to whom, with thee and the Holy Ghost, be all honor and glory, world without end.[38]

The Celebration: The Covenant, the Water, and the Spirit

Holy Spirit means newness of life, an existence in "the full stature of Christ."[39] The celebration of baptism calls for a liturgical expression of the radicalness of this purpose and this process.

There is nothing in baptism that suggests that the sacramental action and the new life are matters of little significance: "Your guarantee is binding, not on earth but in heaven."[40] The seriousness of Christian initiation demands an answer to the call for repentance, the biblical *metanoia*, the turning from the old way of life to the life in Christ. The catechumenate, a period which is provided in *The Book of Occasional Services*,[41] is not so much a time for prolonged intellectual pursuits but for learning to walk in the ways of life, to show a personal redirection of one's goals and means, "the practice of life in accordance with the Gospel."[42] The liturgical expressions of this "turning around" in the celebration of baptism are the renunciation of the old way of sinful life, the confession of following Christ, and the affirmation of the Christian faith and life.

The renunciation has always been a part of the baptismal liturgy[43] and highlights the definite break with all forces that fight against God's love and human response to it. "A Christian has to renounce something and . . . this 'something' is not a few obviously sinful and immoral acts, but above all a certain vision of life, a 'set of priorities,'a fundamental attitude towards the world."[44] The phrasing of the renunciation suggests that the process of turning from the old ways goes deeper than a change of habits and an alteration of attitudes in order to become "a nice person;" it involves a totally different personality core which is no longer determined by destructive and corrupting forces which tear down and do not build up. It is a profoundly personal choice and decision: "He who is not with me is against me, and he who does not gather with me scatters." (Mt 12:30)

The void that has been created by publicly renouncing the evil ways and leaving the old allegiance is filled with a public declaration of adherence to Christ, who is accepted as the

---

[38] "Holy Eucharist: Rite One," The Breaking of the Bread, Postcommunion prayer: *Book of Common Prayer 1979*, p. 339. Cf. Brightman, *English Rite*, II, 708. See Hatchett, *Commentary*, pp. 392-94; Shepherd, *Prayer Book Commentary*, ad pp. 83-84.

[39] "Holy Baptism," Promise by the parents and godparents: *Book of Common Prayer 1979*, p. 302.

[40] "Chirographum tuum tenetur non in terra sed in caelo.": Ambrose of Milan, *De sacramentis* i,6, in his *Des sacrements, des mystères, l'explication du symbole*, éd. Bernard Botte, Sources chrétiennes, 25 bis, nouvelle éd. revue et augmentée (Paris: Cerf, 1961), pp. 62-64; English translation: Yarnold, *Awe-Inspiring Rites*, p. 102. See Hugh M. Riley, *Christian Initiation: A Comparative Study of the Interpretation of the Baptismal Liturgy in the Mystagogical Writings of Cyril of Jerusalem, John Chrysostom, Theodore of Mopsuestia, and Ambrose of Milan*, The Catholic University of America Studies in Christian Antiquities, 17 (Washington, D.C.: The Catholic University of America Press, 1974), pp. 63-64. Cf. John Chrysostom, *Baptismal Homilies* ii,17, in his *Huit catéchèses baptismales inédites*, éd. Antoine Wenger, Sources chrétiennes, 50 (Paris: Cerf, 1957), p. 143. See Riley, *Christian Initiation*, pp. 92-94.

[41] *Book of Occasional Services*, pp. 112-25.

[42] *Book of Occasional Services*, p. 112. For the history and objective of the catechumenate, see Kretschmar, "Geschichte," pp. 63-81, 152-65, 303-07; Stenzel, *Taufe*, pp. 132-64.

[43] Kretschmar, "Geschichte," pp. 96-99, 117-18, 181-83, 255; Stenzel, *Taufe*, pp. 72-75, 98-104, 167-68.

[44] Schmemann, *Of Water and the Spirit*, p. 29.

living guide to salvation--not an impersonal force, power, and desire, but someone to trust, to follow, and to obey. The same personality center that has been cleansed from following the disturbing directions of confusion now puts its energy into trusting the one who is "the way, and the truth, and the life" (John 14:6). "Trusting" here means more than presumption; rather, it is the one all-encompassing attitude of complete commitment and dedication to the other person, to the Savior and Lord whose grace and love are the new sustenances of life. "I pledge myself, Christ, to you."[45]

The commitment to Christ includes faith in the Trinity. The baptizand and all persons present declare their personal and irreplaceable knowledge about God's works, the salvation wrought by His Son, and the life under the Holy Spirit. The knowledge about God here turns into the knowledge of God: "This is eternal life, that they know thee the only true God, and Jesus Christ whom thou hast sent." (John 17:3) Believing is eternal life, and the formulary of faith becomes an expression of fidelity towards the source of life. Commitment to Christ is more than "following Jesus:" it is the acknowledgment that the Trinity is the deepest fountain of all existence. In baptism the Trinity gives of this fountain to those confessing the faith in the Triune God.[46]

Christian faith signifies three distinct yet interrelated aspects: an intellectual knowledge of God and His wonderful deeds; absolute loyalty to the "fountain of life and source of all goodness;"[47] and a life style corresponding to the high demands expressed in the baptismal service and to the grace abundantly given for pursuing. This conduct, especially its spiritual and social aspects, are the scope of the next five questions. They prevent baptism from being seen as a beautiful service, even with a deep theological meaning, without consequences for the everyday life of a Christian. Although each participant in the celebration, baptizands and the other people alike, answer the questions about the belief with "I believe," and the questions about the Christian life style with "I will," nobody can be a Christian without the social implications of one's faith, and the dignity of being baptized claims not only an adherence to a certain standard of knowledge and discipline but also the reaching out to all persons, all people, and every human being.[48]

The prayer concluding the petitions for the candidates is a summary of what is asked of God for these persons. God's grace, his "favor towards us, unearned and undeserved" by which He "forgives our sins, enlightens our minds, stirs our hearts, and strengthens our wills,"[49] is promised to the candidates because God is faithful and gives the means to sustain a baptismal living. The prayer adds one important point to the Christian way: to look for Christ's coming again in glory when the limitations and confinements of the creation are lifted and "the fullness of [God's] peace and glory"[50] is revealed and given to those who have lived up to the covenant God made with them in baptism.

The *Book of Common Prayer* explains a covenant with God as "a relationship initiated by God, to which a body of people responds in faith."[51] It is clear from this interpretation that it is God who offers the relationship, and the people who can accept or reject it. It depends on God's will to grant, and on the willingness of the people to accept. A relationship with God is

---

[45] "Kai syntassomai soi, Christe.": John Chrysostom, *Baptismal Homilies* ii,21, p. 145; English translation: Yarnold, *Awe-Inspiring Rites*, p. 166. Cf. Theodore of Mopsuestia, *Homilies* xiii,13, in *Les homélies catéchétiques de Théodore de Mopsueste*, éd. Raymond Tonneau et Robert Devreesse, repr. phototypique du ms. Mingana yr. 561 (Selly Oak Colleges' Library, Birmingham), Studi e Testi, 145 (Città del Vaticano: Bibliotheca Apostolica Vaticana, 1949), p. 391. See Riley, *Christian Initiation*, pp. 53-54.

[46] Ambrose of Milan, *De sacramentis* vi,5.8, p. 140; John Chrysostom, *Baptismal Homilies* ii,26, pp. 147-48. See Hardy and Ford, *Jubilate*, p. 55.

[47] "Holy Eucharist: Rite Two," The Great Thanksgiving, Eucharistic Prayer D, Preface: *Book of Common Prayer 1979*, p. 373.

[48] Theodore of Mopsuestia, *Homilies* xv,40, p. 523.

[49] "An Outline of the Faith," The Sacraments: *Book of Common Prayer 1979*, p. 858.

[50] "Holy Baptism," Prayers for the Candidates: *Book of Common Prayer 1979*, p. 306.

[51] "An Outline of the Faith," The Old Covenant: *Book of Common Prayer 1979*, p. 846.

always a saving event: He makes available a share in His life for the benefit of those to whom it is offered. God and human beings become partners, although not on equal footing: the latter depend on the former for their existence. But the means for keeping the relationship are given, freely, undeservedly, and abundantly. God, who is faithful to the relationship because He is faithful to Himself, does not abandon His favor when human beings cancel the bond and retract. That is why baptism is called a covenant: God offers newness of life to the baptizand who wants to adhere to the triune God. Because God does not withdraw His grace even if a person lapses into the old way of sin, the covenant once made in baptism can be renewed by that person who again wants to follow Christ as Savior and Lord. That is the deepest meaning behind the theological statement that "[t]he bond which God establishes in Baptism is indissoluble."[52]

The indissoluble bond in baptism is God's grace and favor towards those with whom He establishes it, but they have to receive it in faith. Faith itself is a gift of God:

> it is our God-given capacity to perceive him at work in the person of Jesus and in the waters of Baptism. Furthermore faith is our capacity to receive what God offers us in Christ and in Baptism. Both grace and faith are relational words: God is gracious to us; we respond faithfully to him.[53]

Faith is also the response on the human side to God's call and offfer of life. First and foremost it is trust that what God offers is to the benefit of those He approaches, and worth even a conversion and redirection of life: "Do you turn to Jesus Christ and accept him as your Savior? Do you put your whole trust in his grace and love? Do you promise to follow and obey him as your Lord?"[54] It is a committal of the whole person to the acceptance of salvation, which God established in the redeeming act of Christ's paschal mystery and which he wants to establish in the "application" of this liberation in baptism.

Faith is the loving surrender of the whole person to God's mercy and compassion. That is why the Church in the first two centuries apparently did not have any difficulty baptizing persons without proposing and demanding the knowledge of an explicit text, the "symbol of faith."[55] The intellectual apprehension of a formula summarizing the wonderful deeds of God in the history of salvation is important but not decisive. The compendiums are "statements of our basic beliefs about God,"[56] and in this capacity they have their function as constant reminders of the cause of Christian existence and as a testimony to baptism in which God's life is received. As such their importance in the Church's life is irreplaceable, and rightly is the Apostles' Creed as the ancient baptismal creed "used in the Church's daily worship to recall our Baptismal Covenant" and the Nicene Creed as the creed of the universal Church used at the eucharist[57] to keep the Church from falling from its Head and out of truth. Furthermore, by declaring God's saving acts in history they fulfill a crucial role of praise and thanksgiving.[58] But the recitation of them cannot substitute for the trust of, and submission to, the life-giving will of God and the operation of the Holy Spirit. This act enables a person to receive what God wants to bring about: "If you will not believe, surely you shall not be established." (Is 7:9)[59] As normally this trust cannot be produced in an instant but is a matter

---

[52] "Holy Baptism," Concerning the Service: *Book of Common Prayer 1979*, p. 298.

[53] Eugene Louis Brand, *Baptism: A Pastoral Perspective* (Minneapolis: Augsburg Publishing House, 1975), p. 35.

[54] "Holy Baptism," Questions of Adherence to Christ: *Book of Common Prayer 1979*, pp. 302-03.

[55] Adolf Martin Ritter, "Glaubensbekenntnis(se): V. Alte Kirche," *Theologische Realenzyklopädie* 13, p. 407; Stenzel, *Taufe*, pp. 93-98, 106 note 102.

[56] "An Outline of the Faith," The Creeds: *Book of Common Prayer 1979*, p. 851.

[57] "An Outline of the Faith," The Creeds: *Book of Common Prayer 1979*, p. 852.

[58] Hans Schwarz, "Glaubensbekenntnis(se): IX: Dogmatisch," *Theologische Realenzyklopädie* 13, pp. 439-40; Wainwright, *Doxology*, pp. 182-83, 188.

[59] Klaus Haacker, "Glaube: II/2. Altes Testament," *Theologische Realenzyklopädie* 13, pp. 280-82.

of growth and nourishment, adult candidates for baptism are expected to undergo a period in which this development is supported.

The liturgy of the Church makes clear that baptism is given to infants just as to adults, although the personal commitment which is required of adult candidates cannot be expected of infants. The repentence of sins and acceptance of Christ as Lord and Savior is not at that stage possible for them. Infants nonetheless are baptized "so that they can share citizenship in the Covenant, membership in Christ, and redemption by God."[60] Parents and godparents answer on their behalf the renunciations and questions of adherence to Christ, but oblige themselves to be responsible for a Christian upbringing of the infants and a growth "into the full stature of Christ."[61] These promises are made so as to "guarantee that the infants will be brought up within the Church, to know Christ and be able to follow him."[62] The case of infant baptism, although theologically not the normative practice of the Church, is the as yet normal custom in most of the parishes. It makes clear that it is the faith of the Church as a whole on which the candidates are baptized. The personal agreement of the adult candidates and their trust and promises are irreplaceable. Yet the congregation as the representative of the universal Church affirms its faith, thereby reestablishing the trust in God's love, its union with Christ who is Head of the Church, and its life in the Holy Spirit. This means for the individual candidate that what happens to him or her in baptism is accepted as the salvation mediated through the Church; but it has to be personally affirmed through the loving trust and answer which are given on the basis of the life that is offered in baptism.[63] The candidates are initiated into a pre-existing Body which, however much deserving the forgiveness of its own sins and a renewal of its surrender to God's will, is given the divine life which is also to be bestowed on the candidates in baptism. This central mystery of the Church's life is renewed before the actual baptism of candidates so that the Spirit can add the candidates to the fellowship of Christ's Body. In this same action God also gives all members renewed power "to be obedient all the days of their life to the rule of faith which they received in that Sacrament."[64]

The life in Christ is established by water and the Holy Spirit. Christian baptism has never been administered but with water.[65] Water has throughout the religious history been associated with both destruction and salvation, death and life, tomb and womb.[66] It is therefore the perfect "matter" for the depth of meaning of baptism, and the liturgy recognizes this.[67]

The Great Vigil of Easter, the eminent baptismal time, interprets the water in its cosmic and paschal dimensions. It is the matter of life for everything on earth, and even in the beginning of time already blessed by the presence of God's Spirit upon it.[68] The water is

---

[60] "An Outline of the Faith," Holy Baptism: *Book of Common Prayer 1979*, p. 858.

[61] "Holy Baptism," Promise by the parents and godparents: *Book of Common Prayer 1979*, p. 302.

[62] "An Outline of the Faith," Holy Baptism: *Book of Common Prayer 1979*, p. 859.

[63] Rudolf Pesch, "Zur Initiation im Neuen Testament," *Liturgisches Jahrbuch*, 21 (1971), 103.

[64] "The Weekdays of Easter Season," Collects from Monday after 4 Easter until Ascension Day, no. 12: *Lesser Feasts and Fasts*, p. 63. The basis is the collect "Deus, qui ecclesiam tuam:" Mohlberg, *Sacramentarium Gelasianum*, no. 624.

[65] According to the commentaries to the Acts of the Apostles, the question whether a baptism of 3,000 persons was technically possible (2:41) is missing the point. It is not with a ritualistic detail that St. Luke is concerned here but with the personal reaction to the summons by St. Peter to a turning around and with the consequences for each person.

[66] See Gerardus van der Leeuw, *Phänomenologie der Religion*, 3. Aufl. (Tübingen: Mohr, 1970), pp. 46-48, 387-93; Photina Rech, *Inbild des Kosmos: Eine Symbolik der Schöpfung* (Salzburg: Müller, 1966), II, 303-49.

[67] Stenzel, *Taufe*, pp. 22-23.

[68] "The Great Vigil of Easter," first lesson: Gen 1:1--2:2: *Book of Common Prayer 1979*, p. 288. See Daniélou, *Bible*, pp. 99-104.

destruction of sin and wickedness, and yet from it rises the sign of God's covenant with all creation which will stand for ever.[69] The destroying water will be a saving one for humanity and even more so for the baptized.[70] The water is the ruin of all that is inimical to God's merciful plans for all nations, and it is salvation for those who adhere to the one true God. "It is a passage from sin to life, from guilt to grace, from vileness to holiness. He who passes through these waters [of the font] will not die: he rises again."[71] It is the water of life for the thirsty; it is the necessary precondition for existence of everything on earth; and as the earth can bring forth fruit through the water, so those who are baptized can bring forth a life according to the riches given in the waters of baptism.[72] Water cleanses from every stain and dirt; the baptismal water cleanses from sin.[73] Besides, being purified and endowed with God's Spirit, all who are reborn into the fellowship of the Church are God's people to whom He binds Himself as their God.[74] Water is presented in the economy of salvation of the Easter Vigil as the one great symbol of death and life.

> Creation, Fall and Redemption, Life and Death, Resurrection and Life Eternal: all the essential dimensions, the entire content of the Christian faith, are thus united and "held together" in their inner interdependence and unity in this one symbol; and it is indeed the initial and essential meaning, but also the power of this symbol that it "holds together," brings together (symbolon, from the Greek symballo, to bring together) that which was broken, dislocated and mutilated.[75]

The entire history of salvation is once more condensed in the great Thanksgiving over the Water,[76] and it is here that the doxological aspect of baptism prevails most. The parallels to the Great Thanksgiving of the eucharistic celebration are striking and theologically relevant.

---

[69] "The Great Vigil of Easter," second lesson: Gen 7:1-5,11-18; 8:6-18; 9:8-13: *Book of Common Prayer 1979*, p. 288. See Daniélou, *Bible*, pp. 104-18.

[70] "The Great Vigil of Easter," collect after the second lesson (Gen 7:1-5,11-18; 8:6-18; 9:8-13): *Book of Common Prayer 1979*, p. 289. The basis is an earlier composition by Harry Boone Porter. (Hatchett, *Commentary*, p. 246); "Preparation of Adults for Holy Baptism," During the Catechumenate, prayer 6: *Book of Occasional Services*, p. 119. Cf. Ambrose of Milan, *De sacramentis* i,23--ii,1, p. 72-74.

[71] "Hic est enim transitus, ideo pascha, hoc est transitus eius, transitus a peccato ad uitam, a culpa ad gratiam, ab inquinamento ad sanctificationem--qui per hunc fontem transit, non moritur sed resurgit.": Ambrose of Milan, *De sacramentis*, i,12, p. 66; English translation: Yarnold, *Awe-Inspiring Rites*, p. 104. "The Great Vigil of Easter," fourth lesson: Ex 14:10--15:1: *Book of Common Prayer 1979*, p. 289. See Daniélou, *Bible*, pp. 119-35.

[72] "The Great Vigil of Easter," sixth lesson: Is 55:1-11: *Book of Common Prayer 1979*, p. 290.

[73] "The Great Vigil of Easter," seventh lesson: Ez 36:24-28: *Book of Common Prayer 1979*, p. 290.

[74] "The Great Vigil of Easter," seventh lesson: Ez 36:24-28: *Book of Common Prayer 1979*, p. 290; collect after the seventh lesson: pp. 290-91. The basis is the collect "Omnipotens sempiterne deus qui paschale sacramentum:" Jean Deshusses, éd., *Le sacramentaire, le supplement d'Aniane*, T. I du *Sacramentaire grégorien: Ses principales formes d'après les plus anciens manuscrits, édition comparative*, Spicilegium Friburgense, 16, 2e éd. revue et corrigée (Fribourg Suisse: Editions Universitaires, 1979), no. 423. (Hatchett, *Commentary*, p. 247.)

[75] Schmemann, *Of Water and the Spirit*, p. 40.

[76] See Walter Maurice Bedard, *The Symbolism of the Baptismal Font in Early Christian Thought*, The Catholic University of America Studies in Sacred Theology: Second series, 45 (Washington, D.C.: The Catholic University of America Press, 1951); Johannes Petrus de Jong, "Benedictio fontis: Eine genetische Erklärung der römischen Taufwasserweihe," *Archiv für Liturgiewissenschaft*, 8,1 (1963), 21-46; Emil Joseph Lengeling, "Die Taufwasserweihe der römischen Liturgie: Vorschlag zu einer Neuformung," in *Liturgie--Gestalt und Vollzug*, hrsg. Walter Dürig (München: Hueber, 1963), pp. 176-251; Alexander Olivar, "Vom Ursprung der römischen Taufwasserweihe," *Archiv für Liturgiewissenschaft*, 6,1 (1959), 62-78; Hubert Scheidt, *Die Taufwasser-Weihegebete im Sinne vergleichender Liturgie-Forschung untersucht*, Liturgiewissenschaftliche Quellen und Forschungen, 29 (Münster: Aschendorff, 1935); Eduard Stommel, *Studien zur Epiklese der römischen Taufwasserweihe*, Theophaneia, 5 (Bonn: Hanstein, 1950).

The prayer begins with the salutation and the *Gratias agamus*. The first two paragraphs are an anamnesis of the wonderful deeds God has done in and through the water. The creation, the exodus from Egypt, and the baptism of Jesus are recalled. All use of water is seen through the Holy Spirit as pointing to its deepest meaning: the symbol of Christ's triumph over sin and death, a victory through which we are given everlasting life. This first paragraph shows that through Christ's paschal mystery the cosmos and the history are restored to their original dignity, from chaos to order, from slavery to freedom. A hint of what is yet to be revealed in its totality is shown at the descent of Jesus into the water at his own baptism: the Father manifests Jesus as His Son, and the Holy Spirit anoints him for his work to be Messiah for all the world. The first great revelation of the Trinity takes place in the water as it has been sanctified by Christ's descent into it.[77] The cosmic and Trinitarian aspects are expressed in this first paragraph.

The second paragraph speaks about Christ and our inclusion in his paschal mystery: the christological and ethical character of baptism are manifested. Specifically it is the water of baptism now through which we have our share in the paschal mystery. In this water we are buried with Christ and yet live in the power of his resurrection: new life through death. As much as the water is a tomb, it also is a womb: new life through a new birth, a spiritual birth in which not flesh and blood but the Holy Spirit effects the life.[78] As in the Great Thanksgiving, so here, too, the institution narrative of this sacrament by Christ is recalled; it is based on the command of the Risen One.[79] This is the clearest connection between the paschal mystery and baptism, and the Church, that wants and has to be faithful to Christ, cannot but "joyfully obey" and baptize.

The third paragraph is the epiclesis over the water. The water has been shown to point in its creational value to its use for baptism. And the baptismal water is--as a tomb and a womb--the means of new life for the faithful. Now it is prayed over the water present that the Holy Spirit may work through it so that it become a cleansing bath and a new birth for those who are baptized and, therefore, share in the new life of Christ. This paragraph serves to remove every hint of magic from the Church's rite; it is solely and only the Holy Spirit who works through the water:

> All waters, when God is invoked, acquire the sacred significance of conveying sanctity: for at once the Spirit comes down from heaven and stays upon the waters, sanctifying them from within himself, and when thus sanctified they absorb the power of sanctifying.[80]

This is also the central passage which justifies that "Holy Baptism is full initiation by water and the Holy Spirit into Christ's Body the Church."[81] Immediately after the water rite another thanksgiving associates both the cleansing and the regeneration aspects with the action by the Holy Spirit.[82] Without this power the Church's rites are empty and ritualistic human work, idolatry and sinful magic:

---

[77] Ambrose of Milan, *De sacramentis*, i,19, p. 70.

[78] Cyril of Jerusalem, *Mystagogical Catecheses* ii,4-5, in his *Catéchèses mystagogiques*, éd. Auguste Piédagnel, Sources chrétiennes, 126 (Paris: Cerf, 1966), pp. 110-14. See Riley, *Christian Initiation*, pp. 228-33, 302-04. Theodore of Mopsuestia, *Homilies* xiv,9, pp. 419-23. See Riley, *Christian Initiation*, pp. 325-36.

[79] George R. Beasley-Murray, *Baptism in the New Testament*, Mount Radford Reprints, 14 (London; New York, 1962; rpt. Exeter: Paternoster Press, 1979), pp. 77-92.

[80] "Omnes acquae de pristina originis praerogatiua sacramentum sanctificationis consecuntur inuocato deo: superuenit enim statim spiritus de caelis et aquis superest sanctificans eas de semetipso et ita sanctificatae uim sanctificandi combibunt.": Tertullian, *De baptismo* iv,4, p. 280; English translation: Whitaker, *Documents*, p. 7. Cf. Cyril of Jerusalem, *Mystagogical Catecheses* v,7, p. 154. See Riley, *Christian Initiation*, p. 370 note 64.

[81] "Holy Baptism," Concerning the Service: *Book of Common Prayer 1979*, p. 298.

[82] "Holy Baptism," Prayer for the Gifts of the Spirit: *Book of Common Prayer 1979*, p. 308.

There is a difference between the matter and the consecration, between the action and the effect. The action belongs to the water, its effect to the Holy Spirit. The water does not heal unless the Spirit descends and consecrates the water.[83]

Nor can the Spirit be ordered by the Church to assist in its works; the Church can only implore the Spirit to do what he has been sent to do by the Risen Christ. And "in fulfillment of Christ's true promise, the Holy Spirit came down from heaven . . . giving to your Church the power to serve you as a royal priesthood, and to preach the Gospel to all nations."[84] In consequence of this dignity and task, the Church can be sure of the presence of the Holy Spirit when it does what Christ has commanded it to do.

The Thanksgiving over the Water thus summarizes the salvation by water and the Holy Spirit in one great praise of God who is the source of salvation. At the same time it serves as a compendium of the dignity of baptism and as a beautiful and profound piece of theological penetration of what is, and remains, the creature of water. This thanksgiving is

> the epiphany, the revelation of the true meaning of Baptism as a cosmical, ecclesiological and eschatological act: cosmical, because it is the sacrament of the New Creation; ecclesiological, because it is the sacrament of the Church; eschatological, because it is the sacrament of the Kingdom. It is by entering into this mystery of water that we begin to understand why, in order to save a man, we must first of all immerse him in water.[85]

This now is done, after a possible consecration of the chrism by the bishop at baptism. Each person is presented by name to the baptizing officiant. Notwithstanding its character as incorporation into the community of the Church, baptism is as intimate and personal to each candidate as one's physical birth; the bringing into the fellowship of the Church, the regeneration, and the burial with Christ and share in his resurrection, as well as forgiveness of sin are effects of God's merciful grace bestowed on each individual. As to the mode of baptizing, immersion of the candidate in the water,[86] symbolizing better the tomb and the womb character of baptism, is given preference over aspersion, which nonetheless carries the same cluster of meanings.[87] The candidate is baptized, fully initiated "in the Name of the Father, and of the Son, and of the Holy Spirit."[88] It is the action of the Church: the congregation present assents to the act by saying "Amen." Salvation has become a reality for the baptized, and by water and the Holy Spirit this person has been raised to newness of life and is now part of the new creation in the kingdom of God.

---

[83] "Aliud est elementum, aliud consecratio, aliud opus, aliud operatio. Aquae opus est, operatio spiritus sancti est. Non sanat aqua nisi spiritus sanctus descenderit et illam consecrauit.": Ambrose of Milan, *De sacramentis* i,15, p. 68; English translation: Yarnold, *Awe-Inspiring Rites*, p. 105.

[84] "Holy Eucharist: Rite Two," Preface of Pentecost: *Book of Common Prayer 1979*, p. 380.

[85] Schmemann, *Of Water and the Spirit*, p. 40.

[86] Kretschmar, "Geschichte," pp. 271-73. As the archeological evidence shows, "immersion" means standing in the water up to the hips, and baptismal water being effused over the head of the candidate like a "shower." See John Gordon Davies, *The Architectural Setting of Baptism* (London: Barrie & Rockliff, 1962), pp. 25-26.

[87] Cyprian, *Letter 69 to Magnus*, 12, in *Sancti Thasci Caecilii Cypriani opera omnia*, ed. Guilelmus Hartel, Corpus Scriptorum Ecclesiasticorum Latinorum, 3,2 (Vindobonae: Gerold, 1868), pp. 760-61.

[88] "Der dreigliedrig-eine Name weist . . . auf den Heilszusammenhang hin, dem der Täufling eingefügt wird: das Heilshandeln Gottes in dem Sohn, desen eschatologisch-endgültiger Charakter durch die Sendung des Geistes erwiesen ist. . . . Die Taufe 'auf den (im) Namen . . .' fügt dem Heilsgeschehen ein, das an den Namen (Jesu) gebunden ist.": Gerhard Delling, *Die Zueignung des Heils in der Taufe: Eine Untersuchung zum neutestamentlichen "taufen auf den Namen"* (Berlin: Evangelische Verlagsanstalt, 1961), pp. 96-97. See Edward Charles Whitaker, "The History of the Baptismal Formula," *Journal of Ecclesiastical History*, 16 (1965), 1-12.

The operation of the Holy Spirit in baptism is efficacious in the water rite through which he bestows all that is theologically linked to this act. The Holy Spirit is not only the giver of the newness of life--he himself is given to the person in baptism.

Whether this needed another ritual action by the Church or not has been a point of--sometimes heated--discussion among Anglican theologians almost from the time of the Reformation on, and Anglicanism at times has looked like the debating club on this matter. Since the Oxford Movement this problem has been one of the most hotly argued ones. It centered around the question whether Christian initiation was complete in baptism or needed an additional rite, performed by the bishop afterwards, the commonly called "Confirmation."[89] The arrangement of the rite of baptism in the 1979 *Book of Common Prayer* settles this argument for the Episcopal Church. It has restored to baptism, immediately after the water rite, the prayer historically associated with the conferral of the Holy Spirit and the laying on of hands (with chrism if desired) after this prayer. The presiding priest, whether bishop or presbyter, says this prayer and lays a hand on each candidate. This action, so closely linked to the water rite, is an integral part of the initiatory rites of the Church which needs no substitute or addition some time afterwards.[90]

The person has been baptized, has been buried with Christ to receive a share in his new life, and is reborn to this life by the Holy Spirit. The first and indeed most important response by the Church to this action is that of praise and thankfulness, for what more can a human being receive than "all things that pertain to life and godliness," and what can one become more than "partaker of the divine nature" (2 Pet 1:3,4)? Because in baptism we have become what the prayers requested, by the operation of the Holy Spirit, gratitude for this undeserved favor of God's mercy and compassion is the fundament upon which the life of a Christian is built. The prayer specifies the objects of gratefulness: the heavenly Father has bestowed, by water and the Holy Spirit, the forgiveness of sins and the raising to new life of grace. The Old Adam has died, and a share in the life of the New Adam, Christ himself, has been given, although the baptized person physically remains the same. Yet it is a new human being, someone whose personality core has been changed, as regards spiritual realities, to a life patterned after Christ's death and glorification. "For you have died, and your life is hid with Christ in God." (Col 3:3) Such is the status of baptized persons that the dignity of the transformation, although not visible from outside, is the real life, the one thing that has to determine the whole course of attitude and action.

This newness of life of life has to be supported because of human frailty. Therefore God is asked to "sustain them in your Holy Spirit." The baptized persons are to be held *in* the Holy Spirit, not (only) *by* the Holy Spirit. This sentence makes clear that the Spirit has come to dwell with them and to be in them. Because Christ lives, the baptized persons live also, and the Holy Spirit has been given for the sustenance of this transformed life.[91] The Church bases its petition for this nourishment of the new life on the promise of the Lord that whatever it asks of the Father He will give it in Christ's name.

The Spirit is the great gift in baptism, but he is also the giver, the donor of the traditional "seven gifts of the Spirit." The phrasing in the *Book of Common Prayer* suggests that those are the distinctive marks of a Christian life: inquiry as to what has to be done; discernment whether this action or response is based upon Christ's will and commandment; willpower to overcome the obstacles for a realization of what has to be done; perseverance in the good works without the loss of courage; knowledge of God which is eternal life; love of God which

---

[89] For a bibliography of the different standpoints and the confirmation confusion in Anglicanism, see Leonel Lake Mitchell, "The Theology of Christian Initiation and The Proposed Book of Common Prayer," *Anglican Theological Review*, 60 (1978), 399 note 1.

[90] Charles P. Price and Louis Weil, *Liturgy for Living*, The Church's Teaching Series, 5 (New York: Seabury, 1979), pp. 127-30.

[91] "pantos gar hu an ephapsetai to hagion Pneuma, tuto hegiastai kai metabebletai.": Cyril of Jerusalem, *Mystagogical Catecheses* v,7, p. 154. See Riley, *Christian Initiation*, p. 370 note 64.

is the first and greatest commandment of Christ's; and the Christian joy and wonder in God's works which leads to adoration of God and to a proper use of the bounty.

The following action by the bishop or the priest ritualizes this gift of the Holy Spirit by the laying on of a hand on the baptized person's head, marking on the forehead the sign of the cross.[92] The use of chrism for this rite is optional. Contrary to the decision at the reform of the Roman Catholic rite of confirmation, where it was decided that "the Sacrament of Confirmation is conferred through the anointing with chrism on the forehead, which is done by the laying on of the hand,"[93] the essential rite in the *Book of Common Prayer* is that of imposition, not of chrismation. The ensuing formula in the prayer book reads, "*N.*, you are sealed by the Holy Spirit in Baptism and marked as Christ's own for ever." "Amen."[94] Two interpretations are possible. The first one sees the sealing by the Holy Spirit as actually happening at the laying on of hands and marking. This would make it a "second mystery," a sacramental action next to and after the administration of the water. This explanation is corroborated by the requirement that a person baptized in an emergency baptism ought after recovery to take part in a public celebration of the sacrament where the emergency baptism is recognized and everything is done according to the rubrics except for the very water rite. The second explication says that, because human life consists in a natural sequence of times and periods, even two things that intrinsically belong together have to be done successively so that what appears as two different rites, the administration of water and the imposition of hands, are two sides of one coin. This exposition is supported by the fact that the imposition of the hand may, according to the rubrics, be done immediately after the administration of the water and before the preceding prayer. Furthermore, the following act, the acknowledgment of the incorporation into the Church, is done "when all have been baptized" and with the invitation "Let us welcome the newly baptized," suggesting that the water rite and laying on of the hand together form the one baptism and cannot theologically be separated.

The baptized person is the possession of Christ,[95] but it is a possession in which the servant shares in the fate of the Lord and thereby shares in his dignity. This dignity is expressed in the prayer of consecration of the chrism as a "share in the royal priesthood of Jesus Christ." It is a sacrificial term and means the communication with God, the desire and obligation "to present your bodies as a living sacrifice, holy and acceptable to God." (Rom 12:1) It means a life style that is in accord with the renewal, the new creation to which the baptized person belongs. God as the giver of all good gifts is the goal of everything which a Christian does, so that everything will ultimately find its fulfillment in the communion with God. The royal priesthood is a life of adoration, praise, and thanksgiving directed to the source and end of all creation. It is also the communication of God's will to the world so that it will hear the will of God, the truth that makes free. Sharing in the royal priesthood of Christ means to do the works which God has determined for us to do. Those who in baptism have been conformed to the image of Christ can cooperate in setting the creation free from its bondage to decay in order so that it, too, can be a part of the kingdom of God to which the

---

[92] Joseph Ysebaert, *Greek Baptismal Terminology: Its Origins and Early Development*, Graecitas Christianorum primaeva, 1 (Nijmegen: Dekker & Van de Vegt, 1962), pp. 254-88 (imposition of hands, anointing, sealing in the New Testament).

[93] Apostolic Constitution on the Sacrament of Confirmation: *The Rites of the Catholic Church: As Revised by Decree of the Second Vatican Ecumenical Council and Published by Authority of Pope Paul VI*, trans. International Commission on English in the Liturgy (New York: Pueblo, 1976), p. 296. Obviously, the Congregation for Divine Worship had decided that the sacrament would be conferred through the imposition of hands, but the Congregation for the Doctrine of the Faith intervened at the last minute in favor of the chrismation as the central sacramental rite. See the embarrassing account by Bugnini, *Riforma liturgica*, pp. 601-02, especially note 16; and Louis Ligier, *La Confirmation: Sens et conjoncture oecuménique hier et aujourd'hui*, Théologie historique, 23 (Paris: Beauchesne, 1973), pp. 34-35.

[94] "Holy Baptism," The Baptism: *Book of Common Prayer 1979*, p. 308.

[95] As to the seal as mark of ownership, see Ysebaert, *Terminology*, pp. 390-421.

baptized person has once and for all been admitted through water and the Holy Spirit. This admission has to bear fruit in an existence according to the newness of life.

The recognition of the incorporating character of baptism expresses well what this existence according to the newness of life means: "Confess the faith of Christ crucified, proclaim his resurrection, and share with us in his eternal priesthood."[96] The whole life of a Christian is delineated as an emanation of the paschal mystery which so permeates everything that the entire existence depends on it. Since the gospel, the power of God for salvation, is something not to be ashamed of, the center of God's redemption of humanity--the crucified and risen Christ--is to be confessed in word and deed, like the questions of life style after the baptismal creed have suggested. This proclamation is possible because with the obligation to it God has also given the assistance for it, the Holy Spirit, who as the constant giver of life enables the service of God and neighbor. It is here that the "Confirmation" has its foundations and rationale. One could rightly call "Confirmation" a "service of reminder to the ethics of baptism" since Christian life has to be spent in a way which shows both the dignity and the duty of baptized people.[97] The sacramental aspect of a Spirit-giving and sealing action has been completely restored to the baptismal office so that the baptismal rite with its several climaxes is indeed "full initiation by water and the Holy Spirit" into the Church; there is no need for any additional service or action. This later service is rather the extension of the covenant aspect of baptism. Those who because of age have not been able to answer the questions and make the promises by themselves, are "expected" to grow even further in their existence as baptized people and, after a mature decision for the Christian way of life which otherwise they would have made during the catechumenate, to come forward and to make a "public affirmation of their faith and commitment to the responsibilities of their Baptism."[98] They then receive the laying on of hands by the bishop for the strengthening of their faith and an increase in a life sustained by the Holy Spirit. If the word "initiation" has to be associated with "Confirmation," then it is not in terms of sacramental action but in the area of psychology of religion. Christian life is not a series of habits but demands a conscious decision for Christ and his commandments.[99] Insofar as this requires personal convictions apart from the support by social values and environmental influences, the importance of this office of confirmation will increase for the benefit of the church members and the sustenance of their personal faith. But as infant baptism more and more decreases in numbers and candidates for baptism are more likely to apply at a later, possibly adult, stage, confirmation might vanish from the liturgical books or at least form the liturgical experience of the parish. Then the "mature public affirmation of faith and commitment to the responsibilities of Baptism" will be made at baptism itself, after a prolonged period in which

---

[96] "Holy Baptism," Acknowledgment of the Reception into the Church: *Book of Common Prayer 1979*, p. 308.

[97] See Günther Bornkamm, "Taufe und neues Leben bei Paulus," in his *Gesammelte Aufsätze 1: Das Ende des Gesetzes*, Beiträge zur evangelischen Theologie, 16, 5. Aufl. (München: Kaiser, 1966), pp. 34-50; Niklas Gäumann, *Taufe und Ethik: Studien zu Römer 6*, Beiträge zur evangelischen Theologie, 47 (München: Kaiser, 1967); Hans Halter, *Taufe und Ethos: Paulinische Kriterien für das Proprium christlicher Moral*, Freiburger Theologische Studien, 106 (Freiburg: Herder, 1977); Hans-Friedrich Weiß, "Taufe und neue Existenz im deuteropaulinischen Schrifttum," in *Taufe und neue Existenz*, hrsg. Erdmann Schott (Berlin: Evangelische Verlagsanstalt, 1973), pp. 53-70.

[98] "Confirmation," Concerning the Service: *Book of Common Prayer 1979*, p. 412. No appropriate or desired age is anywhere indicated except that a "mature" affirmation is expected. See John Douglas Close Fisher, "Gifts of the Spirit and a Confession of Faith: The Age for Confirmation," in *The Sacrifice of Praise: Studies on the Themes of Thanksgiving and Redemption in the Central Prayers of the Eucharistic and Baptismal Liturgies, in honour of Arthur Hubert Couratin*, ed. Bryan D. Spinks, Bibliotheca "Ephemerides Liturgicae" "Subsidia," 19 (Roma: CLV Edizioni Liturgiche, 1981), pp. 247-57.

[99] See André Rousseau, "Hérédités sociales et initiation religieuse," *La Maison-Dieu*, 132 (1977), 141-55.

regular association with the worshipping community, the practice of life in accordance with the Gospel (including service to the poor and neglected), encouragement and instruction in the life of prayer, and basic instruction in the history of salvation as revealed in the Holy Scriptures of the Old and New Testaments[100] are featured.

In the confirmation service God's help for the task set before the baptized person is asked. But here again, the first reaction of the Church to baptism, expressed in the prayer for the candidates for confirmation, reception, or reaffirmation, is that of thankfulness for the victory of Christ over sin by his death and resurrection. His paschal mystery has brought redemption to humanity, and it has brought the community of the saved ones, the Church, to God where its life is hid with Christ. In the same "application" of salvation in baptism, God has called and bound the persons to His service "by the sealing of your Holy Spirit" which expresses in the strongest possible terms that the Holy Spirit has been given in baptism. These wonderful deeds which God rendered to every person in baptism and which are now set before Him in grateful memorial, enable the Church to ask Him for a renewal of the covenant He made with the baptized. Yet it is not so much a renewal on the side of God which is necessary but "in these your servants" "who have once been enlightened, who have tasted the heavenly gift, and have become partakers of the Holy Spirit." (Hebr 6:4) For those God is asked to empower them to let the Holy Spirit work in them so that they can lead a Christian life even more convincing than before. In essence this is a petition which is not restricted to just one occasion in life; the strengthening power of the Holy Spirit is needed daily. This is the reason why this prayer is a "collect" said for those who come either for confirmation, or for the reception of persons baptized within another church into the communion of the Episcopal Church, or for the reaffirmation of the baptismal commitment by those whose Christian life had lapsed.

The formulas for these occasions, accompanying the laying on of hands, petition that the Holy Spirit may "strengthen," "empower," "sustain," "direct," and "uphold" the candidate in the service of God; His grace may do the work in the candidate for the sake of the kingdom of God.[101]

The concluding prayer after the imposition of hands over the candidates for the different occasions summarizes the work of the Trinity for these people and the response in their lives. The hand of the Father might always be over the persons who have received the laying on of hands, the hand of the Lord which is not shortened that it cannot save, the hand of which it is promised that it is with His servants (Is 66:14). The Holy Spirit given in baptism ought to be with these people with all the gifts he has given so that they can carry out their service. These persons may be led in the knowledge and obedience of God's Word, both the intellectual knowledge and actual obedience to God's commandments, and the knowledge of God's incarnate Word who gives power to become children of God to those who receive and follow him. This knowledge and obedience is the basis for individuals serving God in this life and through the newness of life, until they are united with Christ not only in his death by their baptism but live with him in the fulness of life in "the joy of that heavenly Jerusalem, where all tears are wiped away and where your saints forever sing your praise."[102]

---

[100] "Concerning the Catechumenate:" *Book of Occasional Services*, p. 112.

[101] "Holy Baptism," At Confirmation, Reception, or Reaffirmation: *Book of Common Prayer 1979*, pp. 309-10.

[102] "The Great Vigil of Easter," Collect after the fifth lesson (Is 4:2-5): *Book of Common Prayer 1979*, p. 290. The basis is an earlier composition by Harry Boone Porter. (Hatchett, *Commentary*, p. 247.) Cyril of Jerusalem knew of these dynamics of baptism: "epi de tu hagiu tes palingenesias lutru, apheilen ho Theos pan dakryon apo pantos prosopon:" *Mystagogical Catecheses* i,10, p. 100. See Riley, *Christian Initiation*, pp. 176-78.

The Interpretation: The Dignity of a Faithful

The texts of the *Book of Common Prayer* unfold what happens at baptism in its several aspects. The richness of the baptismal covenant has many aspects, each of which was highlighted in different regions and at different times. But a certain pattern can be detected in the adoption of those themes. Whereas the Church in the East was slow in taking up the Pauline vision of incorporation into Christ and participation in his death and new new life and the baptismal texts before the middle of the fourth century do not express these aspects at all,[103] the Church in the West focused on the features of cleansing from sin and regeneration. The *Book of Common Prayer* acknowledges as most prominent among the characteristics of baptism the incorporation into Christ's Body, the Church, the dying and rising to new life, the adoption as sons and daughters of God, and the new birth. By doing so it tries to avoid the emphasis on just one aspect to the detriment of the others; both the Pauline and the Johannine theologies are represented, the former by the first two types, the latter by the regenerative aspect, while the adoption as children of God is common to both. Numerically, however, the balance tips in favor of the ecclesiological and paschal character, and the emphasis on Easter and its Great Vigil shows where, for the *Book of Common Prayer*, the center lies.

Initiation means a total change in the condition of human existence; after the initiatory process the person is totally different from the one who he or she was before the initiation. In the course of the rites developed in the history of religion for this purpose, the imagery of death and new life takes a prominent place.

> The majority of initiatory ordeals more or less clearly imply a ritual death followed by resurrection or a new birth. The central moment of every initiation is represented by the ceremony symbolizing the death of the novice and his return to the fellowship of the living. But he returns to life a new man, assuming another mode of being.[104]

This is the background upon which St. Paul could build his arguments about the new existence of a Christian through baptism into Christ's death.[105] His line of thought, complex

---

[103] Kretschmar, "Geschichte," pp. 93, 174; Gabriele Winkler, *Das Armenische Initiationsrituale: Entwicklungsgeschichtliche und liturgievergleichende Untersuchung der Quellen des 3. bis 10. Jahrhunderts*, Orientalia Christiana Analecta, 217 (Roma: Pontificium Institutum Studiorum Orientalium, 1982), pp. 434-41, 444-46.

[104] "La majorité des épreuves initiatiques impliquent, d'une façon plus ou moins transparente, une mort rituelle suivie d'une résurrection ou d'une nouvelle naissance. Le moment central de toute initiation est représenté par la cérémonie qui symbolise la mort du néophyte et son retour parmi les vivants. Mais il revient à la vie un homme nouveau, assumant un autre mode d'être.": Mircea Eliade, *Naissances mystiques: Essai sur quelques types d'initiation*, 4e éd. ([Paris:] Gallimard, 1959), p. 14; English translation: *Birth and Rebirth: The Religious Meanings of Initiation in Human Culture*, trans. William R. Trask, The Library of Religion and Culture (New York: Harper & Brothers, 1958), p. xii. Cf. Eliade, *Quest*, p. 112.

[105] Here is not the place to discuss the implications of a possible link of St. Paul's theological argument with the hellenistic mystery religions. For the pro and con, see Odo Casel, "Mysteriengegenwart," *Jahrbuch für Liturgiewissenschaft*, 8 (1928), 145-224; "Zur Kultsprache des heiligen Paulus," *Archiv für Liturgiewissenschaft*, 1 (1950), 1-64; Rudolf Schnackenburg, *Das Heilsgeschehen bei der Taufe nach dem Apostel Paulus: Eine Studie zur paulinischen Theologie*, Münchener Theologische Studien, 1,1 (München: Zink, 1950); English translation: *Baptism in the Thought of St. Paul: A Study in Pauline Theology* (Oxford: Blackwell, 1964); "Todes- und Lebensgemeinschaft mit Christus: Neue Studien zu Röm 6,1-11," *Münchener Theologische Zeitschrift*, 6 (1955), 32-53; Günter Wagner, *Das religionsgeschichtliche Problem von Röm 6,1-11*, Abhandlungen zur Theologie des Alten und Neuen Testaments, 39 (Zürich: Zwingli, 1962); English translation: *Pauline Baptism and the Pagan Mysteries: The Problem of the Pauline Doctrine of Baptism in Romans VI,1-11, in the Light of Its Religio-*

and controversial, centers around the liberation from sin in and through baptism as expressed above all in Romans 6:1-11. Through our baptism into Christ we were handed over to Christ, in effect being incorporated into his redemptive death.[106] This burial with Christ in baptism had as a goal that, as Christ was raised to new life by the glorious power of God, so, too, should the Christians who were baptized into Christ's death live a new life, no longer a life in sin but in newness. The newness of life for the faithful corresponds to the resurrection of Christ to his new life. To the same extent that the raising of Christ from the dead was a drastic event wrought by God's power, so the newness of life, which is given to the faithful in their baptism into Christ's death, has to be a drastic turning away from sin to living the existence of a person who has shared Christ's death. "To be baptized, then, according to Paul, is to undergo a drastic experience. The overworked term 'existential' is not amiss in application to his exposition of baptism given in Rom. 6."[107] St. Paul's intention is not to deal with the ritual aspects of baptism.[108] Rather it is the ethical aspect of a Christian life: the new nature of life has to conform to Christ's resurrection in which it finds its fundament. This is the reason why the pre-eminent baptismal time has been and is the Great Vigil of Easter in which Christ's passing from death to life is celebrated as the turning point for the life of all creation.

The newness of life of a believer is the newness of the Spirit (Rom 7:6), the Spirit who hovers and vivifies the new creation of those who are in Christ (2 Cor 5:17). To acquire, rather receive this new life, we have been united with the likeness of Christ's death. It is Christ's death on the cross in which he conquered death, the one all-ending point which had come into this world because the First Adam had rejected God's love and life for him, and after him all his children were subject to this death, the separation from God's love and life. "Sin came into the world through one man and death through sin, and so death spread to all men because all men sinned." (Rom 5:12) Christ destroyed this death, the result of sin and rejection of God's love and life, in his death. "As one man's trespass led to condemnation for all men, so one man's act of righteousness leads to acquittal and life for all men." (Rom 5:18) In his death on the cross there was no "death," no rejection of God's love towards all (Rom 5:8). Therefore, the result of sin, the death of separation from God, was conquered by Christ's death and destroyed, the reign of death overcome by the reign of God's love and life. "Both death and resurrection are to our advantage: for death is the end of sin and the resurrection is the reformation of our nature."[109] To this act of salvation we have been united through the likeness of Christ's death which is baptism. "By his death he has destroyed death, and by his rising to life again he has won for us everlasting life."[110] Our life in God comes through Christ's death into which we are united in baptism. Our life with God is patterned after Christ's life which he gained in being raised from the dead. It is the complete newness of life. But it is also a life that is not to continue in sin.

The unity with Christ in his death and burial is narrowly linked with the incorporation into Christ; baptism is baptism into Christ and, therefore, into his Body. St. Paul expresses this as the operation of the Holy Spirit: "By one Spirit we were all baptized into one body--Jews or Greeks, slaves or free--and all were made to drink of one Spirit." (1 Cor 12:13) The Holy Spirit is the agent by which, or the element in which, one is baptized so that one is in the Body; the Spirit constitutes the faithful as members of the one Body. Baptism is always by

---

Historical "Parallels" (Edinburgh: Oliver & Boyd, 1967); Viktor Warnach, "Taufe und Christusgeschehen nach Römer 6," *Archiv für Liturgiewissenschaft*, 3,2 (1954), 284-366.

[106] Pesch, "Initiation," 100-01.

[107] Beasley-Murray, *Baptism*, p. 142.

[108] Ysebaert, *Terminology*, pp. 40-63 (washing, immersion in the New Testament).

[109] "Vtrumque ergo pro nobis, quia et mors finis est peccatorum et resurrectio naturae est reformatio.": Ambrose of Milan, *De sacramentis* ii,17, p. 84; English translation: Yarnold, *Awe-Inspiring Rites*, p. 116. See Riley, *Christian Initiation*, pp. 244-47; cf. pp. 222-27.

[110] "Holy Eucharist: Rite Two," Preface of Easter: *Book of Common Prayer 1979*, p. 379.

water and the Spirit, and the one agent cannot be separated from the other because the effects are the same: any one who has the Spirit of Christ belongs to him (Rom 8:9). The result of this event is the obliteration of social distinctions which in "this world" are the basis of everyday living but are non-existent in the Body of Christ. The only difference that counts are the different functions carried out for the benefit of the life of the entire Body. "We are all baptized by the one Spirit into one Body, and given gifts for a variety of ministries for the common good."[111] There is no special commission or mandate necessary to carry out the work for which one has received the gift. The corporate nature of the Church depends on the cooperation of the different vocations for its mission. "The mission of the Church is to restore all people to unity with God and each other in Christ. The Church carries out its mission through the ministry of all its members."[112]

The Body of Christ exists as the social entity before one is baptized. In baptism one is added to it. Each time someone is incorporated into it, the Body is built up and renewed. The individual believers do not select with whom they might want to mingle and to live according to the baptismal promises; they are added to the pre-existing Body and inseparably linked to it. Christian life cannot be spent privately; it is always a social and open vocation.

The phrase for expressing this social nature of baptism is only slightly different in Galatians 3:2: "As many of you as were baptized into Christ have put on Christ. There is neither Jew nor Greek, there is neither slave nor free, there is neither male nor female; for you are all one in Christ Jesus." The "unitive power of baptism"[113] makes one of those who have put on Christ. "The spiritual Christ 'in' whom the baptized lives, is, so to speak, his new uniform which renders inexistent the distinctive signs of the former life. . . . Christ is the eschatological 'pattern of existence.'"[114] The social distinctions are superseded by the higher dignity of being Christ's property (Gal 3:29) and one with him in his Body. The aspect of being one in Christ and, therefore, in communion with Christ and his members is well expressed in the collect for All Saints' Day, one of the four prominent baptismal days: "Almighty God, you have knit together your elect in one communion and fellowship in the mystical body of your Son Christ our Lord."[115]

This text leads to the deepest fountain of unity and communion. God joins together those who are baptized by water and the Spirit into Christ. On the deepest level, "the unity of the Body of Christ is not simply sociality but a *koinonia* in the Spirit after the pattern of the *koinonia* of the Blessed Trinity."[116] Here we are at the source of all being: the unity of the Father with the Son and the Spirit: "They may all be one even as thou, Father, art in me, and I in thou, that they also may be in us, so that the world may believe that thou hast sent me." (John 17:21) Baptism, then, does not mean simply "imitating Jesus." The Body of Christ is taken up to where the Head of the Body is also: in the unity with the Father and the communion with the Spirit. Every fellowship is a mirror of this communion, and every visible unity reflects the *koinonia* of the Trinity. Among human beings the reflecting rays are broken through frailty and sin. But the distorted and often almost blind image will, when the perfect comes, pass away and fully reveal the deepest origin of communion and corporate identity.

---

[111] "Commissioning for Lay Ministries in the Church," Address to the congregation at the beginning of the Examination: *Book of Occasional Services*, p. 161.

[112] "An Outline of the Faith," The Church: *Book of Common Prayer 1979*, p. 855.

[113] "einheitsstiftende Kraft der Taufe:" Franz Mußner, *Der Galaterbrief*, Herders Theologischer Kommentar zum Neuen Testament, 9, 3., erweiterte Aufl. (Freiburg: Herder, 1977), p. 264.

[114] "Der pneumatische Christus, 'in' dem der Getaufte lebt, ist gleichsam sein neues Einheitskleid, . . . das die unterscheidenden Zeichen der früheren Existenz wesenlos macht. . . . Christus ist das eschatologische 'Existenzmodell.'": Mußner, *Galaterbrief*, p. 263. As to the "uniform," see John Chrysostom, *Baptismal Homilies* iv,17, pp. 191-92.

[115] "Collects: Contemporary," All Saints' Day: *Book of Common Prayer 1979*, p. 245.

[116] Beasley-Murray, *Baptism*, p. 281.

St. Paul also says this in the same chapter of his letter to the Galatians: "God sent forth his Son . . . so that we might receive adoption as sons. And because you are sons, God has sent the Spirit of his son into our hearts, crying, 'Abba! Father.' So through God you are no longer a slave but a son, and if a son then an heir." (4:4-7) Although baptism is not mentioned here, the adoption as sons and daughters by God has been counted among the effects of baptism, and the number of explicit references to this result in the *Book of Common Prayer* is an eloquent witness to it.[117] The whole economy of salvation is seen in this passage as "sonship." In juridical terms this means adoption which, however lacking a physical relation, gives the full privilege of a son, including the right to become an heir to the father.[118]

This new quality is nothing but grace: it is given, not earned. The adoption is effected in baptism through the agent of the Holy Spirit who is sent into the hearts of the baptized. The fact ensues that, as God gives a share of His own nature--His Spirit--into the hearts, there is a hitherto impossible intimacy and personal relationship which exceeds all merely juridical terms.[119] God may be addressed with the word which by right is the prerogative of His Son only: Father. In baptism, by conforming us to the image of His Son and giving His Spirit into our hearts, God reveals His nature, which cannot be known otherwise unless it is given. In His Son God beholds those named after Christ and conformed to him. The gift of the Holy Spirit in baptism entitles those to whom he is given to know God and to serve not a distant deity but a God who has become Father for them, who accepts the service of His sons and daughters as the most eminent sign of gratitude and relationship. This Holy Spirit is the guarantee of our inheritance to which we have been predestined and appointed because in Christ God destined us to be His sons and daughters (Eph 1:3-14). Together with His Son the baptized are heirs to all the promises.

It is at this point, where the adoption as children of God is one of the explications of the mystery of baptism, that the Pauline and Johannine interpretations of baptism converge; it is an elucidation common to both.[120] Persons believing in Christ and receiving him for what he is--the life and the light of the world--are given power by Christ to become children of God (John 1:12-13). Here again the nature of children of God is not something which human beings have out of their own and in their own capacity; it has to be given to them by grace. Being children of God is a gift that comes from the love of the Father. Because this source is the reality that permeates everything and fulfills what it wills, we are not only called children of God, we are (1 John 3:1-2). It is clear from John 1:13 how this privilege is given: in the birth, not from the physical world but from above, which in John 3:3,5 is identified as birth of water and the Spirit. Being children of God is the gift in baptism. "The generation by God is

---

[117] "Collects: Contemporary," Christmas Day, III: *Book of Common Prayer 1979*, p. 213; Easter Day, II (Vigil): p. 222; "Holy Baptism," Alternative Ending, Prayer after the Lord's Prayer: p. 311; "Holy Eucharist: Rite Two," Preface for Baptism: p. 381; "Thanksgiving for the Birth or Adoption of a Child," For an Adoption: p. 441; Prayer for a child not yet baptized: p. 444; Blessing of the family: p. 445; "Reconciliation of a Penitent," Form II, Bidding before the Confession: p. 450; "Dedication and Consecration of a Church," Dedication of the Font: p. 569; Litany of Thanksgiving for a Church: p. 578. "The Weekdays of Easter Season," Collects from Monday after 2 Easter until 4 Easter, no. 7: *Lesser Feasts and Fasts*, p. 60; Collects from Monday after 4 Easter until Ascension Day, no. 16: p. 65. "Blessing in Homes at Epiphany," Blessing I: *Book of Occasional Services*, p. 47 (identical with "Blessing in Homes at Easter," Blessing I: p. 99); "Candlemas Procession," Stational collect during the Procession: p. 53; "Preparation of Adults for Holy Baptism," During the Catechumenate, prayer 1: p. 117.

[118] Mußner, *Galaterbrief*, p. 271.

[119] John Chryostom, *Baptismal Homilies* ii,26, pp. 147-48.

[120] Any sound theology of baptism must not be a vivisection of the mystery but rather an expression in different terms with the same starting point and end: the Christ-event through which we are freed, and our ingrafting into the new life of Christ. Different accents are very legitimate, but as accents, not as main points.

work of the divine Spirit which is not at human disposal or comprehensible."[121] The only condition for this gift, this "power," is faith and trust in Christ. It is the one and all-decisive basis for acquiring salvation. When there is this faith in Christ--in him who is the life and the light of the world, who is the Son from the Father, who became flesh to be lifted up on the cross, and who has sent the Counselor, the Spirit--Christ himself can exercize his power and make these believers in baptism his equal: children of God.

The birth not from the physical world but from above is an explanation much favored in the *Book of Common Prayer*,[122] taking up the regenerative themes of the book's predecessors; numerically it is the most frequent allusion to baptism. Unlike Eastern liturgies of the first four centuries,[123] it is not applied exclusively--for that, the all-penetrating dimension of the paschal mystery is too strong to be in any way neglected--but it complements the otherwise heavy reliance on the interpretation of baptism as a tomb, following the explications of St. Paul in Romans 6.[124]

The birth from above[125] by water and the Spirit for entering the kingdom of God is most clearly expressed in John 3:3-5. The birth from above here is seen as a womb, the place where the all-decisive birth takes place. For a Christian the reference of this image to the beginning of salvation in baptism is inevitable. The birth from above is given by God, preceding all human efforts, and freely given: the Spirit dwells where he wills (John 3:8). The entirely new being generated by the birth from above is the basis for a life directed towards the kingdom of God. This kingdom cannot be reached by human means or efforts; it is by God's grace that a person enters it, and the entrance to this kingdom is the birth "by water and the Spirit." The accent lies on the Spirit. He cannot be separated from the water and the administration of the water in baptism. But it is not the water which effects the regeneration but the Spirit, the giver of life: "That which is born of the flesh is flesh, and that which is born of the Spirit is spirit." (John 3:6) It is spiritual life, no longer merely earthly life. The Spirit bestows a new nature in baptism; he effects the new creation. All this was foretold as a promise for the future:

> I will sprinkle clean water upon you, and you shall be clean from all your uncleanness. . . . A new heart I will give you, and a new spirit I will put within you. . . . And I will put my spirit

---

[121] "Die Zeugung ist menschlich unverfügbares und unbegreifliches Werk des göttlichen Geistes:" Rudolf Schnackenburg, *Das Johannesevangelium: 1. Teil*, Herders Theologischer Kommentar zum Neuen Testament, 4,1 (Freiburg: Herder, 1965), p. 239.

[122] "Collects: Contemporary," Christmas Day, III: *Book of Common Prayer 1979*, p. 213; Thursday in Easter Week: p. 223 (identical with Second Sunday of Easter: p. 224); At Baptism: p. 254; "The Great Vigil of Easter," Concluding prayer after the Renewal of Vows: p. 294; "Holy Baptism," Invitation to Prayers for the Candidates: p. 305; Thanksgiving over the Water: pp. 306, 307; Prayer for the Gifts of the Spirit: p. 308; "The Burial of the Dead: Rite Two," Concluding prayer at the Prayers of the People: p. 498. "The Weekdays of Lent," Tuesday in the Fifth Week of Lent: *Lesser Feasts and Fasts*, p. 49; "The Weekdays of Easter Season," Collects from Monday after 2 Easter until 4 Easter, no. 1: p. 57; no. 2: p. 58; no. 6: p. 59; From Monday after 4 Ester until Ascension Day, no. 12: p. 63; no. 16: p. 65; From Friday after Ascension Day until Pentecost, no. 17: p. 65. "Blessing in Homes at Epiphany," Blessing II: *Book of Occasional Services*, p. 47; "Preparation of Adults for Holy Baptism," During the Catechumenate, prayer 2: p. 118; prayer 3: p. 118; Enrollment of Candidates for Baptism, Concluding prayer after the Litany: p. 123; "Vigil on the Eve of Baptism," Litany, Form II, Introduction: p. 129.

[123] Winkler, *Initiationsrituale*, pp. 443, 446.

[124] Cyril of Jerusalem combines both interpretations in one idea: "Kai en to auto aphthneskete kai egennasthe, kai to soteriu ekeino hydor kai taphos hymin egineto kai meter. . . . kai heis kairos amphoteron tuton poietikos, kai syndromos egineto to thanato he gennesis he hymetera.": *Mystagogical Catecheses* ii,4, p. 112. See Riley, *Christian Initiation*, pp. 228-33, 302-04.

[125] "Anothen" in this context is more likely to mean "from above" than "new:" Beasley-Murray, *Baptism*, p. 226; Schnackenburg, *Johannesevangelium*, pp. 381-82.

within you, and cause you to walk in my statutes and be careful to observe my ordinances. You shall dwell in the land which I gave to your fathers; and you shall be my people, and I will be your God. (Ez 36:25-28)[126]

The Spirit of God creates a new heart, which means a new human being who is able to fulfill the commandments of God and to live as God proposes. St. John sees this fulfilled at the moment when the Spirit causes the birth from above: the kingdom of God is open to the baptized. It is no longer a promise but an invitation; the door is open.

The operation of the Spirit and, therefore, the efficacy of baptism depends upon the glorification of Jesus when "the Son of man is lifted up" and the Spirit is given (John 3:14; 7:39). This in Johannine parlance is nothing less than the cross where Jesus gave the Spirit and established the mysteries of the New Covenant.[127] Just as the Christ-event cannot be vivisected into different clear-cut divisions to the detriment of the understanding of the economy of salvation, so here the Johannine and Pauline visions upon the origin of the efficacy and operation of baptism coincide. Baptism by water and the Spirit is in its effects a creation of the cross--rather, of the Son of God who for the redemption of humanity and all creation suffered death on the cross so that, by laying down his life, he could give life in his Spirit abundantly. Cross and death, exaltation and glorification are identical for St. John. Through his death and glorification by the Father Christ gives new life, his Spirit. St. Paul is different in his expression yet means the same origin: Christ's death and burial are the destruction of sin, and his being raised from the dead is the sign and pledge of newness of life. This newness of life is bestowed by the Spirit in baptism, be it regarded as a birth from above, a spiritual womb, or as a tomb out of which life arises. The newness of life, given in baptism by the Spirit, is what it is all about. This life is God's life in the baptized; it makes them, together with all the others before them, next to them, and after them in Christ's Body, the Church, children of God and heirs of the kingdom of God. This kingdom, as St. John relates, is open to those born by water and the Spirit to join in the festal banquet with the heavenly food of the new creation.

The Fulfillment: The Eucharist

There are inner links between baptism and the eucharist, not only because they are "the two great sacraments of the Gospel given by Christ to his Church,"[128] but as relates to promise and fulfillment, pledge and reality, newness of life and constant renewal. The baptismal liturgies of the first centuries culminated in the first full participation of the newly baptized in the eucharist;[129] the Church Fathers and teachers commented on this link;[130] and

---

[126] "The Great Vigil of Easter," sixth lesson (including verse 24): *Book of Common Prayer 1979*, p. 290.

[127] See Hans-Urs von Balthasar, "Mysterium Paschale," in *Das Christusereignis*, Bd. III/2 von *Mysterium salutis*, hrsg. Johannes Feiner and Magnus Löhrer (Einsiedeln: Benziger, 1969), pp. 216-21; Sebastian Tromp, "De nativitate Ecclesiae e Corde Iesu," *Gregorianum*, 13 (1932), 488-527.

[128] "An Outline of the Faith," The Sacraments: *Book of Common Prayer 1979*, p. 858.

[129] Aidan Kavanagh, *The Shape of Baptism: The Rite of Christian Initiation*, Studies in the Reformed Rites of the Catholic Church, 1 (New York: Pueblo, 1978), pp. 41, 43-44, 46-47, 50, 63, 65; Kretschmar, "Geschichte," pp. 109-14, 124-25, 180, 243, 246-47, 264, 268; Stenzel, *Taufe*, pp. 129, 158, 182, 190; Winkler, *Initiationsrituale*, pp. 104, 126, 166, 171-75.

[130] Raymond Burnish, *The Meaning of Baptism: A Comparison of the Teaching and Practice of the Fourth Century with the Present Day*, Alcuin Club Collections, 67 (London: SPCK, 1985), pp. 21-22; Kretschmar, "Geschichte," pp. 110, 125, 180, 246. See Adrian J. Jacobs, "The Sacraments of Salvation," in *The Sacrifice of Praise: Studies on the Themes of Thanksgiving and Redemption in the Central Prayers of the Eucharistic and*

the Orthodox churches always kept at least the distribution of some of the eucharistic species to the newly baptized in the baptismal liturgy itself, even in the case of infants.[131] The renewal of the rites of the Christian initiation of adults in the Roman Catholic Church provides for the participation in the eucharist and the first reception of the communion after the initiation liturgy.[132] Since "Holy Baptism is full initiation by water and the Holy Spirit into Christ's Body the Church,"[133] and "Confirmation" no longer is a part of the sacramental initiation process, there are no provisions in the *Book of Common Prayer* which demand or suggest a delay of full participation in the eucharist, including the reception of the communion, even in the case of children.[134] As "Holy Baptism is appropriately administered within the Eucharist as the chief service on a Sunday or other feast,"[135] the newly initiated people are expected to take part in the eucharist which continues, after baptism (and confirmation or the other occasions for a laying on of hands by the bishop), with the Prayers of the People or the offertory.[136] At the offertory "the oblations of bread and wine at the baptismal Eucharist may be presented by the newly baptized or their godparents."[137] The connection of the eucharist with baptism, then, must lie in the realm of the full initiation which the newly baptized have undergone, and in the dynamics of baptism which point to the eucharist as the climax of the entire initiation process.[138]

Baptism is full initiation into Christ's Body, the Church. The social character of it is evident: the accent lies not on the forgiveness of sins or personal salvation--which are "side-effects" of the initiation--but on the grafting into Christ and his Body. This Body is constituted by the people whom God has "called out of darkness into his marvelous light." (1 Pet 2:9) He has called them out so that those who once were no people are now His people (1 Pet 2:10). It belongs to the essence of those whom God has called out that they become a social entity which receives the new quality of not only being called by Christ's name[139] but being his Body and each individual a member of this Body.[140]
This Body gathers together regularly to hear God's word and celebrate the eucharist, acts in which it is at the center of its own origin and is constantly renewed by the source of its existence. The Church here receives the life stream again that keeps it the Body of Christ. This

---

Baptismal Liturgies, in honour of Arthur Hubert Couratin, ed. Bryan D. Spinks, Bibliotheca "Ephemerides Liturgicae" "Subsidia," 19 (Roma: CLV Edizioni Liturgiche, 1981), pp. 261-72.

[131] Burnish, *Meaning*, p. 119; Schmemann, *Of Water and the Spirit*, pp. 115-21. The distribution is mentioned in *L'Office divin, la liturgie, les sacrements*, éd. E. [= Feuillen] Mercier et François Paris, La prière des Eglises de rite byzantin, 1, 2e éd. (Chevetogne: Monastère de Chevetogne, 1947), p. 351. As to the theological links in the sacramental theology of the Eastern churches, see Robert Hotz, *Sakramente - im Wechselspiel zwischen Ost und West*, Ökumenische Theologie, 2 (Zürich: Benziger; Gütersloh: Mohn, 1979), pp. 192-98.

[132] *Ordo initiationis christianae adultorum*, Rituale Romanum ex decreto Sacrosancti Oecumenici Concilii Vaticani II instauratum auctoritate Pauli Pp. VI promulgatum ([Romae:] Typis Polyglottis Vaticanis, 1972), pp. 96-97; *Rites*, p. 116. See Kavanagh, *Shape*, pp. 139, 176-77.

[133] "Holy Baptism," Concerning the Service: *Book of Common Prayer 1979*, p. 298.

[134] Price and Weil, *Liturgy for Living*, pp. 130-31; Weil, *Sacraments and Liturgy*, pp. 80-84.

[135] "Holy Baptism," Concerning the Service: *Book of Common Prayer 1979*, p. 298.

[136] "Holy Baptism," At the Eucharist: *Book of Common Prayer 1979*, p. 310.

[137] "Holy Baptism," Additional Directions: *Book of Common Prayer 1979*, p. 313.

[138] Ambrose of Milan calls baptism an "eye-opener" for what happens at the eucharist: "Isti, lauisti, uenisti ad altare, uidere coepisti quae ante non uideras, hoc est: per fontem domini et praedicationem dominicae passionis tunc aperti sunt oculi tui; qui ante corde uidebaris esse caecatus, coepisti lumen sacramentorum uidere.": *De sacramentis* iii,15, p. 100.

[139] "Holy Eucharist: Rite Two," The Great Thanksgiving, Eucharistic Prayer B, Epiclesis and Intercessions: *Book of Common Prayer 1979*, p. 369: Christ as "head of the Church and the author of our salvation."

[140] "Holy Eucharist: Rite One," The Breaking of the Bread, Postcommunion prayer: *Book of Common Prayer 1979*, p. 339.

means that it cannot live without coming together to celebrate this mystery. The Church lives by gathering. Even, the gathering itself is the first mode of Christ's presence (Mt 18:20).[141] In order to live up to their dignity as members of the Body of Christ, the baptized are bound to come together to celebrate the eucharist, for in coming together they can act as the People of God, become renewed by celebrating the memorial of Christ's death and resurrection, and can go forth in the strength of the Spirit. God's grace will keep and assist them so "that we may continue in that holy fellowship, and do all such good works as thou hast prepared for us to walk in."[142] The intimate connection between the individual members is expressed in the Peace which is given to each other and into which the newly baptized are drawn for the first time at their baptismal eucharist:

> As soon as they come up from those sacred waters all present embrace them, greet them, kiss them, congratulate and rejoice with them, because those who before were slaves and prisoners have all at once become free men and sons who are invited to the royal table.[143]

This Peace is the sign of what the eucharist, among other dignities, stands for: peace with God and, therefore, with each other;[144] unity in the Holy Spirit with Christ, the Head of the Church and, therefore, with the members of his Body; communion through Christ in the Holy Spirit with God and, therefore, with those whom He has also called out to be His Church. Being baptized inevitably means baptism into a Church, into the Church as Christ intended it to be (John 17:11,15-26). "Remember, Lord, your one holy catholic and apostolic Church, redeemed by the blood of your Christ. Reveal its unity, guard its faith, and preserve it in peace."[145]

The densest symbol of that unity and of the intimate communion with Christ is the communion of the one Bread and the one Cup. At the Breaking of the Bread (and the pouring of consecrated Wine into any additional chalices), anthems may be sung which clearly express the unitive and communicative characer of the sacrament to the received:

> The bread which we break is a sharing in the Body of Christ.
> We being many are one bread, one body,
> for we all share in the one bread.[146]

> The disciples knew the Lord Jesus
> in the breaking of the bread.
> The bread which we break, alleluia,
> is the communion of the body of Christ.

---

[141] See Horacio E. Lona, "In meinem Namen versammelt: Mt 18,20 und liturgisches Handeln," *Archiv für Liturgiewissenschaft*, 27 (1985), 373-404.

[142] "Holy Eucharist: Rite One," The Breaking of the Bread, Postcommunion prayer: *Book of Common Prayer 1979*, p. 339.

[143] "Eutheos gar anointas autus ek ton hieron ekeinon namaton pantes hoi parontes periplekontai, aspazontai, kataphilusi, sunedontai, sunchairusin hoti hoi proteron duloi kai aichmalotai athroon eleutheroi kai hyioi gegonasi kai eis ten basiliken eklethesan trapezan.": John Chrysostom, *Baptismal Homilies* ii,27, p. 148; English translation: Yarnold, *Awe-Inspiring Rites*, p. 169. See Riley, *Christian Initiation*, p. 351.

[144] "Holy Eucharist: Rite Two," Confession of Sin; The Peace: *Book of Common Prayer 1979*, pp. 359-60.

[145] "Holy Eucharist: Rite Two," The Great Thanksgiving, Eucharistic Prayer D, Intercessions: *Book of Common Prayer 1979*, p. 375. As to a summary of the theological meaning of the eucharistic prayers in the *Book of Common Prayer* 1979, see Harry Boone Porter, "An American Assembly of Anaphoral Prayers," in *The Sacrifice of Praise: Studies on the Themes of Thanksgiving and Redemption in the Central Prayers of the Eucharistic and Baptismal Liturgies, in honour of Arthur Hubert Couratin*, ed. Bryan D. Spinks, Bibliotheca "Ephemerides Liturgicae" "Subsidia," 19 (Roma: CLV Edizioni Liturgiche, 1981), pp. 181-96.

[146] "Anthems at the Breaking of the Bread," no. 2: *Book of Occasional Services*, p. 15.

> One body we are, alleluia,
> for though many we share one bread.[147]

This sharing of one bread is the climax of the sacramental life of the Church. It is the strengthening of the union between the Head of the Body and its members, both between Christ and the individual believer, and among the faithful themselves; it is also the high point of the entire celebration of the eucharist. The strengthening and climactic aspects of the eucharist underscore the close connection between baptism and the eucharist. It is, therefore, towards the celebration with the whole community of baptized that the inner dynamics of Christian initiation are aimed.[148]

The grace of the communion revives, invigorates, and tightens the bond within the Body which was established in baptism and is, therefore, constantly renewed in the eucharist. In "these holy mysteries," in the entire celebration of "the Liturgy for the Proclamation of the Word of God and Celebration of the Holy Communion,"[149] God has assured "that we are living members of the Body of your Son and heirs of your eternal kingdom,"[150] the promise given in baptism and again and again fulfilled in the eucharist. The People of God, thus renewed and sustained, can live up to what the bishop asks for them in the confirmation prayer: that they be sent forth in the power of the Spirit to perform the service God has set before them.[151] They can love and serve God "with gladness and singleness of heart"[152] and so become witnesses in the world to the wonderful deeds of God and extend to others the mercy they themselves have received, first in their baptism and then again in the eucharist.

In baptism a fundamental and existential change occurs: the Holy Spirit makes those who receive the sacrament new persons. Whether the phrasing as a burial with Christ in order to walk in the newness of life, used by St. Paul, or the parlance as a birth from above by water and the Holy Spirit, employed by St. John, is applied, the results are the same: "If any one is in Christ, he is a new creation." (2 Cor 5:17) A new, spiritual creation demands a life style and an expression of this essence.

The first and foremost manifestation of this newness of life is doxological living, a life

> to the praise of his glorious grace: In Christ, according to the purpose of him who
> accomplishes all things according to the counsel of his will, we who first hoped in Christ have
> been destined and appointed to live for the praise of his glory. (Eph 1:11-12)

This doxological living in communion with the whole assembly of the believers concretizes in the "principal act of Christian worship on the Lord's Day and other major Feasts," the eucharist.[153] In it the baptized express their gratitude for the mercy they have found and for the new creation they have become. They give themselves totally over to God, the origin of

---

[147] "Anthems at the Breaking of the Bread," no. 9: *Book of Occasional Services*, p. 17; cf. no. 10: p. 18.

[148] This point again advocates the dismissal of the catechumens before the Peace or the offertory as it is the privilege of baptized people to join in the eucharistic prayer and to receive communion. The distinction of being included in the second part of the celebration, then, ought not to be whether someone is a Christian (by name) but whether someone is baptized; for catechumens belong to the community of Christians (see "Concerning the Catechumenate:" *Book of Occasional Services*, p. 113).

[149] Title-page for Holy Eucharist: *Book of Common Prayer 1979*, p. 315.

[150] "Holy Eucharist: Rite Two," The Breaking of the Bread, Postcommunion prayer II: *Book of Common Prayer 1979*, p. 366.

[151] "Holy Baptism," At Confirmation, Reception, or Reaffirmation, Prayer for the candidates: *Book of Common Prayer 1979*, p. 309.

[152] "Holy Eucharist: Rite Two," The Breaking of the Bread, Postcommunion prayer I: *Book of Common Prayer 1979*, p. 365.

[153] "Concerning the Service of the Church:" *Book of Common Prayer 1979*, p. 13.

their new existence, in "this sacrifice of praise and thanksgiving"[154] for what He has done to them in His Son's mission and salvation, "rendering unto thee most hearty thanks for the innumerable benefits procured unto us by the same."[155] As the eucharist celebrates the memorial of the paschal mystery, the praise and thanksgiving for it is essential, for it is the fountain of the new dignity of the baptized.[156]

The worship they bring is also done on behalf of the entire creation. Even, the "revelation of the sons of God" (Rom 8:19) for which the creation waits has occured in baptism. The spirit of sonship given in it enables the baptized to say, "Abba, Our Father in heaven." In the eucharist the sons and daughters of God are revealed in their "glorious liberty" (Rom 8:21), the liberty to acknowledge and adore the Father: "Joinig with them [the countless throngs of angels], and giving voice to every creature under heaven, we acclaim you, and glorify your Name."[157] The eucharist is the worship of the new creation.

As the congregation of the faithful presents bread and wine, nourishment from the creation, these oblations become the food of the new creation through the sanctifying operation of the Holy Spirit. It is the same Spirit who in baptism gave the newness of life:

> We offer our sacrifice of praise and thanksgiving to you, O Lord of all; presenting to you, from your creation, this bread and this wine. We pray you, gracious God, to send your Holy Spirit upon these gifts that they may be the Sacrament of the Body of Christ and the Blood of the new Covenant.[158]

They become the symbol of Christ's presence and the Body of Christ itself. In the memorial of the paschal mystery and the reception of the gifts, the faithful celebrate the renewal of their own change. Every celebration of the eucharist initiates anew into the Body of Christ because the Holy Spirit sanctifies both the gifts which come to be the Body of Christ and the Blood of the new Covenant, and the assembly of the faithful who come to receive the sacrament.[159] The reception of the Bread and Wine revives the union of the sons and daughters of God with the Son of God; it is the food for strength on the way in the newness of life. The assembly of the faithful, therefore, needs the eucharist in order to express its worship, praise, and adoration, and to receive the renewal of its own dignity as children of God.

In baptism the faithful have been made to conform to Christ the Priest. They have become "a holy priesthood, to offer spiritual sacrifices acceptable to God through Jesus Christ." (1 Pet 2:5) Being made like Christ and having received a share in his priestly office, they are called to carry out their dignity,[160] and this they do by pre-eminence in the eucharist.

---

[154] "Holy Eucharist: Rite Two," The Great Thanksgiving, Eucharistic Prayer A, Anamnesis: *Book of Common Prayer 1979*, p. 363. Cf. Eucharistic Prayer B, Anamnesis: p. 309; Eucharistic Prayer C, Anamnesis: p. 371. See Geoffrey Grimshaw Willis, "Sacrificium laudis," in *The Sacrifice of Praise: Studies on the Themes of Thanksgiving and Redemption in the Central Prayers of the Eucharistic and Baptismal Liturgies, in honour of Arthur Hubert Couratin*, ed. Bryan D. Spinks, Bibliotheca "Ephemerides Liturgicae" "Subsidia," 19 (Roma: CLV Edizioni Liturgiche, 1981), pp. 73-87.

[155] "Holy Eucharist: Rite One," The Great Thanksgiving, Eucharistic Prayer I, Anamnesis: *Book of Common Prayer 1979*, p. 335.

[156] "Holy Eucharist: Rite Two," The Great Thanksgiving, Eucharistic Prayer D, Anamnesis: *Book of Common Prayer 1979*, p. 374.

[157] "Holy Eucharist: Rite Two," The Great Thanksgiving, Eucharistic Prayer D, Preface: *Book of Common Prayer 1979*, p. 373.

[158] "Holy Eucharist: Rite Two," The Great Thanksgiving, Eucharistic Prayer B, Anamnesis and Epiclesis over the gifts: *Book of Common Prayer 1979*, p. 369.

[159] "Holy Eucharist: Rite Two," The Great Thanksgiving, Eucharistic Prayer B, Epiclesis over the gifts and over the communicants: *Book of Common Prayer 1979*, p. 369.

[160] See Ernest Best, "Spiritual Sacrifices: General Priesthood in the New Testament," *Interpretation*, 14 (1960), 273-99; Lucien Cerfaux, "Regale Sacerdotium," in *Recueil Lucien Cerfaux: Etudes d'Exégèse et d'Histoire Religieuse* (Gembloux: Cuculot, 1954), II, 283-315; Paul Dabin, *Le sacerdoce royal des fidèles dans*

They offer their gifts, they are partakers of sacred mysteries, they are united to Christ in his sacrifice, and they affirm the eucharistic action.

The people bring their gifts of bread, wine "and money or other gifts."[161] This activity is more than a mere provision for the elements necessary for celebrating the eucharist. It is the presenting of the representation of the whole creation to the sacrifice of praise and thanksgiving to the Creator, and it is the priestly function of separating the symbols of their own sustenance for the change by the Spirit into the food of the new creation.[162] The priestly office is not confined to the sacramental celebration, though, and other gifts are set aside for other members of the Body of Christ who deserve them.

The baptized--and they only[163]--are invited to join in the sacred mysteries. The admonition "Lift up your hearts" can be answered "We lift them to the Lord" only by those who have "been raised with Christ" (Col 3:1) in baptism. Without the "illumination of the Holy Spirit in the Sacrament of Baptism"[164] no one is able to understand what the congregation is about to do. Baptism is the door to this mystery, but the privilege of joining it is tantamount to the obligation to do what the People of God are called to do. The privilege finds an adequate expression in the Great Thanksgiving: "In him [Christ], you have delivered us from evil, and made us worthy to stand before you. In him, you brought us out of error into truth, out of sin into righteousness, out of death into life."[165]

The obligation is made plain in the same prayer: "Unite us to your Son in his sacrifice, that we may be acceptable through him, being sanctified through the Holy Spirit."[166] The life of a baptized person stands under the imperative to be so led that it is acceptable to God. It is a life of unity with the High Priest who came to fulfill the will of his Father. The one-ness with Christ and his total surrender to "the mystery of his [God's] will according to his purpose" (Eph 1:18) is taken up in the Great Thanksgiving as the active share of the faithful in Christ's sacrifice: "Here we offer and present unto thee, O Lord, our selves, our sould and bodies, to be a reasonable, holy, and living sacrifice unto thee."[167] The submission of the whole being is the logical consequence from the fact that in baptism one has become the property of God[168] and marked as Christ's own for ever[169] so "that those who live might live no longer for themselves." (2 Cor 5:15) Royal Priesthood and a share in Christ's dignity as Great High Priest means being united to Christ in his death and burial "so that as Christ was raised from the dead by the glory of the Father, we too might walk in newness of life." (Rom 6:4) The circuit is closed: in baptism the person is baptized into Christ Jesus, into his death; in the

---

la tradition ancienne et moderne, Museum Lessianum: Section théologique, 48 (Bruxelles: Edition Universelle, 1950).

161 "Holy Eucharist: Rite Two," The Holy Communion, Rubric governing the offertory: *Book of Common Prayer 1979*, p. 361.

162 "Holy Eucharist: Rite Two," The Great Thanksgiving, Eucharistic Prayer C, Epiclesis over the gifts: *Book of Common Prayer 1979*, p. 371.

163 Casel, *Opfermysterium*, pp. 151-67.

164 "Preparation of Adults for Holy Baptism," During Candidacy, Invitation to prayer for the candidates: *Book of Occasional Services*, p. 124. As to the interpretation of baptism as enlightenment, see Ysebaert, *Terminology*, pp. 170-72.

165 "Holy Eucharist: Rite Two," The Great Thanksgiving, Eucharistic Prayer B, Post-*Sanctus*: *Book of Common Prayer 1979*, p. 368.

166 "Holy Eucharist: Rite Two," The Great Thanksgiving, Eucharistic Prayer B, Epiclesis over the communicants: *Book of Common Prayer 1979*, p. 369. See Louis Dussaut, *L'eucharistie, Pâque de toute la vie: Diachromie symbolique de l'eucharistie*, Lectio divina, 74 (Paris: Cerf, 1972).

167 "Holy Eucharist: Rite One," The Great Thanksgiving, Eucharistic Prayer I, Epiclesis over the communicants: *Book of Common Prayer 1979*, p. 336; cf. Eucharistic Prayer II, Epiclesis over the communicants: p. 342.

168 "Preparation of Adults for Holy Baptism," Prayer during the catechumenate, no. 6: *Book of Occasional Services*, p. 119.

169 "Holy Baptism," Consignation formula: *Book of Common Prayer 1979*, p. 308.

eucharist the baptized is united to Christ's sacrifice of his life. The priestly office which has been given in baptism means that by celebrating the eucharist this intimate connection with Christ and thereby the newness of life is renewed and deepened.

Encouraged and strengthened itself by the Spirit of God, the congregation can ask the Father to accept its prayers and praises through Christ. The entire community assents to what has been said in its name, enters the sacrifice of Christ, and summarizes its willingness to live the newness of life in union with Christ by saying "Amen," the one great priestly word of the baptized.[170]

It is evident from what has been said so far that Christ's life, death, and glorified existence is the reason for our redemption and newness of life. This is given in baptism by the Spirit as we are taken into the movement of Christ's self-sacrifice and join his surrender to the redemptive will of the Father. By being united to Christ we are changed into a new existence; we emerge from baptism as a saved people. In Christ's death, burial, and resurrection we are clearly at the center of the entire economy of salvation. In baptism we are drawn into it and are changed into the new creation for which this paschal mystery of Christ is the beginning and source of life. This mystery into which we are once and for all drawn at baptism is celebrated in its representation in the eucharist.[171] In it the assembly of the faithful makes the memorial of the focus of salvation history. By doing so the cause of new life and new dignity is made open and available every time the eucharist is celebrated; the redemption and new life given in the beginning is renewed and strengthened.

The celebration of the eucharist is necessary for the sustenance of the existence of the baptized. The memorial which the Church makes of Christ's redeeming life and his paschal mystery sets, as it were, Christ as the crucified and risen Lord before the Father. This renders it possible that the redemption wrought by Christ's self-sacrifice, its acceptance by the Father, and the bestowal of risen and transformed life, is open again so that those who celebrate the eucharist are drawn into the salvation. As they were once in their whole existence united with Christ in his death and resurrection in their baptism, they are in the eucharist united with him again so that the newness of life, the existence through the birth from above, is sustained and nourished. A baptized life without the celebration of the eucharist would perish.

Being drawn into Christ's paschal mystery is the operation of the Spirit, whom Christ as the exalted and glorified Lord has given and who takes what is Christ's and gives it to the Church (John 16:14). As in the water baptism, so in the memorial of Christ's death and resurrection the Holy Spirit is the "mediator" of salvation of which Christ is "the author."[172] "Unite us to your Son in his sacrifice, that we may be acceptable through him, being sanctified by the Holy Spirit."[173] There is one source of salvation and one agent, and this "applier" is operative for the same reason in baptism and the eucharist: to give new life to the people and to sanctify them. The redemption bestowed in baptism, then, is renewed every time the memorial of just that source of salvation is made in the eucharist. This is not a denial that "[t]he bond which God establishes in Baptism is indissoluble."[174] Rather, this bond is strengthened and invigorated by God whenever the eucharist is celebrated so that those who through their initiation into the Body of Christ have entered the bond, may be able to live according to the promises they made, and according to the newness of life the Holy Spirit gave them.

---

[170] Casel, *Opfermysterium*, pp. 561-65.

[171] See François Xavier Durrwell, *L'Eucharistie, sacrement pascal* (Paris: Cerf, 1980); Max Thurian, *L'Eucharistie: Mémorial du Seigneur, sacrifice d'action de grâce et d'intercession* (Paris: Delachaux & Niestlé, 1959).

[172] "Holy Eucharist: Rite Two," The Great Thanksgiving, Eucharistic Prayer B, Epiclesis over the gifts and over the communicants, Intercessions: *Book of Common Prayer 1979*, p. 369.

[173] "Holy Eucharist: Rite Two," The Great Thanksgiving, Eucharistic Prayer B, Epiclesis over the communicants: *Book of Common Prayer 1979*, p. 369.

[174] "Holy Baptism," Concerning the Service: *Book of Common Prayer 1979*, p. 298.

"Pasch" in the original Christian meaning indicated a transition from one existence into another, from death to life, from sorrow to joy.[175] In this interpretation "paschal mystery" can rightly be applied not only to Christ's passing from the sufferings and death to the risen life with his Father but also to the fundamental change in baptism from "no people" to "God's people" (1 Pet 2:10), from "sin into righteousness and out of death into life."[176] It is a transitional action by God: uniting in the Holy Spirit the baptized to Christ and giving them a full share in his passing to his new existence, so that "they may be with me where I am." (John 17:24) And it is this memorial of their redemption, of their "paschal mystery" as their unity with and share in Christ's paschal mystery, which the baptized celebrate in the eucharist.

Baptism is the entrance to the kingdom of God (John 3:5). To it the baptized have been admitted and have even been made heirs of the eternal kingdom because they have received the title and privilege of children of God and made to conform to the image of the Son of God "in order that he might be the first-born of many brethren" (Rom 8:29). Life in the kingdom of God is described in the New Testament, among other metaphors, as a banquet or a supper, although it is "not food and drink but righteousness and peace and joy in the Holy Spirit." (Rom 14:17)[177] Taking up this figure of speech, the eucharist can be described as the "Supper of the Lamb" (Rev 19:9)[178] at which the baptized, having put on Christ like a wedding dress (Gal 3:27), are invited to take the food and drink of the kingdom, the Body and Blood of Christ. The banquet at the kingdom of God is the logical consequence from baptism, for a kingdom that is set to destroy and not to build up its inhabitants, that is bound to let the people starve and not to give them food, is not worth entering but being left.[179]

The food which the sons and daughters of God receive at the banquet table is "the bread of heaven," and the drink they are served is "the cup of salvation."[180] This again shows that there is no feast without the prior sacrifice of life; the cup of salvation cannot be dispensed without the redemption through Christ's blood. In the bread of heaven and the cup of salvation the baptized are given the pledge of their own liberation from sin and their own new life acquired through Christ's sacrifice. The Body and Blood of Christ are in effect the memorial of this passion and resurrection and, therefore, the means through which the baptized are united with Christ. This union brings them back to the source of their own new life.[181] The Bread and Wine hold them in this life and renew the grace which they originally received in the font. It is "the holy food and drink of new and unending life in him [your Son]."[182] When the feast is kept, it is because "Christ our Passover is sacrificed for us."[183]

There is one sting attached to this concept of the heavenly banquet in the kingdom of God which does not render it invalid but rather brings to the fore another, unexpected aspect:

---

[175] Auf der Maur, *Feiern*, pp. 69-70.

[176] "The Great Vigil of Easter," Collect after the eighth lesson (Ez 37:1-14): *Book of Common Prayer 1979*, p. 291. The basis is an earlier composition by Harry Boone Porter and alludes to the seal of the Holy Spirit in baptism. (Hatchett, *Commentary*, p. 248.)

[177] This verse of course is not in opposition to the banquet character of the kingdom. St. Paul discusses real eating and drinking as such, with no transcendental openness, whereas the parables use eating and drinking as metaphors for the unending feast and the fulfillment of all desires in the kingdom.

[178] "Anthems at the Breaking of the Bread," no. 11: *Book of Occasional Services*, p. 18.

[179] "Holy Baptism," Renunciations: *Book of Common Prayer 1979*, p. 302.

[180] "Holy Eucharist: Rite Two," The Breaking of the Bread, Words of Administration, II: *Book of Common Prayer 1979*, p. 365.

[181] Cyril of Jerusalem, *Mystagogical Catecheses* v,19, p. 168.

[182] "Holy Eucharist: Rite Two," The Great Thanksgiving, Eucharistic Prayer A, Epiclesis over the gifts: *Book of Common Prayer 1979*, p. 363.

[183] "Holy Eucharist: Rite Two," The Breaking of the Bread, Anthem at the Breaking of the Bread: *Book of Common Prayer 1979*, p. 364.

> The eucharist falls short of the final kingdom ... because it is a *periodic and not a perpetual celebration*. We do not yet glorify God unceasingly, not open ourselves without interruption to the abundant life and glory which God intents to give us. The fault lies in our continuance of sin; and therefore the Lord's supper remains, until Christ comes, under the banner of His death, which is the divine judgement on all sin.[184]

Despite the new life which is in reality given to us in baptism, with all the promises this transformation carries, human nature remains frail and needs constant support. This is why it must again and again be strengthened through being placed in touch with its source so that the union with Christ is invigorated on the side of human beings. But God's mercy prevails even over sin which is committed by those "who have once been enlightened, who have tasted the heavenly gift, and have become partakers of the Holy Spirit." (Hebr 6:4) At the eucharist, before the Peace and the beginning of holy communion with the offertory, a confession of sin is made in which the sinners "humbly repent"[185] and ask that God, for the sake of His Son, "forgive us all that is past; and grant that we may ever hereafter serve and please thee in newness of life, to the honor and glory of thy Name."[186]

The periodic celebration also is an incentive to pattern the everyday life after the praise and adoration given to God in the eucharist; to spend the days in faith, hope, and charity; to be a witness to others of God's mercy; and to let the Spirit determine the actions so that the white garment of Christ's life, which was put on in baptism, can be worn spotlessly. This requirement and God's purifying grace are summarized in the Collect for Purity at the beginning of the eucharistic celebration, so that hereafter the garment is a proper wedding garment (Mt 22:11-12):

> Almighty God, to you all hearts are open, all desires known, and from you no secrets are hid:
> Cleanse the thoughts of our hearts by the inspiration of your Holy Spirit, that we may
> perfectly love you, and worthily magnify your Holy Name.[187]

At the end of this brief survey of the links between baptism and the eucharist, there are some expressions for the sacramental communion in the liturgical texts which border to a certain degree on mystic speech, yet are revealing that it is comunication with Life itself, the very source of life, which baptism gives access to and which the eucharist grants.

Those who in baptism have been made the People of God receive "the gifts of God"[188] in communion:

> The bishop announces: "What is holy for the holy". For our Lord's body and blood, which are our food, are indeed holy and immortal and full of holiness, since the Holy Spirit has come upon them. Not everyone may receive this food, but only those who have been sanctified, and therefore only the baptized who have undergone a new birth, and "have the first fruits of the Holy Spirit", which enables them to receive the favour of sanctification. This is why the bishop says: "What is holy for the holy", and urges everyone to recall the dignity of what is laid on the altar.[189]

---

[184] Geoffrey Wainwright, *Eucharist and Eschatology*, 2nd ed. (London 1978; rpt. New York: Oxford University Press, 1981), p. 120. Emphasis by Wainwright.

[185] "Holy Eucharist: Rite One," Confession of Sin, II: *Book of Common Prayer 1979*, p. 331.

[186] "Holy Eucharist: Rite One," Confession of Sin, I: *Book of Common Prayer 1979*, p. 355.

[187] "Holy Eucharist: Rite Two," The Word of God, Collect for Purity: *Book of Common Prayer 1979*, p. 355.

[188] "Holy Eucharist: Rite Two," The Breaking of the Bread, Invitation: *Book of Common Prayer 1979*, p. 364.

[189] "Le pontife crie: 'Le Saint aux saints', parce qu'en effet sainte et immortelle est cette nourriture qui est le corps et le sang du Notre-Seigneur, et pleine de sainteté, puisque l'Esprit-Saint est descendu sur elle. Or, ce n'est pas tout le monde qui prend cette nourriture, mais ceux-là qui déjà ont été sanctifiés: c'est pourquoi, ce sont les seuls baptisés qui la prennent, ceux qui, par une naissance nouvelle reçue au baptême, ont les prémices

These gifts are not only spiritual food but they have power to keep those who eat and drink them "in everlasting life."[190] This ability is derived from the reality that lies behind the symbols: the crucified and glorified Lord himself whose broken life in its self-sacrifice they represent. Because of the acceptance of this offering by God and transformation of Christ into exalted life with Him, the Bread and Wine are filled through the Spirit with Christ's presence, who is the first-born of the new creation (Col 1:15,18) and the image of God's merciful grace for the world. That is why the communicants can beseech God

> that we, and all others who shall be partakers of this Holy Communion, may worthily receive
> the most precious Body and Blood of thy Son Jesus Christ, be filled with thy grace and
> heavenly benediction, and made one body with him, that he may dwell in us and we in him.[191]

These gifts are the assurance of God's favor and goodness towards those who receive them.[192]

The strongest parlance, however, is reserved for anthems taken from John 6 and applied in the liturgy to the bread broken and the cup shared, thereby declaring the deepest union between the receiver and the received:

> My flesh is food indeed, and my blood is drink indeed, says the Lord.
> Those who eat my flesh and drink my blood dwell in me and I in them.[193]

> Whoever eats this bread will live for ever.
> This is the true bread which comes down from heaven and gives life to the world.
> Whoever believes in me shall not hunger or thirst,
> for the bread which I give for the life of the world is my flesh.[194]

> Those who eat my flesh and drink my blood abide in me and I in them.[195]

Because these words are employed in the Spirit-filled reality of the liturgy, they accomplish what they express, and the spiritual food and drink are the means by which Christ unites each faithful individually to himself, the faithful to each other, and the whole Body to himself, the Head.

> In this way, by communion in the blessed mysteries, we shall be united among ourselves and
> joined to Christ our Lord, whose body we believe ourselves to be, and through whom we
> "become partakers of the divine nature".[196]

---

de l'Espirt-Saint et par là obtenu la faveur de recevoir la sanctification. C'est pour celà que le pontife dit le 'Saint aux saints' et amène le coeur de tout le monde à être attentif à la grandeur de ce qui est (là) déposé.": Theodore of Mopsuestia, *Homilies* xv,22, p. 565; English translation: Yarnold, *Awe-Inspiring Rites*, p. 251.

[190] "Holy Eucharist: Rite Two," The Breaking of the Bread, Words of Administration, I: *Book of Common Prayer 1979*, p. 365.

[191] "Holy Eucharist: Rite One," The Great Thanksgiving, Eucharistic Prayer I, Epiclesis over the communicants: *Book of Common Prayer 1979*, p. 336. Cf. The Breaking of the Bread, Prayer of Humble Access: p. 377; The Great Thanksgiving, Eucharistic Prayer II, Epiclesis over the communicants: p. 342.

[192] "Holy Eucharist: Rite One," The Breaking of the Bread, Postcommunion prayer: *Book of Common Prayer 1979*, p. 339.

[193] John 6:55,56. "Anthems at the Breaking of the Bread," no. 5: *Book of Occasional Services*, p. 16.

[194] John 6:58b,33,35,51c. "Anthems at the Breaking of the Bread," no. 6: *Book of Occasional Services*, pp. 16-17.

[195] John 6:56. "Anthems at the Breaking of the Bread," no. 13: *Book of Occasional Services*, p. 18. Cf. Ambrose of Milan, *De sacramentis* vi,1-6, pp. 138-40.

[196] "Et ainsi, nous unirons-nous dans la communion aux saints mystères, et, par celle-ci, serons nous conjoints à notre tête, le Christ Notre-Seigneur, dont, nous le croyons, nous sommes le corps et par qui nous obtenons communion à la nature divine.": Theodore of Mopsuestia, *Homilies* xv,13, p. 555; English translation: Yarnold, *Awe-Inspiring Rites*, p. 247.

After baptism this is the strongest possible union in this life: Christ penetrating and permeating everybody so that the community of fate begun in baptism continues. He as the image of God's love and life itself abiding in the community of the Church and dwelling in each baptized individual: this is communion of divine and inexhaustible life. It is received first at the font when by water and the Holy Spirit one is buried with Christ in order to be born a new person and to walk in the newness of life. And it is sustained, nourished, and strengthened every time the baptized feeds on Christ's Body and Blood in order to continue to walk in the newness of life, despite all trials and temptations, until we are forever changed into the Lord's likeness from one degree of glory to another (2 Cor 3:18).

Epilogue

It has been said in the prologue to this study that the *Book of Common Prayer* is the realization of a great dream of the Church about its own life as a body that walks before God and expresses its trust that its deepest roots are in His life-giving mercy and compassion. And God's delight in all those who turn to Him makes it possible that the Church joyfully celebrates its new life without fear that it would miss the most essential and prominent duty of its life: all those who in Holy Baptism have handed themselves over to Christ's love in complete trust are "destined and appointed to live for the praise of God's glory" (Eph 1:12). The experience that the Church would not fall short of its own end because and (only) insofar as it has put all its hope in God releases its energies to lead a life before God which is not caught up in cleverly devised restrictions, restrictions that are clapped on its life by human authorities or its own anxieties, but which can be spent in the assurance that this body, celebrating before God, is in its worship life in touch with its deepest roots (God's love) and historical origin. This awareness can set the community free from malformations which have crept up at a time when the Church owed its existence more to human powers than to the divine purpose of its life. In turn this liberation from things dead or, worse, idols the Church ran after generates the ability to be flexible in the worship life so that God's saving health is able to reach the participants and is not getting hidden under layers of crusted forms carried over in a narrow interpretation of historical continuity, to the detriment of the flourishing of life which is in its divine abundance open to all who co-celebrate the liturgy.

There is nothing secret or apocryphal about the interdependence between the three guiding principles in the course of the prayer book history, uniformity in the execution of worship, the search for a close approach to the liturgy of the apostolic times, and the demand and gradual permission for greater flexibility and adaptation in the use of the material in public services, nor is there any need for a dogmatic or apologetic rationale behind it. The center of this correlation, from which the answers to the questions around the uniformity, apostolic liturgy, and adaptation come, is the degree to which the Church trusts first and foremost in God's gracious love. It is divine, not human, life that is the last authority for the Church. This applies to all churches and denominations, no matter how rigid their canonical rules are. This study here has been concerned with only one part of the Church catholic, the Episcopal Church.

The first premise, so unequivocally expressed in the four Acts of Uniformity of 1549, 1552, 1559, and 1662, and officially binding to every person in England, has in the life of the former Church of England in the American colonies been abandoned to the point of giving up the rule even within the Episcopal Church. Although the 1979 *Book of Common Prayer* is the one and only constitutionally established prayer book, its 1928 predecessor may under certain circumstances continue to be used, even while the church has taken pains to provide different rites for the church's regular worship life as well as some other occasions. The establishment of certain frames for the liturgy in the "Orders" of Worship for the Evening, for Celebrating the Holy Eucharist, for Marriage, and for Burial point into the direction of a liturgical life which is regulated to a minimal extent only. This, however, asks for thorough education in theological principles of the liturgy, which is far from easy to disseminate among all people concerned. Nonetheless, uniformity has to give way to a profound experience of the riches of the church's liturgical life.

The desire to pattern the church's liturgy after whatever was thought to be "apostolic liturgy" has been a hallmark of the reforms of both the sixteenth and twentieth centuries. Had the compilers of the *Book of Common Prayer* in 1549 and 1552 still to accomodate their own liturgical wishes with the political expediences of the ruling authorities and was their knowledge of the first Christian centuries still severely restricted, there was no outside pressure to be exercized at the period of the latest reforms, and the information about the primitive Church and the first few centuries could not in the least be compared with the inhibitions of four centuries ago. Yet, the ideal of an "apostolic liturgy" in the strict sense of the word has not been accomplished; the question of whether this is desirable or possible remains open. The history of the liturgy cannot be left without damage for the integrity of the Church's self-understanding, even if redundant accretions of especially medieval and early modern origins have been cut back, unless the underlying theological ideas are deemed to be wrong so that the results that have been built upon them would have to be corrected. It is interesting to observe that the silent agreement among the liturgical commissions, not only of the Episcopal Church but obviously also of other great Western churches, must have been a return to the worship forms in the third to sixth or seventh centuries, the "golden era" of patristic literature and formation of the liturgical families. Witness to that is the widespread use of the ordination prayers of Hippolytus of Rome, of the eucharistic prayer of Basil of Caesarea, and of a common structure of the eucharistic celebration. Apart from the fact that the ecclesiastical situation in the fourth quarter of the twentieth century resembles more the circumstances of a minority group--at least as far as profound belief is concerned--than those of the Imperial Church after Constantine, can it be that this apparent correspondence among the liturgical orders of the churches is a gradual and slow fulfillment of the wish for unity among them, maybe not even realized as such but nonetheless real? The common forms of the liturgy as promotor of unity in faith: this is much more than official dialogues can achieve. It would be one of the gifts of the Holy Spirit present in the liturgical assemblies of the congregations.

The demands for flexibility and adaptation are so apparent that they hardly need any endorsement or even encouragement. The vastly different shapes of congregations and parishes leave no other alternative. In essence this situation does not contrast much with the circumstances of the sixteenth century when more likely than not there was just as much variety in a parish as nowadays. Yet, society as a whole has become a mobile one with constant new challenges. A once-and-for-all fixed liturgy would do injustice to the people and would be detrimental to the incarnational principle so dear to Anglicanism. This means that the presence of God's love in this world through the Spirit is not limited to one appearance and that each congregation may claim the same dignity as members in the Body of Christ. To their needs the liturgical forms have to answer so that the contents of what is celebrated in the liturgy, Christ's paschal mystery and our union with him, can be understood and lived. The Episcopal Church advances the limits of the balancing act between a total uniformity and a total surrender to spontaneity much farther than previously; the flexibility goes to the center of the Church's liturgy, the eucharist, which can be celebrated according to a model which has to be filled in by the congregation, although this permission is not given for the principal Sunday eucharist.

In other words: it has become obvious that the first and third of the guiding principles, uniformity and adaptation, exclude each other if aimed at simultaneously. The history of the *Book of Common Prayer* attests to it. Total comprehensiveness cannot be accomplished within a church that subscribes to a fixed liturgy. Yet, the fixation of the liturgy can be opened up to allow for as much adaptation, within certain confines, as possible. And exactly this the Episcopal Church has done in its 1979 *Book of Common Prayer*.

Dreams do not only, and not even in the first instance, serve as an assimilation of experiences and impressions of the day or period past but always have an inherent purpose: to guide to a life which is devoid of the limitations of the present state, to show that newness of life is not a luxury but a necessity for survival, not a web of ideas promoted for the sake of change but the prerequirement for an existence that is not determined by the pressures and expectations of other people or oneself but by the potential for development into that person who is at unity with oneself, who has the healthy center of life in oneself, not in other people.

What is true for humanity in general, applies equally to Christians. Newness of life for them means leaving the way of (theologically speaking) sin and death and turning to the way of grace and life, and for bearing witness to God's saving act in baptism. A Christian cannot survive ("save his life:" Mk 8:35) by treading the old ways of habitual Christianity in all its cozy arrangements with the expectations of "this world." For a baptized person newness of life is a commitment to Christ as the Way who leads to complete loving surrender of one's existence to God's purposes which is possible in the trust that His will is salvation, not damnation, redemption from the "demons" of inhumane existence and slavery to determination of one's life by anxiety and fear, in order to acknowledge the supremacy of God's graciousness and to serve Him in perfect freedom and fullness of joy.

Again there is nothing arcane or "mystical" about this newness of life seen in a perspective of Christian initiation. Baptism is not the reward for a perfect life style but the commitment by God that, come what may, He will not renounce His covenant with that person; He has opened wide the door that lets all the waters of life flow so that not waterless pits and broken cisterns await the person who looks for the deepest meaning of life but the never-ending river of God's delights; He has shut the door that traps and holds persons in the abyss of having to live with ever-increasing circles of fear; He has promised and will never renege on it that the baptized has the inalienable dignity of being the heir to a kingdom whose hallmark is divine life.

This dignity of baptism, which the Anglican Reformers tried to rediscover and reestablish, was never questioned and was even strengthened in the course of the latest process of prayer book revision; the baptismal theology of the 1979 *Book of Common Prayer* is superbly rich and marvelous. Forgiveness of sin, regeneration to new life, bestowal of the Holy Spirit, and support for a Christian life worthy of that name--all these divine acts are manifest in the church's liturgy of baptism. The persons thus baptized are fully initiated and enjoy the privilege of joining the congregation, gathered around the Table of the Lord, in receiving the Body and Blood of Christ. Theologically speaking, there is no deficiency in the fullness of Christian initiation thus accomplished.

For all its superb qualities, the present *Book of Common Prayer* has not succeeded in getting rid of the ghost of the Reformation misunderstanding of confirmation. The issue centers around the understanding of a "mature public affirmation" of one's faith and commitment to the responsibilities of one's baptism, which is "expected" of those baptized at an early age or by a person who is not a bishop. Nobody denies the good that comes from such a public witness if it is truly personal and not simply a custom because "it is done;" nobody doubts the right of the church, either, to request such a testimony so that its members are living ones and not only nominal numbers. The controversy goes about the theological quality of an episcopal laying on of hands which is the "reward" for such an affirmation and about the appropriateness of the name "Confirmation" for this service. Confirmation is understood as a renewal of the covenant first--and indissolubly--made at baptism. Whereas in baptism the persons are "sealed by the Holy Spirit" by the imposition of hands and the mark of the cross on the forehead (with chrism if desired), in confirmation they are "strengthened" with the Holy Spirit by the laying on of hands by a bishop. There is no challenge to the appropriateness of this rite, either.

The rite that in Anglican parlance is called confirmation is left outside the pattern which is observed in the baptismal rite of the Episcopal Church. The washing, the bestowal of the seal of the Holy Spirit, and the nourishment at the Lord's Table (if the circumstances allow) are the three stages of Christian initiation which the candidates undergo. "Confirmation" is left outside this sacramental order. It is connected with persons fully initiated years ago, and lies in the realm of a maturing process which is to be supported by the strength and daily increase of the Spirit. The name of this rite and the role of the bishop in it are understandable only from a historical standpoint--and from a liturgical dichotomy which belongs to the past, as the conferral of the Spirit has been restored to baptism. It is suggested here that the one prominent flaw in the otherwise excellent initiation process and liturgy in the Episcopal Church is the existence of yet another "Confirmation" rite in the 1979 *Book of Common Prayer*. It is due not to the necessity for a liturgy in which the previously given Holy Spirit would have to be confirmed, but to an interpretation of their own pastoral office by the bishops which apparently is centered around the laying on of hands at confirmation. It is revealing that the final version of the prayer book speaks about *a* bishop in the presence of whom the public affirmation of the faith has to be made. It needs not be the ordinary bishop as the chief priest and pastor of the diocese who presides over the rite, *a* bishop suffices. The history of the revision process resulting in the 1979 *Book of Common Prayer* has shown that the preeminence of baptism has not yet come through to the bishops, however worthy their attempts of finding pastorally suitable ways of being in contact with the members of their dioceses. The insistence of the body of bishops to retain their privileged liturgical rite has marred the otherwise admirable recovery of the totality of Christian initiation in the one rite called "Holy Baptism." As far as the confirmation is concerned, the disadventageous effects of the Reformation have not yet been overcome.

A future revision of the prayer book will have to begin by educating the church at large, and the bishops in particular, about the dignity and integrity of Christian initiation, of the eminent role of bishops in it, and about ways and means to find a better solution to the necessary public commitment to the responsibilities of one's baptism.

There will never be an end to the great dream about the Church's celebration before the Living God because His treasures are much too vast to ever become exhausted. But to those who celebrate before Him with all their trust in His compassion He gives His life in all its divine abundance.

Select Bibliography

Sources

The Bible, Patristic Texts, and Ancient Liturgical Material

Ambroise de Milan. "Des sacrements." In his *Des sacrements, de mystères, l'explication du symbole*. Ed. Bernard Botte. Sources chrétiennes, 25 bis. Nouvelle éd. revue et augmentée. Paris: Cerf, 1969, pp. 60-155.

Augustinus, Aurelius. *Sancti Aurelii Augustini in Iohannis evangelium tractatus CXXIV*. Ed. Radbodus Willems. Corpus Christianorum Series Latina, 36. Turnholti: Brépols, 1954.

Brightman, Frank Edward, ed. *Liturgies Eastern and Western: Being the Texts Original or Translated of the Principal Liturgies of the Church*. Vol. I. 1896; rpt. Oxford: Oxford University Press, 1965.

Cyprianus, Thascius Caecilius. "Epistula LXVIIII." In his *Sancti Thasci Caecilii Cypriani opera omnia*. Ed. Guilelmus Hartel. Corpus Scriptorum Ecclesiasticorum Latinorum, 3,2. Vindobonae: Gerold, 1868, pp. 749-66.

Cyrille de Jérusalem. *Catéchèses mystagogiques*. Ed. Auguste Piédagnel. Sources chrétiennes, 126. Paris: Cerf, 1966.

Deshusses, Jean, éd. *Le sacramentaire, le supplement d'Aniane*. T. I du *Sacramentaire grégorien: Ses principales formes d'après les plus anciens manuscrits, édition comparative*. Spicilegium Friburgense, 16. 2e éd. revue et corrigée. Fribourg Suisse: Editions Universitaires, 1979.

Jean Chrysostome. *Huit catéchèses baptismales inédites*. Ed. Antoine Wenger. Sources chrétiennes, 50. Paris: Cerf, 1957.

Mohlberg, Leo Cunibert, Hrsg. *Liber Sacramentorum Romanae aeclesiae ordinis anni circuli (Cod. Vat. Reg. lat. 316 / Paris Bibl. Nat. 7193, 41/56) (Sacramentarium Gelasianum)*. Rerum Ecclesiasticarum Documenta: Series maior, Fontes, 4. 3. Aufl., verbessert und ergänzt von Leo Eizenhöfer. Roma: Herder, 1981.

The New Oxford Annotated Bible with the Apocrypha. Revised Standard Version, Containing the Second Edition of the New Testament And an Expanded Edition of the Apocrypha. Ed. Herbert G. May and Bruce M. Metzger. New York: Oxford University Press, 1977.

Tertullianus, Quintus Septimus Florens. "De baptismo." Ed. J. G. Ph. Borleffs. In *Opera catholica*. Vol. I of *Quinti Septimi Florentis Tertulliani opera*. Corpus Christianorum Series Latina, 1. Turnholti: Brépols, 1954, pp. 275-95.

----------. "De resurrectione mortuorum." Ed. J. G. Ph. Borleffs. In *Opera montanistica*. Vol. II of *Quinti Septimi Florentis Tertulliani opera*. Corpus Christianorum Series Latina, 2. Turnholti: Brépols, 1954, pp. 919-1012.

Théodore de Mopsueste. *Les homélies catéchétiques de Théodore de Mopsueste*. Ed. Raymond Tonneau et Robert Devreesse. Repr. phototypique du ms. Mingana syr. 561 (Selly Oak Colleges' Library, Birmingham). Studi e Testi, 145. Città del Vaticano: Bibliotheca Apostolica Vaticana, 1949.

Whitaker, Edward Charles. *Documents of the Baptismal Liturgy*. Large Paperbacks, 32. 2nd ed. rev. and supplemented, rpt. London: SPCK, 1979.

Yarnold, Edward. *The Awe-Inspiring Rites of Initiation: Baptismal Homilies of the Fourth Century*. [Slough:] St. Paul Publications, 1972.

Reformation to 1662

Booty, John E., ed. *The Book of Common Prayer 1559: The Elizabethan Prayer Book.* Folger Documents of Tudor and Stuart Civilization, 22. Washington, DC: Folger Shakespeare Library; London: Associated Universities Press, 1976.

Brightman, Frank Edward, ed. *The English Rite: Being a Synopsis of the Sources and Revisions of The Book of Common Prayer.* 2 vols. 2nd ed. rev. 1921; rpt. Farnborough: Gregg, 1970.

Buchanan, Colin, ed. *Eucharistic Liturgies of Edward VI: A Text for Students.* Grove Liturgical Study, 34. Bramcote, Notts.: Grove Books, 1983.

----------. "The Lord's Supper according to the Book of Common Prayer." In *Coena Domini I: Die Abendmahlsliturgien der Reformationskirchen im 16./17. Jahrhundert.* Hrsg. Irmgard Pahl. Spicilegium Friburgense, 29. Freiburg (Schweiz): Universitätsverlag, 1983, pp. 377-429.

Cardwell, Edward. *A History of Conferences and Other Proceedings: Connected with the Revision of the Book of Common Prayer from the Year 1558 to the Year 1690.* 3rd ed. Oxford 1849; rpt. Ridgewood, NJ: Gregg, 1966.

----------. ed. *Documentary Annals of the Reformed Church of England: Being a Collection of Injunctions, Declarations, Orders, Articles of Inquiry, &c., from the Year 1546 to the Year 1716.* New ed. in 2 vols. Oxford 1844; rpt. Ridgewood, NJ: Gregg, 1966.

Clay, William Keatinge, ed. *Liturgical Services: Liturgies and Occasional Forms of Prayer Set Forth in the Reign of Queen Elizabeth.* Parker Society, 27. Cambridge: Cambridge University Press, 1847.

Collins, Arthur Jefferies, ed. *Manuale ad vsum percelebris ecclesie Sarisburiensis: From the Edition Printed at Rouen in 1543 Compared with Those of 1506 (London), 1516 (Rouen), 1523 (Antwerp), 1526 (Paris).* Henry Bradshaw Society, 91. Chichester: Moore & Tillyer, 1960.

Cox, John Edmund, ed. *Miscellaneous Writings and Letters of Thomas Cranmer.* Cambridge: Cambridge University Press, 1846.

Cuming, Geoffrey John, ed. *The Durham Book: Being the First Draft of the Revision of the Book of Common Prayer in 1661.* London: Oxford University Press, 1961.

Donaldson, Gordon. *The Making of the Scottish Prayer Book of 1637.* Edinburgh University Publications: History, Philosophy and Economics, 3. Edinburgh: Edinburgh University Press, 1954.

Fisher, John Douglas Close, ed. *Christian Initiation: The Reformation Period, Some Early Reformed Rites of Baptism and Other Contemporary Documents.* Alcuin Club Collections, 51. London: SPCK, 1970.

Gairdner, James, ed. *Letters and Papers, Foreign and Domestic, of the Reign of Henry VIII: Preserved in the Public Record Office, The British Museum and Elsewhere in England.* Vol. VII. London: Longmans, Trübner, 1883.

Gee, Henry, and William John Hardy, eds. *Documents Illustrative of English Church History.* London: Macmillan, 1896.

Gibson, Edgar Charles Summer, ed. *The First and Second Prayer Books of Edward VI.* Everyman's Library, 448. 1910; rpt. London: Dent; New York: Dutton, 1964.

Guide to Law Reports and Statutes. 4th ed. London: Sweet & Maxwell; Edinburgh: Green, 1962.

Hatchett, Marion Josiah. "Thomas Cranmer and the Rites of Christian Initiation." M.A. Thesis General Theological Seminary 1967.

Henry VIII. *Assertio septem sacramentorum aduersus Mart[inum] Lutherum.* Parisiis: Guilelmus Desboys, 1562.

Keble, John ed. *The Works of That Learned and Judicious Divine Mr. Richard Hooker: With an Account of His Life and Death by Isaac Walton.* 7th ed., rev. by Richard William Church and Francis Paget. 3 vols. Burt Franklin Research and Source Series, 546: Philosophy Monograph Series, 34. Oxford 1888; rpt. New York: Franklin, 1970.

Legg, John Wickham, ed. *Cranmer's Liturgical Projects: Edited from British Museum ms. royal, 7, B. IV.* Henry Bradshaw Society, 50. London: Harrison, 1915.

Legg, Leopold George Wickham, ed. *English Coronation Records.* Westminster: Constable; New York: Dutton, 1901.

[Lloyd, Charles, ed.] *Formularies of Faith Put Forth by Authority during the Reign of Henry VIII: viz. Articles about Religion, 1536, The Institution of a Christian Man, 1537, A Necessary Doctrine and Erudition for any Christian Man, 1543.* Oxford: Clarendon, 1825.

Maskell, William, ed. *The Ancient Liturgy of the Church of England according to the Uses of Sarum, York, Hereford and Bangor and the Roman Liturgy Arranged in Parallel Columns.* 3rd ed. Oxford 1892; rpt. New York: AMS Press, 1973.

Robinson, Hastings, trans. and ed. *Original Letters Relative to the English Reformation: Written during the Reigns of King Henry VIII., King Edward VI., and Queen Mary, Chiefly from the Archives of Zurich.* 1st portion. Parker Society, 23. Cambridge: Cambridge University Press, 1846.

----------. *Original Letters Relative to the English Reformation: Written during the Reigns of King Henry VIII, King Edward VI., and Queen Mary, Chiefly from the Archives of Zurich.* 2nd portion. Parker Society, 28. Cambridge: Cambridge University Press, 1847.

Whitaker, Edward Charles, ed. *Martin Bucer and The Book of Common Prayer.* Alcuin Club Collections, 55. Great Wakering: Mayhew-McCrimmon, 1974.

Wilson, Henry Albert, ed. *The Order of the Communion, 1548: A Facsimile of the British Museum Copy C. 25, f. 15.* Henry Bradshaw Society, 34. London: Harrison, 1908.

Wriothesley, Charles. *A Chronicle of England during the Reigns of the Tudors, from A.D. 1485 to 1559.* Ed. William Douglas Hamilton. 2 vols. Westminster 1870, 1875; rpt. New York: Johnson, 1965.

American Period to 1928

Ayres, Anne. *The Life and Work of William Augustus Muhlenberg.* New York: Harper, 1881.

The Book of Common Prayer and Administration of the Sacraments and Other Rites and Ceremonies of the Church according to the use of the Protestant Episcopal Church in the United States of America Together with the Psalter or Psalms of David. New York: Church Hymnal Corporation, 1929.

Episcopal Church. General Convention. *Fourth Report of the Joint Commission on The Book of Common Prayer Appointed by The General Convention of 1913.* New York: Macmillan, 1925.

----------. *Report of the Joint Commission on The Book of Common Prayer Appointed by The General Convention of 1913.* Boston: Updike, 1916.

----------. *Second Report of the Joint Commission on The Book of Common Prayer Appointed by The General Convention of 1913.* New York: Macmillan, 1919.

----------. *Third Report of the Joint Commission on The Book of Common Prayer Appointed by The General Convention of 1913.* New York: Macmillan, 1922.

Frere Walter Howard, ed. *Russian Observations upon the American Prayer Book.* Trans. Wilfrid J. Barnes. Alcuin Club Tracts, 12. London: Mowbray; Milwaukee: Young Churchman Co., 1917.

Froude, Richard Hurrell. *The Remains of Richard Hurrell Froude.* Ed. by Friends. Vol. I. London: Rivington, 1838.

Gore, Charles. "The Holy Spirit and Inspiration." In *Lux Mundi: A Series of Studies in the Religion of the Incarnation.* Ed. Charles Gore. 14th ed. London: Murray, 1895, pp. 230-66.

----------. "Preface." In *Lux Mundi: A Series of Studies in the Religion of the Incarnation.* Ed. Charles Gore. 14th ed. London: Murray, 1895, pp. vii-ix.

----------. "Preface to the Tenth Edition." In *Lux Mundi: A Series of Studies in the Religion of the Incarnation.* Ed. Charles Gore. 14th ed. London: Murray, 1895, pp. x-xxx.

Hatchett, Marion Josiah. "The Making of the First American Prayer Book." Dissertation General Theological Seminary 1972.

Lambeth Conference. *Conference of Bishops of the Anglican Communion. Holden at Lambeth Palace, in July 1888: Encyclical Letter from the Bishops, With the Resolutions and Reports.* London: SPCK, 1888.

----------. *Conference of Bishops of the Anglican Communion. Holden at Lambeth Palace, in July 1897: Encyclical Letter from the Bishops, With the Resolutions and Reports.* London: SPCK, 1897.

Manross, William Wilson, ed. *The Fulham Papers in the Lambeth Palace Library: American Colonial Section, Calendar and Indexes.* Oxford: Clarendon, 1965.

----------. *SPG Papers in the Lambeth Palace Library: Calendar and Indexes.* Oxford: Clarendon, 1974.

McGarvey, William. *Liturgiae Americanae or The Book of Common Prayer as Used in the United States of America: Compared with the Proposed Book of 1786 and with the Prayer Books of The Church of England and an Historical Account and Documents.* Philadelphia: [Sunshine,] 1895.

[Newman, John Henry.] "Advertisement." In *Tracts for the Times.* By Members of the University of Oxford. Vol. I for 1833-34. London: Rivington; Oxford: Parker, 1834, pp. iii-v.

----------. "Catena Patrum. No. II: Testimony of Writers in the Later English Church to the Doctrine of Baptismal Regeneration." In *Tracts for the Times.* By Members of the University of Oxford. Vol. III for 1835-36; new ed. London: Rivington; Oxford: Parker, 1840, Tract 76.

----------. "Remarks on Certain Passages in the Thirty-Nine Articles." In *Tracts for the Times.* By Members of the University of Oxford. Vol. VI for 1840-41. London: Rivington; Oxford: Parker, 1841, Tract 90.

----------. "Rites and Customs of the Church." In *Tracts for the Times.* By Members of the University of Oxford. Vol. I for 1833-34. London: Rivington; Oxford: Parker, 1834, Tract 34.

[Pusey, Edward Bouverie.] "Scriptural Views of Holy Baptism: As Established by the Consent of the Ancient Church, and Contrasted with the Systems of Modern Schools." In *Tracts for the Times.* By Members of the University of Oxford. Vol. II, part II for 1834-35. 4th ed. London: Rivington; Oxford: Parker, 1842, Tract 67.

Tiffany, Charles C. *A History of the Protestant Episcopal Church in the United States of America.* The American Church History Series, 7. New York: Christian Literature Company, 1895.

Tocqueville, Alexis de. *De la démocratie en Amérique.* Ed. Harold Joseph Laski. Oeuvres, papiers et correspondences d'Alexis de Tocqueville, 1,2. 7e éd. Paris: Gallimard, 1951.

----------. *Democracy in America.* Abridged and ed. Richard Douglas Heffner. Mentor Book, 2053. New York: New American Library, 1956.

Vitoux, Pierre. *Histoire des idées en Grande Bretagne.* 3e éd. Paris: Colin, 1969.

[Williams, Isaac.] "Indications of a Superintending Providence in the Preservation of the Prayer Book and in the Changes Which It Has Undergone." In *Tracts for the Times.* By Members of the University of Oxford. Vol. V for 1838-40. London: Rivington; Oxford: Parker, 1840, Tract 86.

1928 to 1979, including the Liturgical Movement

The Altar Book containing The Holy Eucharist Rites One and Two. New York: The Church Hymnal Corporation, 1980.

The Book of Common Prayer and Administration of the Sacraments and Other Rites and Ceremonies of the Church Together with The Psalter or Psalms of David according to the use of The Episcopal Church. [New York:] Church Hymnal Corporation, [1979].

The Book of Common Worship As Authorized by the Synod 1962. London: Oxford University Press, 1963.

The Book of Occasional Services. New York: Church Hymnal Corporation, 1979.

Constitution and Canons for the Government of the Protestant Episcopal Church in the United States of America, Otherwise Known as The Episcopal Church, Adopted in General Conventions 1789-1979 together with the Rules of Order. [New York:] Seabury, [1979].

Dix, Gregory. "The Idea of 'The Church' in the Primitive Liturgies." In *The Parish Communion: A Book of Essays.* Ed. Arthur Gabriel Hebert. London: SPCK; New York: Macmillan, 1937, pp. 95-143.

----------. *The Shape of the Liturgy.* 2nd ed. 1945; rpt. London: Dacre, 1975.

Episcopal Church. General Convention. *Journal of the General Convention of the Protestant Episcopal Church in the United States of America, Held in the City of Washington, D.C. From October Tenth to October Twenty-Fifth, inclusive, in the Year of Our Lord 1928.* New York: Abbot, 1929.

----------. *Journal of the General Convention of the Protestant Episcopal Church in the United States of America, Held in Cleveland, Ohio From October Second to October Eleventh, inclusive, in the Year of Our Lord 1943.* N.p.: Printed for the Convention, 1943.

----------. *Journal of the General Convention of the Protestant Episcopal Church in the United States of America, Held in Philadelphia, Pennsylvania From September Tenth to Twentieth, inclusive, in the Year of Our Lord 1946.* N.p.: Printed for the Convention, 1947.

----------. *Journal of the General Convention of the Protestant Episcopal Church in the United States of America, Held in San Francisco, California From September Twenty-Sixth to October Seventh, inclusive, in the Year of Our Lord 1949.* N.p.: Printed for the Convention, 1949.

----------. *Journal of the General Convention of the Protestant Episcopal Church in the United States of America, Held in Detroit, Michigan From September Eighteenth to Twenty-Third, inclusive, in the Year of Our Lord 1961.* N.p.: Rand McNally, 1961.

----------. *Journal of the General Convention of the Protestant Episcopal Church in the United States of America, Held in St. Louis, Missouri From October Twelfth to Twenty-Third, inclusive, in the Year of Our Lord 1964.* N.p.: Printed for the Convention, 1964.

----------. *Journal of the General Convention of the Protestant Episcopal Church in the United States of America, Otherwise Known as The Episcopal Church, Held in Seattle, Washington From September Seventeenth to Twenty-Seventh, inclusive, in the Year of Our Lord 1967.* N.p.: Printed for the Convention, 1967.

----------. *Journal of the Special General Convention of the Protestant Episcopal Church in the United States of America, Otherwise Known as The Episcopal Church, Held in South Bend, Indiana From August Thirty-First to September Fifth, inclusive, in the Year of Our Lord 1969.* N.p.: Printed for the Convention, 1970.

----------. *Journal of the General Convention of the Protestant Episcopal Church in the United States of America, Otherwise Known as The Episcopal Church, Held in Houston, Texas From October Eleventh to Twenty-Second, inclusive, in the Year of Our Lord 1970.* N.p.: Printed for the Convention, 1970.

----------. *Journal of the General Convention of the Protestant Episcopal Church in the United States of America, Otherwise Known as The Episcopal Church, Held in Louisville, Kentucky From September Thirtieth to October Eleventh, inclusive, in the Year of Our Lord 1973.* New York: Seabury, 1973.

----------. *Journal of the General Convention of the Protestant Episcopal Church in the United States of America, Otherwise Known as The Episcopal Church, Held in Minneapolis, Minnesota From September Eleventh to Twenty-Third, inclusive, in the Year of Our Lord 1976.* Ambler, PA: Trinity Press, 1976.

----------. *Journal of the General Convention of the Protestant Episcopal Church in the United States of America, Otherwise Known as The Episcopal Church, Held in Denver, Colorado From September Ninth to Twentieth, inclusive, in the Year of Our Lord 1979.* New York: Episcopal Church Center, 1979.

Episcopal Church. Standing Liturgical Commission. *Authorized Services 1973.* New York: Church Hymnal Corporation, 1973.

----------. *Baptism and Confirmation; The Liturgical Lectionary.* Prayer Book Studies 1; 2. New York: Church Pension Fund, 1950.

----------. *The Draft Proposed Book of Common Prayer and Administration of the Sacraments and Other Rites and Ceremonies of the Church According to the use of the Protestant Episcopal Church in the United States of America otherwise known as The Episcopal Church Together with The Psalter or Psalms of David.* New York: Church Hymnal Corporation, 1976.

----------. *Holy Baptism; A Form for Confirmation, for Reception, and for the Reaffirmation of Baptismal Vows.* [Prayer Book Studies, 26, rev.] New York: Church Hymnal Corporation, 1975.

----------. *Holy Baptism: together with A Form for Confirmation or the Laying-On of Hands by the Bishop with the Affirmation of Baptismal Vows as Authorized by the General Convention of 1973.* Prayer Book Studies, 26. New York: Church Hymnal Corporation, 1973.

----------. *Holy Baptism with the Laying-On-of-Hands.* Prayer Book Studies 18 on Baptism and Confirmation. New York: Church Pension Fund, 1970.

----------. *Minutes of the Standing Liturgical Commission 1967-1979.* Archives of the Episcopal Church, Austin, Texas.

----------. *Services for Trial Use: Authorized Alternatives to Prayer Book Services.* New York: Church Hymnal Corporation, 1971.

Hebert, Arthur Gabriel. *Liturgy and Society: The Function of the Church in the Modern World.* London: Faber & Faber, 1935.

----------. "The Parish Communion in Its Spiritual Aspect, with a Note on the Fast before Communion." In *The Parish Communion: A Book of Essays.* Ed. Arthur Gabriel Hebert. London: SPCK; New York: Macmillan, 1937, pp. 1-29.

----------. "Preface." In *The Parish Communion: A Book of Essays.* Ed. Arthur Gabriel Hebert. London: SPCK; New York: Macmillan, 1937, pp. v-ix.

Ladd, William Palmer. *Prayer Book Interleaves: Some Reflections on How the Book of Common Prayer Might Be Made More Influential in Our English-Speaking World.* 2nd ed. New York: Oxford University Press, 1943.

Lambeth Conference. *The Lambeth Conference 1958: The Encyclical Letter from the Bishops Together With the Resolutions and Reports.* [London:] SPCK; [Greenwich, CT:] Seabury, 1958.

----------. *The Report of the Lambeth Conference 1978.* London: Church Information Office, 1978.

El Libro de Oración Común: Administración de los Sacramentos y otros Ritos y Ceremonias de la Iglesia Junto con el Salterio o Salmos de David Conforme al uso de La Iglesia Episcopal. New York: Church Hymnal Corporation, 1982.

Le Livre de la Prière Commune de l'Administration des Sacrements et des autres rites et cérémonies de l'Eglise avec le Psautier, ou les Psaumes de David selon l'usage de L'Eglise Episcopale. New York: Church Hymnal Corporation, 1983.

Missale Romanum. Missale Romanum ex decreto Sacrosancti Oecumenici Concilii Vaticani II instauratum auctoritate Pauli Pp. VI promulgatum. Ed. typica altera. [Romae:] Typis Polyglottis Vaticanis, 1975.

Ordo initiationis christianae adultorum. Rituale Romanum ex decreto Sacrosancti Oecumenici Concilii Vaticani II instauratum auctoritate Pauli Pp. VI promulgatum. [Romae:] Typis Polyglottis Vaticanis, 1972.

Parsons, Edward Lambe, and Baynard Hale Jones. *The American Prayer Book: Its Origins and Principles.* New York: Scribner, 1937.

"Pocono Statement." *Anglican Theological Review,* 54 (1972), 118-19.

The Proper for the Lesser Feasts and Fasts: Together with The Fixed Holy Days. 3rd ed. New York: Church Hymnal Corporation, 1980.

Proposed The Book of Common Prayer and Administration of the Sacraments and Other Rites and Ceremonies of the Church Together with The Psalter or Psalms of David according to the use of The Episcopal Church. [New York:] Church Hymnal Corporation, [1977].

The Rites of the Catholic Church: As Revised by Decree of the Second Vatican Ecumenical Council and Published by Authority of Pope Paul VI. Trans. International Commission on English in the Liturgy. New York: Pueblo, 1976.

Robeyns, D. A. "Die religiöse und theologische Bedeutung der liturgischen Erneuerung." *Liturgische Zeitschrift,* 5 (1932/33), 1-8.

Shepherd, Massey Hamilton. Letter to author. April 14, 1986.

----------. Letter to author. July 12, 1986.

Stevick, Daniel B. *Holy Baptism: together with A Form for the Affirmation of Baptismal Vows with the Laying-On of Hands by the Bishop also called Confirmation.* Supplement to Prayer Book Studies, 26. New York: Church Hymnal Corporation, 1973.

Suter, John Wallace, and George Julius Cleaveland. *The American Book of Common Prayer: Its Origins and Development.* New York: Oxford University Press, 1949.

Overlapping Periods

Alberigo, Joseph, et al., eds. *Conciliorum Oecumenicorum Decreta.* Ed. tertia. Bologna: Istituto per le scienze religiose, 1973.

Commager, Henry Steele, ed. *Documents of American History.* Crofts American History Series. 5th ed. New York: Appleton-Century-Crofts, 1949.

Grisbrooke, William Jardine. *Anglican Liturgies of the Seventeenth and Eighteenth Centuries.* Alcuin Club Collections, 40. London: SPCK, 1958.

Heffner, Richard Douglas. *A Documentary History of the United States.* Bloomington: Indiana University Press, 1952.
Jagger, Peter John, ed. *Christian Initiation 1552-1969: Rites of Baptism and Confirmation since the Reformation Period.* Alcuin Club Collections, 52. London: SPCK, 1970.
Wattenberg, Ben J., ed. *The Statistical History of the United States from Colonial Times to the Present: Historical Statistics of the United States, Colonial Times to 1970.* Prep. by the United States Bureau of the Census. New York: Basic Books, 1976.
Wigan, Bernard, ed. *The Liturgy in English.* London: Oxford University Press, 1962.

Studies

Addison, James Thayer. *The Episcopal Church in the United States 1789-1931.* 1951; rpt. Hamden, CT: Archon Books, 1969.
Addleshaw, George William Outram, and Frederick Etchells. *The Architectural Setting of Anglican Worship: An Inquiry into the Arrangements for Public Worship in the Church of England from the Reformation to the Present Day.* London: Faber & Faber, 1948.
Ahlstrom, Sydney Eckman. *A Religious History of the American People.* Complete and unabridged in 2 vols. Garden City, NY: Image Books, 1975.
----------. "The Traumatic Years: American Religion and Culture in the '60s and '70s." *Theology Today,* 36 (1980), 504-22.
Albright, Raymond Wolf. *A History of The Protestant Episcopal Church.* New York: Macmillan; London: Collier-Macmillan, 1964.
Arnold, John Henry, and Edward Gerald Penfold Wyatt, eds. *Walter Howard Frere: A Collection of His Papers on Liturgical and Historical Subjects.* Alcuin Club Collections, 35. Oxford: Oxford University Press; London: Milford, 1940.
Auf der Maur, Hansjörg. *Feiern im Rhythmus der Zeit I: Herrenfeste in Woche und Jahr.* Gottesdienst der Kirche, 5. Regensburg: Pustet, 1983.

Beasley-Murray, George R. *Baptism in the New Testament.* Mount Radford Reprints, 14. London; New York, 1962; rpt. Exeter: Paternoster Press, 1979.
Beckwith, Roger Thomas. "Thomas Cranmer and the Prayer Book." In *The Study of Liturgy.* Ed. Cheslyn Jones, Geoffrey Wainwright, and Edward Yarnold. London: SPCK, 1978, pp. 70-74.
Bond, Hugh Lawrence. "Edward, Jonathan." *Theologische Realenzyklopädie* 9, pp. 299-301.
Brand, Eugene Louis. *Baptism: A Pastoral Perspective.* Minneapolis: Augsburg Publishing House, 1975.
Brigden, Susan Elizabeth. "The Early Reformation in London, 1520-1547: The Conflict in the Parishes." Dissertation Cambridge [1979].
Bromiley, Geoffrey William. *Baptism and the Anglican Reformers.* London: Lutterworth, 1953.
Bugnini, Annibale. *La riforma liturgica (1948-1975).* Bibliotheca "Ephemerides Liturgicae" "Subsidia," 30. Roma: CLV Edizioni Liturgiche, 1983.
Burnish, Raymond. *The Meaning of Baptism: A Comparison of the Teaching and Practice of the Fourth Century with the Present Day.* Alcuin Club Collections, 67. London: SPCK, 1985.
Buxton, Richard F. *Eucharist and Institution Narrative: A Study in the Roman and Anglican Traditions of the Consecration of the Eucharist from the Eighth to the Twentieth Centuries.* Alcuin Club Collections, 58. Great Wakering: Mayhew McCrimmon, 1976.

Casel, Odo. *Das christliche Kultmysterium.* 4. durchgesehene und erweiterte Aufl. Hrsg. Burkhard Neunheuser. Regensburg: Pustet, 1960.
----------. *Das christliche Opfermysterium: Zur Morphologie und Theologie des eucharistischen Hochgebetes.* Hrsg. Viktor Warnach. Graz: Styria, 1968.
Chorley, Edward Clowes. *Men and Movements in the American Episcopal Church.* The Hale Lectures. 1946; rpt. Hamden, CT: Archon Books, 1961.

Clebsch, William Anthony. *American Religious Thought: A History*. Chicago History of American Religion. Chicago: University of Chicago Press, 1973.
Clubbe, John, and Ernest J. Lovell. *English Romanticism: The Grounds of Belief*. DeKalb, IL: Northern Illinois University Press, 1983.
Coleman, D. C. *The Economy of England 1450-1750*. London: Oxford University Press, 1977.
Collinson, Patrick. "A Comment: Concerning the Name Puritan." *Journal of Ecclesiastical History*, 31 (1980), 483-88.
----------. *The Elizabethan Puritan Movement*. London: Cape, 1967.
Commager, Henry Steele. *The Empire of Reason: How Europe Imagined and America Realized the Enlightenment*. Garden City, NY: Anchor Press Doubleday, 1978.
Cornish, Francis Warre. *The English Church in the Nineteenth Century*. A History of the English Church, 8. 2 parts. London: Macmillan, 1910.
Coulson, John. "Coleridge, Samuel Taylor." *Theologische Realenzyklopädie* 8, pp. 149-54.
Cross, Claire. *The Royal Supremacy in the Elizabethan Church*. Historical Problems, Studies and Documents, 8. London: Allan & Unwin; New York: Barnes & Noble, 1969.
Cuming, Geoffrey John. *The Godly Order: Texts and Studies Relating to the Book of Common Prayer*. Alcuin Club Collections, 65. London: SPCK, 1983.
----------. *A History of Anglican Liturgy*. 2nd ed. London: Macmillan, 1982.

Dalby, John Mark Meredith. "Christian Initiation: The Background and Formation of the Prayer Book Pattern." Dissertation Nottingham 1977.
Daniélou, Jean. *Bible et liturgie: la théologie biblique et des fêtes d'après les Pères de l'Eglise*. Lex orandi, 11. 2e éd. revue. Paris: Cerf, 1958.
Davies, Horton. *From Andrewes to Baxter, 1603-1690*. Vol. II of *Worship and Theology in England*. Princeton: Princeton University Press, 1975.
----------. *From Cranmer to Hooker, 1534-1603*. Vol. I of *Worship and Theology in England*. Princeton: Princeton University Press, 1970.
----------. *The Worship of the English Puritans*. Westminster: Dacre, 1948.
Delling, Gerhard. *Die Zueignung des Heils in der Taufe: Eine Untersuchung zum neutestamentlichen "taufen auf den Namen."* Berlin: Evangelische Verlagsanstalt, 1961.
Detscher, Alan F. *The Evolution of the Rite for the Ordination of Priests in the Protestant Episcopal Church in the United States of America from Its Pre-Reformation English Origins to the Book of Common Prayer, 1979: An Historical Study*. Dissertation Rome 1981. Romae: Pontificium Institutum Liturgicum, 1981.
Devereux, James Ashton. "The Collects of the First Book of Common Prayer as Works of Translation." Dissertation University of North Carolina 1964.
Dickens, Arthur Geoffrey. *The English Reformation*. 7th ed. New York: Schocken Books, 1980.
----------. *Reformation and Society in Sixteenth Century Europe*. London: Thames & Hudson, 1966.
Doody, Margaret. "Our Fathers, Often Faithless Too." In *No Alternative: The Prayer Book Controversy*. Ed. David Martin and Peter Mullen. Oxford: Blackwell, 1981, pp. 36-56.
Dugmore, Clifford William. "The First Ten Years, 1549-59." In *The English Prayer Book 1549-1662*. London: SPCK, 1963, pp. 6-30.

Echlin, Edward Patrick. "Was Laud's Liturgy Wholly Laud's?" *Historical Magazine of the Protestant Episcopal Church*, 37 (1968), 105-15.
Eliade, Mircea. *Birth and Rebirth: The Religious Meanings of Initiation in Human Culture*. Trans. William R. Trask. The Library of Religion and Culture. New York: Harper & Brothers, 1958.
----------. *Naissances mystiques: Essai sur quelques types d'initiation*. 4e éd. [Paris:] Gallimard, 1959.
----------. *The Quest: History and Meaning in Religion*. Chicago: University of Chicago Press, 1969.
Elton, Geoffrey Rudolph. "Cranmer, Thomas." *Theologische Realenzyklopädie* 8, pp. 226-29.
----------. "Elisabeth I." *Theologische Realenzyklopädie* 9, pp. 509-13.
----------. *Reform and Reformation: England, 1509-1558*. The New History of England. Cambridge, MA: Harvard University Press, 1977.
Episcopal Church. Standing Liturgical Commission. *Introducing the Proposed Book: A Study of the Significance of the Proposed Book of Common Prayer for the Doctrine, Discipline, and Worship of the*

Episcopal Church. By Charles Price. Prayer Book Studies, 29, rev. New York: Church Hymnal Corporation, 1976.
Eslinger, Richard R. "Civil Religion and the Year of Grace." *Worship*, 58 (1984), 372-83.

Faulkner, Harold Underwood. *American Political and Social History.* Educational Manual, 270. New York: Crofts, 1943.
Fisher, John Douglas Close. *Confirmation Then and Now.* Alcuin Club Collections, 60. London: SPCK, 1978.
Florovsky, George Vasilievich. "The Orthodox Churches and the Ecumenical Movement prior to 1910." In *A History of the Ecumenical Movement 1517-1948.* Ed. Ruth Rouse and Stephen Charles Neill. London: SPCK, 1954, pp. 169-218.
Franklin, Ralph William. "Guéranger and Variety in Unity." *Worship*, 51 (1977), 378-99.
----------. "Pusey and Worship in Industrial Society." *Worship*, 57 (1983), 386-412.
Frere, Walter Howard. *A New History of The Book of Common Prayer: With a Rationale of Its Office.* Revised and rewritten on the basis of the former work by Francis Procter. 3rd impr., with corrections and alterations. London: Macmillan, 1910.

Garrett, Samuel M. "Prayer Book Presence in Colonial America." In *Worship Points The Way: A Celebration of the Life and Work of Massey H. Shepherd, Jr.* Ed. Malcolm C. Burson. New York: Seabury, 1981, pp. 60-98.
Garrett, Thomas Samuel. *Worship in the Church of South India.* Ecumenical Studies in Worship, 2. London: Lutterworth, 1958.
Gestrich, Christof. "Deismus." *Theologische Realenzyklopädie* 8, pp. 392-406.
Glamann, Kristof. "European Trade 1500-1750." In *Sixteenth and Seventeenth Centuries.* Ed. Carlo Maria Cipolla. The Fontana Economic History of Europe, 2. Glasgow: Collins, 1974, pp. 427-526.
Glens, Ronald V. "A Select Bibliography of the Writings of Massey Hamilton Shepherd, Jr." In *Worship Points The Way: A Celebration of the Life and Work of Massey H. Shepherd, Jr.* Ed. Malcolm C. Burson. New York: Seabury, 1981, pp. 273-83.
Gray, Donald. *Earth and Altar: The Evolution of the Parish Communion in the Church of England to 1945.* Alcuin Club Collections, 68. Norwich: Canterbury Press, 1986.
Green, Ian M. *The Re-establishment of the Church of England 1660-1663.* Oxford Historical Monographs. Oxford: Oxford University Press, 1978.
Griffin, John R. "The Anglican Policies of Cardinal Newman." *Anglican Theological Review*, 55 (1973), 434-43.
----------. "Dr. Pusey and the Oxford Movement." *Historical Magazine of the Protestant Episcopal Church*, 42 (1973), 137-53.
----------. "The Oxford Movement: A Revision." *Faith and Reason*, 4 (1979), 30-50.
----------. "The Social Implications of the Oxford Movement." *Historical Magazine of the Protestant Episcopal Church*, 44 (1975), 155-65.
Grisbrooke, William Jardine. "The 1662 Book of Common Prayer: Its History and Character." *Studia Liturgica*, 1 (1962), 146-66.

Haaker, Klaus. "Glaube: II/2. Altes Testament." *Theologische Realenzyklopädie* 13, pp. 279-89.
Haas, Steven W. "Martin Luther's 'Divine Right' Kingship and the Royal Supremacy: Two Tracts from the 1531 Parliament and Convocation of Clergy." *Journal of Ecclesiastical History*, 31 (1980), 317-25.
Hall, Basil. "Bibelübersetzungen: III/2. Übersetzungen in andere germanische Sprachen, Übersetzungen ins Englische." *Theologische Realenzyklopädie* 6, pp. 247-51.
----------. "The Early Rise and Gradual Decline of Lutheranism in England (1520-1600)." In *Reform and Reformation: England and the Continent c. 1500 - c. 1750, Dedicated and Presented to Prof. Clifford W. Dugmore.* Ed. Derek Baker. Studies in Church History: Subsidia, 2. Oxford: Blackwell, 1979, pp. 103-31.
Hall, Jeremy. "The American Liturgical Movement: The Early Years." *Worship*, 50 (1976), 472-89.
Handy, Robert Theodore. *A History of the Churches in the United States and Canada.* Oxford: Oxford University Press, 1979.
Hardy, Daniel W., and David F. Ford. *Jubilate: Theology in Praise.* London: Darton, Longman & Todd, 1984.

Harvey, Margaret. "Ecclesia Anglicana, cui Ecclesiastes noster Christus vos prefecit: The Power of the Crown in the English Church during the Great Schism." In *Religion and National Identity: Papers Read at the Nineteenth Summer Meeting and the Twentieth Winter Meeting of the Ecclesiastical History Society.* Ed. Stuart Mews. Studies in Church History, 18. Oxford: Blackwell, 1982, pp. 229-41.

Hatchett, Marion Josiah. *Commentary on the American Prayer Book.* New York: Seabury, 1981.

----------. "Draft Proposed Prayer Book." *Worship,* 50 (1976), 213-37.

----------. *The Making of the First American Book of Common Prayer: 1776-1789.* New York: Seabury, 1982.

----------. Review of *No Alternative: The Prayer Book Controversy,* ed. David Martin and Peter Mullen. *Worship,* 57 (1983), 463-64.

----------. "A Sunday Service in 1776 or Thereabouts." *Historical Magazine of the Protestant Episcopal Church,* 45 (1976), 369-85.

Haugaard, William Paul. "The Coronation of Elizabeth I." *Journal of Ecclesiastical History,* 19 (1968), 161-70.

----------. *Elizabeth and the English Reformation: The Struggle for a Stable Settlement of Religion.* Cambridge: Cambridge University Press, 1968.

Heimert, Alan. *Religion and the American Mind: From the Great Awakening to the Revolution.* Cambridge, MA: Harvard University Press, 1966.

Herklots, Hugh Gerard Gibson. *The Church of England and the American Episcopal Church: From the First Voyages of Discovery to the First Lambeth Conference.* London: Mowbray; New York: Morehouse Barlow, 1966.

Hill, Christopher. *Reformation to Industrial Revolution: A Social and Economic History of Britain 1530-1780.* London: Weidenfels & Nicolsen, 1967.

Holdsworth, William. *A History of English Law.* Vol. I. Ed. Arthur Lehman Goodhart and Harold Greville Hanbury. 7th ed. rev. London: Methuen; Sweet & Maxwell, 1966.

Holmes, Urban Tigner. "Education for Liturgy: An Unfinished Symphony in Four Movements." In *Worship Points The Way: A Celebration of the Life and Work of Massey H. Shepherd, Jr.* Ed. Malcolm C. Burson. New York: Seabury, 1981, pp. 116-41.

Hotz, Robert. *Sakramente - im Wechselspiel zwischen Ost und West.* Ökumenische Theologie, 2. Zürich: Benziger; Gütersloh: Mohn, 1979.

Hughes, Philip. *"The King's Proceedings."* Vol. I of *The Reformation in England.* 3rd ed. London: Hollis & Carter, 1954.

----------. *Religio depopulata.* Vol. II of *The Reformation in England.* London: Hollis & Carter, 1954.

Hutin, Serge. *La philosophie anglaise et américaine.* "Que sais-je?, 796. Paris: Presses Universitaires de France, 1958.

Jasper, Ronald Cloud Dudley. "Christian Initiation: The Anglican Position." *Studia Liturgica,* 12 (1977), 116-25.

Johnson, Cuthbert. *Prosper Guéranger (1805-1875): A Liturgical Theologian, An Introduction to His Liturgical Writings and Work.* Studia Anselmiana, 89: Analecta Liturgica, 9. Roma: Pontificio Ateneo S. Anselmo, 1984.

Johnson, Sherman Elbridge. "Massey Shepherd and the Episcopal Church: A Reminiscence." In *Worship Points The Way: A Celebration of the Life and Work of Massey H. Shepherd, Jr.* Ed. Malcolm C. Burson. New York: Seabury, 1981, pp. 5-17.

Kavanagh, Aidan. *The Shape of Baptism: The Rite of Christian Initiation.* Studies in the Reformed Rites of the Catholic Church, 1. New York: Pueblo, 1978.

Keller-Hüschenmenger, Max. *Die Lehre der Kirche im frühreformatorischen Anglikanismus: Struktur und Funktion.* Gütersloh: Mohn, 1972.

King, Peter. "The Reasons for the Abolition of the Book of Common Prayer in 1645." *Journal of Ecclesiastical History,* 21 (1970), 327-39.

Kretschmar, Georg. "Die Geschichte des Taufgottesdienstes in der Alten Kirche." In *Der Taufgottesdienst.* Vol. V of *Leiturgia: Handbuch des evangelischen Gottesdienstes.* Hrsg. Karl Ferdinand Müller und Walter Blankenburg. Kassel: Stauda, 1970, pp. 1-348.

Landauer, Carl. *Sozial- und Wirtschaftsgeschichte der Vereinigten Staaten von Amerika*. Stuttgart: Metzler, 1981.
Legg, John Wickham. "The Regalism of the Prayer-book." In *Some Principles and Services of The Prayer-Book Historically Considered*. Ed. John Wickham Legg. London: Rivington, 1899, pp. 155-74.
Lehmberg, Stanford Eugene. *The Reformation Parliament 1529-1536*. Cambridge: Cambridge University Press, 1970.
Leuchtenberg, William E. *Franklin D. Roosevelt and the New Deal: 1932-1940*. The New American Nation Series. New York: Harper & Row, 1963.
Ligier, Louis. *La Confirmation: Sens et conjoncture oecuménique hier et aujourd'hui*. Théologie historique, 23. Paris: Beauchesne, 1973.

McKenna, John William. "How God Became an Englishman." In *Tudor Rule and Revolution: Essays for G. R. Elton from His American Friends*. Ed. Delloyd J. Guth and John William McKenna. Cambridge: Cambridge University Press, 1982, pp. 25-43.
McLoughlin, William Gerald. *Revivals, Awakenings, and Reform: An Essay on Religion and Social Change in America, 1607-1977*. Chicago History of American Religion. Chicago: University of Chicago Press, 1978.
Mills, Frederick Vandever. *Bishops by Ballot: An Eighteenth-Century Ecclesiastical Revolution*. New York: Oxford University Press, 1978.
----------. "Mitre Without Sceptre: An Eighteenth Century Ecclesiastical Revolution." *Church History*, 39 (1970), 365-71.
Minchinton, Walter. "Patterns and Structure of Demand 1500-1750." In *Sixteenth and Seventeenth Centuries*. Ed. Carlo Maria Cipolla. The Fontana Economic History of Europe, 2. Glasgow: Collins, 1974, pp. 83-176.
Mitchell, Leonel Lake. "The Alexandrian Anaphora of St. Basil of Caesarea: Ancient Source of 'A Common Eucharistic Prayer.'" *Anglican Theological Review*, 58 (1976), 194-206.
----------. "The Collects of the Proposed Book of Common Prayer." *Worship*, 52 (1978), 138-45.
----------. "Revision of the Rites of Christian Initiation in the American Episcopal Church." *Studia Liturgica*, 10 (1974), 25-34.
----------. "The Theology of Christian Initiation and The Proposed Book of Common Prayer." *Anglican Theological Review*, 60 (1978), 399-419.
Mokrosch, Reinhold. "Devotio moderna: II. Verhältnis zu Humanismus und Reformation." *Theologische Realenzyklopädie* 8, pp. 609-16.
Mols, Roger. "Population in Europe 1500-1700." In *Sixteenth and Seventeenth Centuries*. Ed. Carlo Maria Cipolla. The Fontana Economic History of Europe, 2. Glasgow: Collins, 1974, pp. 15-82.
Moorman, John Richard Humpidge. *A History of the Church in England*. 3rd ed. rpt. with corrections. London: Black, 1980.
Morgan, J. Hallock. "The Economic Policies of Archbishop Laud." *Anglican Theological Review*, 57 (1965), 217-26.
Morison, Samuel Eliot, and Henry Steele Commager. *The Growth of the American Republic*. 5th ed. rev. and enlarged. 2 vols. New York: Oxford University Press, 1962.
Morris, Richard Brandon, and Jeffrey Branon Morris, eds. *Encyclopedia of American History*. Bicentennial Edition. New York: Harper & Row, 1976.
Mußner, Franz. *Der Galaterbrief*. Herders Theologischer Kommentar zum Neuen Testament, 9. 3., erweiterte Aufl. Freiburg: Herder, 1977.

Neale, John Ernest. *Elizabeth I and Her Parliaments 1559-1581*. London: Cape, 1953.
Neunheuseer, Burkhard. "Odo Casel in Retrospect and Prospect." *Worship*, 50 (1976), 489-504.
Nijenhuis, Willem. "Calvin, Johannes." *Theologische Realenzyklopädie* 7, pp. 568-92.
Noakes, K. W. "Initiation: From New Testament Times until St. Cyprian." In *The Study of Liturgy*. Ed. Cheslyn Jones, Geoffrey Wainwright, and Edward Yarnold. London: SPCK, 1978, pp. 80-94.

Parker, Dorothy Mills. "The Issue of the American Prayer Book." In *No Alternative: The Prayer Book Controversy*. Ed. David Martin and Peter Mullen. Oxford: Blackwell, 1981, pp. 149-61.

Pawley, Bernard Clinton, and Margaret Pawley. *Rome and Canterbury through Four Centuries: A Study of the Relations between the Church of Rome and the Anglican Churches 1530-1973.* London: Mowbray, 1974.

Pesch, Rudolf. "Zur Initiation im Neuen Testament." *Liturgisches Jahrbuch,* 21 (1971), 90-107.

Piepkorn, Arthur Carl. "Episcopal Churches." In *Protestant Denominations.* Vol. II of *Profiles in Belief: The Religious Bodies of the United States and Canada.* Ed. Arthur Carl Piepkorn. San Francisco: Harper & Row, 1978, pp. 133-258.

Poll, Gerrit Jan van de. *Martin Bucer's Liturgical Ideas.* Dissertation Groningen 1954. Assen: Van Gorcum, [1954].

Porter, Harry Boone. "Toward an Unofficial History of Episcopal Worship." In *Worship Points The Way: A Celebration of the Life and Work of Massey H. Shepherd, Jr.* Ed. Malcolm C. Burson. New York: Seabury, 1981, pp. 99-115.

Powicke, Frederick Maurice, and Edmund Boleslaw Fryde, eds. *Handbook of British Chronology.* Royal Historical Society: Guides and Handbooks, 2. 2nd ed. London: Royal Historical Society, 1961.

Price, Charles P. *Introducing the Proposed Book of Common Prayer.* A rev. ed. of Prayer Book Studies 29. New York: Seabury, 1977.

----------, and Louis Weil.. *Liturgy for Living.* The Church's Teaching Series, 5. New York: Seabury, 1979.

Quinn, Frank Currer. "Contemporary Liturgical Revision: The Revised Rites of Confirmation in the Roman Catholic Church and in the American Episcopal Church." Dissertation Notre Dame 1978.

Quitslund, Sonya A. *Beauduin: A Prophet Vindicated.* New York: Newman, 1973.

Ramsey, Arthur Michael. *From Gore to Temple: The Development of Anglican Theology between Lux Mundi and the Second World War 1889-1939.* The Hale Memorial Lectures of Seabury-Western Theological Seminary, 1959. London: Longmans, Green & Co., 1960.

Ratcliff, Edward Craddock. "The Liturgical Work of Archbishop Cranmer." *Journal of Ecclesiastical History,* 7 (1956), 189-203.

----------. "The Savoy Conference and the Revision of the Book of Common Prayer." In *From Uniformity to Unity 1662-1962.* Ed. Geoffrey Fillingham Nuttall and Owen Chadwick. London: SPCK, 1962, pp. 89-148.

Reardon, Bernard M. G. *From Coleridge to Gore: A Century of Religious Thought in Britain.* London: Longman, 1971.

Reed, Luther Dotterer. *The Lutheran Liturgy: A Study of the Common Liturgy of the Lutheran Church in America.* 2nd ed. rev. Philadelphia: Muhlenberg, 1959.

Ridley, Jasper. *Thomas Cranmer.* Oxford: Clarendon, 1962.

Riley, Hugh M. *Christian Initiation: A Comparative Study of the Interpretation of the Baptismal Liturgy in the Mystagogical Writings of Cyril of Jerusalem, John Chrysostom, Theodore of Mopsuestia, and Ambrose of Milan.* The Catholic University of America Studies in Christian Antiquity, 17. Washington, DC: The Catholic University of America Press, 1974.

Ritter, Adolf Martin. "Glaubensbekenntnis(se): V. Alte Kirche." *Theologische Realenzyklopädie* 13, pp. 399-412.

Scarisbrick, John Jay. *Henry VIII.* English Monarchs. 4th impr., rpt. London: Eyre Methuen, 1981.

Schlosshauer-Selbach, Stefan. *Staat und Kirche in England.* Europäische Hochschulschriften: Reihe 2, 153. Dissertation München 1976. Frankfurt: Lang, 1976.

Schmeemann, Alexander. *Of Water and the Spirit: A Liturgical Study of Baptism.* Crestwood, NY: St. Vladimir's Seminary Press, 1974.

Schnackenburg, Rudolf. *Das Johannesevangelium: 1. Teil.* Herders Theologischer Kommentar zum Neuen Testament, 4, 1. Freiburg: Herder, 1965.

Schnitker, Thaddäus August. "Das amerikanische Book of Common Prayer." *Theologische Revue,* 78 (1982), cols. 265-72.

----------. "Kirche, Staat und Liturgie: Zwei bedeutsame Jahre im Leben der Kirche von England, 1533 und 1833." *Liturgisches Jahrbuch,* 33 (1983), 105-17.

Schramm, Percy Ernst. *A History of the English Coronation.* Trans. Leopold George Wickham Legg. Oxford: Clarendon, 1937.

Schwarz, Hans. "Glaubensbekenntnis(se): IX. Dogmatisch." *Theologische Realenzyklopädie* 13, pp. 437-41.
Sella, Domenico. "European Industries, 1500-1700." In *Sixteenth and Seventeenth Centuries*. Ed. Carlo Maria Cipolla. The Fontana Economic History of Europe, 2. Glasgow: Collins, 1974, pp. 354-426.
Shannon, David A. *Between the Wars: America, 1919-1941*. Houghton Mifflin Books in American History. Boston: Houghton Mifflin, 1965.
Shepherd, Massey Hamilton. "The Berakah Award: Reponse." *Worship*, 52 (1978), 299-313.
----------. "The History of the Liturgical Renewal." In *The Liturgical Renewal of the Church: Addresses of the Liturgical Conference, Held in Grace Church, Madison, May 19-21, 1958*. Ed. Massey Hamilton Shepherd. New York: Oxford University Press, 1960, pp. 19-52.
----------. "The Liturgy." In *The Second Vatican Council: Studies by Eight Anglican Observers*. Ed. Bernard Clinton Pawley. London: Oxford University Press, 1967, pp. 149-74.
----------. *The Oxford American Prayer Book Commentary*. New York: Oxford University Press, 1950.
Shoemaker, Robert W. *The Origin and Meaning of the Name "Protestant Episcopal"*. New York: American Church Publication, 1959.
Shriver, Frederick. "Hampton Court Revisited: James I and the Puritans." *Journal of Ecclesiastical History*, 33 (1982), 48-71.
Stenzel, Alois. *Die Taufe: Eine genetische Erklärung der Taufliturgie*. Forschungen zur Geschichte der Theologie und des innerkirchlichen Lebens, 7/8. Innsbruck: Rauch, 1958.
Stevenson, Kenneth W. *Gregory Dix - Twenty-Five Years On*. Grove Liturgical Study, 10. Bramcote, Notts.: Grove Books, 1977.
Stewart, Columba. Review of *Gregory Dix. The Shape of the Liturgy*. Ed. with additonal notes by Paul V. Marshall. *Worship*, 57 (1983), 88-90.
Streatfield, Frank. *Latin Versions of the Book of Common Prayer*. Alcuin Club Pamphlet, 19. London: Mowbray, 1964.
Stupperich, Robert. "Bucer, Martin." *Theologische Realenzyklopädie* 7, pp. 258-70.
Sumner, David E. *The Episcopal Church's History 1945-1985*. Wilton, CT: Morehouse Barlow, 1987.
Sydnor, William. *The Real Prayer Book: 1549 to the Present*. Wilton, CT: Morehouse Barlow, 1978.

Tawney, Richard Henry. *Religion and the Rise of Capitalism: A Historical Study*. 1926; rpt. Harmondsworth, Middlesex: Penguin Books, 1984.
Teubner, Werner. *Kodifikation und Rechtsreform in England: Ein Beitrag zur Untersuchung des Einflusses von Naturrecht und Utilitarismus auf die Idee einer Kodifikation des englischen Rechts*. Berlin: Duncker & Humblot, 1974.

Ullmann, Walter. "'This Realm of England is an Empire.'" *Journal of Ecclesiastical History*, 30 (1979), 175-203.

Wainwright, Geoffrey. *Doxology: The Praise of God in Worship, Doctrine and Life, A Systematic Theology*. London: Epworth, 1980.
----------. "'E pluribus unum:' Questions of Unity and Diversity on the Ecumenical and Liturgical Scene in the USA." In *Communio Sanctorum: Mélanges offerts à Jean-Jacques von Allmen*. Genève: Labor et Fides, 1982, pp. 291-305.
----------. *Eucharist and Eschatology*. 2nd ed. London 1978; rpt. New York: Oxford University Press, 1981.
----------. "Recent Eucharistic Revision." In *The Study of Liturgy*. Ed. Cheslyn Jones, Geoffrey Wainwright, and Edward Yarnold. London: SPCK, 1978, pp. 280-88.
----------. "Il rinnovamento liturgico nelle chiese dell'America del Nord." *Rivista Liturgica*, 68 (1981), 400-12.
----------. "The Rites and Ceremonies of Christian Initiation: Developments in the Past." *Studia Liturgica*, 10 (1974), 2-24.
Weil, Louis. "Christian Initiation in the Anglican Communion: A Reponse." *Studia Liturgica*, 12 (1977), 126-28.
----------. *Sacraments and Liturgy, The Outward Signs: A Study in Liturgical Mentality*. Faith and the Future. Oxford: Blackwell, 1983.

----------. "Worship and Sacrament in the Teaching of Samuel Johnson of Connecticut: A Study of the Sources and Development of the High Church Tradition in America, 1772-1789." Dissertation Institut Catholique 1972.

Whiteman, Anne. "The Restoration of the Church of England." In *From Uniformity to Unity, 1662-1962*. Ed. Geoffrey Fillingham Nuttall and Owen Chadwick. London: SPCK, 1962, pp. 19-88.

Winkler, Gabriele. *Das Armenische Initiationsrituale: Entwicklungsgeschichtliche und liturgievergleichende Untersuchung der Quellen des 3. bis 10. Jahrhunderts*. Orientalia Christiana Analecta, 217. Roma: Pontificium Institutum Studiorum Orientalium, 1982.

Wolf, Frederick B. "Christian Initiation." In *Prayer Book Renewal: Worship and the New Book of Common Prayer*. Ed. Hayden Barry Evans. New York: Seabury, 1978, pp. 35-44.

Woolverton, John F. "W. R. Huntington: Liturgical Renewal and Church Unity in the 1880's." *Anglican Theological Review*, 42 (1966), 175-99.

Yarnold, Edward. "Initiation: The Fourth and Fifth Centuries." In *The Study of Liturgy*. Ed. Cheslyn Jones, Geoffrey Wainwright, and Edward Yarnold. London: SPCK, 1978, pp. 95-110.

Ysebaert, Joseph. *Greek Baptismal Terminology: Its Origins and Early Development*. Graecitas Christianorum primaeva, 1. Nijmegen: Dekker & Van de Vegt, 1962.

Index

In all instances, page references include the footnotes, too.

Index of Names

Umlaute [ä ö ü] have been treated as ae oe ue.

Addison, J. Th.   ix, 53, 54, 59, 65, 69, 73, 83, 87
Addleshaw, G. W. O.   20
Ahlstrom, S. E.   ix, 34, 51, 52, 54, 55, 56, 57, 59, 60, 65, 69, 71, 72, 83, 85, 89, 90, 91, 97, 106, 107, 108, 116, 117, 118, 119
Alberigo, J.   63, 125, 126
Albright, R. W.   ix, 52, 59, 65, 70, 79, 80, 81, 83, 85, 86, 87, 90, 92, 119
Allen, M. B.   58
Allen, R. Ch.   76
Ambrose of Milan   186, 187, 190, 191, 192, 198, 203, 211
Armstrong, N. A.   118
Arnold, J. H.   109
Auf der Maur, Hj.   182, 209
Augustine of Hippo   143, 153, 181
Ayres, A.   81, 82

Balthasar, H.-U. v.   202
Barlow, W.   38
Barnes, R.   9
Barnes, W. J.   95
Barth, K.   107
Basil of Caesarea   177, 216
Battifol, P.-H.   110
Baumgartner, J.   xiii
Beam, Ch. M.   51
Beasley-Murray, G. R.   191, 198, 199, 201
Beauduin, L.   110
Becker, Hj.   184
Becket, Th.   10
Beckwith, R. T.   22, 23, 26
Bedard, W. M.   190
Bell, A. G.   84
Bellah, R. N.   118
Bellenger, D.   75
Benson, E.   86, 93
Berger, T.   74, 183, 184
Berens, J. F.   59

Best, E.   206
Best, G.   74
Biggs, J. W.   32
Bird, D. J.   125
Blake, W.   75
Blankenburg, W.   181
Block, J. S.   10
Boleyn, A.   6, 31
Bond, H. L.   57
Bonner, E.   23
Booty, J. E.   32, 33
Borleffs, J. G. Ph.   181, 182
Bornkamm, G.   195
Botte, B.   186
Bouyer, L.   109
Brand, E. L.   188
Brandeth, H. R. T.   74
Bray, Th.   54
Brent, Ch. H.   158
Bridgen, S. E.   14
Brightman, F. E.   14, 18, 19, 20, 21, 22, 23, 26, 27, 28, 29, 32, 33, 38, 40, 45, 46, 47, 54, 109, 178, 179, 184, 185, 186
Bromiley, G. W.   34
Brooks, R.   152
Bucer, M.   16, 24, 25, 27
Buchanan, C.   16, 18, 20, 26, 41, 42, 46, 66, 74
Bugnini, A.   123, 194
Bullinger, H.   18, 23, 24
Burnish, R.   202, 203
Burson, M. C.   35, 68, 113, 114, 115
Buxton, R. F.   179
Byrd, W.   37

Calvin, J.   31, 32, 33, 34
Cardwell, E.   15, 16, 18, 23, 24, 30, 31, 33, 34, 38, 39, 42, 44
Carnegie, A.   88-89
Carr, D. W. T.   24
Carter, J.   118
Casel, O.   110, 111, 115, 125-26, 184, 197, 207, 208
Catherine of Aragón   2, 29
Caughron, T. M.   31
Cerfaux, L.   206
Chadwick, O.   43, 45
Chapuys, E.   4, 6
Charles I   38-40, 43
Charles II   43-45
Charles V   6, 9
Chorley, E. C.   69, 70, 74, 79, 80, 81, 82, 85, 109
Church, R. W.   35, 74
Cipolla, C. M.   8, 9

Clark, L. 160
Clark, W. 70
Clay, W. K. 32, 33
Cleaveland, G. J. ix, 17, 104
Clebsch, W. A. 55
Clement VII 9
Clubbe, J. 75, 76
Coleman, D. C. 8, 36
Coleridge, S. T. 75, 76, 92
Collins, A. J. 17, 20, 21
Collinson, P. 33, 34, 35
Commager, H. S. 52, 58, 59, 60, 68, 71, 83, 97
Cornish, F. W. 75
Cosin, J. 45
Coulson, J. 76
Couratin, A. H. 184, 195, 203, 204, 205
Coverdale, M. 11, 156
Cox, J. E. 28
Coyle, E. L. 29
Cranmer, Th. xiii, 5, 9-10, 12, 13, 14, 15, 16, 20, 21, 22, 23, 24, 25, 27, 28, 29, 30, 113, 150, 155, 156, 185
Cromwell, Th. 8, 10
Croesmann, a. W. 39
Cross, C. 32, 33, 34
Cuming, G. J. ix, xiii, 14, 16, 17, 20, 21, 24, 27, 28, 33, 40, 44, 45, 47, 62, 98, 109, 110, 115, 120
Currie, S. 68
Curry, Th. J. 60
Cyprian 192
Cyril of Jerusalem 186, 191, 193, 196, 201, 209

Dabin, P. 206
Dalby, J. M. M. 21, 28, 29
Danbeny, Ch. 75
Daniélou, J. 182, 189, 190
Davies, H. 22, 34, 35
Davies, J. G. 192
Delling, G. 192
Deshusses, J. 190
Detscher, A. F. 24, 83, 86, 87, 101, 119, 148, 160
Devereux, J. A. 22
Devreesse, R. 187
Dickens, A. G. ix, 3, 5, 10, 11, 13, 17, 22, 23, 26
Diffendal, A. E. P. 54
Dix, G. 10, 17, 22, 26, 108, 112-13, 175
Donaldson, G. 40, 41, 42, 66
Donovan, M. S. 81
Doody, M. 147
Dowden, J. 109

Dowland, J. 37
Dressner, R. B. 89
Dryander, F. 18
DuBose, W. P. 158
Dürig, W. 190
Dugmore, C. W. 26
Dujarier, M. 181
Durbin, L. D. 19
Durrwell, Fr.-X. 208
Dussaut, L. 207

Echlin, E. P. 41
Edison, Th. A. 84
Edward VI 6, 15, 18, 23, 29, 32, 37
Edwards, J. 51, 57
Einstein, A. 106
Eisenhower, D. D. 117
Eizenhöfer, L. 130
Eliade, M. 51, 57, 197
Elizabeth I 6, 31-37, 45
Elton, G. R. ix, 2, 5, 10, 26, 34
Emswiler, S. 160
Emswiler, Th. N. 160
Erasmus of Rotterdam 24
Erickson, J. H. xiii
Eslinger, R. L. 118
Etchells, F. 20
Evans, H. B. 131

Faber, G. C. 74
Faulkner, H. U. 49, 50, 68, 69, 70, 71, 72, 84, 88, 90, 97
Fawcett, T. J. 63
Feiner, J. 202
Fessender, R. A. 96
Fishburn, J. F. 90
Fisher, J. D. C. xi, 12, 13, 14, 20, 21, 122, 195
Fitch-Lytle, G. 8
Florovsky, G. V. 94, 95
Ford, D. F. 183, 187
Franklin, B. 57
Franklin, R. W. 77, 81, 108
Frere, W. H. 14, 22, 26, 94, 95, 96, 109, 110, 113, 154
Froude, R. H. 75, 77, 79
Fryde, E. B. 2, 4, 7, 9, 39
Furnas, J. C. 71

Gäumann, N. 195
Gagarin, Y. 117
Gairdner, J. 5, 7
Garrett, S. H. 35, 52, 54, 55, 59
Garrett, Th. S. 115
Gaßmann, G. 36

Gee, H. 2, 3, 4, 5, 6, 7, 10, 12, 15, 16, 17, 25, 30, 31, 32, 33, 34, 37, 38, 39, 42, 43, 44, 45, 49
George III 58
Gerardi, D. F. M. 55
Gestrich, Ch. 57
Gibson, E. C. S. 18, 19, 20, 21, 22, 23, 26, 27, 28, 29, 179
Gladden, W. 90
Glamann, K. 9
Glenn, J. H. 117
Glens, R. V. 115
Goodhart, A. L. 6
Gore, Ch. 75, 76, 92-93, 110
Graham, W. F. 107
Gray, D. 108, 110, 111, 112
Gray, N. 105
Green, I. M. 43
Gregory VI 94
Grey, J. 29
Griffin, J. R. 74, 77, 78, 79
Grisbrooke, W. J. 22, 26, 40, 42, 62
Griswold, A. V. 70
Guardini, R. 110, 115
Guéranger, P. 108
Guth, D. J. 2

Haaker, K. 188
Haas, St. W. 5
Haddon, W. 33
Härdelin, A. 74
Hahn, J. 50
Hahn, O. 106
Hailman, D. L. 59
Hales, J. R. 51
Hall, B. 11
Hall, J. 110
Halter, H. 195
Hamilton, W. D. 15
Hanbury, H. G. 6
Handy, R. Th. 107, 108
Hardy, D. W. 183, 187
Hardy, E. R. 82
Hardy, W. J. 2, 3, 4, 5, 6, 7, 10, 12, 15, 16, 17, 25, 30, 31, 32, 33, 34, 37, 38, 39, 42, 43, 44, 45, 49
Hartel, G. 192
Harvard, J. 50
Harvey, M. 8
Hatchett, M. J. ix, xiii, 9, 12, 13, 14, 20, 21, 22, 27, 28, 29, 55, 59, 61, 62, 65, 66, 67, 68, 86, 102, 115, 145, 146, 148, 150, 152, 156, 157, 166, 167, 176, 177, 182, 183, 184, 185, 186, 190, 196, 209
Haugaard, W. P. 7, 22, 31, 33, 35

Hayes, A. L. 10
Hebert, A. G. 110-12
Heffner, R. D. 73, 84, 88, 89
Heimert, A. 57
Hennesey, J. 54
Henry IV 8
Henry VII 16, 37
Henry VIII xi, 1-15, 18, 23, 29, 31, 32, 37, 49
Henly, N. 1
Hensley, F. S. 71
Herklots, H. G. G. 51, 59, 61
Herwegen, I. 110, 111
Hill, Ch. 9, 37
Hippolytus of Rome 112, 116, 176, 216
Hobart, J. J. 70
Hoedemaker, L. A. 107
Holdworth, W. 6
Holmes, U. T. 113, 114, 128, 147, 150, 167
Hooker, R. 22, 35-36, 78
Hooper, J. 23
Hopkins, Ch. H. 89
Hotz, R. 203
Hughes, Ph. 4, 7, 17, 22, 23, 25
Huntington, W. R. 85-87, 92, 158
Hutchinson, W. R. 89
Hutin, S. 50

Islif, S. 9
Ives, L. S. 80

Jacobs, A. J. 202
Jagger, P. J. 27, 28, 29, 41, 46, 47, 115, 116
James I 37-39
James II 49, 61
Jasper, R. C. D. x, 125
Jefferson, Th. 57, 58, 60
Jenkyns, H. 28
John XXIII 125
John Chrysostom 184, 185, 186, 187, 199, 200, 204
Johnson, C. 108
Johnson, E. 51
Johnson, L. B. 117
Johnson, S. 36, 55, 57
Johnson, S. E. 114, 115, 132
Jones, B. H. 113-14
Jones, Ch. 22, 113, 182
Jones, W. 75
Jong, P. de 190
Jüngel, E. 107
Justin Martyr 116
Juxon, W. 40

Kaczynski, R. 184

Kalu, O. U.   38
Kavanagh, A.   202, 203
Keble, J.   35, 36, 74
Kegley, Ch. W.   107
Keller-Hüschenmenger, M.   21
Kendall, R. T.   32
Kennedy, J. F.   117 118
Kennedy, R. F.   118
Kilgour, R.   60
King, M. L.   117, 118
King, P.   42
Know, A.   75
Krahe, M. J.   184
Kretschmar, G.   181, 182, 186, 192, 197, 202

Ladd, W. P.   114, 115
Landauer, C.   72, 83, 84, 105
Larocca, J. J.   31
Laski, H. J.   73
Laud, W.   39-41, 43, 52
Leeuw, G. v. d.   189
Legg, J. W.   17, 19, 109
Legg, L. G. W.   1
Legg, L. W.   1
Lehmberg, S. E.   3, 5
Lengeling, E. J.   190
Leo X   2
Leuchtenberg, W. E.   106
Lewis, M.   70
Ligier, L.   194
Lincoln, A.   118
Lindbergh, Ch. A.   96
Lipkin, J. A.   7
Lloyd, Ch.   11, 12, 13, 14, 21, 22, 75
Lloyd, G.   46
Locke, J.   50, 58
Löhrer, M.   202
Lona, H. E.   204
Longland, J.   9
Loveland, C. O.   59
Louisa, A. J.   31
Lovell, E. J.   75 76
Loyer, O.   36
Luoma, J. K. R.   36
Luther, M.   2, 5, 8, 9, 20, 99, 103
Lyons, St. M.   24

Macsorley, R. H.   51
Manross, W. W.   54
Margerie, B. de   107
Marlowe, Ch.   37
Marshall, P. V.   112
Marsiglio of Padua   8
Martin, D.   147, 148

Martin, J. J.   8
Martyr, P.   24
Martyrs of New Guinea   158
Mary I   6, 18, 23, 29-31, 32
Mary II   49, 61
Maskell, W.   17
Mason, Th. A.   40
Maximilian I   5, 6
McCarthy, J.   117
McClintock, D. A.   90
McGarvey, W.   62, 63, 64, 65, 66, 67, 87, 179
McGoldrick, J. E.   9
McKenna, J. W.   2
McLoughlin, W. G.   55, 56, 57, 69, 91
Mead, M.   129
Meade, W.   70
Mercier, D.   110
Mercier, E.   203
Mernitz, S. C.   89
Mews, St.   xi, 8
Michel, V.   110
Miller, J. B.   8
Miller, R. S.   90
Mills, F. V.   54, 65
Milton, J.   75
Minchinton, W.   8, 9, 37, 53
Mitchell, L. L.   x, 129, 150, 156, 177, 184, 193
Mohlberg, L. C.   130, 182, 183, 184, 189
Mokrosch, R.   8
Mols, R.   8, 36
Moody, D. L.   91
Moorman, J. R. H.   ix, 25, 26, 30, 45, 75, 109, 110
More, Th.   7
Morgan, J. H.   40
Morison, S. E.   52
Morris, J. B.   70, 71, 72, 84, 96, 106
Morris, R. B.   70, 71, 72, 84, 96, 106
Morse, S.   72
Müller, K. F.   181
Muhlenberg, H. M.   81
Muhlenberg, W. A.   81-83, 85, 86
Mullen, P.   147, 148
Mullin, R. B.   70
Murray, S. C.   55
Mußner, F.   199, 200

Neale, J. E.   31
Neill, St. Ch.   94
Neunheuser, B.   126
Newman, J. H.   75, 76-77, 78, 79, 81
Niebuhr, H. R.   107
Niebuhr, R.   107
Nijenhuis, W.   34

Nixon, R. M. 118
Noakes, K. W. 182
Nuttall, G. F. 43, 45

Oakeley, F. 75
Old, H. O. 24
Olivar, A. 190
Ollard, S. L. 109
Osiander, A. 9

Paget, F. 35
Pahl, I. 16
Paris, F. 203
Parker, D. M. 147
Parker, M. 33
Parsch, P. 110
Parsons, E. L. 98, 113-14
Paul VI 183, 194, 203
Pawley, B. C. 75, 110, 125
Pawley, M. 75, 110
Peabody, F. G. 90
Pesch, R. 189, 198
Petri, A. 60
Philip II 30
Piédagnel, A. 191
Piepkorn, A. C. 54, 73, 83, 96
Pol, G. J. v. d. 24
Pole, R. 30
Porter, H. B. 68, 103, 104, 182, 183, 190, 196, 204, 209
Powell, Ch. 135, 148
Powicke, F. M. 4, 7, 9, 39
Price, Ch. P. 128, 135, 136, 146, 156, 159, 178, 193, 203
Procter, F. 14, 113
Provoost, S. 60
Pusey, E. B. 78-79

Quinn, F. C. 131
Quitslund, S. A. 110

Raleigh, W. 49
Ramsey, A. M. 92, 93
Ratcliff, E. C. 22, 26, 45
Rauschenbusch, W. 90
Reading, Ph. 59
Reardon, B. M. G. 75, 76, 92
Rech, Ph. 189
Reed, L. D. 22
Ridley, J. 9, 10, 12
Riley, H. M. 186, 187, 191, 193, 196, 198, 201, 204
Ritter, A. M. 188
Robeyns, D. A. 111

Robinson, H. 18, 23, 24
Roey, J. E. v. 110
Rogers, J. 11
Ronan, M. 160
Roosevelt, F. D. 105, 106
Rota, T. 72
Rouse, R. 94
Rousseau, A. 195

Sancroft, W. 61
Sanderson, R. 45
Scarisbrick, J. J. 1, 3, 5, 6, 10, 11
Scheidt, H. 190
Schereschewsky, S. I. J. 158
Schleifer, J. Th. 72
Schlosshauer-Selbach, St. 18
Schmemann, A. 182, 186, 190, 192, 203
Schmidt, G. R. 160
Schmidt, R. F. 110
Schnackenburg, R. 197, 201
Schnitker, Th. A. 1, 2, 74
Schott, E. 195
Schramm, P. E. 1
Schulte, A. 6
Schwartz, P. H. 43
Schwarz, H. 188
Scopes, J. Th. 91
Seabury, S. [sr.] 60
Seabury, S. [bishop] 60-62, 64-65, 67
Sella, D. 8
Seymor, E. 15, 29
Shakespeare, W. 37
Shannon, D. A. 105, 116
Shaw, P. E. 74
Shephard, A. B. 117
Shepherd, M. H. ix, xiii, 35, 68, 102, 108, 109, 113, 114, 115, 116, 122, 125-26, 132, 135, 146, 150, 153, 186
Shoemaker, R. W. 62, 98
Shriver, F. 38
Sikes, Th. 75
Skinner, J. 60
Smuts, R. M. 39
Spencer, B. 184
Spinks, B. D. 184, 195, 203, 204, 205
Stam, D. H. 32
Standish, H. 9
Stenzel, A. 181, 186, 188, 189, 202
Stevens, W. 75
Stevenson, K. W. 112, 113
Stevick, D. 135, 142-44
Stewart, C. 112
Stommel, E. 190
Stowe, H. B. 71

Streatfield, F. 33
Strong, J. 90
Stupperich, R. 24
Sumner, D. E. ix, 127, 158, 160
Sunday, W. A. 91
Suter, J. W. ix, 17, 104
Sutter, J. A. 72
Sydnor, W. 35, 40, 87, 98, 99, 100, 101, 119

Talley, Th. J. 152
Tawney, R. H. 40
Temple, F. 92, 93, 94
Tertullian 181, 182, 191
Teubner, W. 3
Theodore of Mopsuestia 186, 187, 191, 211
Thomas of Aquino 183
Thome, B. 160
Thompson, H. P. 54
Thurian, M. 208
Tiffany, Ch. C. 82
Tikhon [Russian-Orthodox archbishop] 94
Tillich, P. 107
Tocqueville, A. de 72-73
Tonneau, R. 187
Trask, W. R. 197
Tromp, S. 202
Truman, H. S. 106
Turner, F. J. 84
Tyndale, W. 9 11

Ullmann, W. 3

Van Mildert, W. 75
Vitoux, P. 50
Vos, W. 184
Voysey, J. 9

Wagner, G. 197
Wainwright, G. ix, 22, 99, 113, 132, 160, 170, 177, 182, 184, 210
Walker, E. 160
Walker, W. Th. 31
Walsh, J. H. 90
Walton, I. 35
Warham, W. 9
Warnach, V. 184, 198
Washington, G. 68, 118
Watson, J. 75
Wattenberg, B. J. 49, 53, 58, 68, 71, 73, 83, 84, 85, 88, 90, 96, 97, 105, 107, 116, 117
Watts, M. W. 49
Wedderburn, J. 40, 41
Weil, L. x, xiii, 36, 55, 74, 79, 155, 193, 203
Weingart, J. W. 6

Weiß, H.-F. 195
Wenger, A. 186
Whitaker, E. C. 24, 25, 150, 181, 182, 191, 192
White, G. xi
White, G. L. 31
White, W. 60, 67, 81
Whiteman, A. 43, 44
Wied, H. 16
Wigan, B. 66
Wilberforce, R. 75
Willems, R. 181
William III 49, 61
Williams, I. 77-78, 79
Willis, G. G. 206
Wilson, H. A. 16, 109
Winkler, G. 197, 201, 202
Wolf, F. B. 131
Wolsey, Th. 5, 7
Woolverton, J. F. 86, 87
Wordsworth, W. 75
Wren, M. 40, 42
Wright, O. 96
Wright, W. 96
Wriothesley, Ch. 15, 16, 18, 23, 24, 29, 30
Wyatt, E. G. P. 109
Wyeth, N. J. 1

Yarnold, E. 22, 113, 181, 182, 186, 187, 190, 192, 198, 204, 211
Ysebaert, J. 194, 198, 207

The Bible, Patristic Texts, and Ancient Liturgical Material

The Bible

Gen 1:1--2:2   164, 189
    7:1-5,11-18; 8:6-8; 9:8-13   164, 190
    22:1-18   164, 183

Ex 14:10--15:1   164, 182, 190
    20:1-17   66, 87, 102, 172

Ps 1   160, 170
    8:5-7   160
    15   164
    23   164, 169
    27   164
    27:1,4f,7-11,13,14f   122
    42   169
    42:1-7   164
    84   164
    96:9   40
    124:6   81
    139:1-9   170

Is 4:2-6   164, 183, 196
    7:9   188
    12:2-6   164
    55:1-11   164, 182, 190
    61:1-9   170
    66:14   196

Jer 31:31-34   141, 170

Ezek 36:24-28   129, 138, 164, 190, 202
    36:25-28   122, 201-02
    37:1-14   164, 209
    37:1-10   170

Zeph 3:12-20   164, 182, 183

Mt 5:1-12   170
    12:30   186
    16:24-27   170
    18:20   204
    22:11-12   210
    22:37-40   66, 87, 102
    28:18-20   99, 103
    28:19   21, 46, 129

Mk 1:9-11   129, 164
    8:35   216
    10:13-16   20, 47, 103, 129, 164

Lk 4:16-22   170

Jn 1:12-13   200
    1:13   200
    3:1-8   47, 99, 103, 121, 129, 137, 164
    3:1-6   137, 164
    3:3-5   201
    3:3,5   200
    3:5   209
    3:6   201
    3:8   201
    3:14   202
    6   211
    6:33,35,51c   211
    6:55,56   211
    6:56   211
    6:58b   211
    7:39   202
    14:6   187
    14:15-21   141, 170
    16:14   208
    17:3   187
    17:11,15-26   204
    17:21   199
    17:24   209
    19:34   21, 46, 121

Acts 1:8   122
    2:41   189
    8:14-17   87, 170

Rom 5:12   198
    5:18   198
    6   195, 198, 201
    6:1-11   197, 198
    6:3-11   163
    6:3-5   129, 164
    6:3-4   13
    6:4   207
    7:6   198
    8:9   199
    8:14-17   129, 164
    8:18-27   170
    8:19   206
    8:21   206
    8:29   209
    12:1-8   170
    12:1   194
    14:17   209

1 Cor 5:7b,8a   174
    12:13   198

2 Cor 3:18   212
    4:6   102
    5:15   207
    5:17-20   129, 164
    5:17   198 205
    13:13   179

Gal 3:2   199
    3:27   209
    3:29   199
    4:4-7   200
    5:16-25   170

Eph 1:3-14   200
    1:11-12   205
    1:12   215
    1:18   207
    3:14-19   101, 168
    4:4-6a   129, 164
    4:7,11-16   141, 170

Col 1:15,18   211
    3:1   207
    3:3   193

Heb 6:4   196, 210
    12:1-2   102

1 Pet 2:5   206
    2:9   203
    2:10   203, 209

2 Pet 1:3,4   193

1 Jn 3:1-2   200

Rev 19:9   209

Church Fathers

Ambrose, *De sacramentis*
    i,6   186
    i,12   190
    1,15   192
    i,19   191
    i,23--ii,1   190
    ii,17   198
    iii,15   203

    vi,1-6   211
    vi,5.8   187

Augustine, *Tractatus in Iohannis evangelium*
    xliv,2   181

Cyprian, "Letter 69 to Magnus"
    12   192

Cyril of Jerusalem, *Mystagogical Catecheses*
    i,10   196
    ii,4-5   191
    ii,4   201
    v,7   191, 193
    v,19   209

Hippolytus of Rome, *Apostolic Tradition*
    iii   216
    iv   176
    vii   216
    viii   216

John Chrysostom, *Baptismal Homilies*
    ii,17   186
    ii,21   187
    ii,26   187, 200
    ii,27   204
    iv,17   199

Tertullian, *De baptismo*
    iv,4   191
    xix,1   182
    De resurrectione mortuorum
    viii,3   181

Theodore of Mopsuestia, *Homilies*
    xiii,13   187
    xiv,9   191
    xv,15   211
    xv,22   211
    xv,40   187

Ancient Liturgical Material

Gelasian Sacramentary
  292 20
  297 20
  419 20
  432 182, 183
  434 183
  435 182
  451 130, 184
  454 183
  624 189

Gregorian Sacramentary
  423 190

Liturgy of St. Basil 177, 216

Liturgy of St. John Chrysostom 184, 185

Index of Subjects

Acts of Parliament x, 2, 3, 4, 5, 6, 12-13, 15, 16, 17-18, 23, 25, 30, 31, 32, 34, 37, 45, 60, 75, 134, 215
Adaptation x, xi, 45-46, 62-63, 67, 68, 98, 99, 104, 114, 124, 143, 149, 150, 154, 159, 160, 176, 215, 216
Adoption as Sons and Daughters 21, 130, 138, 163, 168, 183, 197, 200-01, 202, 209
Altar Book 153-54, 177
American Churches ix, 51-52, 53-54, 55-57, 63, 64, 68, 69, 70, 71, 72, 81, 82, 89-91, 106, 107-08, 117-18, 132, 146, 176, 177
American Colonies 37, 46, 47, 49-52, 53-54, 56, 57, 58-60, 215
American Mind 50-51, 55-57, 69, 71, 72, 84, 87, 99, 117-18
Anglican Communion ix, x, xi, 60, 74, 81, 86, 92, 93,-94, 96, 98, 100, 108, 109, 114, 119, 120, 122-25, 126, 132, 142-43, 147, 150, 158, 159, 193, 216
Anglo-Catholicism 13, 74, 79, 91, 108-09
Anointing 20, 27, 28, 78, 95
Anticlericalism 7, 42
Apostolic Liturgy x, xi, 15, 61, 62, 68, 78, 123, 149, 150, 157, 215-16
Awakening 51, 55-57, 58, 69, 72, 90-91

Baptism x, xi, 11, 12, 13, 20-21, 25, 27-28, 34, 35, 36, 38, 41, 44, 46-47, 54, 55, 63-64, 66-67, 74, 78, 79, 85, 86, 87, 95, 98-101, 103, 115, 117, 120-21, 122, 123, 124, 128-31, 133, 134, 135-36, 137-41, 142, 143, 144, 150, 152, 155, 159, 161, 162-69, 170, 170, 171, 177, 181-202, 217
Bible 11, 18, 70, 75, 76, 80, 91, 92-93, 94, 151
Bishop(s) xi, 4, 6, 7, 24, 26, 42-43, 44, 52-53, 54, 64, 65, 69, 76, 77, 78, 80, 82-83, 85, 128, 129, 130, 131, 133, 135, 136, 137, 138, 141-42, 144, 147, 148, 149, 150, 151, 155, 156, 157, 158, 159, 160, 163, 164, 166, 167, 168, 169, 170, 171, 172, 179, 193, 203, 205, 210, 217, 218
Bishops' Book 11-12
Black Population 49, 53, 71, 83, 117, 118
Book of Common Prayer [general] ix, 1, 14, 34, 35, 42, 44, 45, 46, 75, 80, 86, 93, 94, 98, 108, 109, 113-14, 119, 120, 122, 123, 124, 126, 147, 149, 158, 216
Book of Common Prayer 1549 16-23, 25, 26, 27, 29, 33, 41, 42, 45, 61, 63, 67, 94, 102, 113, 120, 122, 128, 154, 159, 184, 185-86, 215
Book of Common Prayer 1552 25-29, 32-33, 41, 45, 102, 113, 154, 167, 184, 215
Book of Common Prayer 1559 32-33, 154
Book of Common Prayer 1604 38, 41, 43, 154
Book of Common Prayer 1637 40-42, 45, 61, 66, 176, 178
Book of Common Prayer 1662 x, xi, 45-47, 51, 55, 57, 61, 63, 64, 66, 67, 78, 79, 93, 94, 108, 109, 112, 123, 178, 179, 184
Book of Common Prayer [proposed] *1786* 62-64, 65, 66, 67, 85
Book of Common Prayer 1789 ix, 65-68, 70, 78, 83, 85, 86, 87, 93, 101, 109, 134
Book of Common Prayer 1892 65, 66, 87-88, 93, 94-96, 98, 100, 102, 109, 134
Book of Common Prayer 1928 xi, 65, 66, 88, 96, 98, 101-04, 108, 114, 115, 119, 120, 121, 122, 130, 134, 136, 142, 144, 146, 147, 148, 149, 155, 156, 159, 162, 164, 168, 171, 172-75, 176, 179, 184, 215
Book of Common Prayer [proposed] *1976* 137, 145, 146, 147, 160
Book of Common Prayer 1979 ix, xi, xii, 60, 62, 65, 66, 86, 113, 115, 129, 130, 131, 132, 134, 135, 136, 139-41, 148, 149, 150, 151-79, 181-212, 215, 216, 217, 218
Book of Occasional Services 152-53, 171, 181, 185, 186, 190, 196, 199, 200, 201, 204, 205, 207, 209, 211

Catechism (Outline of the Faith)   19, 21, 22, 28, 29, 38, 47, 95, 155-56, 172, 179, 185, 187, 188, 189, 199, 202
Catechumenate   152, 181, 185, 186, 189, 190, 195-96, 200, 201, 205, 207
Catholicity of the Church   12, 13, 75, 76, 77, 79, 81, 94, 108
Ceremonies   11, 12, 13, 15-16, 18, 19, 25, 28, 30, 32, 34, 36, 38, 42, 45, 74, 85, 108, 121, 162, 197
Chrismation   14, 21, 130, 135, 138, 144, 145, 166, 193, 194
Christian Initiation   x, xi, xiii, 12, 13, 21, 27, 28, 115-16, 121, 122, 124, 128-31, 132, 133, 134, 135-36, 137, 141, 142-44, 147, 149, 150, 151, 162-69, 181-212, 217, 218
Church of England   x, 6, 10, 12, 13, 14, 26, 33-35, 36, 37, 39, 40, 41, 42-43, 44, 45, 50, 51-53, 54-55, 57, 59, 60, 61, 62, 63, 74, 75, 76, 77, 79, 80, 92, 94, 109-10, 112, 123, 125, 143, 155, 159, 215
Confirmation   x, xi, 12, 14, 21-22, 25, 28-29, 35, 38, 41, 47, 52, 54, 64, 67, 74, 78, 87, 95, 101, 104, 115-16, 120, 121-22, 123, 124, 128, 130, 131, 133, 134, 135-36, 137, 141-42, 143, 144, 145, 147, 149, 150, 151, 159, 165, 166, 167-68, 169-71, 172, 181, 193, 194, 195-96, 202, 205, 217, 218
Constitution of the Episcopal Church   ix, 62, 65, 85, 87, 122, 126, 134, 148, 149, 151, 154, 155, 158, 160
Constitution of the United States   52, 59-60, 71, 83, 97, 118, 119
Constitution on the Sacred Liturgy   115, 125-26, 132, 150
Convocations   4, 5, 11, 14, 39, 45
Covenant   13, 21, 36, 115, 140, 141, 167, 170, 186-88, 190, 195, 196, 197, 202, 206, 208, 217

Deism   57-58, 64, 67, 69, 75
Devotio moderna   7-8

Economy   x, 8-9, 23, 36-37, 49, 55, 56, 70-71, 72, 83-85, 88-91, 96-97, 105-08, 116
Ecumenical Movement   74, 81, 82, 85, 86, 109-10, 123
England   x, 3, 8-9, 23, 29, 30, 37, 42-43, 49, 50, 51, 53, 54, 60, 62, 74, 77, 109, 143, 215
Enlightenment   57-58, 59, 68, 69, 75
Episcopal Church   ix, x, xi, xii, 1, 41, 42, 51, 59, 62, 64, 65, 68-69, 70, 73, 79-83, 85-88, 90, 91-96, 98-101, 109, 113-15, 119-22, 124, 126-50, 151, 152, 158, 159, 160, 161, 162, 181, 193, 215, 216-18

Ethical Consequences of Baptism   13, 21, 28, 103, 124, 129, 137-38, 141, 164, 165, 167, 170, 183-84, 185, 187, 194-95, 196, 198, 199, 205, 210, 216-17
Erastianism   8, 10, 76, 79
Eucharist   x, xi, 11, 12, 13, 19-20, 23-24, 25, 26, 28, 32-33, 35, 36, 38, 41, 42, 46, 55, 61, 63, 66, 74, 82, 85, 86, 87, 88, 88, 95, 101, 102-03, 112-13, 114, 115, 116, 121, 122, 123, 124, 127, 128, 129, 130, 132, 133, 134, 135, 136, 137, 138, 141, 142, 143, 144, 145, 146, 147, 149, 151, 153, 155, 156, 157, 158, 159, 161, 162, 163, 164, 166, 168, 169, 170, 171-79, 181, 183, 184-86, 202-12, 216, 217
Eucharistic Prayer   19, 24-25, 26-27, 41-42, 61, 63, 65, 66, 95, 102, 112-13, 114, 124, 146, 154, 157, 161, 175-78, 184, 185, 187, 190, 191, 203, 204, 205, 206, 207, 208, 209, 211
Evening Prayer   15, 16, 20, 27, 33, 55, 82, 98, 102, 122, 127, 129, 151, 152, 155, 156, 157, 161, 165, 172
Exhortation   16, 19, 20, 21, 26, 63, 66, 67, 87, 98, 99, 102, 103, 114, 121, 124, 162, 163, 174
Exorcism   11, 20, 27, 95

Frontier   49, 54, 56, 69, 71, 84, 90, 117

General Convention 1789   60, 65, 66, 67
General Convention 1792   67
General Convention 1808   67
General Convention 1811   67
General Convention 1838   70
General Convention 1844   80
General Convention 1853   82
General Convention 1856   82-83, 87
General Convention 1862   94
General Convention 1868   85
General Convention 1871   85, 94
General Convention 1874   85, 86
General Convention 1880   86
General Convention 1883   86
General Convention 1886   86
General Convention 1889   85, 87
General Convention 1895   87
General Convention 1913   98
General Convention 1916   98, 99
General Convention 1919   99
General Convention 1922   100
General Convention 1925   101
General Convention 1928   101, 119
General Convention 1943   120
General Convention 1946   120
General Convention 1949   120
General Convention 1961   126, 131, 149

General Convention 1964   62, 126, 131, 149, 153
General Convention 1967   62, 127-28, 131, 153
Special General Convention 1969   131-32
General Convention 1970   131, 132-33, 153
General Convention 1973   129, 135, 136-37, 145, 153
General Convention 1976   137, 145-46, 148, 152, 153, 160, 177
General Convention 1979   137, 146, 147-48, 149, 152, 153

Holy Spirit   xi, 13, 20, 21, 25, 27, 28, 64, 66, 67, 77, 92, 99, 111, 121, 122, 124, 128, 129, 130, 135, 136, 138, 140, 141, 142, 144, 145, 147, 162, 163, 165, 166, 167, 168, 169, 170, 176, 177, 178, 182, 183, 185, 186, 187, 188, 189, 190, 191, 192, 193, 194, 195, 196, 198, 199, 200, 201, 202, 203, 204, 205, 206, 207, 208, 209, 210, 211, 212, 216, 217
House of Bishops   65, 80, 85, 86, 119, 120, 120, 122, 126, 128, 133-34, 135, 137, 142, 144, 146, 148, 149, 160
House of Deputies   65, 80, 85, 119, 126, 128, 146, 148, 149, 155
Humanism   7-8

Imposition of Hands   14, 21, 28, 29, 47, 128, 129, 130, 133, 134, 135, 136, 142, 143, 145, 149, 166, 167, 170, 171, 193, 194, 195, 196, 203, 217
Incarnation   92-93, 108, 111, 168, 176, 177, 216
Incorporation into Church   20, 27, 28, 35, 64, 79, 99, 103, 121, 128, 130, 135, 138, 141, 162, 163, 166-67, 168, 185, 189, 190, 191, 192, 194, 195, 197, 198-99, 202, 203, 204, 205, 208
Industrial Revolution   68, 70, 71
Interrogatories   35, 36, 46, 64, 66, 99, 100, 103, 121, 122, 129, 137-38, 139-40, 165

Justification   11, 79, 81

King's Book   13-14
Kingdom of God   20, 28, 99, 100, 103, 130, 138, 168, 182-83, 185, 195, 201, 209

Lambeth Conference 1867   51
Lambeth Conference 1888   86, 93-94
Lambeth Conference 1897   94
Lambeth Conference 1948   124
Lambeth Conference 1958   122-25
Lambeth Conference 1978   147, 150

Lesser Feasts and Fasts   153, 183, 189, 200, 201
Libro de Oración Común   154
Livre de la Prière Commune   154
Litany   10, 14, 31, 32, 55, 87, 88, 101, 155, 157
Liturgical Movement   98, 103, 108-16, 120, 122
Lutheranism   9, 11, 22

Millenialism   50-51, 56, 57, 58, 69, 86-87, 90, 99
Missale Romanum   183
Morning Prayer   15, 16, 20, 26, 27, 33, 55, 66, 82, 87, 88, 98, 102, 122, 127, 129, 151, 152, 155, 156, 157, 161, 165, 172

Newness of Life   124, 130, 164, 166, 170, 181-202, 205, 207, 208, 216-17
Non-Jurors   61

Order for Celebrating the Holy Eucharist   157, 158, 161, 178, 215
Order of Communion   16, 19, 20, 25, 26
Oxford Movement   74-81, 82, 85, 91, 108, 110, 114, 155, 193

Participation in Christ's Death (and Resurrection)   21, 28, 99, 101, 128, 129, 141, 164, 165, 166, 170, 182, 183, 185, 191, 192, 193, 197-98, 202, 205, 208, 209, 212, 216
Paschal Mystery   125, 134-35, 138, 159, 163, 176, 177, 181-83, 185, 188, 191, 195, 196, 197, 198, 201, 206, 208-09, 216
Paschal Vigil   152, 159, 162, 163, 164, 168, 182, 189-90, 197, 198, 201, 209
Prayer Book Studies 1;2   xi, 120-22, 124, 149
Prayer Book Studies 4   122
Prayer Book Studies 11   153
Prayer Book Studies 15   126
Prayer Book Studies 17   127
Prayer Book Studies 18   128-31, 132, 133, 134, 136, 137, 138, 139-41, 142, 149, 150, 164, 165, 166, 167, 169
Prayer Book Studies 26   129-30, 135, 136, 137-42, 143, 144, 150, 162, 164, 165, 166, 167, 170
Prayer Book Studies 26, rev.   144-45
Prayer Book Studies 26, suppl.   142-44
Prayer Book Studies 29   145
Prayer Book Studies 29, rev.   145
Primitive Church   x, 23, 25, 62, 68, 78, 123, 124, 125, 128, 150, 215

Puritanism   34-35, 37, 38, 39-40, 42-43, 51-52, 53, 55, 57, 63, 64, 121

Questions of Belief   20, 27, 103, 121, 129, 187

Reformation   x, xi, 1, 2-6, 7-10, 14, 15-16, 17, 22, 30, 49, 63, 78, 79, 81, 108, 113-14, 125, 136, 150, 151, 156, 158, 159, 161, 193, 217, 218
Regeneration   21, 27, 28, 35, 64, 67, 79, 81, 85, 99, 100, 103, 121, 129, 166, 170, 185, 190, 191, 192, 193, 197, 200, 201-02, 205, 208, 210, 212, 217
Remission of Sins   11, 13, 20, 28, 67, 128, 129, 129, 130, 136, 166, 168, 187, 190, 191, 192, 197, 203, 209, 217
Renunciation   20, 27, 46, 64, 67, 100, 101, 103, 129, 137, 139, 164, 165, 186, 189, 209
Restoration   43-45
Ritualist Movement   78, 80, 81, 85, 108-09, 110, 114, 155
Romanticism   74, 75-76
Russian Observations upon the American Prayer Book   94-96

Second Vatican Council   115, 123, 125-26, 150, 183, 194, 203
Social Gospel   89-90, 91
Social Situation   x, 8-9, 23, 36, 42-43, 49, 53, 55, 68, 69, 70-72, 81, 82, 83-85, 88-91, 96-97, 98, 105-08, 109, 116-19, 160
Special Days   16, 19, 146, 154, 155, 157, 159, 162
Standing Liturgical Commission   119-22, 124, 126, 127-28, 131-37, 142, 144-46, 147-48, 149, 150, 152, 153, 156, 175, 185
Supremacy over the Church   2, 4, 5, 6, 7, 8, 10-12, 13, 14, 15, 17, 19, 29, 30, 31-32, 34, 36, 38, 39, 59

Ten Articles   11
Thanksgiving over the Water   11, 20, 21, 27, 41, 101, 103, 121, 129, 138, 140, 145, 163, 165-66, 169, 184, 190-92

Uniformity   x, xi, 6, 10, 11, 14, 15, 16, 17, 18, 23, 33, 34, 36, 39, 41, 43, 86, 109, 124, 125, 126, 134, 149-50, 158, 215, 216
United States   x, 49, 51, 54, 58-60, 67, 68, 70-73, 83-85, 88-91, 94, 96-97, 105-08, 116-19, 157, 163
Uses   17, 23, 30

Vestments   19, 26, 29, 32, 33, 34, 44

www.ingramcontent.com/pod-product-compliance
Lightning Source LLC
Chambersburg PA
CBHW050847230426
43667CB00012B/2191